W9-CUA-352

EDUCATING EXCEPTIONAL CHILDREN

Eighth Edition

Editor

Karen L. Freiberg
University of Maryland, Baltimore

Dr. Karen Freiberg has an interdisciplinary educational and employment background in nursing, education, and developmental psychology. She received her B.S. from the State University of New York at Plattsburgh, her M.S. from Cornell University, and her Ph.D. from Syracuse University. She has worked as a school nurse, a pediatric nurse, a public health nurse for the Navajo Indians, an associate project director for a child development clinic, a researcher in several areas of child development, and a university professor. She is the author of an award-winning textbook, *Human Development: A Life-Span Approach*, which is now in its fourth edition. She is currently on the faculty at the University of Maryland, Baltimore County.

A Library of Information from the Public Press

Cover illustration by Mike Eagle

The Dushkin Publishing Group, Inc.
Sluice Dock, Guilford, Connecticut 06437

The Annual Editions Series

Annual Editions is a series of over 65 volumes designed to provide the reader with convenient, low-cost access to a wide range of current, carefully selected articles from some of the most important magazines, newspapers, and journals published today. Annual Editions are updated on an annual basis through a continuous monitoring of over 300 periodical sources. All Annual Editions have a number of features designed to make them particularly useful, including topic guides, annotated tables of contents, unit overviews, and indexes. For the teacher using Annual Editions in the classroom, an Instructor's Resource Guide with test questions is available for each volume.

VOLUMES AVAILABLE

Africa
Aging
American Foreign Policy
American Government
American History, Pre-Civil War
American History, Post-Civil War
Anthropology
Archaeology
Biology
Biopsychology
Business Ethics
Canadian Politics
Child Growth and Development
China
Comparative Politics
Computers in Education
Computers in Business
Computers in Society
Criminal Justice
Developing World
Drugs, Society, and Behavior
Dying, Death, and Bereavement
Early Childhood Education
Economics
Educating Exceptional Children
Education
Educational Psychology
Environment
Geography
Global Issues
Health
Human Development
Human Resources
Human Sexuality
India and South Asia

International Business
Japan and the Pacific Rim
Latin America
Life Management
Macroeconomics
Management
Marketing
Marriage and Family
Mass Media
Microeconomics
Middle East and the Islamic World
Money and Banking
Multicultural Education
Nutrition
Personal Growth and Behavior
Physical Anthropology
Psychology
Public Administration
Race and Ethnic Relations
Russia, the Eurasian Republics, and Central/Eastern Europe
Social Problems
Sociology
State and Local Government
Urban Society
Violence and Terrorism
Western Civilization, Pre-Reformation
Western Civilization, Post-Reformation
Western Europe
World History, Pre-Modern
World History, Modern
World Politics

Cataloging in Publication Data
Main entry under title: Annual editions: Educating exceptional children. 8/E.
   1. Exceptional children—Education—United States—Periodicals. 2. Educational innovations—United States—Periodicals. I. Freiberg, Karen, comp. II. Title: Educating exceptional children.
ISBN 1-56134-354-4   371.9'05   76-644171

Eighth Edition

Printed in the United States of America

Editors/ Advisory Board

WITHDRAWN

To the Reader

In publishing ANNUAL EDITIONS we recognize the enormous role played by the magazines, newspapers, and journals of the *public press* in providing current, first-rate educational information in a broad spectrum of interest areas. Within the articles, the best scientists, practitioners, researchers, and commentators draw issues into new perspective as accepted theories and viewpoints are called into account by new events, recent discoveries change old facts, and fresh debate breaks out over important controversies.

Many of the articles resulting from this enormous editorial effort are appropriate for students, researchers, and professionals seeking accurate, current material to help bridge the gap between principles and theories and the real world. These articles, however, become more useful for study when those of lasting value are carefully *collected, organized, indexed,* and *reproduced* in a *low-cost format,* which provides easy and permanent access when the material is needed. That is the role played by *Annual Editions.* Under the direction of each volume's *Editor,* who is an expert in the subject area, and with the guidance of an *Advisory Board,* we seek each year to provide in each ANNUAL EDITION a current, well-balanced, carefully selected collection of the best of the public press for your study and enjoyment. We think you'll find this volume useful, and we hope you'll take a moment to let us know what you think.

Inclusive education is changing the face of our public school system. Integration of "special needs" students is becoming increasingly common. *All children have special needs. Good teaching is good teaching. Separate is unequal.* Such euphemistic phrases run off the tongue quite easily. Teaching a class where children with few special needs are combined with children with many special needs due to problems such as mental retardation, learning disabilities, behavioral disorders, visual impairments, hearing impairments, communications disorders, physical or health impairments, multiple disabilities, or special gifts and talents is not easy! *Regular classroom teachers should not show favoritism. Each child should be taught in the most appropriate way every day. No child should be shunted off, or ignored.* The "shoulds" and "should nots" may seem overwhelming, especially when the regular classroom teacher feels unprepared, unassisted, underpaid, and has a crowded classroom. Can inclusive education be good for all students? Can good regular education teachers still be effective? Can special education teachers make the transitions required of them if special education and regular education merge?

Inclusive education is not a controversy that will go away. The Individuals with Disabilities Education Act, PL 94-142, formerly known as the Education for All Handicapped Children Act, has been the law since 1975. It has been made more explicit with three amendments. Numerous court cases have upheld its legality and made it a binding force on our public school systems. PL 94-142 does not mandate regularized education classrooms. It does, however, require the least restrictive environment for the education of every child with special needs. The number of children being assessed as having "special needs" has been growing annually. It now includes babies and toddlers considered "at-risk" of developing disabilities, and adolescents and young adults making school-to-adult life transitions. The large majority of students being assessed as having disabilities or special needs are only mildly or moderately affected. The least restrictive environment for their education is the regular classroom. Special schools and special classes are not appropriate for their individualized educational programs.

This anthology includes many articles that can provide assistance to regular and special education teachers, future teachers, administrators, consultants, psychologists, social workers, therapists, health clinicians, speech-language pathologists, allied educational professionals, and parents. The selection of articles was made with an eye to the controversy surrounding inclusion. The editor addressed the goal of finding articles to provide support and encouragement for teachers facing the inevitable change in the way special educational services are provided.

The introductory unit contains articles whose primary focus is inclusion: what it means; what it takes to make it work; how teachers, parents, and students react to it. Units 2 through 9 contain articles whose secondary focus is inclusion. Each unit is primarily concerned with eight areas of special needs: learning disabilities, mental retardation, behavioral disorders, communication disorders, hearing impairments, visual impairments, physical and health impairments, and students with special gifts and talents. Units 10 and 11 address the amendments to The Individuals with Disabilities Education Act, which together require comprehensive multidisciplinary services for infants and toddlers and their families and transition services for students with disabilities exiting the public school system.

To improve future editions of this anthology, the editor and advisory board would like comments, suggestions, and constructive criticisms from you, the reader. You are encouraged to use the article rating form on the last page of this book.

Good luck in using this anthology to make your own and others' lives a little easier and a lot more rewarding.

Karen Freiberg

Karen Freiberg
Editor

Contents

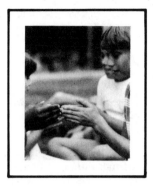

Unit 1

Inclusive Education

Six articles present strategies for establishing positive interactions between students with and without special needs.

The concepts in bold italics are developed in the article. For further expansion please refer to the Topic Guide and the Index.

Unit 2

Children with Learning Disabilities

Four selections address the assessment and special needs of students with learning disabilities.

Unit 3

Children with Mental Retardation

Three articles discuss concerns and strategies for providing optimal educational programs for students with mental retardation.

Unit 4

Children with Behavioral Disorders and Autism

Four articles discuss the regular education initiative and ways to teach emotionally and behaviorally disordered students in mainstream classes.

Unit 5

Children with Communication Disorders

Four selections discuss disorders of communication and suggest ways in which adults can assist students' learning and development in speech and language.

Children with Visual Impairments

Three selections discuss the special needs of visually impaired and blind children from infancy through secondary school.

Children with Physical and Health Impairments

Four articles examine the educational implications of medical treatments and physical impairments on children.

The concepts in bold italics are developed in the article. For further expansion please refer to the Topic Guide and the Index.

Unit 9

Children with Special Gifts and Talents

Four articles examine the need for special services for gifted and talented students, assessment of giftedness, and ways to teach these students.

Unit 10

Early Childhood Exceptionality

Four articles discuss the implementation of special services to infants and preschoolers with disabilities.

Unit
11

Transition to Adulthood

Two articles examine the problems and issues
regarding transitions within school or from school to
the community and work force.

The concepts in bold italics are developed in the article. For further expansion please refer to the Topic Guide and the Index.

Topic Guide

This topic guide suggests how the selections in this book relate to topics of traditional concern to students and professionals involved with educating exceptional children. It is very useful in locating articles that relate to each other for reading and research. The guide is arranged alphabetically according to topic. Articles may, of course, treat topics that do not appear in the topic guide. In turn, entries in the topic guide do not necessarily constitute a comprehensive listing of all the contents of each selection.

TOPIC AREA	KNOWLEDGE (These articles provide information about a handicap or about a special education concept.)	ATTITUDES (These articles contain personal experiences of exceptional persons or discussions about changing children's attitudes toward a handicap.)	TEACHING (These articles contain practical suggestions about how to apply special education principles to the teaching of exceptional children.)
Assessment	3. Privacy of School Records 8. Young Children with Attention Deficits 34. Poor and Minority Students Can Be Gifted, Too!	4. Separate and Unequal 9. Identifying Students' Instructional Needs 15. They Can But They Don't 17. The Culturally Sensitive Disciplinarian	16. Do Public Schools Have an Obligation? 20. Do You See What I Mean?
Behavioral Disorders	14. Autism 15. They Can But They Don't	16. Do Public Schools Have an Obligation? 17. Culturally Sensitive Disciplinarian 30. Physical Abuse	
Communication Disorders	14. Autism 18. Preschool Classroom Environments That Promote Communication 19. Toward Defining Programs and Services		20. Do You See What I Mean? 21. Using a Picture Task Analysis to Teach Students
Computers and Technology	6. Selection of Appropriate Technology 22. Hearing for Success in the Classroom	25. Developing Independent and Responsible Behaviors 26. Efficacy of Low Vision Services	1. Inclusion 10. Adapting Textbooks for Children with Learning Disabilities 39. Children Who Use Assistive Technology
Cultural Diversity	4. Separate and Unequal 17. Culturally Sensitive Disciplinarian	2. Commentary on Inclusion and Self-Identity	19. Toward Defining Programs and Services
Early Childhood Exceptionality	8. Young Children with Attention Deficits 11. Prenatal Drug Exposure 14. Autism 37. Infants and Toddlers with Special Needs	38. Preschool Mainstreaming: Attitude Barriers	18. Preschool Classroom Environments 36. Meeting the Needs of Gifted and Talented Preschoolers 39. Children Who Use Assistive Technology 40. Play for All Children
Family Impact	3. Privacy of School Records 11. Prenatal Drug Exposure 25. Developing Independent and Responsible Behaviors	9. Identifying Students' Instructional Needs 15. They Can But They Don't 30. Physical Abuse	5. Peer Education Partners 19. Toward Defining Programs and Services
Gifted and Talented	33. How Schools Are Shortchanging the Gifted	34. Poor and Minority Students Can Be Gifted, Too 35. Gifted Girls in a Rural Community	36. Meeting the Needs of Gifted and Talented Preschoolers

TOPIC AREA	KNOWLEDGE (These articles provide information about a handicap or about a special education concept.)	ATTITUDES (These articles contain personal experiences of exceptional persons or discussions about changing children's attitudes toward a handicap.)	TEACHING (These articles contain practical suggestions about how to apply special education principles to the teaching of exceptional children.)
Hearing Impairments	22. Hearing for Success in the Classroom 23. Roles of the Educational Interpreter	24. Establishment Clause as Antiremedy	25. Developing Independent and Responsible Behaviors
Inclusive Education	1. Inclusion 3. Privacy of School Records 13. Effects of Social Interaction Training	2. Commentary on Inclusion and Self-Identity 4. Separate and Unequal 31. Inclusion Revolution	5. Peer Education Partners 6. Selection of Appropriate Technology 7. Enabling the Learning Disabled
Individualized Education Program (IEP) and Individualized Family Service Plan (IFSP)	3. Privacy of School Records	16. Do Public Schools Have an Obligation? 19. Toward Defining Programs and Services 31. Inclusion Revolution	6. Selection of Appropriate Technology 40. Play for All Children
Learning Disabilities	7. Enabling the Learning Disabled 8. Young Children with Attention Deficits	9. Identifying Students' Instructional Needs	10. Adapting Textbooks for Children with Learning Disabilities
Legal Processes	3. Privacy of School Records 24. Establishment Clause as Antiremedy	4. Separate and Unequal 16. Do Public Schools Have an Obligation? 32. Physically Challenged Students 38. Preschool Mainstreaming: Attitude Barriers	6. Selection of Appropriate Technology 23. Roles of the Educational Interpreter 39. Children Who Use Assistive Technology 40. Play for All Children
Mental Retardation	11. Prenatal Drug Exposure 14. Autism	12. Integrating Elementary Students	13. Effects of Social Interaction Training 28. Teaching Choice-making Skills
Multiple Disabilities	11. Prenatal Drug Exposure 14. Autism	12. Integrating Elementary Students	13. Effects of Social Interaction Training 28. Teaching Choice-making Skills
Physical and Health Impairments	29. Medical Treatment and Educational Problems in Children	30. Physical Abuse 31. Inclusion Revolution	32. Physically Challenged Students
Transition to Adulthood	25. Developing Independent and Responsible Behaviors 41. Transition: Old Wine in New Bottles 42. Is a Functional Curriculum Approach Compatible?	13. Effects of Social Interaction Training	10. Adapting Textbooks for Children with Learning Disabilities

Inclusive Education

The education of exceptional children has been undergoing a revolution since 1975 and the passage of The Individuals with Disabilities Education Act, PL 94-142, formerly known as The Education for All Handicapped Children Act. The key principles of Public Law 94-142 call for zero reject of exceptional individuals, parental participation in their care plans, nondiscriminatory evaluations, individualized education programs, equal protection by the law/due process, and education in the least restrictive environment. This last principle, least restrictive environment (LRE), has created considerable controversy. Inclusive education is the term currently used to describe the least restrictive environment. Terms also associated with LRE include normalization, mainstreaming, and deinstitutionalization. Does LRE mean that every exceptional child should be placed in a regular classroom? No. Inclusive education means that every exceptional child should be educated with nondisabled children to the maximum extent appropriate. What is appropriate for one exceptional child might not be appropriate for another. The LRE is the placement that meets both the educational needs and the normalization needs of each unique child.

Inclusive education does not require the regular classroom for every exceptional child, every hour, or every day. Some children with exceptionalities still attend specialized nonpublic day or residential schools full time. This is considered most restrictive and is usually only deemed appropriate for a few children with the most severe problems. A few children with more severe problems may also attend public day schools that specialize in an area of exceptionality. Public Law 94-142 defines an exceptional child as one who differs from a nondisabled child in mental characteristics and/or sensory abilities, and/or communication abilities, and/or social behavior, and/or physical characteristics. While most exceptional children have one small area of disability and many abilities, some exceptional children have multiple disabilities. The children with multiple disabilities generally have the most severe problems and thus are more appropriately placed in specialized facilities or special schools.

Inclusive education encompasses a continuum of educational services for children with exceptional conditions. The regular classroom now admits the vast majority of exceptional children to its rolls. The regular classroom teacher helps provide the prescribed special education services according to an individualized education program (IEP). This instructional program is developed with input from a transdisciplinary team of specialists in the child's area of exceptionality, with input from the regular classroom teacher, input from the family, and input from the child (when appropriate). It defines the nature of the child's problem, long- and short-term goals, and criteria for gauging the effectiveness of the IEP. Inclusion in the regular classroom does not mean that the regular classroom teacher provides all of the prescribed instruction alone. The continuum of services provides consultation to the teacher for the least disabled students and supplementary instruction and services for more disabled students. The supplemental instruction may be done by an itinerant specialist or a school-based specialist, in the regular classroom, in a resource room (pull-out room), or in a special class. Some children with disabilities are enrolled in a regular classroom (inclusive education) in order to have daily contact with nonexceptional children in extracurricular activities. They may, however, have the largest percentage of their educational curriculum provided in a special class with a special education teacher.

Inclusive education, when appropriate, is now provided to children with disabilities from birth through age 21, thanks to two amendments to PL 94-142. Public Law 99-457, passed in 1986, mandates services for exceptional infants and toddlers (age 0–5) and their families. Public Law 101-476, passed in 1990, mandates transitional services for students moving from school to post-school activities through age 21.

Several strategies can help to make inclusive education beneficial. The articles selected for this unit emphasize what works. In the best situations the ratio of students to teachers, and exceptional students to nondisabled students, is low. Each exceptional child's abilities and strengths are stressed. Nondisabled peers are helped to accept each child's area of disability with understanding and empathy, and without fear. Terms such as "afflicted," "burdened," "crippled," "unfortunate," "victimized," or "sick" are avoided. Nondisabled students help teach disabled students as peer tutors and serve as their buddies in extracurricular activities. When a regular classroom teacher has adequate resources, a strong support system, and responsive parental feedback, inclusive education can be very rewarding for all concerned.

The first unit article about inclusion articulates what works. It also discusses what sometimes can go wrong and why. The authors include a checklist of important topics to help make inclusion succeed in public school classrooms. The second unit article addresses the controversy about self-esteem and people with disabilities. Will inclusion in the mainstream with predominantly nondisabled individuals make the disabled person feel badly about him- or herself? The authors suggest that positive self-identity is enhanced by some association with other

persons sharing the same or similar disabilities. However, the affiliations should be chosen by the people with disabilities, not mandated by any segregation procedures. The third article addresses the problem of privacy of school records of persons with disabilities. Assessment, IEPs, and inclusive education make some confidential information more likely to be disclosed. The article discusses what should remain confidential. The next article addresses the problems of assessment of possible exceptionalities. While labeling a child's exceptionality can create problems, nondiscriminatory evaluation is the right of every child. Good screening, diagnosis, classification, placement, planning, and evaluation of IEPs can make special educational services and inclusionary education beneficial. The last two articles in this section stress teaching strategies that help make inclusive education work. "Peer Education Partners" details the benefits of letting nondisabled students help teach disabled students as peer tutors. The last selection in this unit on inclusion details the benefits of housing computers and other tech-

nological aids in the regular education classroom as supplements to the special services provided for each disabled child.

Looking Ahead: Challenge Questions

How do teachers really feel about inclusion? How can they make it work for them?

Do you think disabled students placed in classes with nondisabled peers develop good self-concepts? Why, or why not? How can this be enhanced?

What information about a disabled student is confidential? What may a teacher disclose and to whom?

Is inclusion giving disabled students an edge? How can assessment, labeling, and service be reformed to ensure a positive impact on all our children?

Can peer tutoring strengthen academic skills? Can it also have a beneficial effect on social and vocational skills?

How can teachers select the most appropriate technology for supplemental educational services for their students with disabilities?

INCLUSION

*What it takes to make it work, why it sometimes fails,
and how teachers really feel about it*

**Marilyn Friend
and Lynne Cook**

Everrett is a student in Jeannette Forschner's third-grade class. He has a learning disability that causes him to read at a first-grade level. He also lacks self-confidence; he won't begin his work unless assisted, and he often refuses to do his work at school so his mother can help him with it at home. He is easily distracted.

In another time and place, Everrett would have been in a special class or school, but Jeannette Forschner's class is *inclusive*. Jeanette and a special-education teacher have developed strategies to help Everrett. Reading is structured so that every student has a buddy; parent volunteers audiotape books for Everrett and other students; two desks in a quiet corner of the room are set up for students who have trouble concentrating. These are just a few of the many strategies they have adopted.

A Growing Movement

More and more classrooms resemble Jeannette Forschner's as the nationwide move toward inclusion picks up speed. Whether your school is already becoming inclu-

sive or is just learning about the inclusion movement, you undoubtedly have questions about what it may mean for you as a professional. To help answer your questions, we talked with teachers who are involved in inclusion to get their firsthand accounts, advice, and honest appraisals of the movement.

What Inclusion Is

The term *inclusion* has been defined in many ways by many people, and your school district may even have its own definition. Generally, though, inclusion is an educational philosophy based on the belief that all students are entitled to fully participate in their school community.

Inclusion is most often used to describe programs for students with disabilities, but it also pertains to students from different cultures

Students at Columbus Grove Elementary in Columbus, Ohio, are all smiles during their first week of school. The school is taking its first steps toward inclusion this year.

whose first language is not English, students at risk for failure because of alcohol or drug abuse, and other students with special needs.

Disabilities and Abilities

In the case of children with disabilities, the aim is to integrate them—with the supports they need—into classrooms with nondisabled peers. When inclusion works, these children become members of their classroom communities, valued for their abilities and for who they are.

In inclusive schools, the terms *special-education student* and *special-education teacher* are seldom used. A third-grade teacher who works in an inclusive school in suburban Chicago described it this way: "As a staff, we used to worry about which kids belonged to which teachers, and we'd wonder whether we-were trained to teach those kids. We would discuss whether the special-education teachers were working as hard as the other teachers. Now none of those things matter. We are all teachers; we have a school full of students. We get on with what we're here to do."

In an inclusive classroom, the arrangement between the teacher and the specialist (often a special-education teacher, though it may be a speech pathologist, school psychologist, audiologist, or other support specialist) varies depending upon the students' needs. In most cases, the specialists are in the classroom periodically, but in rare instances, some students with complex multiple disabilities may need full-time classroom assistance. The special-education teacher may also help the classroom teacher create behavior programs, adapt instructional strategies, or develop alternative curriculum.

What Inclusion Isn't

A common misconception about inclusion is that it means that students with disabilities never leave the classroom for special help. But in fact, a student may have a need, such as physical therapy or a treatment that involves highly specialized equipment, that is best handled outside the classroom. Or a student may be moved to a special-education setting if his or her needs truly can't be met in the regular classroom. A child who is medically fragile or a child whose violent behavior cannot be managed should not remain in a regular classroom.

However, in an inclusive classroom, students do not leave just

because they are learning at a different rate or with different materials than their classmates. Instead, instruction is adapted to meet their current needs. Pullout services are the final option, not the first.

What Makes Inclusion Work?

Warren Harris, a sixth-grade teacher in Fairview Elementary School in Bloomington, Indiana, suggests, "Move toward inclusion gradually and allow ample time to talk about kids and the types of help they need. When we started becoming inclusive, we hadn't thought about a lot of things, and we didn't know how to work with each other. We spent the first year in a crisis because we didn't realize how many little things we needed to resolve."

To ensure that your move toward inclusion goes more smoothly, Harris and colleagues Barbara Horvath, Janis Foos, Yvonne Aubin, and Carolyne Ambrose, all of whom work in the Monroe County Community School Corporation, share their advice on how to prepare:

● Inclusion takes time. Schedule regular planning meetings.

● Support from the principal is

Columbus Grove fifth graders help each other with an assignment. Peer tutoring is a common strategy in inclusive classrooms.

crucial. If you and other teachers feel that you need more support, do everything you can to get it sooner rather than later.

● Inclusion is about attitudes. It works when teachers focus on students' abilities, not their disabilities.

● Be flexible, be ready to change. You have to do what's best, and not always be concerned with whether this follows the rules.

● Be willing to teach in a classroom with another teacher. Special-education teachers have to be willing to try to teach a whole class and to help other students, too.

● Remind yourself: "A kid is a kid. I know how to teach kids. If I get stuck, I'll ask for help."

● Address logistical problems such as scheduling, and broader issues such as assessment, as they arise.

● Visit and draw on the experiences of other schools in which students with disabilities are already included in classrooms.

1. INCLUSIVE EDUCATION

Support Is the Key

In a perfect world, all school districts would provide all the assistance needed to make inclusion successful for students and feasible for teachers. Unfortunately, some schools are jumping on the inclusion bandwagon without lining up the necessary supports. In others, inclusion is seen as a cost-saving approach, and sufficient supports are eliminated. In both situations, problems are likely to occur.

What constitutes sufficient support depends on the individual situation. Here are some ways help is delivered:

- The classroom teacher and special-education teacher or other support staff meet periodically to discuss a student's needs and develop strategies to meet them.
- The special-education teacher may create alternative materials for the student or come into the classroom more frequently.
- The teacher and special-education teacher may coteach the class—a popular approach to inclusion.

TECHNOLOGY CONNECTION

Technology can help support learning by all students in an inclusive class—with all of their different learning styles. Technology tools can include:

- Adaptive computer devices for disabled children, such as touch screens and "talking" software.
- Tool software such as word processors and printing programs, which help students communicate ideas they may have trouble getting onto paper by hand.
- Tape recorders for storytelling, data collecion, and oral journals.
- VCRs and camcorders to bring an audiovisual dimension to student projects. For more information about technology and children's special needs, contact the Council for Exceptional Children, Technology and Media Division, 1920 Association Dr., Reston, VA 22091; (703) 630-3660.

Are You Ready for Inclusion? A Checklist for Your School

It's likely that your school will move toward inclusion in the near future. To help you get ready, we've created a checklist of important topics to discuss with your coworkers and principal.

- [ ] Does your school have a mission statement that expresses the belief that the professionals and other staff strive to meet the needs of all students?
- [ ] Have teachers had opportunities to discuss their concerns about inclusion and have steps been taken to address these concerns?
- [ ] Has planning for inclusion included classroom teachers, special-education teachers, other support staff, administrators, parents, and students?
- [ ] Have you clarified the expectations for students with disabilities who will be integrated into classrooms?
- [ ] Has shared planning time been arranged for teams of teachers?
- [ ] Have staff members become comfortable with working collaboratively?
- [ ] Has the plan for creating an inclusive school addressed the needs of all students, not just the needs of students with identified disabilities?
- [ ] Has a pilot program been planned prior to full implementation?
- [ ] Have start-up resources been allocated for the inclusion effort?
- [ ] Have steps been taken to ensure that teachers will be rewarded for experimentation and innovation, even if efforts are sometimes not successful?
- [ ] Have all teachers, even those who may not at first participate in teaching students integrated into classroom programs, learned that inclusion can only exist as a schoolwide belief system?
- [ ] Have students without disabilities had opportunities to learn about all types of diversity, including individuals with disabilities?
- [ ] Have teachers and other staff identified benchmarks so that they have attainable goals to celebrate after one year? Two years? Three years?

Teachers Speak Out About Inclusion

What is it really like to work in an inclusive school? We asked teachers to share their successes and their struggles. Here's what they said.

THE SUCCESSES

"Inclusion is good for kids. It helps students really understand diversity. And students learn how to help each other. It teaches students that they can learn from each other; that the teacher is not the only source in the classroom."
—Karen Adams
Fairview Elementary School
Bloomington, Indiana

"Students with disabilities benefit from being with their peers. Some students learn much more than they would if they received the same instruction in a special-education classroom. And they learn how to get along with their classmates who don't have special needs." *—Eileen Kearney*
Gary Elementary School
West Chicago, Illinois

"Inclusion is really about effective education. We're doing it because it's right for kids." *—Missy Douglas*
Fairview Elementary School
Bloomington, Indiana

"Inclusion brings the staff together. We had to talk through a lot of issues to get ready for inclusion. Now we all talk about what we're teaching and how we're teaching it. If we have a problem with a student, we talk about it. We support each other more than we ever did before." *—Rhonda Caldwell*
Broadview Elementary School
Bloomington, Indiana

THE STRUGGLES
(The names of teachers quoted in this section have been omitted.)

"I had 29 third graders, four with disabilities. There wasn't anyone to help me. I didn't know what to expect of them; I didn't want to do something that would hurt those students. If I had known what the expectations were, I could have done a better job."
— Enfield, Connecticut

"I had a student with an emotional disability placed in my class. He would bite other students and blow in their faces. He wouldn't stay in one place for a minute. I spent the entire year worrying that he would seriously injure another student. I don't think he should have been in my classroom. I think I should have had more help."
—Indianapolis, Indiana

"I had a fifth-grade student reading at a first-grade level. I didn't have materials for her. She wanted to read, but just couldn't. I don't know why she was in my class. She should have been with other kids who couldn't read. I had nothing for her." *—Chicago, Illinois*

"Sometimes I felt like I wasn't a teacher, more like a traffic cop. The special-education teacher came in sometimes. The aide came in every day. The speech therapist was here twice a week. I didn't have time to do my own planning, much less planning for everyone else. It almost would have been better to be left alone."
—Philadelphia, Pennsylvania

A Commentary on Inclusion and the Development of a Positive Self-Identity by People with Disabilities

ABSTRACT: *A growing number of concerned individuals throughout the world, including people with disabilities, their parents, and educators, are advocating that students with disabilities be educated in the mainstream of neighborhood classrooms and schools. However, some disability-rights advocates believe that if people with disabilities are to have a well-developed sense of identity as adults, they need to have had opportunities in their school years to associate with other people (both children and adults) having similar characteristics and interests. In this article, we examine this issue and provide one perspective on how it might be addressed.*

SUSAN STAINBACK
WILLIAM STAINBACK
KATHERYN EAST
MARA SAPON-SHEVIN

SUSAN STAINBACK, Professor; WILLIAM STAINBACK, Professor, College of Education, University of Northern Iowa, Cedar Falls. KATHERYN EAST, Ed.D, Adjunct Instructor, Educational Psychology and Foundations, University of Northern Iowa, Cedar Falls. MARA SAPON-SHEVIN, Associate Professor, Elementary and Special Education, Syracuse University, Syracuse, New York.

The issue of educational integration or inclusion has been the focus of much debate over the past several years in many articles published in *Exceptional Children* (e.g., Blackman, 1989; Braaten, Kauffman, Braaten, Polsgrove, & Nelson, 1988; Davis, 1988; Lieberman, 1985; Messinger, 1985; Stainback & Stainback, 1984, 1985). Few researchers, however have focused on how inclusion into the educational mainstream influences the development of a positive self-identity among students with disabilities.

Branthwaite (1985) has contended that a person's self-identity—confidence and feelings of worth—influences the way he or she interacts with the environment. Gliedman and Roth (1980) have provided evidence that it is important for people with disabilities to develop a positive self-identity that incorporates their disabilities. Fer-

guson and Asch (1989) described the issue as follows:

> How do disabled people come to think of themselves in ways that incorporate their disability as an important part of their personal and social identity? It is a theme that complicates the call for educational integration. In both the literature and our personal reflections we find an undeniable recognition that a well-developed sense of identity as a disabled adult needs some significant involvement as a child with other people (children and adults) who have similar disabilities. (p. 131)

Although the goal of inclusion is to create a community in which all children work and learn together and develop mutually supportive repertoires of peer support, the goal has never been to become oblivious to children's individual differences. Within the field of multicultural education, the goal of "color blindness" (of not noticing differences) has been discredited and replaced by models that acknowledge and support the development of positive self-identity for diverse groups. Similarly, the goal of inclusion in schools is to create a world in which all people are knowledgeable about and supportive of all other people, and that goal is not achieved by some false image of homogeneity in the name of inclusion.

From *Exceptional Children*, Vol. 60, No. 6, May 1994, pp. 486-490. © 1994 by The Council for Exceptional Children. Reprinted by permission.

Rather, we must look carefully at the ways schools have typically organized around individual differences and come up with alternatives. Typical models of special education services have involved identifying individual differences, labeling them, and then providing segregated services for people similarly labeled. The alternative to segregation is not dumping students in heterogeneous groups and ignoring their individual differences. This is the expressed fear of many who oppose inclusion—that students' individual needs will get lost in the process. We must find ways to build inclusive school communities that acknowledge student differences and meet students' needs, yet do so within a common context.

Given the importance of this issue, we need to examine how we might enhance the development of self-identity when considering the integrated/inclusive schooling movement. The purposes of this commentary are to outline why the issue of developing a positive self-identity exists within the integration/inclusion movement and to discuss how we might address that issue.

THE MOVEMENT TOWARD INTEGRATION AND THE PROBLEM IT CREATES IN DEVELOPING POSITIVE SELF-IDENTITY

Many educators consider grouping or clustering students homogeneously, based on a common characteristic, to be inappropriate for moral reasons involving equality (e.g., Biklen, 1985; Fullwood, 1990; Lipsky & Gartner, 1989; Stainback, Stainback, & Forest, 1989). As Chief Justice Warren pointed out in the *Brown v. Board of Education* decision, segregation produces ill effects—and "separate is not equal" (Warren, 1954, p. 493). Other educators have recognized that homogeneous grouping is less than optimal for people with disabilities who must learn to live and work in integrated communities (Disability Rights, 1983).

On the other hand, integrated classrooms often have a low incidence of students with certain disabilities (such as blindness or spina bifida) who have few opportunities to get to know and interact with other students with similar characteristics. To prevent this isolation, we need to find ways for these students to positively identify with others with similar characteristics. We could, however, provide planned opportunities for people who share common characteristics to get together, either in school or in community settings.

ACKNOWLEDGING INDIVIDUAL CHARACTERISTICS THROUGH PURPOSEFUL ACCESS

Students could meet and spend time with individuals with characteristics similar to theirs in ad hoc groups formed around specific characteristics or issues. In these groups, students may share information, support, and strategies for transforming prejudice, discrimination, and practice. In much the same way, the women's movement sought to empower women by forming consciousness-raising groups in which members could feel safe so that they could then deal with the broader society. Young people with disabilities may have similar needs.

Such support groups are characterized by *purposeful access*—planned opportunities for people who share common characteristics to get together. These groups provide opportunities for voluntary affiliations, yet allow their members to retain involvement in the community as a whole. Adrienne Asch, a colleague who is blind, pointed out that although it was important for her educational and social development that she attend regular neighborhood public school classes, having the opportunity to "compare notes" and share experiences with peers who were also blind was helpful to her. She stated:

> We talked about how our parents, teachers, and the kids in our schools treated us because we were blind. Sometimes someone who solved a problem told the rest of us what s/he figured out. Sometimes we complained together about those problems none of us had managed to solve. It was important to compare notes, have solid friendships where sight or lack of it did not affect the terms of the interaction, and just in general not feel alone. (Ferguson & Asch, 1989, pp. 132-133)

The benefits of formal and informal support or interest groups have been cited for students of divorced parents, students who are deaf, victims of abuse or rape, future farmers, religious groups, wheelchair athletes, teenage girls, and so on (Hahn, 1985). Such groups have several important components. One is that their membership and participation is neither imposed (people can choose whether they will participate) nor exclusionary (anyone who wants to be part of the group is accepted). Group membership is based on a person's expressed needs and interests, not on an adult or authority figure's perception of that person's identifying characteristic (e.g., blindness or deafness). In this way, young people can truly have free access to form friendships and identify with whomever they choose. As an illustration of this, in a work situation in which people who were labeled mentally retarded were learning job skills, several staff members expressed concern over a young woman who chose to interact socially with the staff rather than the other workers. When asked, the woman explained, "I am normal inside, and I can't seem to get that out" (Kauffman, 1984, p. 89). All people are "normal" inside and must be allowed ample opportunity to express that normality in their choice of talents, characteristics, friendships, and interests if they are to develop a healthy sense of personal identity. If people who share a common characteristic, such as being disabled or black or female or Catholic, want to get together, share experiences, or form an advocacy group, that is their personal choice. Though authority figures may assist in group formation, mandated participation may be counterproductive, particularly if the goal is to enhance the positive self-identity of the person.

There is a danger when those in authority make assumptions about who should be grouped together and around what characteristic or issue. In other words, if the principal decided that all bilingual students should be grouped together because their primary language is not English or the special education coordinator decided that all students who are mobility-impaired should meet with one another, the potential for that group to achieve individual and group empowerment would automatically be limited because the group was formed, not out of common concern or mutual identification, but because of definition from outside the group.

Groups also need to be initiated and defined by the members to avoid violating the interests, needs, and basic rights of the members (Stainback et al., 1989). Hazards exist when people in authority, including educators and parents, focus on any one of an individual's characteristics (e.g., disability, race, or religion) and organize the individual's life around that characteristic. According to Strully and Strully (1985), parents and educators who encourage children with disabilities to have only friends who have disabilities and to participate only in social events for people with disabilities perpetuate the well-intentioned segregation of years past. The real danger here is that affinity groups become the only safe haven for people who have been defined as "different" and thereby remove from those in the mainstream the responsibility to make the broader community accessible and welcoming.

THE ROLE OF SCHOOL PERSONNEL

There is growing evidence from the experiences of people with disabilities that developing a positive self-identity that incorporates disability does not necessarily have to conflict with achieving school and community integration (see Ferguson & Asch, 1989; Hahn, 1989; People First, 1987). These experiences indicate that integration/inclusion in schools and communities can be achieved without restricting the rights of any person or group to freely form friendships and bonds or identify with whomever they choose. However, school personnel may need to be sensitive to some students' desire to identify with others who have similar characteristics and interests.

Schools can provide the framework necessary to allow students to form such groups, just as they have enabled students to initiate other student-centered groups such as pep clubs, circles of friends, or photography clubs. Some schools, for example, sponsor special support groups for students whose parents are divorcing so that students can combat their sense of isolation and alienation about what is happening in their lives.

The opportunity for such student-initiated interest groups could be made available at all levels of schooling, from preschool through high school. Varying degrees of facilitation by adults may be required. Schools supporting flexible groups guided by student-expressed interest and made up of volunteers could allow the benefits to positive self-identity to accrue. Schools simply assume the role of providing opportunities for students to become acquainted and to interact with other people who have characteristics similar to theirs, should they choose to do so.

It is important that affinity groups be self-chosen, that is, initiated by the members. Though an adult or authority figure can certainly facilitate the formation of a group when there is expressed interest, any member of the school community should have the opportunity to initiate a group. A mechanism could be in place for any student to do so. For example, if one student decides that he would like to meet with others who are having problems with older siblings, or with others who are concerned about fights on the playground, that is how the group would be defined. When groups are structured this way, they become special interest groups related to a specific area or topic and not necessarily disability-oriented groups. If several students who are hearing impaired decide to meet together to discuss their experiences in Jefferson Middle School as students with hearing impairments, they can seek others who are so identified or interested, and form a group. Groups might also involve students who wish to identify themselves as allies for a particular group—people who will help to counter oppression that students in the group are experiencing and commit to being there with them and for them in their struggles to achieve their goals. When groups choose to form in this way, the concern that resegregation of people with disabilities will occur is minimized.

Also, school personnel should facilitate groups that are self-defined. Self-defined groups are those that decide not only who will be in them, but what their focus and purpose will be. A group of students who are visually impaired might decide that their goal is mutual support only, sharing issues and concerns in a safe setting. Or they might decide that their goal is self-advocacy, educating students or teachers about ways in which their needs might be better met.

Finally, the emerging professional literature on mutual support groups (Vaux, 1988) indicates that they should be flexible. Flexible groups are those that remain intact only as long as they are useful and meet the needs of the individual members. Just as newly divorced or widowed people might seek out a transitional support group, leaving that group when they no longer feel the need for that particular kind of support, groups should not be initiated for a fixed or inflexible duration. Joining the group and deciding how long the group will operate should be the decision of the group members.

A CALL FOR RESEARCH

There is little or no research in special education on issues surrounding the development of a self-identity. One route such research might take is to ask students how their sense of self-identity is being or could be enhanced at school. Another could be to ask students who have moved beyond school what changes would have made their educational experience more positive. Using the data gathered from students, combined with the understanding of how schools and other community organizations have developed and facilitated interest/support groups, educators could develop a process for ensuring purposeful access for all young people. After implementation, the effects of such groups on the young people involved and their peers, family, and teachers might be investigated.

CONCLUSION

To develop a positive self-identity, young people need opportunities to exercise and express choices about friendships and group affiliations. To allow this choice, the mainstream of the schools and the community must be flexible, adaptive, and sensitive to the unique needs of all its members. Purposeful access can introduce these qualities into the mainstream by allowing each individual an opportunity to develop a positive sense of identity. School can become a place where purposeful access groups are facilitated and where each student is given the opportunity to develop positive feelings about the unique qualities he or she brings to the educational community. After all, the goal of inclusion is not to erase differences, but to enable all students to belong within an educational community that validates and values their individuality.

As inclusion continues to be a hotly debated issue, it is critical that the voices of students be heard. One way of ensuring that students have a voice is to provide them with opportunities to meet together, form friendships among themselves, generate allies across groups, and learn to take charge of their education and their lives.

REFERENCES

Biklen, D. (Ed.). (1985). *Achieving the complete school*. New York: Teachers College Press.

Blackman, H. P. (1989). Special education placement. Is it what you know or where you live? *Exceptional Children, 55,* 459-462.

Braaten, S., Kauffman, J., Braaten, B., Polsgrove, L., & Nelson, C. (1988). The regular education initiative: Patent medicine for behavioral disorders. *Exceptional Children, 55,* 21-27.

Branthwaite, A. (1985). The development of social identity and self-concept. In A. Branthwaite & D. Rogers (Eds.), *Children growing up* (pp. 34-42). Philadelphia: Open University Press.

Davis, W. (1988). The regular education initiative debate: Its promise and problems. *Exceptional Children, 55,* 440-449.

Disability Rights, Education, and Defense Fund. (1983). *The Disabled Women's Education Project: Report of survey/results: Executive summary.* Berkeley, CA: Author.

Ferguson, P., & Asch, A. (1989). Lessons from life: Personal and parental perspectives on school, childhood, and disability. In D. Biklen, D. Ferguson, & A. Ford (Eds.), *Schooling and disability* (pp. 108-140). Chicago: National Society for the Study of Education.

Fullwood, D. (1990). *Chances and choices.* Baltimore: Paul H. Brookes.

Gliedman, J., & Roth, W. (1980). *The unexpected minority: Handicapped children in America.* New York: Harcourt, Brace Jovanovich.

Hahn, H. (1985). Toward a politics of disability: Definitions, disciplines, and policies. *The Social Science Journal, 22,* 87-105.

Hahn, H. (1989). The politics of special education. In D. Lipsky & A. Gartner (Eds.), *Beyond special education* (pp. 225-242). Baltimore: Paul H. Brookes.

Kauffman, S. (1984). Socialization in sheltered workshop settings. In R. Edgerton & S. Bercovici (Eds.), *Mental retardation* (pp. 73-92). Washington, DC: American Association for Mental Deficiency.

Lieberman, L. (1985). Special and regular education: A merger made in heaven? *Exceptional Children, 51,* 513-517.

Lipsky, D. & Gartner, A. (1989). *Beyond separate education.* Baltimore: Paul H. Brookes.

Messinger, J. (1985). A commentary on "A rationale for merger of special and regular education." *Exceptional Children, 51,* 510-513.

People First. (1987). *People first* [Video]. Downsview, Ont.: Canadian Association for Community Living.

Stainback, S., & Stainback, W. (1985). The merger of special and regular education: Can it be done? *Exceptional Children, 51,* 517-521.

Stainback, S., Stainback, W., & Forest, M. (Eds.). (1989). *Educating all students in the mainstream of regular education.* Baltimore: Paul H. Brookes.

Stainback, W., & Stainback, S. (1984). A rationale for the merger of special and regular education. *Exceptional Children, 51,* 102-111.

Strully, J., & Strully, C. (1985). Friendship and our children. *Journal of the Association for Persons with Severe Handicaps, 1,* 224-227.

Vaux, A. (1988). *Social support: Theory, research, and intervention.* New York: Praeger Press.

Warren, E. (1954). *Brown v. Board of Education of Topeka.* 347 U.S. 483, 493.

PRIVACY
OF SCHOOL RECORDS:
What Every Special Education Teacher Should Know

Timothy S. Hartshorne
and Lyman W. Boomer

Timothy S. Hartshorne, Associate Professor of Psychology, Central Michigan University, Mr. Pleasant. Lyman W. Boomer (CEC Chapter #76), Professor, Department of Psychology, Western Illinois University, Macomb.

Schools gather a great deal of information, some of it highly personal, regarding each child with exceptionalities. This must be done to fulfill the requirements of the Education for All Handicapped Children Act of 1975 (EHA). When the school conducts a comprehensive evaluation, it gathers personal information on such factors as the child's health, vision, hearing, social and emotional status, level of intelligence, and academic achievement. When an individualized education program (IEP) is developed, it includes the child's level of educational performance along with annual goals and short-term objectives. The information used to make a placement decision must be documented.

Following placement, the special education teacher may conduct a curriculum-based assessment or use teaching probes to gather further information regarding the child's unique learning needs. A daily chart of the child's academic performance and a record of self-management skills may be maintained. The list goes on of tests and inventories, rating scales and checklists, and charts and records concerning each child with exceptionalities.

The problem with such information collection is the natural conflict between the individual's right to privacy and society's need for information concerning individual behavior (Stevens, 1980). To protect the privacy of students and their families while at the same time ensuring access to information by those with a legitimate interest in a child's education, Congress enacted the Family Educational Rights and Privacy Act (FERPA) in 1974. Additional safeguards were provided for children with disabilities through EHA.

This article examines issues in the disclosure of student records—the release of information regarding a child or permitting access to the child's educational records—and invasion of privacy.

WHAT INFORMATION MUST TEACHERS DISCLOSE?

Teachers are required to report known and suspected incidents of child abuse and neglect. Federal assistance for child abuse programs requires that each state enact a child abuse and reporting statute (Child Abuse Prevention and Treatment Act of 1974, 45 CFR 1340.1). Educators in all 50 states and the District of Columbia are now required to report child abuse (Meddin & Rosen, 1986), and 45 states impose criminal penalties for failure to report abuse and neglect (cited in *State v. Grover*, 1989).

The principal of a Minnesota elementary school was charged with two counts of failing to report suspected child abuse following two alleged incidents of sexual misconduct by a teacher (*State v. Grover*, 1989). The mothers of two boys informed the principal that a teacher had made sexual advances toward their sons, but the principal failed to notify police. During the investigation police discovered that the principal had also failed to report two other incidents of alleged child abuse involving the same teacher. During the trial, the principal argued that the statute requiring educators to report known and suspected instances of child abuse was unconstitutionally vague and overbroad. The Minnesota Supreme Court found otherwise. The Court held that the statute does not require the espousal of an ideological point of view, but only mandates the reporting of information. An individual making such a report would be free to indicate that while there is reason to suspect abuse,

From *Teaching Exceptional Children*, Vol. 25, No. 4, Summer 1993, pp. 32-35. © 1993 by The Council for Exceptional Children. Reprinted by permission.

he or she does not hold a personal belief to that effect. Thus whether the principal believed them to be true or not, he was required to report the incidents.

Teachers in most states are also required to report to law enforcement officials any information communicated to them by a student that may bear on the commission of a felony. For example, if a student confides to a teacher information about violations of drug laws, that information must be reported (Overcast & Sales, 1982).

WHAT INFORMATION MUST BE SAFEGUARDED?

Teachers must safeguard educational records. An educational record is *any* form of information directly related to a child that is collected, maintained, or used by the school (FERPA, 1974, 34 CFR 99.3). An educational record may include the results of a child's psychological evaluation or the IEP. It may also include a videotape of the class taken by the teacher or an audiotape made by the teacher of a child's oral reading performance. For students under the age of 18, psychiatric hospital treatment plans may be considered educational records (Bellamy to Woodson, 1989). Any form of information collected, maintained, or used by the school that relates to a child is considered an educational record and must be safeguarded.

Records that a school district collects or uses but does not originate must also be considered an educational record under FERPA and EHA. For example, if a school were to receive a medical evaluation regarding a child and that report were placed in the child's file, the medical report would be considered an educational record (Tyrrell to Janda, 1980). Reports from juvenile court or social service agencies that the school maintains in its files are also considered educational records. Use, not origination, defines an educational record under FERPA and EHA.

WHO HAS ACCESS TO CONFIDENTIAL INFORMATION?

Parents must be permitted to inspect any and all confidential information related to their child (FERPA, 1974, 34 CFR 99.10[a]; EHA, 1975, 300.562[a]). Such inspection must be afforded without unnecessary delay and before any meeting regarding an IEP or hearing relating to the identification, evaluation, or placement of the child. In no case may access be delayed more than 45 days.

The parents may also request explanations and interpretations of their child's records from school officials. Furthermore, parents may have a representative such as an attorney inspect the records (EHA, 1975, 34 CFR 300.562[b]).

The school district is required to provide the parents with *access to,* but not necessarily *copies of* their child's educational records. If, however, a parent were unable to go to the school to inspect the records because of illness or injury, school officials would be required to provide copies of the records. A fee may be charged for copies unless it would effectively prevent parents from exercising their right to inspect the records. However, the school district may not charge an administrative fee for searching for and retrieving educational records (FERPA, 1974, 34 CFR 99.11).

Access to educational records must be afforded to custodial and noncustodial parents alike. When Robert Fay, a noncustodial parent, tried to obtain information regarding his children's school activities and educational progress, the superintendent wrote that the school system would "provide information to any person or organization whom the courts decide have a legal right to it" (*Fay v. South Colonie Central School District,* 1986, p. 24). Fay then sued the school district in federal court, alleging that he had been denied access

to his children's educational records. The court found the school district liable under the Civil Rights Act of 1871 for denying Fay his statutory right under FERPA to inspect school records. The judgment, along with compensatory damages, was upheld by the Second Circuit Court of Appeals.

Students who are 18 years old or older or who are enrolled in a postsecondary educational institution, exclusive of their parents, have the right to inspect their own educational records. Parents, however, retain the right to inspect records if the student is claimed as a dependent for income tax purposes (FERPA, 1974, 34 CFR 99.31 [a][8]).

School officials, including teachers and administrators who have a legitimate educational interest, may access educational records (FERPA, 1974, 34 CFR 99.31[a][1]). The names of children with disabilities may also be disclosed to school board members if the district's policies define the board members as school officials with a legitimate educational interest (Tyrrell to Grossman, 1980).

Records may also be disclosed to officials of another school system or agency in which the child intends to enroll (FERPA, 1974, 34 CFR 99.31[a][2]). If the parent has notified the school district that the child will be transferring to another school, the child's educational records may be sent to the new school. **Upon request, written notice and copies of the records must also be sent to the parent (FERPA, 1974, 34 CFR 99.34[a][2]).**

Federal or state program auditors, representatives of accrediting organizations, and organizations conducting studies may access personally identifiable information in order to carry out their responsibilities (FERPA, 1974, 34 CFR 99.31[a][5,6,7]).

Finally, information from educational records may be disclosed in order to comply with a judicial order or subpoena or to protect the health and safety of the child (FERPA, 1974, 34 CFR 99.31[a][9,10]).

With written consent of the parent, personally identifiable information may be disclosed to a third party (FERPA, 1974, 34 CFR 99.30). For example, with written consent of the parent, copies of a child's educational records may be sent to a physician. Likewise, personal information concerning a child may be discussed with a private psychologist provided that the school district has obtained prior written consent from the parent. Teachers and administrators with access to educational records may disclose information to third parties only after written consent of the parent has been obtained.

WHAT RECORD OF ACCESS MUST BE MAINTAINED?

EHA and FERPA both require that the school district maintain a record of each disclosure of personally identifiable information or request for disclosure (FERPA, 1974, 34 CFR 99.32; 300.563). The record of access must include the name of the person seeking information, the date access was given, and the purpose for which access was given. The record of access requirement does not apply to school officials, parents, students over the age of 18 or enrolled in postsecondary educational institutions, or individuals with written consent from the parent. Requests for "directory information"—information that would not generally be considered harmful or an invasion of privacy if disclosed to the public—need not be recorded.

WHAT INFORMATION MAY TEACHERS DISCLOSE?

Teachers may disclose directory information (FERPA, 1974, 34 CFR 99.3). For example, disclosure of a child's name, address, telephone number, or date and place of birth is usually considered harmless. However, disclosure of other information that would ordinarily be considered harmless may be harmful to a child with disabilities. Disclosure of the name of the child's previous school, for example, may be considered harmless enough, but disclosure that the child had previously attended a special school for children with severe emotional disturbances is an invasion of privacy of a greater magnitude.

The school district must notify parents of the information that has been designated directory information and thus subject to public disclosure. Parents may, in turn, notify the school of any or all information that should not be released without their consent (FERPA, 1974, 34 CFR 99.37). Thus, prior to disclosing even directory information, the teacher should check to verify that a child's parent has not requested that it be withheld.

WHAT INFORMATION IS NOT SUBJECT TO DISCLOSURE?

Not subject to disclosure are personal notes made by a teacher, kept in his or her sole possession, and revealed to no one except a temporary substitute teacher (FERPA, 1974, 34 CFR 99.3). For example, if a teacher kept a written record in a notebook of a child's behavioral outbursts and showed it to no one, the notebook would not be subject to disclosure. However, if the teacher shared the notebook with anyone other than a substitute teacher, the notebook would be considered an educational record.

A 4th-grade teacher in Massachusetts wrote a college term paper describing a child with disabilities in her classroom (*Alinovi v. Worcester School Committee*, 1985). The paper referred to the child by his first name only and identified no other person or place. Before the start of a reevaluation conference for the child, the teacher gave the term paper to the school district special education supervisor and told him that it might provide additional understanding of the child's special needs. The supervisor placed the paper in his briefcase but did not read it, and returned the paper to the teacher after the meeting. When the building principal asked to see the term paper, the teacher refused, claiming that the paper was private. The U.S. Court of Appeals held, however, that by taking the term paper to the reevaluation conference, the teacher had forfeited her expectation of privacy.

Private notes are just that: notes. Once they become the basis for a special education decision or intervention, they may no longer be considered private notes (FERPA, 1974, 34 CFR 300.562). Mary K. has a doctorate in counseling psychology and is qualified to administer and interpret the Rorschach Inkblot Test. When her daughter was administered the Rorschach along with other instruments by a school psychologist, Mary and her husband, John K., requested access to the verbatim Rorschach responses in order to better evaluate the school psychologist's recommendations and to possibly obtain a second opinion. The Circuit Court's ruling against the parents was overturned by the Illinois Court of Appeals (*John K. v. Board of Education for School District 65, Cook County*, 1987). The Court ruled that raw psychological test data are a part of a student's record and are subject to disclosure under Illinois law. The judge stated, "We cannot consider the verbatim transcript of [the child's] responses as [the psychologist's] `speculations, reminders, hunches, or impressions'" (p. 803).

INVASION OF PRIVACY

Justice Brandeis wrote, "The makers of our constitution…conferred, as against the Government, the right to be let alone—the most comprehensive of rights and the right most valued by civilized men" (*Olmstead v. U.S.*, 1928, p.

478). In the creation of voluminous educational records for children placed in special education, school personnel observe the children, interview them, test them, and intervene with them; they are hardly "let alone." While the rights of minors are protected by the Constitution, states still retain the power to restrict the rights of children (Fleming & Fleming, 1987). The rights of children must be balanced against specific governmental interests in the educational setting that may not be present in society at large (Stevens, 1980). Students' rights to privacy may need to be violated in the form of search and seizure when there is a reasonable suspicion of illegal behavior (Avery & Simpson, 1987); disclosure in order to provide appropriate supervision to protect other pupils from aggressive or violent behavior (Baker, 1987); reporting suspected child abuse (Meddin & Rosen, 1986); and creating, maintaining, and releasing educational records.

However, to avoid infringing on the privacy rights of students, teachers should take the advice of Eades (1986) and make certain that the reports they write, the statements they make, and the records they create are *only* as required and permitted by their employment in the school.

REFERENCES

Alinovi v. Worcester School Committee, 777 F.2d 776 (1st Cir. 1985).

Avery, C. W., & Simpson, R. J. (1987). Search and seizure: A risk assessment model for public school officials. *Journal of Law and Education, 16,* 403-433.

Baker, M. G. (1987). The teacher's need to know versus the student's right to privacy. *Journal of Law and Education, 16,* 71-91.

Bellamy to Woodson, (1989, July 28). *Education for the Handicapped Law Reporter, 213,* p. 224.

Child Abuse Prevention and Treatment Act of 1974, 42 USC 5100 (1983); 45 CFR 1340.

Civil Rights Act of 1871, 42 USC 1983 (1981).

Eades, R. W. (1986). The school counselor or psychologist and problems of defamation. *Journal of Law and Education, 15,* 117-120.

Education for All Handicapped Children Act of 1975, 20 USC 1400 (1978); 34 CFR 300.

Family Educational Rights and Privacy Act of 1974, 20 USC 1232g (1978); 34 CFR 99.

Fay v. South Colonie Central School District, 802 F.2d 21 (2nd Cir. 1986).

Fleming, E. R., & Fleming, D. C. (1987). Involvement of minors in special education decision-making. *Journal of Law and Education, 16,* 389-402.

John K. v. Board of Education for School District 65, Cook County, 504 N.E.2d 797 (Ill. App. 1 Dist. 1987).

Meddin, B. J., & Rosen, A. L. (1986). Child abuse and neglect: Prevention and reporting. *Young Children, 41*(4), 26-30.

Olmstead v. U.S., 277 U.S. 438 (1928).

Overcast, T. D., & Sales, B. D. (1982). The legal rights of students in the elementary and secondary public schools. In C. R. Reynolds & T. B. Gutkin (Eds.), *The handbook of school psychology* (pp. 1075-1100). New York: Wiley.

State v. Grover, 437 N.W.2d 60 (Minn. 1989).

Stevens, G. E. (1980). Invasion of student privacy. *Journal of Law and Education, 9,* 343-351.

Tyrrell to Grossman. (1980, October 3). *Education for the Handicapped Law Reporter, 211,* p. 227.

Tyrrell to Janda. (1980, October 8). *Education for the Handicapped Law Reporter, 211,* p. 205.

The authors gratefully acknowledge the assistance of Janis P. Stucky in the development of this article.

SEPARATE AND UNEQUAL

*America's special education system was intended to give disabled kids an edge.
But it is cheating many—and costing the rest of us billions*

Billy Hawkins speaks softly as he tells his students of the promise of special education. "Every child," he says, "can learn." Billy Hawkins should know. For the first 15 years of his life, he was labeled by his teachers as "educable mentally retarded." That meant "special education"—and a stigma that too often in America was a passport to failure.

Things changed for Hawkins one crisp fall night 23 years ago. A backup quarterback, Hawkins came in off the bench and rallied his team from far behind. In the stands, the principal watched the high school sophomore in amazement. The "retarded kid" could play. He ran complicated plays; he clearly had a gift for the game. Soon after, the principal had Hawkins enrolled in regular classes, his teachers instructed to give him extra help. Today, Billy Hawkins is 39. He holds a Ph.D. and is the associate dean of the school of education at Michigan's Ferris State University.

It is an inspiring story, but in the world of special education, it is the exception, not the rule. Just a few years after Billy Hawkins moved out of a special classroom to rejoin the rest of his schoolmates, Congress passed a law requiring public schools to educate all children with disabilities. In the 18 years since, the good intentions have yielded decidedly mixed results. While millions of American children have received educations as a result of the Individuals with Disabilities Education Act (IDEA), the school system created by the law hurts many of the very children it is intended to help even as it costs taxpayers billions.

A five-month examination of the nation's special education system by *U.S. News* has documented a network of programs that regularly use subjective testing criteria, that rely on funding formulas and identification procedures that funnel ever greater numbers of children into special programs each year and that, in state after state, include disproportionately high numbers of black schoolchildren. The system has ballooned into more than a $30 billion-a-year industry, and the costs are climbing. More

troubling, nearly 40 years after *Brown v. Board of Education*, the U.S. Supreme Court's landmark school desegregation ruling, Americans continue to pay for and send their children to classrooms that are often separate and unequal.

Presented with the results of the *U.S. News* investigation, Secretary of Education Richard Riley last week acknowledged serious flaws in the special education system. As a result of that, Riley pledged to make fundamental reforms in the special education system next year. Says Riley: "The need for disabled students coming out of high school to be productive citizens is much, much greater today than in the past.

The magazine's principal findings:

■ **Funding.** Special education programs often operate in ways specifically designed to attract state and federal dollars to local school districts—not to best serve students. In nearly two thirds of the 50 states, *U.S. News* found that reimbursement formulas for special education programs had an effect in determining the number and type of such programs funded. Texas, for instance, pays local school districts 10 times more for teaching special education students in separate classrooms than in classrooms with other students. The result? Despite generally accepted evidence that some special education students benefit from regular classrooms, only 5 percent of all special education students in Texas are taught in regular classrooms. That's the lowest rate in the nation. In Tennessee, thousands of special education students who had been receiving training just a few hours a week in separate classrooms were assigned to nearly all-day classes in separate rooms. The reason: a change in the state's special education funding formula that gave school districts more money to teach special education students in separate rooms.

■ **Growth.** Imprecise state and federal regulations not only allow frequent misdesignation of special education students, they also drive up the size and cost of the special education system. Since the implementation of the IDEA legislation, the number of students in special education has increased every year without exception. Today, there are 5 million special education students in the nation's schools—10 percent of all students enrolled. One result of the system's growth: a bloated bureaucracy that even advocates of special education say is unnecessarily expensive. In Connecticut, for instance, a separate transportation system costs taxpayers 10 times more to bus a special ed student than one attending regular classes. Separate transit systems for special education students exist in most states. Some cost more than Connecticut's. Nationally, the bill for all special education services has rocketed from roughly $1 billion in 1977 to more than $30 billion today.

■ **Incentives.** Many principals have raised their schools' scores on statewide competency exams by placing low-scoring students in special education programs—children who might otherwise not be in special education. In most states, special education students are exempted from reading and mathematics exams; average school test scores, as a result, are higher. Such scores are important to administrators' performance and compensation reviews. Researchers Richard Allington and Anne McGill-Franzen of the State University of New York at Albany found this pattern widespread in New York. *U.S. News* documented numerous other examples.

■ **Classification.** Special education labels are so ambiguous that classifications vary from state to state—and even from school district to school district. Fifteen percent of all Massachusetts students wind up in special education programs, for instance. Yet in Hawaii, just 7 percent of all students are in special education; in Georgia and Michigan, only 8 percent. Classifications vary wildly from state to state, even within special education categories. In Alaska, only 3 percent of all special education students are classified as retarded; in Alabama, 28 percent.

There are not even hard and fast rules on how to define a retarded child. In Ohio, a child with an IQ level below 80 is considered mentally retarded. Move across the border to Kentucky, and the same child is placed in a regular classroom and taught along with all the other students. The anomalies are endless. Should special education students be taught in separate classrooms or regular classrooms? There are few meaningful guidelines. The result: In North Dakota, 72 percent of the state's special education students are taught in regular classrooms. In South Dakota, a state with almost identical demographics, only 8 percent of special ed students go to class with nondisabled children.

■ **Race.** In 39 states, according to a *U.S. News* analysis of Department of Education data, black students are overrepresented in special education programs, compared with their percentage of the overall student population. Significantly, the analysis found that black students are most likely to be overrepresented in special education classes when they are students in predominantly *white*

By the numbers

Criteria for classifying special education students vary from state to state and are often highly imprecise. One result: Disproportionately high numbers of African-American students wind up in such programs. Socioeconomic factors account for some of the disproportionality, experts say, but not all.

	Blacks among all students	Blacks in special ed	Whites among all students	Whites in special ed
Delaware	29%	41%	66%	54%
South Carolina	42	51	57	49
Connecticut	14	22	72	78
Louisiana	46	53	51	45
North Carolina	33	40	63	57
Nevada	12	19	70	69

USN&WR—Basic data: USN&WR analysis of U.S. Dept. of Education Office of Civil Rights 1990 Survey of Schools

school districts. In some school districts, neither the number of black students nor household demographics accounted for the high percentage of black students, the *U.S. News* analysis found. Among those with the highest percentage of black special ed students not accounted for by demographics or black enrollment: South Country Central, in East Patchogue, N.Y.; Fordyce, Ark.; Compton Unified, Calif.; and Emerson, Ark. These findings tend to support arguments by critics of the special education system who attribute the overrepresentation of African-American students in the system to cultural bias in testing and placement procedures—not to any inherently high level of disability.

■ **Oversight.** Lax enforcement by state and federal agencies has allowed classification problems to persist. A *U.S. News* analysis of 10,147 discrimination complaints reviewed by the Department of Education's Office of Civil Rights since 1987 found just *one* case in which the office imposed the most severe penalty—revoking federal funds. School districts usually are allowed to work with regulators to design corrective measures. But with penalties invoked so rarely, critics say, there is little incentive for educators to address some recurrent problems.

Federal regulators often don't even know about some problems because information they receive is frequently misleading. New York State recently submitted data on graduation rates of special education students for a report to Congress. A *U.S. News* reporter reviewed the submission and found that it included information on just 9,418 of New York's 324,677 special education students. New York officials admit the misreporting.

■ **Service.** Special education classrooms often become convenient places for teachers to send struggling students they don't want in their classrooms; academics, in such cases, takes a back seat. Indeed, special ed instructors often do as much social work—sometimes known as "life skills"—as teaching. In one special ed classroom in Ohio, students learned how to bake a frozen pizza in an oven.

In and out of the classroom

States with the largest shares of special education students in regular classes		States with the smallest shares of special education students in regular classes	
Vermont	83%	California	27%
North Dakota	72	Colorado	24
Massachusetts	62	Iowa	22
Wyoming	62	District of Columbia	16
New Mexico	62	Minnesota	11
Nebraska	61	Arizona	10
Oregon	61	South Dakota	8
Idaho	61	New York	8
Montana	60	West Virginia	6
North Carolina	54	Texas	5

USN&WR—Basic data: Fifteenth Annual (1993) Report to Congress on the Implementation of the Individuals with Disabilities Education Act

In theory at least, special education is simple. A child thought by his parents or teachers to have a learning problem is given a test, any problem is identified and necessary assistance is provided. Federal regulations list 13 types of disabilities that affect learning: autism, deaf-blindness, deafness, hearing impairment, mental retardation, multiple disabilities, orthopedic impairment, chronic or acute health problems (like a heart condition or epilepsy), serious emotional disturbance, specific learning disability, speech or language impairment, traumatic brain injury and visual impairment, including blindness. Only a few of these disabilities, such as deafness or blindness, can be measured by objective tests.

The rest can be highly subjective, and this is where mislabeling can occur. Consider "learning disabilities." By far the largest class of special education students, at 49.9 percent, learning-disabled pupils are the most difficult to identify properly. One reason is definition. A learning-disabled child, according to the Department of Education, is one who has "a severe discrepancy between achievement and intellectual ability." This is squishy territory. The perceptual or processing difficulties that many think of as learning disabilities—dyslexia, for instance, in which a person reads letters in reverse order—account for just a small percentage of all learning-disabled students.

The definitional problem is compounded by another. It is up to state education departments to suggest which tests and procedures are used to measure a learning disability, and as a result, school practices can vary widely. Federal law requires that more than one test be used to identify a learning disability and that more than one individual be involved in making the determination. But such precautions are thin protection against the possibility of mislabeling a child. In fact, says University of Minnesota researcher James Ysseldyke, more than 80 percent of *all* schoolchildren in America could qualify as learning-disabled according to one or more of the various definitions now used by states.

Nothing drives the special education system like money. No state has more students classified as emotionally disturbed than Connecticut, for example. But it's not that there is more stress, paranoia or pathology there. It's simply that the state's complex funding formula encourages school districts to send emotionally disturbed students to separate schools, according to special education expert Thomas Nerney, who takes Connecticut's system to task in a new report published by the Western Connecticut Association for Human Rights. Nerney notes that some cities, like New Haven, actually save money when they send students to out-of-district schools, even though these schools can cost more than $100,000 per student, because the state picks up the bulk of the cost (see "Beating the System").

The Constitution State is hardly alone. Twenty-three states have funding formulas that reward school districts with more tax dollars if they place more students in special ed programs. Two decades ago, when most disabled kids received little or no education, "weighted" programs made sense: The financial incentives induced school districts to start providing services to children with learning problems. Now, however, such weighted formulas often serve as money magnets. By identifying students with only minor disabilities, educators can demand more money for their schools—and get it. The trouble is, besides the financial burdens created, kids can be hurt by stigmatizing special education labels.

■ **Labels matter.** Funding formulas also determine what kind of teachers are hired—and what kind of special education schools deliver. Contrary to national trends, for example, since the mid-1980s, Ohio has had just a tiny increase in learning-disabled students. During this same period, the state stopped providing extra money to school districts that hired instructors for children with learning disabilities.

There are reasons for differences in special education enrollment from community to community, but because of the subjective criteria employed throughout the system, such differences are often exaggerated. In Georgia, educators classify 32 percent of the state's special educa-

A breakdown by race

The most troubling anomaly in special education has to do with mental retardation. More than twice as many blacks as whites are classified as mentally retarded.

Percentage of black, white and Hispanic special education students who are classified as—

	Black	White	Hispanic
Retarded	26%	11%	18%
Learning-disabled	43	51	55
Emotionally disturbed	8	8	4
Speech-impaired	23	30	23

USN&WR—Basic data: U.S. Dept. of Education Office of Civil Rights 1990 Survey of Schools

tion students as having learning disabilities. Rhode Island, employing different criteria, categorizes twice that many learning-disabled students, 63 percent. "Who has a disability," says Brian McNulty, Colorado's special education director, "is much more a function of *where* one lives than anything else."

And labels *do* matter. They determine how teachers choose to educate children—or whether they attempt to teach them at all. Alfred Profeet is a case in point. Struggling to read, he was forced to switch schools and ended up in a separate class for learning-disabled children. Assigned to a classroom where academic subjects were not emphasized, Alfred's basic math and reading abilities plummeted. His mother, Zipporah Profeet, saw her son's self-confidence deteriorate. She found a lawyer and a specialist who ran new tests. Alfred's real problem—he has trouble focusing his eyes—is minor and could be dealt with in a regular classroom. Last month, the 10-year-old was allowed to return to his old school in Queens, N.Y. His classmates greeted him with hugs at the front door. Today, Alfred is working hard to catch up academically. But his mother is bitter. Her son, she says, "lost two years out of his life."

The vagaries in the special education system can make children and parents prisoners of geography. This is what happened to the Flair family. Connie Flair wants her daughter Katie to go to her local school so she can develop ties to her community. Instead, affluent Bloomfield Hills, Mich., chooses to transport the mentally retarded 14-year-old—on a bus by herself—to an out-of-district school. If the Flairs moved 2 miles north on the street they live on now, they would be in another district, which would allow Katie to attend the local school. The same would be true if they moved 3 miles south. Connie Flair thinks this is unfair. Why, she asks, "should a family have to move?"

Of all problems with the nation's special education system, none is more troubling than its racial imbalance, particularly in categories like retardation. Mental retardation can be caused by the conditions of poverty—as when a mother fails to get prenatal care or an infant chews lead paint chips. But the large number of blacks in special ed programs cannot be explained by socioeconomic factors alone.

A tale of two counties. The *U.S. News* analysis found that blacks are twice as likely as whites to be classified as mentally retarded while white students are placed much more often than blacks in the less stigmatizing category of "learning-disabled." Some critics, like Harold Dent of the Center for the Study of Minorities in Special Education at Hampton University, argue that "culturally biased" IQ tests used to classify students are at least partially responsible for the disproportionate numbers of black students in special education. California seems to prove the point. Contrary to national trends, 68 percent of blacks in special education in California are classified as learning-disabled. The reason: A federal court barred the

Race and retardation

An absence of federal standards for classifying children as mentally retarded has caused great disparities between whites and blacks—and from state to state

States with highest percentages of black special ed students labeled retarded		States with the lowest percentages of black special ed students classified as retarded	
Alabama	47%	Nevada	9%
Ohio	41	Connecticut	7
Arkansas	37	Maryland	8
Indiana	37	New Jersey	6
Georgia	36	Alaska	3

USN&WR—Basic data: USN&WR analysis of U.S. Dept. of Education Office of Civil Rights 1990 Survey of Schools

state from using IQ tests to classify black students for special education.

The role of race can be starkly clear. The Perry County and Mountain Brook school districts in Alabama have the same number of special education students. In Perry County, in the state's impoverished, cotton-farming "Black Belt," 236 students are labeled mentally retarded and 14 learning-disabled. The Mountain Brook district is farther north, a wealthy suburb of Birmingham. There, the numbers are reversed: 271 youngsters are classified as learning disabled, only 15 as mentally retarded. Demographically, the two districts could not be more different. Perry County's residents are 96 percent black. Mountain Brook is 99 percent white.

In such situations, race can be a self-fulfilling prophecy. Geraldine Tubbs Moore teaches some of Perry County's mentally retarded students at West Side Middle School. She recalls vividly the advice she heard at the college where she was studying for her teaching degree: Get certified in mental retardation, she was told, because that is a black disorder. Thirteen of Perry County's 18 special education teachers are certified to teach mentally retarded children. Each year, there always seem to be enough mentally retarded students to keep them busy.

"Low expectations." In Mountain Brook, by contrast, school officials bend over backward to classify kids as learning-disabled. The label is less stigmatizing, and it typically results in the placement of students in more rigorous academic programs than if they were classified as mentally retarded. That is clear at Mountain Brook High School, where nearly every student with a learning disability takes all regular classes and 97 percent go on to college. Almost all of Mountain Brook's few children who are labeled mentally retarded have some clear genetic condition. Just three teachers are retained to teach them. "When kids are inappropriately labeled mentally retarded," says Carol Standifer, Mountain Brook's special education coordinator, "there are low expectations from those around them."

One reason for such disparities is lax enforcement by federal regulators. Although the U.S. Department of Edu-

PRIVATE SCHOOLS

Beating the system

Not too long ago, a California school system paid $188,000 to send an emotionally troubled student to a Texas psychiatric institution for 14 months. A Georgia school system paid $42,600 toward the cost of sending a mentally retarded student to private schools in Japan and Boston.

The students' parents won the right to send them to distant private institutions at public expense under the Indi- viduals with Disabilities Education Act. If parents can convince hearing officers or the courts that local schools are not providing disabled students with an "appropriate" education, the law says, they may put them in private schools at taxpayers' expense. And parents aren't shy about pursuing "private placements": fully 25 percent of requests for hearings under IDEA involve demands for private placement, a Pennsyl- vania study shows. Nationally, 100,000 students, 2 percent of the special ed population, are in private programs.

Big bills. In many instances, costly private placements are justified: They offer additional staffing and specialized equipment that local schools can't or won't provide. But many special education experts say IDEA also allows well-to-do parents with savvy lawyers to have taxpayers pick up the tab for Cadillac-quality private treatment — even, in many instances, when students have relatively mild disabilities. It has helped make private placements by far the most expensive sector of special education.

For affluent parents, the pursuit of private placement has low risk. IDEA and the courts let them put their children in private special ed schools and then sue public school systems to recover the tuition. Parents must prove that the private placement is "appropriate" and public schooling isn't. But that's often not difficult, because test scores frequently rise once students benefit from the increased individualized attention of private schools.

BY THOMAS TOCH

---

cation's Office of Civil Rights received several hundred complaints of excessive bunching of minority students in low-ability tracks in 1991, it scheduled only eight investigations. According to a critical report by the U.S. General Accounting Office, the civil rights office rarely followed up when it found evidence of violations.

7 percent solution? America's special education system today is a far cry from what Congress envisioned when it passed the path-breaking IDEA legislation in 1975. Disabled children, the law's sponsors vowed, would be guaranteed a "free appropriate public education." Lawmakers, says Lisa Walker, a key Senate aide who helped draft the law, envisioned disabled youngsters being taught alongside other students, with additional aides and support as needed. To make that happen, IDEA promised that Washington would reimburse 40 percent of a state's costs to educate handicapped children.

That promise has proved hollow. Today, just 7 percent of a special education student's cost is repaid by Washington, and the resentment in state capitals has resulted in considerable apathy toward or hostility to special education. The U.S. Supreme Court appeared to take note of this just a few weeks ago, ruling that a South Carolina school district must reimburse the family of a learning-disabled teenager for the tuition paid to send the youngster to private school. Finding for the family, the justices agreed with lower courts that South Carolina officials had failed to educate the youngster properly.

Today, more special educators are looking for ways to cut costs and make the system work better. There is much room for improvement. About 1 in 4 special education students drops out of high school; 43 percent of those who graduate remain unemployed three to five years after high school, and nearly one third—primarily those with learning and emotional disabilities—are arrested at least once after leaving high school.

**ABOUT THIS REPORT:
THE METHODOLOGY**

■ In its examination of special education programs, *U.S. News* analyzed computerized U.S. Department of Education records on student enrollment. Separately, the magazine examined computerized records of 23,106 discrimination cases filed with the Education Department's Office of Civil Rights. In addition, reporters obtained paper and computerized records from 11 states. These records provided detailed breakdowns of special education data by school district. The information was entered into a computerized database for analysis along with the federal records.

To analyze the disproportionate numbers of African-American students enrolled in special education programs, the magazine obtained U.S. Census Bureau information on the socioeconomic characteristics of school districts. Consultant John Bare, a doctoral student in the journalism school at the University of North Carolina at Chapel Hill, conducted a statistical analysis to explore the extent to which household demographics contributed to the labeling of black children in special education. Bare's analysis was factored into the magazine's analysis of enrollment data.

Finally, the magazine's reporters traveled to eight states to visit special education classrooms. The reporters conducted more than 250 interviews with students, parents, teachers, administrators, researchers and academics.

Parents and some special educators are trying a number of solutions. Inclusion of children with learning problems in ordinary classrooms is a concept that is growing in favor. It is also one that is close to the intent of the IDEA legislation. Carlos Oberti of New Jersey says it has allowed his young son with Down's syndrome to grow socially and academically. Other parents note that it can save money on overlapping services—like the separate bus Ginger Spiers's daughter was required to take even after she transferred from a special education program in Norwalk, Conn., to a regular classroom. Yet for every parent with a story of inclusion's wonders, there is another with a cautionary tale. Some students, such as deaf children, may learn best in segregated classrooms. Inclusion also can be problematic when schools try to cut costs by placing a child with learning problems into a regular classroom without supports. The regular teacher then has to do two jobs, causing all students to suffer.

Riley's reforms. There are few other beacons of hope. New York City has a promising pilot program that is moving many children from pre-kindergarten through second grade out of special education and into mainstream classrooms. Two fifths of the children who have completed the program have been reclassified as regular students. In Vermont, a new funding formula stops rewarding school districts for putting students in special education. The result: The number of special education students in the state has dropped by 18 percent in the past three years.

Additional reason for hope comes from the changes Education Secretary Riley promises from Washington. In the interview last week with *U.S. News* reporters, Riley and Tom Hehir, the department's director of special education, said they plan to propose fundamental changes when Congress considers reauthorization of the IDEA law next year. While Riley, Hehir and Assistant Secretary Judith Heumann are committed to preserving the educational opportunities protected by the law, they intend to recommend that lawmakers:

■ Make sure that children served by the special education system are truly disabled. "We are concerned," says Hehir, "about the misidentification of students and the overidentification of students."

■ Encourage school systems to educate more special education students in their neighborhood schools. "Let's bring services to kids," Hehir says, "not kids to services as we do now."

■ Raise academic standards in special education. Riley believes that special ed students should not be exempt from state testing programs.

■ Shift federal oversight of special education away from its present emphasis on whether school systems are following bureaucratic procedures to a new emphasis on the performance of local special education efforts to end the overrepresentation of minorities and return children to local schools.

The reforms, if implemented, could change the lives of thousands of the nation's schoolchildren.

By Joseph P. Shapiro, Penny Loeb and David Bowermaster with Andrea Wright, Susan Headden and Thomas Toch

PEER EDUCATION PARTNERS

A PROGRAM FOR LEARNING AND WORKING TOGETHER

Louise Fulton, Christopher LeRoy, Martha L. Pinckney, and Tim Weekley

Louise Fulton (CEC Chapter #530), Professor of Education and Director, California Transition Center, California State University, San Bernardino. Christopher LeRoy, Transition Program Manager, San Bernardino Unified School District, California. Martha L. Pinckney, Principal, and Tim Weekley, Teacher, Hillside University Demonstration School, San Bernardino, California.

"He acts like he doesn't know how to do something, but he really does."

This comment was made by Erika, a fourth grader at Hillside University Demonstration School participating in the Peer Education Program (PEP). PEP is a future-oriented program that gives typical fourth-, fifth-, and sixth-grade students opportunities to share activities with peers who have intensive needs. This program is a powerful tool for teachers in the 1990s, who must bring together core academic courses and the skills needed for living, learning, and working in future community environments.

This article describes how PEP provides mutually beneficial experiences for students as they learn, work, and play together. Teachers, parents, and students believe that PEP participants have shown gains in social, academic, and career vocational skills. More important, they have developed positive attitudes toward themselves and others that cross home, school, and community environments.

PROGRAM OVERVIEW

PEP has been a collaborative effort from the beginning. The program was initially motivated by a mainstreaming model described by Almond, Rodgers, and Krug (1979) and by other research and development reported in the literature (Brown et al., 1979; Sailor et al., 1989; Voeltz, 1980). Development and field testing of PEP occurred during the 1988–1989 school year. Initially the PEP planning committee, composed of regular and special educators, parents, two school principals, a program specialist, and a university professor, met many times to develop the model and procedures. These efforts resulted in joint problem solving and shared ownership of the program as well as the development of the *PEP Handbook*. The handbook, which includes all PEP procedures, forms, and handouts, has been useful for replicating PEP at other school sites.

PEP was originally conceived as a special education effort; however, the program thrust changed early in the developmental stages. Discussions at planning committee meetings revealed a need to emphasize academic, social, and vocational benefits for all students. This was viewed as an important means for capturing the interest of teachers and parents as well as for providing beneficial experiences for students in the regular education program.

During the final 6 weeks of the 1989–1990 school year, 16 students participated in PEP as student leaders. Three were from grade 6, four from grade 5, and nine from grade 4. These students were assigned to their partners by the PEP supervising teacher, who teaches students with severe disabilities at Hillside School. PEP leaders worked with seven of the classroom partners on reading, math, art, physical education, and computer skills. The disabilities among these first- and second-grade students included Down syndrome and severe cognitive or behavioral disorders.

PROCEDURES

Establishment of the PEP program at Hillside followed a step-by-step procedure now being implemented at five other school sites. In order to replicate the PEP model, the following sequence of activities is suggested:

1. Obtain administrative support and schedule an overview of the PEP program at the potential school site. Review the *PEP Handbook* and show slides or a videotape of typical PEP activities.
2. Identify a PEP coordinating teacher, who begins by establishing an implementation schedule.
3. Schedule a PEP School Awareness Day. Typical activities include classroom visits by individuals with disabilities, a poster contest with an appropriate one-school/community-for-all theme, and films or other activities depicting normalized experiences of individuals with a variety of disabilities.
4. Have special educators develop specific descriptions of jobs, which are advertised in conspicuous spots around the school.
5. Have interested students obtain job applications from their teachers. The students complete and submit the application forms with signatures from parents, teachers, and the principal.
6. Interview all student applicants for available PEP leader positions, and give them constructive feedback about their interviews and skills.
7. Following consideration of interviews and teacher recommenda-

From *Teaching Exceptional Children*, Vol. 26, No. 4, Summer 1994, pp. 6-8, 10-11. © 1994 by The Council for Exceptional Children. Reprinted by permission.

tions, "hire" PEP leaders for the 6-week experience. Have the PEP leaders complete the pre-PEP survey form.

8. Conduct weekly PEP training sessions for 4 weeks. Training components specified in the *PEP Handbook* include (a) job procedures, forms, expectations, and reports; (b) development of job skills; (c) terminology, specific techniques, and behavior management; and (d) procedures and expectations for daily journal writing.

9. Establish schedules for student workers in consultation with the teachers and the students. Continue hiring PEP leaders as needed to work on specific volunteer jobs for 6 weeks. These jobs entail 30-minute sessions 3 to 5 days a week for a period of 6 weeks. Students participate in weekly conferences with the supervising teacher. Using the PEP progress conference form provides a forum for both the teacher and the student to talk about progress, successes, and areas of needed skill improvement.

10. At the end of 6 weeks, complete a final post-PEP survey. Interested students must then reapply for their current position or a different job.

11. Organize a social activity for students to enjoy, and recognize them at a school awards assembly for leadership and work success.

12. Make sure that all teacher and parent surveys are completed as a means to increase participation and gain input for program improvement.

BENEFITS OF PEP

"When we practiced math and reading together we both learned."

This typical comment was made by a fifth grader at the post-PEP interview. It supports the premise that student participants benefit academically and socially regardless of whether they are tutors or tutees (Jenkins & Jenkins, 1982; Osguthorpe & Scruggs, 1986). Moreover, cross-age peer education programs such as PEP provide a means for maximizing resources. Levin, Glass, and Meister (1984) found such programs to be more cost effective and successful in improving academic skills than reducing class size or increasing instructional time.

Vocational experiences are also emphasized in the PEP program. The PEP leader assists a fellow student with core academic and social skills while working at jobs with titles such as "Reading Friend," "Art Partner," "Playground Pal," "Library Friend," "PE Pal," "Computer Buddy," "Community Helper," and "Math Mentor." While "on the job," students learn or improve vocational skills such as punctuality, dependability, self-initiative, problem solving, leadership, and work evaluation. They also develop confidence in themselves as leaders among their peers. This job-oriented recruitment and participation of students has been highly motivating, with 60 students requesting interviews for the first 9 positions.

Students in the special education classroom also have been enthusiastic about PEP. This result is consistent with the findings of Kohl, Moses, and Stettner-Eaton (1983) who reported increased motivation among special education students who participated in learning activities with their general education peers.

"It's not just helping somebody. It's learning to work together"; "I learned not to 'blow up' but to keep trying to help him"; and "In the beginning Matt had to follow along with his fingers and

PEP participants develop positive attitudes toward themselves and others in home, school, and community environments.

count bears. Now he can count." In these comments two sixth graders summarized their feelings about PEP and how the program combines academic, social, and vocational experiences for lessons in learning together.

Students in the PEP program also have demonstrated significant growth in positive attitudes toward individuals with disabilities, as expressed in the following comments: "If you believe in someone they believe in themselves"; "When you get to know Sara she doesn't seem disabled"; and "If Joshua says no, just be patient and he'll do it."

The rich environment encouraged by the PEP program allows typical students to gain positive experiences with students who have special educational needs. These experiences have immediate and potential long-term implications. Fenrick and Petersen (1984) found an increase in positive attitudes toward students with severe disabilities following 7 weeks of peer tutoring. Stainback and Stainback (1982) reported that students participating in integrated school activities expressed positive feelings about their experiences and a desire to continue such experiences. Short-term interactions may reach beyond the school to future living and working environments as PEP leaders grow to assume other roles in the school and community. The students' mutual enjoyment of the experience is evidenced in Josie's statement: "Natalie used to not jump rope. Now we jump rope together."

PEP encourages partnerships that begin with an assigned task but may develop into sustained friendships. Kishi (1985) noted that friendships develop from peer tutoring as well as special friends programs. The philosophy of PEP has been to emphasize reciprocal activities that move beyond tutorial partnerships to mutual relationships of personal choice. As one PEP student commented, "I want to be a PEP leader next year 'cause I want to be Sarah's partner." Another said, "I want to be with Adam again."

Friendships often develop as a result of peer tutoring.

EVALUATION

Program evaluation procedures were incorporated early. The PEP planning committee wanted to know the opinions of students, parents, and teachers toward the program. Evaluation data were gathered in five ways.

First, PEP leaders completed a pre-

and postparticipation survey. Prior to participation, students were asked to respond to the following four questions: What do you feel a student with a disability can learn? In what activities do you feel the student could participate? How could you help the student? What could you learn from the experience? Student responses were scored with points given for key expressions reflecting attitude, expectation, self-contribution, and self-benefit. Their individual comments also helped in identifying areas of strength as well as topics to discuss with the students throughout the next 6 weeks.

At the end of 6 weeks of employment, a post-PEP survey was given. Comparisons of pre- and post-PEP participation

responses revealed positive changes in expectations and attitudes of PEP leaders toward their peers with special educational needs. In addition, all PEP leaders asked to reapply for a PEP position. Lindy summed it up when she said, "They can learn anything if they just try hard."

Second, PEP leader growth was examined at weekly progress conferences with the PEP supervising teacher. Topics included discussions about successes and areas of needed improvement in dependability, attitude, praise giving, helpfulness, and overall quality of work.

Third, at the end of each semester PEP leaders were interviewed and asked to talk about what they learned, what they taught, and what methods they used. According to Gracie, "I learned to use reverse psychology. When Carl doesn't want to work at the computer I tell him he doesn't have to. Then he wants to." Another student explained, "I was able to teach him more math than he knew." Arzebet described his teaching techniques by saying, "I tell Chris he's doing a good job, and it seems to make him feel good inside." Linda summarized her approach by saying, "I just make up games. Sometimes she already knew. I just helped her try."

Fourth, the students with special needs were observed for changes in socialization as well as progress in the tutored academic areas. PEP peers developed enhanced social confidence. With PEP intervention, these students began to initiate peer interactions more frequently, and they exhibited greater choice in selecting friends and activities.

Improvement in academic skills among the students with special needs was also documented. Progress in language arts was assessed by pre-post measures, with rewarding results. For example, students showed gains in reading, with three of the seven moving from preprimer to first grade level in 1 year. Similar results were recorded in mathematics, with several students moving from rote counting to simple addition. When asked about her teaching success, Michelle replied, "In the beginning he used his fingers to count bears. Now he can add."

Finally, parents and teachers were surveyed to gain their opinions and input. The program achieved 100% parental approval, with all parents supporting their child's continued participation. One of the most significant measures of the program's effectiveness was evidenced in the following comments by parents: "I think it's wonderful that Josie can help another child and at the same time help

herself"; "It increases the children's understanding of each other"; "Summer is now talking about making a career of teaching." Teachers also were supportive in their comments and felt the program was well organized and beneficial. Valuable suggestions and input from parents and teachers are being incorporated into the program for continued improvement.

These suggestions included preparing an instructional video that outlined program procedures and depicted PEP student instructional sessions. Both parents and teachers suggested that such a video would be useful at implementation sites and for sharing the program at PTA meetings. Both parents and students indicated a need for the PEP program to continue at the middle school. Parents and teachers strongly approved of the 6-week periods with 30-minute sessions as ideal time frames. Finally, several teachers and parents asked that the number of PEP sessions in regular classrooms be increased.

CONCLUSION

The PEP program is but one model for increasing peer interaction while at the same time strengthening academic, social, and vocational skills among elementary school students. One of the greatest benefits of the program has been the positive attitude and cooperative spirit of the entire campus in assisting with its implementation. This spirit of partnership can only stand to benefit all children as they continue to learn, play, and work together in current and future environments.

REFERENCES

Almond, P., Rodgers, S., & Krug, S. (1979). A model for including elementary students in the severely handicapped classroom. *TEACHING Exceptional Children, 11*(4), 135–139.

Brown, L., Branston, M., Hamre-Nietupski, Johnson, E, Wilcox, B., & Gruenewald, L. (1979). A rationale for comprehensive longitudinal interactions between severely handicapped students and non-handicapped students and other citizens. *AAESPH Review, 4*(1), 3–14.

Fenrick, N., & Petersen, T. (1984). Developing positive changes in attitudes toward moderately/severely handicapped students through a peer tutoring program. *Education and Training of the Mentally Retarded, 19,*(2), 83–90.

Jenkins, J., & Jenkins, I. (1982). *Cross-age and peer tutoring.* Reston, VA: The Council for Exceptional Children.

Kishi, G. (1985, December). *Long-term effects of a social interaction program between non-handicapped and severely handicapped children.* Paper presented at the 12th annual conference of the Association for Persons with Severe Handicaps, Boston.

Kohl, E., Moses, L., & Stettner-Eaton, B. (1983). The results of teaching fifth graders to be instructional trainers with students who are severely handicapped. *Journal of Association for Persons with Severe Handicaps, 8*(4), 32–40.

Levin, H., Glass, G., & Meister, G. (1984). *Cost effectiveness of four educational interventions.* Stanford, CA: Stanford University Institute for Research on Education, Finance, and Governance.

Osguthorpe, R., & Scruggs, T. (1986). Special education students as tutors: A review and analysis. *RASE, 7*(4), 15–26.

Sailor, W., Anderson, J., Halvorsen, A., Doering, K., Filler, J., & Goetz, L. (1989). *The comprehensive local school.* Baltimore: Paul H. Brookes.

Stainback, W., & Stainback, S. (1982). Non-handicapped students' perceptions of severely handicapped students. *Education and Training of the Mentally Retarded, 17,* 177–182.

Voeltz, L. (1980). Special friends in Hawaii. *Education Unlimited, 2,* 10–11.

For information about the PEP Handbook contact, California Transition Center, California State University San Bernardino, 5500 University Parkway, San Bernardino, CA 92407, 909/880-5495.

Selection of Appropriate Technology for Children with Disabilities

Howard P. Parette, Jr., Jack J. Hourcade and Alan Van-Biervliet

Howard P. Parette, Jr., *is The Americans with Disabilities Act Coordinator, Arkansas Easter Seal Society, Little Rock.* **Jack J. Hourcade** *(CEC Chapter #626) is Professor, Department of Teacher Education, Boise State University, Idaho.* **Alan VanBiervliet** *is Professor, Department of Rehabilitation Medicine, University of Arkansas for Medical Sciences, Little Rock.*

Technology plays an important role in the lives of individuals who have disabilities. As used in this article, technology is defined as any item, device, or piece of equipment that is used to increase, maintain, or improve the functional abilities of persons with disabilities. These items, devices, or pieces of equipment may be commercially available or customized [Technology Related Assistance for Individuals with Disabilities Act of 1988, (Public Law 100-407) 29 U.S.C. 2202, §3(1)]. They are available for a variety of age and grade levels ranging from infants and toddlers to adults.

The devices that are available are as diverse as the needs and characteristics of the people who benefit from them. Augmentative communication aids are available for persons who are unable to speak that allow them to communicate their needs to others. Motorized wheelchairs are available for those who are unable to walk that allow them to move about in the environment. For infants and young children with disabilities, microswitches are used with adaptive toys to help them manipulate objects in their environment and learn about cause and effect. Talking alarm clocks and calculators are used by individuals with visual problems, allowing them to access important information that sighted people often take for granted. These and many other technological advancements are greatly improving the quality of life for individuals with disabilities. More specifically, these technologies enhance their independence and productivity and increase their ability to participate in the mainstream of society (Garner & Campbell, 1987; Vanderheiden, 1985).

Most schools have had some experience in providing devices and equipment to students with disabilities. Both P.L. 94-142, the Education for All Handicapped Children Act of 1975, and P.L. 99-457, the Education of the Handicapped Amendments of 1986, provided school systems with the flexibility to fund assistive devices and other related services as indicated in the child's individualized education program (IEP). However, since technology was not specifically defined in either legislation, considerable variation existed across the country regarding the provision of devices and equipment to students in educational settings (National Information Center for Children and Youth with Disabilities, 1991).

With the recent reauthorization of P.L. 94-142, now known as the Individuals with Disabilities Education Act, or IDEA (P.L. 101-476), assistive technology devices were finally defined using the earlier language of P.L. 100-407. This places schools in the position of having even greater responsibility for providing devices and equipment to students in special education settings. Additionally, school districts must provide "assistive technology services" to eligible students with disabilities. These services are defined by the IDEA as "any service that directly assists an individual with a disability in the selection, acquisition, or use of an assistive technology device" [20 U.S.C. 33, § 1401(26)]. Thus, schools are now responsible for helping students select and acquire devices and equipment as well as instructing them in their use.

The increasingly expanding possibilities of technologies to help children in academic settings will require educational and related services personnel to rethink the scope of instructional opportunities for students with disabilities. In the past, many instructional activities may have been viewed from an administrative perspective to be impractical due to cost constraints or the degree of the student's disability (Cavalier, 1989; Cohen, 1989; Mendelsohn, 1989; National Information Center for Children and Youth with Disabilities, 1991). Unfortunately, while it is clearly a violation of IDEA, it has been suggested that in the past the limited resources of

From *Teaching Exceptional Children*, Vol. 25, No. 3, Spring 1993, pp. 18-22. © 1993 by The Council for Exceptional Children. Reprinted by permission.

school systems have, on occasion, played a role in the decisions made about technology provided for children with disabilities.

A Challenge to the Schools

In the future, devices and equipment will become easier to obtain as the costs of producing them decline (Esposito & Campbell, 1987). With decreases in the costs associated with technologies that can help children to benefit from special education, a wider variety of devices and equipment is likely to be provided with greater frequency. Already, many schools have acknowledged a willingness to invest in more sophisticated technologies such as computers for children with special needs (Bennett & Maher, 1984; Office of Technology Assessment, 1988). Since information about and instruction in the use of the many different types of technologies used in school settings is an often-cited need of teachers (Office of Technology Assessment, 1988; RESNA, 1989), teachers will increasingly be encouraged to acquire more information about devices and assume more skills in technology service provision. As they acquire these skills, teachers must, in turn, use them to assist in the selection and use of equipment in the schools. Important meetings where teachers can obtain information and acquire skills are indicated in Table 1.

■ A Team Approach

Within the public schools, the design and application of adaptations and technological devices are usually accomplished through a multidisciplinary IEP team of professionals and other interested parties including occupational, physical, and speech/language therapists; special and regular education teachers; and parents. Part of the assignment of the team is to ensure that all dimensions of a child's present level of performance are considered. This team approach is most effective when persons who have expertise in instructional programming—including technology and its applications—work cooperatively with parents and professionals who are involved in day-to-day instruction of students.

Special education teachers who participate in such team processes may be called upon to assume important responsibilities as team members. Unfortunately, many teachers have had inadequate training and/or experience with technology and its applications. When teachers are not prepared for the responsibility of selecting devices for students and using them in classroom settings, they may rely too heavily on the judgment of other professionals (e.g., the occupational, physical, or speech/language therapist). These professionals may see the child and his or her needs from a very different (and more limited) perspective than does the teacher.

Selection of Appropriate Technology

It is important for the teacher, as well as all other team members, to develop a philosophical base around which decisions will be made when selecting appropriate technology for children with disabilities. It is also important to remember that the concept of "appropriateness" takes on several dimensions. P. L. 94-142 was drafted to encompass any need the child has related to learning and/or development, including the need to learn basic self-help skills, have appropriate adaptive equipment, develop appropriate social integration skills, acquire basic prevocational skills, and receive therapy services. In each of these areas, devices and equipment can play critical roles in ensuring the provision of appropriate learning experiences for children with disabilities in public school settings.

From a more traditional perspective, a technology is appropriate when its application meets one of three criteria. First, it should be in response to (or in anticipation of) specific and clearly defined goals that result in enhanced skills for the student. Second, it should be compatible with practical constraints such as the available resources or amount of instruction required for the student and the teacher to use the technology. Third, it should result in desirable and sufficient outcomes (Office of Technology Assessment, 1982).

Determining the Fit

To match technology most effectively with any given student, the teacher and other team members must keep in mind two parallel considerations: characteristics of the student and characteristics of the technology.

■ Student Characteristics

The characteristics of the child are of the utmost importance and must be considered first. The comprehensive assessment procedures that determine the child's present levels of functioning and precede the actual program development process provide the initial basis for selection of any devices or equipment. In addition to the obvious selection implications of such characteristics as the child's academic skills, intellectual level, behavioral and social skills, and physical abilities, the teacher and other team members must consider the child's preferences for certain types of technology. An assistive device that appears excellent on paper but remains unused because the child is uncomfortable with it is the equivalent of no assistance at all.

Since the development of the IEP is a joint effort of a team that includes the child (when appropriate), the child can express his or her preferences during the decision-making process. Interviews with the parent and child can yield significant information that is not otherwise obtainable. For example, a girl may be uncomfortable using an augmentative communication system that employs a male adult voice. Alternatively, the IEP team may wish to determine which devices and equipment the child has had successful previous experiences with at school or at home. Once this information is acquired, the team may wish to purchase a similar technology for use in the school setting with appropriate modifications being made to meet the needs of the child. For example, a particular type of adaptive spoon may have made it possible for the child to feed himself or herself at home. The same type of spoon should be given consideration by the IEP team to assist the child with self-help skill development at school if this is deemed to be an important area of concern.

Additional considerations include anticipating the child's needs in the future. This is especially important with older students who are entering transition programs. For example, an older student with physical disabilities who has significant academic strengths may be a potential candidate to receive a modified computer system with adapted input and/or output modes.

The IEP team may feel that development of computer skills may make it possible for the student to enter a career with a telecommunications firm such as AT&T or a business corporation such as IBM, both of which employ persons with disabilities. Many government agencies such as the IRS also employ significant numbers of persons with disabilities.

Given the concern that all school systems have for the equitable distribution of resources, cooperative arrangements for funding may sometimes become an alternative for IEP team consideration if a child is to receive a needed technology. Alternative financial avenues include the use of the Medicaid program and private insurance. Teachers must bear in mind the argument that any device identified and recommended by the IEP committee should be paid for with public funds. In practicality, it must be recognized that not all equipment that can benefit children can be subsidized by the schools. Space-age technology is available through the National Aeronautics and . Space Administration (NASA, 1988) that has limitless possibilities for technology applications for persons with disabilities. These technologies, such as robotics and artificial intelligence devices, are not yet commercially available on a wide-scale basis, and their expense would be impossible for most school systems to consider for all children with disabilities. In a case where a costly, commercially unavailable technology is deemed to be a desirable alternative for a child with a disability, the IEP

team may choose to find partial external funding for the device. This may enable the school to provide a specific technology that would not otherwise be possible.

■ Technology Characteristics

Once relevant characteristics of the child have been identified and considered, the focus is placed on the characteristics of the various technologies that will be considered for the child. Goals for the use of devices should emerge as a result of the assessment of the needs, desires, and capabilities of the child. In examining the range of technologies that might be useful for a child with a disability, a variety of factors should be considered carefully.

The availability of the equipment is crucial. Sometimes technologies are not in vendors' stock, and they require lengthy periods of time to manufacture. This is particularly true of small firms that market products that are in large demand and are modestly priced. Delivery of such equipment sometimes can take 2 to 3 months once an order has been placed. It must also be remembered that most commercially available equipment cannot be modified by the manufacturer to meet the unique needs of a child with disabilities. Generally, devices must be customized or modified by others once the technology has been purchased for the child. This may require significant amounts of both time and money.

The simplicity of operation of the equipment is an important area of consideration. Too often schools purchase technologies that are overly complex and require tremendous investments in instruction of teachers and the children who are recipients of the equipment. When devices require large amounts of teacher time to learn to operate and maintain, most teachers will understandably be reluctant to use them. Such devices often are relegated to a storage closet in the school.

The initial and ongoing costs of the technology are one of the most frequently expressed concerns of school personnel at the administrative level (Cavalier, 1989; Office of Technology Assessment, 1982). Installation costs (if

any) must be considered, and this additional significant expense may not be reflected in the price quote provided to the IEP team by the vendor. The cost of daily, monthly, or annual operation must also be given consideration. Some devices, particularly those that require power packs or batteries, may incur frequent and unanticipated replacement expenses. Augmentative communication devices and power wheelchairs are two examples. Other equipment may require periodic maintenance, with its associated costs.

Since many technologies will be used for a long period of time, adaptability to meet the changing needs of children over time must be carefully considered. For example, a communication device that can be modified over time to continue to meet the evolving needs of a child with a disability would be more desirable than a device that could be used only for 1 year.

Another important consideration in the selection of technologies is the reliability and repair record of the devices. Some technologies, or certain brands or models of those technologies, require lengthy or frequent repairs. In fact, most augmentative communication boards and power wheelchairs require ongoing repair. Since communication boards are used frequently throughout the course of a day's activities, they become worn, soiled, and damaged. Children who sit in wheelchairs daily will cause wear and damage to the seats, armrests, and other padded surfaces of the equipment. In either case, once the technology is removed to be repaired, the child is denied access to a device that enhances the quality of life.

Teachers and other members of the IEP team may ask representatives of companies that sell certain types of equipment about the reliability and repair records of their devices. Sometimes there may be product testing information regarding specific technologies that is available to the IEP team on request. However, the best information about device reliability can probably be obtained from children who use the devices. In Arkansas, for example, a user-to-user network will be developed in the state technology system that has been funded under P.L. 100-407 (Arkansas Division of Rehabilitation Services, 1991). This system will be patterned after the parent-to-parent network established by the Association for Retarded Citizens in many states. Basically, such a network is made up of volunteers who agree to act as contact persons within the system for anyone wishing to get information about a particular type of technology. Thus, a teacher or anyone else who is considering buying a specific device for a child with a disability can learn of the personal experiences of a person who has used the technology. In states where such a network is not being developed, teachers may contact local advocacy groups and attempt to identify people who are using certain technologies. These individuals may then be contacted and questioned about the reliability of the equipment.

Finally, the teacher must examine the ability of the technology to provide performance or evaluation data necessary for the documentation of student progress. Certain technologies, especially computer-based devices, readily lend themselves to objective behavioral recordkeeping strategies. A computer spelling program that maintains an ongoing count of the number of lessons a child has completed and the accuracy of those performances lends itself more readily to recordkeeping for IEP and other purposes than would an instructional program that requires the direct observation of the teacher.

Conclusion

As technological advances continue, assistive devices for students with disabilities will continue to grow in power, usefulness, affordability, and widespread utilization. As core members of the IEP committees, special educators increasingly will be called upon to develop new technological competencies, not only in the use and maintenance of the evolving technologies, but in their prescription as well. By basing such decisions on ethical concerns and completing careful and systematic analyses of the characteristics of both students and technologies, teachers can help to ensure that all children achieve maximum levels of learning and independence.

References

Arkansas Division of Rehabilitation Services. (1991). *Increasing Capabilities Access Network (ICAN)*. (Grant #H224A90020-91). Washington, DC: U.S. Department of Education, National Institute on Disability and Rehabilitation Research.

Bennett, R. E., & Maher, C. A. (1984). *Microcomputers and exceptional children*. New York: Haworth.

Cavalier, A. (1989, May). *Ethical issues related to technology*. Paper presented to the preconference for the Association for Retarded Citizens/Arkansas 1989 annual conference, Little Rock.

Cohen, C. (1989, March). *Funding streams for assistive technology*. Paper presented to the Technology Access for Arkansans DeGray Lodge Retreat, Arkadelphia.

Esposito, L., & Campbell, P. H. (1987). Computers and severely and physically handicapped individuals. In J. D. Lindsey (Ed.), *Computers and exceptional individuals* (pp. 105-124). Columbus, OH: Merrill.

Garner, J. B., & Campbell, P. H. (1987). Technology for persons with severe disabilities: Practical and ethical considerations. *Journal of Special Education, 21,* 122-132.

Mendelsohn, S. (1989, March). *Payment issues and options in the utilization of assistive technology*. Paper presented to the National Workshop on Implementing Technology Utilization, Washington, DC.

National Aeronautics and Space Administration. (1988). *Spinoff*. Washington, DC: U.S. Government Printing Office.

National Information Center for Children and Youth with Disabilities. (1991). Related services for school-aged children with disabilities. *NICHCY News Digest, 1,* 1-25.

Office of Technology Assessment. (1982). *Technology and handicapped people*. New York: Springer.

Office of Technology Assessment. (1988). *Power on! New tools for teaching and learning*. Washington, DC: Author.

RESNA. (1989). *Technology-related assistance for individuals with disabilities. Summaries of 1989 successful grant applications awarded under P. L. 100-407*. Washington, DC: Author.

Vanderheiden, G. C. (1985). Promises and concerns for technological intervention for children with disabilities. In Health Resources and Services Administration (Ed.), *Developmental handicaps: Prevention and treatment III. A cooperative project between University Affiliated Facilities and state MCH/CC programs* (pp. 23-50). Rockville, MD: Office of Maternal and Child Health Services.

Table 1 — Assistive Technology Conferences

Conference	Date	Attendance	Target Audience	Contact
Technology and Persons with Disabilities—Annual Conference on Contemporary Applications of Technology	Spring	2,000	Mixed	Office of Disabled Student Services California State University-Northridge 1811 Nordhoff Street-DVSS Northridge, CA 91330 • 818/885-2587
ConnSENSE	Summer	200-300	Mixed	UCon Special Education Technology Lab 249 Glenbrook Road, U-64 Storrs, CT 06269-2064 • 203/486-0172
RESNA Annual Conference	Summer	1,000-2,000	Mixed	RESNA 1101 Connecticut Avenue NW, Suite 700 Washington, DC 20036 • 202/857-1199
International Society for Augmentative and Alternative Communication	Summer	1,000	Mixed	Applied Science and Engineering Laboratories University of Delaware/A.I. duPont Institute P.O. Box 269 Wilmington, DE 19899 • 302/651-6830
Annual Closing the Gap Conference	Fall	1,200	Mixed	Closing the Gap P. O. Box 68 Henderson, MN 56044 • 612/248-3294
International Technology and Media (TAM) Conference	Winter	400	Educators	TAM c/o The Council for Exceptional Children 1920 Association Drive Reston, VA 22091-1589 • 703/620-3660

Children with Learning Disabilities

Learning disabilities (LDs) are disorders that are intrinsic to the individual and make some area(s) of learning difficult. No one definition of LD is uniformly accepted. However, most states assess the difficulty as LD when there is a discrepancy between the child's ability to learn and what has actually been learned; when there is a need for special assistance to learn in some area(s); and when other causes for difficulties in learning have been excluded. For example, LDs are not due to mental retardation, not due to sensory impairment (vision, hearing, taste, touch, smell), and not due to behavioral disorders, autism, or communication disorders. They may, however, exist concurrently with other conditions of exceptionality; for example, LD plus behavior disorder, or LD plus physical impairment. Some famous individuals have had both an LD and special gifts and talents; for example, Thomas Edison, August Rodin, George Patton, Woodrow Wilson, Albert Einstein, Benjamin Franklin, and Winston Churchill.

Learning disabilities are found three times more frequently in males than in females. They can occur at any age, although the vast majority of LDs are diagnosed in early elementary school. LDs are the most common exceptional condition for which special education services are provided. The enrollment of LD students in special programs almost doubled between 1980 and 1990. This is, in part, due to improved assessment procedures. It also reflects more stringent criteria for diagnosing mental retardation, more acceptability of the diagnosis of learning disabled, and more special services provided for LD preschoolers and LD adolescents in transition-to-adulthood programs.

The causes of learning disabilities are unknown. They are presumed to be due to some localized and minimal area(s) of central nervous system dysfunction, or to some biochemical disturbance(s) affecting small area(s) of the brain, or to some environmental factor(s).

There are many types of learning disabilities. Two broad categories of LD are (1) developmental learning disabilities, and (2) academic learning disabilities. Developmental LDs affect the prerequisite skills that a child needs to learn (attention, memory, perception, perceptual-motor feedback, listening, comprehension, oral expression). Academic LDs are usually not obvious until a child enters school. They affect the ability to perform specific skills (reading, spelling, handwriting, arithmetic calculation, arithmetic reasoning). Deficiencies in reading and spelling are more common than in mathematics. All students with LDs have significant area(s) where they fail to learn despite adequate overall intelligence. Their level of aca-

demic achievement gets progressively worse as their grade level increases unless they get special help.

Children may have only one type of LD, or may have two or more LDs in any possible combination. Some students are very motivated to learn despite the LD; other students give up easily when asked to achieve any challenging task. Some highly motivated students appear to be resisting efforts to teach them because of the nature of their LD. It is not surprising that persons faced with the task of assessing or explaining LDs, or teaching LD students, are often confused about what to say or do.

Learning disabilities and difficulties due to mental retardation, or sensory impairments, or behavioral disorders, or autism, or communication disorders, are difficult to differentiate. Assessment is fraught with ticklish problems. Mislabeling is common. Assessment usually combines the use of a standardized test of intelligence plus several achievement tests. The achievement tests may be process tests, norm-referenced tests, criterion-referenced tests, informal inventories, informal observations, or formal daily measurements of some specific skill(s). Multiple, frequent, direct assessments of the specific problematic skill(s) are recommended, but they are time-consuming, expensive, and may be inconvenient for students, parents, teachers, and assessors.

Attention deficit (often referred to as hyperactivity) and dyslexia (difficulty in reading) are fairly common LDs. They are more readily comprehended and accepted by the lay public. However, because these terms are more readily accepted as labels, they have become "umbrella" terms. They are often misused to cover a multitude of conditions that are neither attention deficit disorders nor reading disorders. In order for each child with an LD to receive an appropriate individualized education program (IEP) and special services tailored to his or her specific needs, each child should have a thorough assessment of the unique area(s) in which he or she is having difficulty learning. An easy label such as attention deficit or dyslexia may suggest an easy program such as drug therapy or dyslexic reading remediation. There are no easy fixes for LDs. Each child's IEP should be based on his or her genuine area(s) of difficulty and meet his or her unique needs.

No one way of teaching has been demonstrated to be the best way to assist all children with learning disabilities. Children with developmental LDs (attention, memory, perception, perceptual-motor feedback, listening, comprehension, oral expression) benefit from early intervention in a preschool with special LD services. The central nervous

system has more plasticity (ability to change) in infancy and early childhood. The earlier intervention begins, the less difficulty the child will have later. However, it is hard to assess LDs, even developmental disabilities, very early in life. Children with academic LDs (reading, spelling, handwriting, mathematics) are seldom assessed until first or second grade. They need annually updated IEPs to meet their constantly changing needs and the types of instructional remediation most suited to their specific performance deficits.

The first article in this unit, "Enabling the Learning Disabled," answers questions about reaching, teaching, and meeting the special needs of LD students who are in regular education classrooms. It includes a definition of LDs and a check-list of signs of LD that may alert a teacher to request an LD assessment for a student. The second article gives a comprehensive review of an attention deficit disorder. It details the problems of assessment and the possibility of incorrect labeling, and it suggests many behavioral ways in which teachers can make their classrooms more appropriate for students with attention deficit LDs. It also discusses the use of drug therapy for

attention disorders with possible effects and side effects. In the third article, James Ysseldyke and his colleagues discuss the usefulness of assessing the instructional environments of both school and home when developing an effective IEP. A table summarizes the components that are desirable in both the school and the home for valuable learning to take place. Selection four of this unit outlines many ways to adapt textbooks in order to enhance the instructional contexts of students with LDs.

Looking Ahead: Challenge Questions

Can teachers recognize characteristics of LDs? Why, or why not? How can teachers help LD students in regular education classrooms?

What is attention deficit hyperactivity disorder (ADHD)? What does successful treatment entail? Who can assist a teacher with an ADHD student?

Why should learning environments be assessed as well as the LD child's disability(ies)?

Can textbooks be adapted for students with LDs who are mainstreamed into regular classes? How?

Enabling The Learning Disabled

Answers to your questions about reaching, teaching, and meeting the special needs of learning-disabled students in the regular classroom

Sally Smith

Sally Smith is the founder and director of The Lab School in Washington, D.C. She is also professor and head of the American University's masters degree program in special education: learning disabilities, and is the author of six books.

Chances are you'll have at least one learning disabled (LD) student in your classroom this year. And if you teach in a district that's already moved toward inclusion (see sidebar "Inclusion"), that number could be higher.

Teaching children with learning disabilities brings with it special joys, and special challenges. To help you manage, INSTRUCTOR went to Sally Smith, founder and director of the Lab School in Washington, D.C., and professor and head of special education at the American University—and asked her to address some of your biggest concerns. Her advice follows.

What does the term *learning disabled* really mean?

Learning disabilities encompass a broad range of neurological problems that are quite distinct from either retardation or emotional disturbances. The LD child is likely to have difficulty with reading, writing, spelling, and math. More sub-tle—and harder to pinpoint—are difficulties the child will have in attending; concentrating; remembering; organizing; sequencing; coordinating; and distinguishing right from left, letters, and numbers. The ability to make these distinctions is essential in learning the rudiments of reading, writing, and mathematics. If not addressed, a child's academic, emotional, and social development is adversely affected.

What instructional strategies work best with LD students?

LD students need opportunities to apply what they're learning. Ask them to reenact events, draw pictures, collect magazine photos to illustrate topics, construct models, and so on. Follow up with discussions that encourage students to verbalize what they've learned.

Also, whenever possible, show photos that will help students comprehend a topic. All children will enjoy the pictures, but for the LD child—who tends to have disabilities with language and tends to learn visually—pictures can mean the difference between not understanding and understanding a subject.

My LD students have trouble grasping abstract concepts. What can I do?

Turn an abstract idea into something concrete by having kids illustrate the

How can I tell if a student is LD?

Learning disabilities affect 10 to 15 percent of all Americans. According to the Learning Disabilities Association of America, if a child demonstrates a number of these signs, it may mean that he or she should be referred to a psychologist who understands learning disabilities for testing. Watch the child who:

- is disorganized,
- is easily distracted,
- has a poor attention span,
- overreacts to noise,
- doesn't enjoy being read to,
- has poor hand-eye coordination,
- can't make sense of what he or she hears,
- uses words inappropriately,
- is hyperactive,
- has limited vocabulary,
- is unable to follow simple directions,
- sometimes has poor emotional control,
- has difficulty remembering or understanding sequences, and
- chooses younger playmates or prefers solitary play.

[For a more in-depth look at detection, see the INSTRUCTOR Guide to Early Diagnosis and Referral, September 1993.]

From *Instructor*, July/August 1993, pp. 88-91. © 1993 by Scholastic, Inc. Reprinted by permission.

concept using their bodies, objects, and pictures. For example, to introduce the concept of our government's balance of power, you might begin with balancing exercises—have students use weights to even out a pair of scales. Then you could divide students into threes—to represent the judicial, executive, and legislative branches—and have them clasp hands and gently tug on one another's arms to illustrate the system's give-and-take. Afterward, kids could draw a triangular chart to show the balance of power and discuss a current example of the balance in action.

Especially during the early part of the year, when I'm trying to get to know all the students in my class, I sometimes have trouble remembering each of my LD students' main problem areas. What do you suggest?
Create a handy profile for each student. On separate index cards list each child's strengths, weaknesses, and interests, as well as the classroom-management methods that he or she responds to and the techniques that don't work. Add other information you've discovered about the student, and you'll have a quick reference tool at your fingertips.

How can I help the LD student feel successful?
Break down tasks into as many steps as necessary to ensure that the student can complete each step successfully. By starting with what a youngster can do and then building from there, you'll give the child a boost of confidence. (Hint: Be sure the student understands each step thoroughly before moving on to the next.)

When a student feels overwhelmed or depressed, how can I help?
I give the student tangible proof of his or her progress and commit to working together on trouble spots. On a sheet of paper folded down the middle, I make a column on the left-hand side called "Your Strengths" and write down such observations as: You work hard, you are a good artist, and so on. I read the list aloud to the child. Then I make a column on the right-hand side called "Needs Work" and write down skills the student needs to work on, such as spelling, subtraction, and reading. I read the list aloud. Next I tear the sheet down the middle, hand the list of strengths to the student, and say something like, "You keep the list of

your strengths. I'll keep the list of what you need to work on because it's my job to take care of those things for a while until you can become responsible for them."

Following my oral instructions is difficult for the LD students in my class. What can I do?
First, to reinforce sound, make sure the children are looking at you when you're giving instructions. It helps to stand near them, too. Be sure you speak slowly and loudly enough to be heard and keep your directions clear, precise, and succinct. Also, break down your instructions into simple steps, give only one or two at a time, and ask students to repeat each one aloud. Consider pairing an LD child with a considerate classmate who can check whether the student understands the instructions and can help explain them when he or she doesn't.

Because concrete reinforcement works well for the LD child, consider giving students gold stars or stickers when they follow instructions properly.

INCLUSION—
A Movement That's Gaining Momentum

If you haven't heard of inclusion, you will soon. It's a movement that's gaining ground in schools across the country. It means bringing the special-education teacher into the regular classroom—instead of pulling students out. The regular teacher and special-ed teacher coteach: planning lessons and delivering instruction together and sharing the responsibility for assessing students' mastery.

How does it work? In some schools, students with disabilities are grouped into a single class at each grade level for subjects like reading

and language arts, and the special-education teacher coteaches in that classroom every day. Sometimes special-education teachers split time among several classrooms, perhaps coteaching in social studies in a third-grade class on Mondays and Wednesdays and in a fifth-grade class on Tuesdays and Thursdays, with Fridays set aside as flexible time to be used according to need. Some schools find that coteaching works well when scheduled by units. For example, if a teacher who has mainstreamed students in her class is

teaching a concept that many children find difficult, she might ask the special-education teacher to coteach that concept.

Through coteaching, special-education students avoid the stigma associated with the daily journey in and out of the regular classroom. Their learning is less fragmented, not only because they don't miss any time in the regular classroom, but also because the special-education teacher is better able to relate remediation to regular instruction.

How can I approach the student who is afraid to admit he or she doesn't know something or is afraid to make mistakes?

When you don't know the answer to something yourself, set an example by saying, "I don't know, but we can find out together."

Send the signal to all students that it's okay to make mistakes and that everyone—even teachers—makes them. When kids do something wrong, tell them about mistakes you've made and talk about how you learned from them.

One of my LD students often has trouble finding her way around the school. For example, I have to show her how to find the resource room nearly every day. What can I do?

Pair the student with a classmate who does not have directional difficulty. Or point out landmarks between your classroom and the resource room—such as the green door, the drinking fountain, and the stairs—that the child can use to help her find her way on her own. If the student is a visual learner, have her draw a map of how to get there.

Sometimes I feel angry or frustrated with my LD students. How can I overcome these feelings?

Your feelings are important diagnostic tools because they may reflect students' feelings. When a student is angry, his or her feelings may be contagious. If you realize you're frustrated because the child is, you'll be better able to diffuse a situation and work patiently with a student. So it's important for you to be solidly in touch with your feelings, recognize and acknowledge them, and use them as a barometer to clue you in to what's happening with a student.

I've noticed that humor works well with my LD students. Why?

Nothing dispels tension faster than laughter, because if students can see the funny side of difficult or uncomfortable situations, usually they can find a way out of them. Because LD children tend to feel that others are laughing at them, it's important for these students to see laughter as a relief and means of togetherness—not as a form of punishment.

Teachers who laugh at themselves in an easy, accepting way are important models for children who tend to see themselves with despair or as a source of worry to others. And humor and the absurd can be an effective tool for anything from disciplining to testing.

Is it true that LD students need additional structure?

Yes. Structure means predictability, and predictability helps make LD children feel more comfortable. Although it takes extra work on your part, give your LD students a list of the topics for the day. The list will help them focus and better prepare them to learn.

If You Want To Know More

No Easy Answers: The Learning Disabled Child at Home and School by Sally Smith (Bantam paperback, 1981). To order call (800) 223-6834 or (212) 354-6500.

Succeeding Against the Odds: How the Learning Disabled Can Realize Their Promise by Sally Smith (Tarcher/Perigee paperback, 1992)

The following organizations offer a variety of publications and services. For more information, write or call:

The Learning Disabilities Association of America 4156 Library Rd. Pittsburgh, PA 15234 (412) 341-1515

The Orton Dyslexia Society Chester Building, Suite 382 8600 Lasalle Rd. Baltimore, MD 21286 (410) 296-0232

National Center for Learning Disabilities 99 Park Ave. New York, NY 10016 (212) 687-7211

Editor's Note: Most children who are diagnosed by competent mental health professionals as having attention-deficit hyperactivity disorder do; but as early childhood educators, we must always ensure that our classrooms are developmentally appropriate and that children are not being inappropriately labeled because our classroom is inappropriate.

Young Children With Attention Deficits

Steven Landau and Cecile McAninch

Steven Landau, Ph.D., is a professor of psychology at Illinois State University. Previously a school psychologist, his research interests include ADHD and problems associated with peer rejection.

Cecile McAninch, M.A., is completing her doctorate in clinical psychology at the University of Kentucky. Her areas of interest include children's self-concept and social cognition.

Three-year-old Jamie was expelled from preschool after frequent fights with other children. If Jamie and the other boys were playing with trucks, Jamie was the first one to start crashes, which escalated into wild behavior. In the sandbox it was always Jamie who threw sand in someone's face or grabbed the shovel from another child. After a month of preschool, Jamie's teacher became worried that Jamie might seriously hurt another child, and she asked Jamie's mother to keep him home.

Jamie's parents were dismayed by this request. They knew that he was a difficult child. They found Jamie hard to manage because he seemed to have an excessive activity level and a short attention span and was prone to numerous temper outbursts. Indeed, he had been "difficult" since infancy; however, they wanted to believe that this was simply a phase he was going through—a difficult period of development—and that he would outgrow these problems sometime soon. They even considered the possibility that Jamie's preschool teacher didn't understand him—that she could intervene more before he became too excited and wound up. These problems were thus simply developmental (i.e., he is just "all boy"), or they were best understood as a function of an intolerant preschool teacher. Maybe a better preschool would be the answer.

Jamie, who was first described by Campbell (1988), is representative of many young children referred for atten-

tion-deficit hyperactivity disorder (ADHD). What is ADHD, and how does it differ from hyperactivity? ADHD is the current psychiatric term used to describe a set of symptoms reflecting excessive inattention, overactivity, and impulsive responding. It is important to note that the presence of these symptoms must be established in the context of what is developmentally appropriate for the child's age and gender group. ADHD is found in 3 to 5% of the childhood population (American Psychiatric Association, 1987) and is clearly a disorder that is far more prevalent in males; sex differences among children referred for treatment average about six males to one female. Because ADHD is the formal diagnostic label from the psychiatric classification scheme (i.e., the *Diagnostic and Statistical Manual of Mental Disorders* [DSM–III–R]; American Psychiatric Association, 1987), this is the term used by family physicians, pediatricians, psychiatrists, and other mental health clinicians. Indeed, all professionals who deal with children, *except* professionals in the public school system, employ the psychiatric classification scheme and, thus, the term ADHD.

The fact that children considered "in need of special services" by their school according to Public Law 94–142 are not required to have a formal DSM–III–R psychiatric diagnosis for placement creates confused communication among parents, school personnel, and community professionals. Confusion is further increased by the fact that the nomenclature pertaining to this disorder has changed several times over the years. The disorder has previously been known as "brain damage syndrome"; "minimal brain dysfunction"; "hyperkinetic reaction to childhood"; "attention deficit disorder (with and without hyperactivity)"; and, most recently, "attention-deficit hyperactivity disorder." Although frustrating for some, this trend of changing terminology clearly represents improved understanding of the disorder (Schaughency & Rothlind, 1991).

Primary symptoms

The preceding overview of evolving terminology makes it apparent that there has been a shift in emphasis regarding what is considered most central to the disor-

---

The column in this issue was edited by Laura E. Berk, Ph.D., professor of psychology at Illinois State University.

From *Young Children*, Vol. 48, No. 4, May 1993, pp. 49-58. © 1993 by the National Association for the Education of Young Children, 1834 Connecticut Avenue, NW, Washington, DC. Reprinted by permission.

der. Many researchers agree that a deficit in *sustained attention,* the inability to remain vigilant, represents the area of greatest difficulty for the child with ADHD (Douglas, 1983); thus, children with ADHD show significantly less persistence than their classmates. Even though many teachers use the term *distractible* to characterize their observations of school performance, distractibility implies that the child with ADHD seems unable to select relevant from irrelevant stimuli that compete for their attention (i.e., a *selective attention* deficit). The bulk of current research, however, suggests that their greatest difficulties stem from an inability to *sustain a response* long enough to accomplish assigned tasks, that is, they lack perseverance in their efforts. As a consequence, parents and teachers attribute to them characterizations such as "doesn't seem to listen," "fails to finish assigned tasks," "can't concentrate," "can't work independently of supervision," "requires more redirection," and "confused or seems to be in a fog"—all apparently the result of this inability to sustain attention (Barkley, 1990).

It is important to stress, however, that even though inattention may be the source of some difficulty in a less structured, free-play setting, highly structured academic settings create the greatest problem for these children (Milich, Loney, & Landau, 1982). The specific expectations within a setting and the degree of structure in that setting thus play important roles in determining the presence of the disorder. This may explain, in part, why parents and teachers do not tend to agree when rating the symptoms of these children (Achenbach, McConaughy, & Howell, 1987). Expectations in the home environment are simply different from those at school. This point was recently reinforced in a study by Landau, Lorch, and Milich (1992). These investigators were intrigued by the surprising but frequent parent report that their child with ADHD is able to attend to television (e.g., "What do you mean he can't pay attention in school? He sits glued to the TV for hours!"). In fact, a recent advice column in *Parents* magazine suggested that parents could rule out thoughts of ADHD if their child was able to pay attention to television. Results of the study by Landau and his colleagues indicated that boys diagnosed with ADHD who were extremely inattentive in the classroom were able to attend to educational television programming to a high degree, and their attention was indistinguishable from that of normal agemates under some circumstances. It seems evident that television may hold greater intrinsic appeal than schoolwork for the child with ADHD, plus TV does not represent the historical source of frustration and failure associated with classroom performance. Apparently the nature of the task seems crucial when determining if the child has significant difficulty paying attention.

Related to problems with inattention, children with ADHD are *impulsive;* they experience difficulty *inhibiting* their response in certain situations (Barkley, 1990). As with inattention, impulsivity is a multidimensional construct; it can be defined in several ways (Olson, 1989). Children with ADHD, for example, are impulsive when confronted with academic tasks. They are extremely quick to respond without considering all alternatives; thus they are known as fast but careless and inaccurate problem solvers. This type of response style can have a profound influence on the child's ability to perform in an academic setting. Besides affecting cognitive performance, impulsivity can also manifest itself as an inability to suppress inappropriate behavior. As such, children with ADHD are also known to be high-risk takers, as evidenced by their running out in traffic. In addition, they seem unable to delay gratification (Campbell, Szumowski, Ewing, Gluck, & Breaux, 1982). In school they experience difficulty waiting their turn in line, blurt out answers in class, constantly touch other children, and tend to be undesirable playmates because of their difficulty with turn taking, sharing, and cooperation, and their low tolerance for frustration while playing games (Landau & Moore, 1991).

The third primary symptom involves motor excess, or *overactivity.* Historically overactivity was considered the hallmark characteristic of the disorder and served as the source for the enduring "hyperactivity" label applied to these children. This is probably because overactivity remains the most salient symptom and possibly the symptom most annoying to others. In fact, parents of children with ADHD retrospectively report overactivity to be an early marker of the disorder (Campbell, 1988), even though it is also a common complaint from parents of normal children (Lapouse & Monk, 1958; Richman, Stevenson, & Graham, 1982). As with the other symptoms, overactivity can take many forms but is especially apparent as excessive body movements (both major and minor motor) and vocalizations; for example, these children are described as "always on the go" or "squirmy and fidgety," or as a child who "can't sit still," "hums and makes other odd noises," "talks incessantly," and "climbs excessively" (Barkley, 1990).

When children with ADHD engage in table activities or academic seatwork, they constantly get up and down from the desk (or do all seatwork while standing). Many show minor motor fidgeting, such as pencil tapping or leg shaking, and they seem unable to keep their hands off objects unrelated to the task at hand. During individual psychological testing, children with ADHD can be extremely challenging subjects because they attempt to manipulate the examiner's test materials throughout the evaluation. Finally, they are often overactive and incessantly talkative in the context of social play—behaviors that seem to have a negative effect on peer relations (Landau & Moore, 1991). Again, it is important to remember that setting demands—in particular, the degree of structure in the environment—affect the extent to which these children are problems to their teachers. The child with ADHD may be considered quite troublesome, for example, in a highly structured academic setting, with desks placed in rows and all work to be accomplished in one's seat. In contrast, in the open-classroom setting where cooperative learning is encouraged and children are expected to move about and collaborate with others, the child with ADHD may be less distinctive and disturbing to others (Jacob, O'Leary, & Rosenblad, 1978).

Secondary symptoms or associated characteristics

Children with ADHD experience numerous difficulties that go beyond inattention, impulsive responding, and overactivity. Although these problems are not related to the diagnosis of ADHD, the fact that children with ADHD present these added difficulties accounts for the extreme heterogeneity among ADHD cases.

First, children with ADHD are at elevated risk for problems related to conduct disorder. Although the rates of overlap vary with each study, most investigators agree that at least one half of all children with ADHD also meet diagnostic criteria for conduct disorder. In these children one finds extreme stubbornness, noncompliance, hostility, rule violations, stealing, lying, and aggressive acts (Hinshaw, 1987). Studies of children with ADHD indicate that those who show conduct disorder not only are more difficult to manage as children but also will have more serious adolescent and adult adjustment problems (Weiss & Hechtman, 1986).

Second, many children with ADHD are rejected by their peers (Landau & Moore, 1991). In fact, many boys with ADHD who are not aggressive seem to be more "disliked" than their classmates who are highly aggressive but do not have ADHD (Milich & Landau, 1989), and this negative reputation may be established after only brief contact with unfamiliar children (Pelham & Bender, 1982). This effect on others is not surprising, as children with ADHD tend to be bossy, intrusive, disruptive, and easily frustrated while in the play group. They have few, if any, friends. Peer rejection is a serious outcome of ADHD because children who are rejected early in life tend to be at high risk for many adult adjustment difficulties, including job terminations, bad-conduct discharge from the military, negative contact with police, and psychiatric hospitalization (Parker & Asher, 1987).

Third, children with ADHD are at high risk for achievement difficulties, and many meet special-education placement criteria as learning disabled (McGee & Share, 1988). Because children with ADHD in the academic setting are typically off task, noisy, disruptive, out-of-seat, and do not finish schoolwork or homework, parents and teachers complain of underachievement. These children's work tends to be highly inefficient and disorganized, and their performance often shows great fluctuations.

Finally, these children seem to experience problems dealing with the numerous transitions in school (such as going from recess back to class). They have difficulty adapting their behaviors as situational expectations change (Landau & Milich, 1988). Consequently, there may be a grave discrepancy between actual achievement in school and the child's estimated potential for learning. As children with ADHD accumulate a history of negative feedback from parents, teachers, and peers, it is little wonder that they are also at risk for low self-esteem and depression as they mature.

Effects on the classroom

Children with ADHD can be an extremely negative force in the classroom setting. They tend to evoke numerous negative interactions with their teachers and take teacher time away from other children. They are disruptive to learning activities; try to dominate social situations; and, to make matters worse, do not perform well academically. Indeed, the presence of a child with ADHD in the preschool setting serves as a catalyst for significantly more negative teacher feedback to all children in the classroom (Campbell, Endman, & Bernfeld, 1977).

Causal hypotheses

Many causal explanations for ADHD have been proposed over the years. First, research indicates that the role of genetic transmission must be taken seriously. Parents and siblings of children diagnosed with ADHD are more likely to have the disorder, and studies of twins indicate that identical twins are much more likely to share the disorder than are fraternal twins. Second, researchers are currently working on identifying a neurobiological cause, such as a deficit in the neurotransmitters that control attention, although none has yet been isolated (Hynd, Hern, Voeller, & Marshall, 1991). Third, there is intriguing correlational evidence that maternal smoking and/or alcohol use during pregnancy may be linked to increased risk for ADHD. Fourth, in spite of widespread belief among lay persons and the popularity of the "Feingold Diet" (1975), sugar consumption does *not* seem to be related to the symptoms of ADHD (Wolraich, Milich, Stumbo, & Schultz, 1985). Finally, there is no evidence to suggest that parenting or childrearing is in any way related to the primary symptoms of the disorder; however, some of the secondary problems associated with ADHD (such as conduct disorder and self-esteem problems) may be the consequence of factors in the child's social environment.

Assessment of ADHD

Because symptoms of impulsivity, poor attention, and excessive activity may differ among children with ADHD and across various situations, a multidimensional approach to assessment is necessary. Parent, teacher, and possibly even peer reports, plus observation in the naturalistic setting, are considered in the evaluation of ADHD. This assessment is designed to go beyond offering an actual diagnosis. A comprehensive school-based evaluation should provide data to develop a thorough intervention plan for the child.

Parents

Parents are, of course, an important source of information about children's behavior because they observe the children daily and in a variety of settings. In addition, parents are in a position to notice fluctuations in behavior in response to different situations and varying responses to treatment. Parent reports are not sufficient in the evaluation of ADHD, however, for two reasons. First, parents do not have exposure to the full range of child behavior. They may be unaware of developmental norms and what constitutes age-appropriate behavior. Second, as stated earlier, the symptoms of ADHD may not be as troublesome in the home, a setting that typically is less structured than school. Although parent reports are necessary, information from other sources must be considered as well.

2. CHILDREN WITH LEARNING DISABILITIES

Teachers

Teachers serve as an essential source in the assessment of ADHD, and there are several rating scales by which teachers may easily communicate their knowledge and concerns regarding the child. These scales provide a normative comparison; teachers are asked to rate the degree to which the child's behavior differs from the behavior of other children in the class. Like parents, teachers have almost daily contact with these children. Unlike parents, teachers are also exposed to many other children of the same age and are able to use their *normative perspective* to determine if the referred child is behaving in age-inappropriate ways. In addition, teachers observe these children in unstructured play settings as well as highly structured academic settings, where symptoms of ADHD are more likely to emerge. Teacher input is thus integral in the assessment of ADHD (see Barkley, 1990, for a review of these rating scales).

Naturalistic observation data

An important source of information regarding the child with ADHD—one that has direct implications for treatment planning—involves systematic observation of the child in classroom and play settings. By using previously defined code categories that quantify the amount of time the child with ADHD spends engaged in on-task behavior and in various inappropriate off-task behaviors, it is possible to get *direct* information about how the child is functioning. In addition, it is helpful to collect these data on the same-sex classmates of the child. In this way it is possible to determine that Billy, who presents symptoms suggestive of ADHD, attends to math or storytime 22% of the time, while the other boys in his class attend an average of 84% during that same observation session. Because parent and teacher reports are based on previous contact with the child (i.e., numerous *retrospective* observations) and may be biased by the disruptive nature of the child's behavior, direct observation of the child with ADHD is the only way to provide data on *current* behavior, and these data will facilitate interpretation of the reports from parents and teachers.

Peers

One final area to be considered in the assessment process involves the child's peer interactions. Classroom sociometric assessment, which can provide information about peer popularity and rejection, in combination with measures of social loneliness and social anxiety offers valuable information about the child's social functioning and may highlight areas for intervention (see Landau & Milich, 1990, for a discussion of appropriate measures).

Preschool issues

Special issues arise in the assessment of preschool-age children. Most measures used to diagnose ADHD, for example, are not normed for preschoolers and may be developmentally inappropriate for this age group (Barkley, 1990). Furthermore, high activity level and non-compliance in very young children may either signify

Many children with ADHD are rejected by their peers. Children with ADHD tend to be bossy, intrusive, disruptive, and easily frustrated while in the play group. They have few, if any, friends. Peer rejection is a serious outcome of ADHD because children who are rejected early in life tend to be at high risk for many adult adjustment difficulties, including job terminations, bad-conduct discharge from the military, negative contact with police, and psychiatric hospitalization.

problems or simply represent normal development. In assessing preschoolers, therefore, special emphasis must be placed on the severity and frequency of a disruptive behavior rather than on its presence or absence (Campbell, 1990). Parents who are unaware of developmental norms tend to overreport problems with their children due to unrealistic expectations, thereby engendering additional conflict. On the other hand, some parents may be overly lenient and thus fail to notice potential problems.

Finally, teacher reports of behavior are obviously unavailable for those young children who do not attend preschool. Problems exist, however, even when teacher reports are obtainable (Barkley, 1990). As mentioned earlier, the public school classroom is an important arena in which to assess ADHD due to its structure; preschool settings are generally less structured and can therefore accommodate children with attentional deficits more easily. Preschool-based assessments thus may yield much less informative information than assessments conducted in grade school. Activities of daily living (e.g., eating, dressing) are more likely to be the source of conflict at this age. Even in this area, however, it is important to not confuse the child's normal attempts at autonomy with ADHD-related management difficulties.

Treatment of ADHD

Once assessment has indicated a possibility of ADHD, what can teachers and caregivers do? It is important to remember that children with ADHD benefit from the same environments that all children do; thus, designing classrooms appropriately for the child's development is an important step toward managing the behavior of a child with ADHD. For young children this means a loosely structured environment in which active involvement is an integral part of the learning process. In addition, tailoring work to fit the child's individual needs and encouraging collaboration and cooperation are practices recommended for children with ADHD, as they are for all children.

The two primary methods of intervention are stimulant medication and behavioral management; however, the most effective treatment involves a combination of the two (Pelham, in press).

Medication therapy

The most common treatment for ADHD is medications that stimulate the central nervous system (Barkley, 1990). Research suggests that children with ADHD may not be as sensitive to feedback from the social and physical environment as other children; stimulant medication appears to render these children more sensitive by lowering response thresholds in the nervous system (Barkley, 1989). Ritalin, or methylphenidate (the generic drug name), is the most common stimulant used. Approximately 70 to 75% of children responded positively to this medication, while about one fourth are unaffected (Pelham, 1987); thus, these medications will help many but not all children with ADHD.

Effects of medication. For those children who do respond positively, the effects are immediate and typically quite strong. Attention, impulse control, and short-term memory may all be improved (Barkley, 1990). Children talk less, are less disturbing, follow rules better, and exhibit less aggression (Pelham, 1987). These changes often lead to improved relations with parents, teachers, and peers. As these children become more cooperative, the need for close adult supervision should diminish; however, in spite of substantial reduction in disruptive behavior, the majority of children with ADHD will still show problem behaviors. Medication is thus often helpful, but not sufficient, in managing the disorder.

In addition to reducing disruptive behavior, stimulant medication has been found to help children attend better when involved in organized athletic play with other children (Pelham et al., 1990). Because these activities, such as soccer or T-ball, involve peer interactions, medication may indirectly improve the peer relations and self-esteem of children with ADHD. Even while on medication, however, it is difficult for most children with ADHD to gain peer acceptance (Pelham & Milich, 1984).

Children with ADHD who are on medication are also better able to concentrate on schoolwork. They complete more assignments and are more careful and accurate; thus, they show improved academic *performance* (Barkley, 1990). Medication is much less effective in improving children's scores on academic *achievement* tests, however. In other words, medication does not necessarily help children with ADHD master more difficult tasks and may not directly relate to enhanced learning; thus, academic achievement *per se* appears to be only minimally improved by medication, if at all.

Recently there has been growing interest in the effects of medication on the attitudes and motivation of children with ADHD. Some experts have suggested, for example, that medication may cause children to believe that they are responsible for their own misbehavior—that they must rely on some external agent (the drug) for control of their difficulties. Consequently, when children behave inappropriately or do not succeed at schoolwork, they might conclude that the medication must not be working that day—in other words, these problems are not their fault. In contrast, other researchers suggest that because medication leads to improved performance, children with ADHD may be able to personalize this newly discovered success and thus feel greater responsibility for their own behavior than

if they had not been medicated—they have greater control than before. Although more study is necessary, current results support the second hypothesis: Medicated children with ADHD seem to credit themselves for good performances (i.e., they *internalize* and personalize their successes) while *externalizing* or blaming poor performance on factors beyond their control (Milich, 1993). The fact that these children attribute successes to their personal responsibility, and not to the medication, may contribute to their self-esteem. In summary, medication seems to improve behavior in a variety of ways and may also help children to feel better about themselves.

Despite the important effects of medication, several cautions should be kept in mind. First, as mentioned earlier, not all children with ADHD benefit from stimulant medication. Second, four- to five-year-old children do not experience improvement to the same extent as do older children (Barkley, 1989). In a review of medication studies with preschoolers, Campbell (1985) noted that few benefits were obtained and that side effects, such as increased solitary play and clinging, appeared serious enough to potentially disrupt social development. Third, all of the medication-induced benefits represent short-term effects only; that is, improvements are noticeable only while the child is taking the medication. In the evenings, weekends, and summers, when children are typically not medicated, their symptoms generally return to pretreatment levels; thus medication brings no lasting benefits.

Side effects. Many parents express concern about potential negative side effects of stimulant medication; for example, there is evidence that mild insomnia and lessened appetite, especially at lunchtime, can occur (Barkley, 1990). This latter effect has been thought to lead to suppressed weight and height gains. Research indicates, however, that effects on growth can be corrected by altering dosage and tend to occur only during the first year of medication therapy (Barkley, 1990). Height and weight tend to catch up to age norms in subsequent years even if medication is continued (Mattes & Gittleman, 1983). There is little research on this side effect in pre-school children, however, even though medication is sometimes given to children as young as age three (Campbell, 1990). As a consequence, medication is not recommended for children in this age group. Because medication effects tend to wear off within a four-hour period, most children with ADHD receive a noontime dose to cover their afternoon activities at school. One simple way to avoid the lunchtime appetite loss is to have the child eat lunch prior to taking the afternoon medication dose.

Mild headaches and stomachaches may also occur, but they tend to disappear within a few weeks (Barkley, 1990). These problems, along with mood changes, such as irritability, and individual reactions (e.g., lip licking, rashes) may be alleviated by a simple dosage adjustment. Research indicates that there are no known long-term side effects; for example, these children do not appear to be at increased risk for drug abuse later in life. Any side effects, therefore, tend to be mild, short term, and easily relieved.

One unfortunate consequence of drug treatment is that many parents and teachers tend to rely on medication exclusively and not invest in other, more lasting interventions. Within the past few years, the lay press has expressed alarm about overmedication of children. If parents seek medication for their child to manage home-based behavior problems, this concern may be valid; however, if medication is used to help the child attend to important classroom instruction and adjust well to school, this concern seems to be exaggerated. It is important to remember that medicated children with ADHD, although improved, are not made symptom free. For these reasons, medication is not adequate by itself as a treatment for children with ADHD. The "best practice," based on research, is to combine medication and behavioral treatments in the management of ADHD. This is done not only because medication is insufficient in the treatment of most cases but also because it permits the use of a lower dose of medication. There is strong evidence that a low dose of Ritalin, in combination with behavioral intervention, results in at least the same improvement—and sometimes greater improvement—in the child as does a high dose of Ritalin alone (Pelham, in press). In addition, when the low dose is used, most undesirable side effects can be avoided. In fact, it has been suggested that behavioral interventions be attempted in school *before* thought is given to the use of medication (National Association of School Psychologists, 1992).

Behavioral treatment

Because many children with ADHD demonstrate an inability to follow rules and govern their own behavior (Barkley, 1989), behavioral treatment is necessary for these self-regulatory difficulties. Aspects of successful behavioral intervention include rewarding appropriate behavior, giving effective directions and requests, and using consistent methods of discipline. If teachers can receive assistance from consultants (such as school psychologists) to implement these procedures, most children with ADHD can have their educational and social needs met in the regular education setting. In addition, collaboration with parents is essential because home-based support for school behavior and performance will enhance the success of programs at school.

Appropriate behavior. Many parents and teachers do not think that children should be rewarded simply for "doing what they ought to do," and most children do not need a heavy overlay of rewards to promote acceptable behavior; however, if a child with ADHD seldom engages in an important behavior (such as playing cooperatively), then rewards may be necessary to promote the behavior. As the child learns the behavior, rewards should be gradually removed. Research shows that the use of rewards is particularly helpful when dealing with children who have ADHD (Pelham, 1992). Their inappropriate behavior tends to be extremely compelling; adults cannot ignore it. As a consequence, much of the feedback these children receive from parents, teachers, and peers is expressed as a complaint or reprimand. It is little wonder that many children with ADHD develop self-concept difficulties and depression. **Rewarding positive behaviors thus not only encourages the child to continue behaving well but also provides the child with desperately needed success, thereby building self-esteem.**

Verbal praise is crucial for a child with ADHD and is especially powerful when the positive behavior is also clarified (e.g., "I like the way you are playing so nicely with the other boys"). Praise may not, however, provide adequate incentive initially due to the child's lower sensitivity to feedback from the social environment; thus children with ADHD often require more frequent and powerful rewards for a time (Barkley, 1990). At first parents and teachers may need to give material rewards along with praise, to teach appropriate behavior; subsequently they may use praise alone to maintain the behavior—for example, smiley faces or gold stars may be given to the child every half hour for engaging in appropriate classroom behavior. A star chart on which different classroom activities (e.g., storytime) are separated as intervals can make implementation of such a reward system easier. To avoid a problem with classroom equity (other children wondering why they do not earn these rewards), the smiley faces could be granted discreetly, perhaps on a special card to be taken home at the end of each day. Even though some teachers may find these procedures intrusive and distracting, the fact remains that the use of behavioral intervention disrupts classroom routine less than does an untreated child with ADHD.

Directions. Unfortunately, the disruptive behavior of children with ADHD causes parents and teachers to often find themselves issuing numerous directives and commands to these youngsters throughout the day. To increase the likelihood that the child will cooperate with adult requests, directions should be specific and brief (Pelham, 1992). Those that are vague or issued in question format (e.g., "Let's get back to work, shall we?") or that involve several directives strung together are not likely to be obeyed. Instead, adults should obtain the child's attention, issue the direction (e.g., "Joey, finish picking up those blocks now"), and wait a few seconds. The child should then be praised for cooperating. Research shows that these techniques are effective. They prevent adult interactions from escalating into impatience and reduce the tendency of children with ADHD to ignore or resist adult direction.

In instances in which a child with ADHD does not respond to adult guidance, school psychologists can work with teachers to implement a variety of other behavioral interventions. Ignoring mildly negative behaviors may prove effective, but often increased adult monitoring and immediate consequences to reduce disruptive acts (e.g., asking the child to sit out an activity) are necessary. If the child engages in aggressive outbursts or is extremely uncooperative, a time-out procedure may also have to be implemented (Barkley, 1990). Consistency is essential for all of these methods to work well.

Daily report card. Parents can serve as an effective back-up to school-based interventions. An important behavior-management strategy involves sending home a brief daily report card reflecting the child's performance for each day (Barkley, 1990). Parents may thus praise the child for success in school, thereby supporting teachers

Acknowledging teachers' need for effective consultation and collaboration in this area, the National Association of School Psychologists (NASP) recently issued the following position statement describing a "best-practice" approach for dealing with children with attention deficits.

NASP believes that effective intervention should be tailored to the unique learning strengths and needs of every student. For children with attention deficits, such interventions will include the following:

1) Classroom modifications to enhance attending, work production, and social adjustment;

2) Behavioral management systems to reduce problems in arenas most likely to be affected by attention deficits (e.g., large group instruction, transitions, etc.);

3) Direct instruction in study strategies and social skills, within the classroom setting whenever possible to increase generalization;

4) Consultation with families to assist in behavior management in the home setting and to facilitate home-school cooperation and collaboration;

5) Monitoring by a case manager to ensure effective implementation of interventions, to provide adequate support for those interventions, and to assess progress in meeting behavioral and academic goals;

6) Education of school staff in characteristics and management of attention deficits to enhance appropriate instructional modifications and behavior management;

7) Access to special education services when attention deficits significantly impact school performance;

8) Working collaboratively with community agencies providing medical and related services to students and their families.

NASP believes appropriate treatment may or may not include medical intervention. When medication *is* considered, NASP *strongly* recommends:

1) That instructional and behavioral interventions be implemented before medication trials are begun;

2) That behavioral data be collected before and during medication trials to assess baseline conditions and the efficacy of medication; and

3) That communication between school, home, and medical personnel emphasize mutual problem solving and cooperation. (National Association of School Psychologists, 1992)

---

efforts. In addition, parents should consider using small toys and special activities (e.g., going to a movie) as back-up rewards for positive school performance because these children need rewards of high salience. Parents should target small successes first (e.g., remaining seated throughout storytime) then gradually increase expectations as the child demonstrates mastery.

Preschool issues. Unfortunately, dealing with ADHD symptoms among preschool-age children can be quite a challenge because some of these problems simply represent individual differences in developmental rates. Excessive activity, impulsive responding, and an inability to pay attention—all symptoms of ADHD among school-age children—may not be particularly unusual behaviors for many preschool-age children. Even so, some preschool children receive a diagnosis of ADHD. In these cases—such as Jamie, who was described earlier in this article—parents may feel overwhelmed with the child's discipline problems at home and with aggressive conduct with playmates. The primary symptoms of ADHD *per se* thus do not represent the major source of difficulty, and a diagnosis of ADHD would be premature. Parent training, however, may be an appropriate intervention, in which Jamie's parents are given systematic guidance on how to manage his behavior at home. If Jamie continues to experience difficulties once he reaches school age, when classroom demands require a greater restraint on activity and more persistent attention, a diagnosis of ADHD may be given serious consideration.

Conclusion

ADHD is a problem that has many facets and affects the child in many areas of functioning, including academic performance, interpersonal relations, and emotional well-being. Because of ADHD's complexity, successful treatment requires a multidisciplinary approach reflecting the collaboration of many professionals. Teachers must have assistance in dealing with children with ADHD.

References

Achenbach, T.M., McConaughy, S.H., & Howell, C.T. (1987). Child/adolescent behavioral and emotional problems: Implications of cross-informant correlations for situational specificity. *Psychological Bulletin, 101*, 213–232.

American Psychiatric Association. (1987). *Diagnostic and statistical manual of mental disorders* (3rd ed., revised). Washington, DC: Author.

Barkley, R.A. (1989). Attention deficit-hyperactivity disorder. In E.J. Mash & R.A. Barkley (Eds.), *Treatment of childhood disorders* (pp. 39–72). New York: Guilford.

Barkley, R.A. (1990). *Attention-deficit hyperactivity disorder: A handbook for diagnosis and treatment.* New York: Guilford.

Campbell, S.B. (1985). Hyperactivity in preschoolers: Correlates and prognostic implications. *Clinical Psychology Review, 5,* 405–428.

Campbell, S. (1988, October). *Longitudinal studies of active and aggressive preschoolers: Individual differences in early behavior and in outcome.* Paper presented at the Second Rochester Symposium on Developmental Psychopathology, Rochester, NY.

Campbell, S.B. (1990). *Behavioral problems in preschool children: Clinical and developmental issues.* New York: Guilford.

Campbell, S.B., Endman, M.W., & Bernfeld, G. (1977). Three year follow-up of hyperactive preschoolers into elementary school. *Journal of Child Psychology and Psychiatry, 18,* 239–249.

Campbell, S.B., Szumowski, E.K., Ewing, L.J., Gluck, D.S., & Breaux, A.M. (1982). A multidimensional assessment of parent-identified behavior problem toddlers. *Journal of Abnormal Child Psychology, 10*(4), 569–592.

Douglas, V.I. (1983). Attentional and cognitive problems. In M. Rutter (Ed.), *Developmental Neuropsychiatry* (pp. 280–329). New York: Guilford.

Feingold, B. (1975). *Why your child is hyperactive.* New York: Random House.

Hinshaw, S.P. (1987). On the distinction between attentional deficits/hyperactivity and conduct problems/aggression in child psychopathology. *Psychological Bulletin, 101,* 443–463.

Hynd, G.W., Hern, K.L., Voeller, K.K., & Marshall, R.M. (1991). Neurobiological basis of attention-deficit hyperactivity disorder (ADHD). *School Psychology Review, 20*(2), 174–186.

Jacob, R.B., O'Leary, K.D., & Rosenblad, C. (1978). Formal and informal classroom settings: Effects on hyperactivity. *Journal of Abnormal Child Psychology, 6*(1), 47–59.

Landau, S., & Milich, R. (1988). Social communication patterns of attention-deficit-disordered boys. *Journal of Abnormal Child Psychology, 16,* 69–81.

Landau, S., & Milich, R. (1990). Assessment of children's social status and peer relations. In A.M. LaGreca (Ed.), *Through the eyes of the child* (pp. 259–291). Boston: Allyn & Bacon.

Landau, S., & Moore, L. (1991). Social skill deficits in children with attention-deficit hyperactivity disorder. *School Psychology Review, 20*(2), 235–251.

Landau, S., Lorch, E.P., & Milich, R. (1992). Visual attention to and comprehension of television in attention-deficit hyperactivity disordered and normal boys. *Child Development, 63,* 928–937.

Lapouse, R., & Monk, M. (1958). An epidemiological study of behavior characteristics in children. *American Journal of Public Health, 48,* 1134–1144.

Mattes, J.A., & Gittleman, R. (1983). Growth of hyperactive children on maintenance regimen of methylphenidate. *Archives of General Psychiatry, 40,* 317–321.

McGee, R., & Share, D.L. (1988). Attention deficit disorder-hyperactivity and academic failure: Which comes first and what should be treated? *Journal of the American Academy of Child and Adolescent Psychiatry, 27,* 318–325.

Milich, R. (1993). *Children's response to failure: If at first you don't succeed, do you try, try again?* Manuscript submitted for publication.

Milich, R., & Landau, S. (1989). The role of social status variables in differentiating subgroups of hyperactive children. In L.M. Bloomingdale & J. Swanson (Eds.)., *Attention deficit disorder: Current concepts and emerging trends in attentional and behavioral disorders of childhood: Vol. 5* (pp. 1–16). Elmsford, NY: Pergamon.

Milich, R., Loney, J., & Landau, S. (1982). The independent dimensions of hyperactivity and aggression: A validation with playroom observation data. *Journal of Abnormal Psychology, 91,* 183–198.

National Association of School Psychologists. (1992, May). Position statement on students with attention deficits. *Communique, 20,* 5.

Olson, S.L. (1989). Assessment of impulsivity in preschoolers: Cross-measure convergence, longitudinal stability, and relevance to social competence. *Journal of Clinical Child Psychology, 8*(2), 176–183.

Parker, J.G., & Asher, S.R. (1987). Peer relations and later personal adjustment: Are low-accepted children "at risk"? *Psychological Bulletin, 102,* 357–389.

Pelham, W.E., Jr. (1987). What do we know about the use and effects of CNS stimulants in the treatment of ADD? In J. Loney (Ed.), *The young hyperactive child: Answers to questions about diagnosis, prognosis and treatment* (pp. 99–110). New York: Haworth.

Pelham, W.E. (1992). *Children's summer day treatment program: 1992 program manual.* Unpublished manuscript, University of Pittsburgh School of Medicine, Western Psychiatric Institute and Clinic, Pittsburgh, PA.

Pelham, W.E. (in press). Pharmacotherapy for children with attention deficit hyperactivity disorder. *School Psychology Review.*

Pelham, W.E., & Bender, M.E. (1982). Peer relationships in hyperactive children: Description and treatment. In D.C. Gadow & I. Bialer (Eds.), *Advances in learning and behavioral disabilities: A research annual: Vol. 1* (pp. 365–436). Greenwich, CT: JAI.

Pelham, W.E., & Milich, R. (1984). Peer relations in children with hyperactivity/attention deficit disorder. *Journal of Learning Disabilities, 17,* 560–567.

Pelham, W.E., Jr., McBurnett, K., Harper, G.W., Milich, R., Murphy, D.A., Clinton, J., & Thiele, C. (1990). Methylphenidate and baseball playing in children with ADHD: Who's on first? *Journal of Consulting and Clinical Psychology, 58,* 130–133.

Richman, N., Stevenson, J., & Graham, J.J. (1982). *Preschool to school: A behavioral study.* London: Academic.

Schaughency, E.A., & Rothlind, J. (1991). Assessment and classification of attention deficit hyperactive disorders. *School Psychology Review, 20*(2), 187–202.

Weiss, B., & Hechtman, L.T. (1986). *Hyperactive children grown up.* New York: Guilford.

Wolraich, M., Milich, R., Stumbo, P., & Schultz, F. (1985). The effects of sucrose ingestion on the behavior of hyperactive boys. *Pediatrics, 106,* 675–682.

Identifying Students' Instructional Needs in the Context of Classroom and Home Environments

James E. Ysseldyke

Sandra Christenson

Joseph F. Kovaleski

James E. Ysseldyke *(CEC Chapter #367), Professor,* and **Sandra Christenson**, *Associate Professor, Department of Educational Psychology, University of Minnesota, Minneapolis.* **Joseph F. Kovaleski** *(CEC Chapter #65), Director, Instructional Support System of Pennsylvania, East Petersburg, Pennsylvania.*

Teachers refer students to intervention assistance teams or related services personnel because they want a change for the student, other students, and themselves. Quite simply, teachers want instructionally relevant information and helpful strategies for teaching the referred student. An excellent and scientific way to determine the referred student's needs is to ascertain whether specific instructional factors correlating with academic achievement are present or absent in the student's instructional environments. The key word in the previous sentence is "correlating." Teachers are not determinants of students' achievement, but they are facilitators of achievement.

Increasingly, teachers and diagnostic personnel are recognizing the impor-tance of assessing student performance and learning outcomes in the context of classroom and home environments (cf. Ysseldyke & Christenson, 1987). Such recognition is leading to new approaches to identifying students' instructional needs. These approaches focus not only on assessing a learner and his or her characteristics but also on learning and the learning context. These new approaches are prescriptive rather than descriptive, and are used to specify the instructional needs of individual students in the context of the surroundings in which learning occurs.

The belief that diagnostic personnel ought to assess the learning environment in addition to assessing the learner is based on the belief that student performance in school is a function of an interaction between the student and the learning or instructional environment. Instructional environments are those contexts in which learning takes place: the schools and homes.

Ysseldyke and Christenson (1993) have developed a system, The Instructional Environment System-II (TIES-II), to provide a framework for assessing instructional environments. They identified 12 instructional and 5 home-support-for-learning components that are critical to consider when assessing learning environments (see Table 1). When instructional environments are assessed using systems like TIES-II, professionals are given essential information for preferral intervention, instructional consultation, intervention assistance, and collaborative intervention planning. Among other premises, such assessment practices are based on the assumptions that: (a) complex diagnostic procedures are not necessary to make a relevant instructional change and (b) assessment should be focused on collecting instructionally relevant information. Information necessary for instructional planning is gathered in classrooms (where problems and concerns typically arise) on variables that teachers can change (like skill level, participation, success rate, and task completion rate).

Steps in the collaborative intervention planning process are shown in

From *Teaching Exceptional Children*, Vol. 26, No. 3, Spring 1994, pp. 37-41. © 1994 by The Council for Exceptional Children. Reprinted by permission.

Figure 1. When teachers encounter difficulty with a student, they describe their concerns by differentiating between actual and desired student performance. They provide for the team's use of information on instructional needs. Team members gather information on the classroom instructional environment by observation, teacher interview, and student interview. Team members (teams must always include the teacher) meet to identify instructional needs and discuss how instruction will be planned, managed, delivered, and evaluated. Team members may also use a parent interview/survey form to document the presence and importance of specific home-support-for-learning components. They use the information obtained to identify ways to involve the student's parent(s) or guardian, and invite parents' assistance.

Team members brainstorm ways to intervene with students. Classroom-based assessment (e.g., curriculum-based assessment, observation, interviewing) is critical to framing the problem and developing the intervention. Practice has shown that brainstorming per se is a waste of time and can lead to ineffective interventions. More effective interventions are developed if the brainstorming is based on a good classroom-based assessment. For example, the classroom-based assessment might point to the need for the student to engage in more relevant practice. The brainstorming then is on alternative ways to provide relevant practice in school and at home, rather than on a broad-based listing of all known strategies. Team members share resources and discuss ways they can work together to implement the selected intervention(s). Throughout the intervention planning process the focus is on intervention and the use of instructionally relevant information to make a change. Questions and/or information tangential to the design of an intervention are temporarily tabled. This is essential to design an intervention expediently. Without this, it is easy for teams to discuss, discuss, and discuss—something the authors have referred to as "admiring the problem."

A Practical Example

The following case description is an example of the use of an analysis of the classroom environment to plan for a student's instructional needs. It assumes that the classroom teacher has access to an intervention assistance team (IAT) providing support in the regular classroom and a resource for use in planning interventions (e.g., Algozzine & Ysseldyke, 1992).

A Request for Assistance

Michael, a third grader, has been identified by his teacher as having difficulty in reading and classroom behavior. His teacher reports that Michael reads in a halting, word-by-word manner and does not connect discourse. He appears to be interested in getting through a passage without regard to its meaning and does not use reading as a skill to obtain information. The teacher is using the beginning 3rd-grade book with Michael and the other members of the lowest reading group. In addition, the teacher has noted that Michael leaves many assignments unfinished, bothers other students, is overactive, and has difficulty attending to task.

Michael's teacher has requested the help of her school's IAT. The IAT has been trained to assist teachers by closely analyzing the instructional environment in the classroom as well as the student's skills in meeting the demands of that setting. In the course of their work with each teacher, various team members thoroughly interview the teacher, the parents, and the student about the presenting problems. Other members conduct classroom observations and curriculum-based assessment in the area of concern. The IAT uses the Instructional Environment System (Ysseldyke & Christenson, 1993) as a framework to organize their work with each student. After selecting the interventions based on their assessment, the IAT assists the teacher in implementing the interventions and carefully monitors the student's response to determine their effectiveness.

In Michael's case, the IAT found Michael's classroom to have a highly positive learning climate. His teacher is lively and presents all of her lessons in an interesting and enthusiastic manner. While the instructional level was appropriate for most of the students in the class, Michael was unable to keep up. The kinds of feedback that worked with other students in the class did not result in improved performance for Michael. And, the team learned that Michael's parents are supportive but are bewildered by what to do about Michael's school problems. They report that Michael is happy at home and has lots of friends in the neighborhood. However, nightly homework time is a stressful event for Michael and his parents.

As a result of their work with Michael, his teacher, and his parents, the IAT has identified three areas of support for Michael: instructional match, evaluation and feedback, and home support. Each has direct relation to instructional interventions that are appropriate.

Instructional Match

Using curriculum-based assessment of Michael's reading, the IATs found that his average oral reading fluency in third-grade material was 16 words per minute (wpm) with seven errors per minute (epm), or about 70% known material. According to curriculum-based assessment guidelines (e.g., Gickling & Thompson, 1985; Shinn, 1989), Michael was working at a frustrational level in his material. He hesitated over many words and displayed no strategies to "unlock" unknown words. He understood little of what he read. While the other students were reading, Michael looked around the room. When presented with other language arts materials based on the third-grade reader (e.g., seatwork), Michael was on task about 40% of the time and finished only about 25% of the work. Interestingly, the IAT found that during math activities Michael's on-task behavior was around 80% and his task completion 95%. Michael was assessed to be working at an instructional level in math.

The IAT hypothesized that Michael's reading and behavior problems could be traced to his frustration in reading, in

Table 1. Instructional-Environment and Home-Support-for-Learning Components

Instructional-Environment Components

Instructional Match: The student's needs are assessed accurately, and instruction is matched appropriately to the results of the instructional diagnosis.

Teacher Expectations: There are realistic, yet high expectations for both the amount and accuracy of work to be completed by the student, and these are communicated clearly to the student.

Classroom Environment: The classroom management techniques used are effective for this student; there is a positive, supportive classroom atmosphere; and time is used productively.

Instructional Presentation: Instruction is presented in a clear and effective manner; directions contain sufficient information for this student to understand what kinds of behaviors or skills are to be demonstrated; and the student's understanding is checked.

Cognitive Emphasis: Thinking skills and learning strategies for completing assignments are communicated explicitly to the student.

Motivational Strategies: Effective strategies for heightening student interest and effort are used with the student.

Relevant Practice: The student is given adequate opportunity to practice with appropriate materials and a high success rate. Classroom tasks are clearly important to achieving instructional goals.

Informed Feedback: The student receives relatively immediate and specific information on his or her performance or behavior; when the student makes mistakes, correction is provided.

Academic Engaged Time: The student is actively engaged in responding to academic content; the teacher monitors the extent to which the student is actively engaged and redirects the student when the student is unengaged.

Adaptive Instruction: The curriculum is modified within reason to accommodate the student's unique and specific instructional needs.

Progress Evaluation: There is direct, frequent measurement of the student's progress toward completion of instructional objectives; data on the student's performance and progress are used to plan future instruction.

Student Understanding: The student demonstrates an accurate understanding of what is to be done in the classroom.

Home-Support-for-Learning Components

Expectations and Attributions: High, realistic expectations about school work are communicated to the child, and the value of effort and working hard in school is emphasized.

Discipline Orientation: There is an authoritative, not permissive or authoritarian, approach to discipline and the child is monitored and supervised by adults.

Home Effective Environment: The parent-child relationship is generally positive and supportive.

Parent Participation: There is an educative home environment, and others participate in the child's schooling, at home and/or at school.

Structure for Learning: Organization and daily routines facilitate the completion of schoolwork and the child's academic learning is supported.

Note: Adapted from *The Instructional Environment System-II* by J. Ysseldyke and S. L. Christenson, 1993, Longmont, CO: Sopris West. Copyright 1993. Reprinted by permission.

that his behavior problems were not as evident in other subjects nor in the home. In consultation with the classroom teacher, the IAT planned to implement strategies for improving Michael's pool of known words through a drill sandwich technique (Gickling & Thompson, 1985; Shapiro, 1992). This technique allows for a systematic presentation of new words along with a structured procedure to ensure adequate repetitions of new learnings. Relevant practice of this newly learned material would be provided by reading the new words in a variety of print contexts. Michael would also be taught to self-monitor his comprehension of reading passages as a further check on passage difficulty. The IAT also assisted his teacher in adapting other tasks (e.g., Huck, Myers, & Wilson, 1989) to maximize engaged time by ensuring that all materials were at his instructional level.

Ongoing Monitoring and Feedback

Once the classroom-based interventions were planned, it became critical to monitor Michael's progress throughout the intervention period. With the assistance of the IAT, Michael's teacher conducted biweekly checks of Michael's acquisition of new words, his retention of learned words, his oral reading fluency, and his comprehension or understanding of the material. This information was fed back to Michael who maintained a chart of his gains. Michael's teacher found that having Michael keep track of his progress was highly motivating to him. He seemed to take pride in his gradual achievement of higher level of performance. As Michael displayed progress, his teacher set increasingly higher goals for him to achieve.

Home Support

The IAT worked closely with Michael's parents throughout the duration of the intervention so that strategies implemented in school could be reinforced at home. Michael's teacher and other team members advised his parents on how to structure Michael's homework time, and taught them the drill sandwich technique to help Michael practice his newly learned words. Particular emphasis was given to avoiding teaching new

Figure 1. The collaborative intervention planning process

1. A teacher or teachers describe their concern(s), differentiating between actual and desired student performance.	*Teacher(s) Describe Concern(s)*
2. Team members or the education professional share information with the teacher(s) about Instructional Environment Components, discussing how instruction will be planned, managed, delivered, and evaluated for the individual student.	*Share Information About Instructional Environment Components*
3. Team members arrive at a consensus about the student's instructional needs.	*Consensus About Needs*
4. Team members describe Home-Support-for-Learning Components	*Home-Support-for-Learning Components*
5. Team members identify ways to involve the student's parent(s) or guardian and invite parents' assistance.	*Invite Parent(s) Assistance*
6. Team members brainstorm ideas/options for interventions.	*Brainstorm Ideas/Options*
7. An intervention (or interventions) is (are) selected.	*Intervention(s) Selected*
8. Team members share resources, discussing ways they can work together to implement the selected intervention(s).	*Share Resources*
9. Teacher/parent questions not directly relevant to intervention are then discussed.	*Teacher/Parent Questions Discussed*

Note: Adapted from *The Instructional Environment System-II* by J. Ysseldyke and S. L. Christenson, 1993, Longmont, CO: Sopris West. Copyright 1993. Reprinted by permission.

tive instructional program for a student at risk of school failure. If the IAT members had limited their focus to variables related to student characteristics (e.g., his ability or background), they would not have designed an intervention that precisely met Michael's needs in this particular classroom. They may also have missed an opportunity to help Michael reach his optimal performance level.

It is worth noting that assessing the instructional environment facilitates a close match between the student's needs and the characteristics of the teacher and the classroom. The interventions developed through this approach will, therefore, be different for different students and different classrooms. In approaching each classroom setting, a careful assessment of the environment as well as the student's skills is needed. This increases the likelihood that an intervention appropriate for that classroom teacher as well as for that student will be developed. The use of this approach focuses on enabling the teacher and parents to be better facilitators of student engagement and outcomes.

concepts or reteaching old ones at home, which typically led to frustration for both Michael and his parents. The IAT also guided the family in the selection of easy reading material so that at home Michael could begin learning to read for pleasure.

Resolution

As the intervention proceeded, Michael began to make slow, but steady gains in his reading skills. As he progressed through more difficult material, he began to perceive himself as a competent reader. Providing tasks appropriate to his instructional level in both reading

and language arts led to a corresponding decrease in inattention and off-task behavior. His teacher indicated that the gap between actual and desired performance decreased. Michael's parents continued their close coordination of school and homework with the classroom teacher and were very gratified by Michael's progress.

Conclusion

This example of a common school situation highlights the usefulness of assessing the instructional environment when developing and implementing an effec-

References

Algozzine, B., & Ysseldyke, J. (1992). *Strategies and tactics for effective instruction.* Longmont, CO: Sopris West.

Gickling, E. E., & Thompson, V. P. (1985). A personal view of curriculum-based assessment. *Exceptional Children, 52,* 205-218.

Huck, R., Myers, R., & Wilson, J. (1989). *ADAPT: A developmental activity program for teachers* (2nd ed.). Pittsburgh: Allegheny Intermediate Unit.

Shapiro, E. S. (1992). Use of Gickling's model of curriculum-based assessment to improve reading in elementary age students. *School Psychology Review, 21,* 168-176.

Shinn, M. R. (1989). *Curriculum-based measurement: Assessing special children.* New York: Guilford.

Ysseldyke, J., & Christenson, S. L. (1987). *The instructional environment scale.* Austin, TX: Pro-Ed.

Ysseldyke J., & Christenson, S. L. (1993). *The instructional environment system-II (TIES-II).* Longmont, CO: Sopris West.

Adapting Textbooks for Children with Learning Disabilities in Mainstreamed Classrooms

Ruth Lyn Meese

Ruth Lyn Meese *(CEC Chapter #955) is an Assistant Professor of Special Education, Department of Education, Special Education, and Social Work, Longwood College, Farmville, Virginia.*

Cooperative efforts between special education and regular education teachers are vital if students with learning disabilities are to be successful in mainstreamed classes in which the textbook is the primary means for disseminating information.

Adapting textbooks to meet the needs of these students can be a complex task. For example, some children with learning disabilities have attentional deficits affecting their ability to differentiate what information they should attend to (Hallahan & Kauffman, 1988). The cluttered appearance of many textbooks complicates the decision as to what does or does not warrant attention. Other children are reading at a level far below that of the textbook. Their reading problems are compounded by the complex sentence and organizational structures, difficult vocabulary, and concept density typically found in expository text material (Carnine, Silbert, & Kameenui, 1990). Still other students may lack efficient strategies to comprehend and remember textbook reading assignments (Seidenberg, 1989).

Special education teachers do not have the time to rewrite textbooks. They can, however, provide adaptations based on the needs of the individual student, the demands of the textbook, and the needs of the regular classroom teacher (Margolis & McGettigan, 1988; Martens, Peterson, Witt, & Cirone, 1986).

A student listens to tape-recorded text in which the teacher has stopped periodically to summarize important information.

This article describes ways in which special educators can help students get the most from content area textbooks.

Modifying the Textbook

Modification usually involves highlighting information in the textbook, tape recording the textbook, or providing the student with a high-interest/low-vocabulary alternative—all of which can be both time consuming and costly. Since little research exists to document the effectiveness of highlighting, the focus here is on the other two alternatives.

Tape Recording the Text

Teachers can ask student or adult volunteer groups to prepare tape-recorded versions of textbooks (Smith &

From *Teaching Exceptional Children*, Vol. 24, No. 3, Spring 1992, pp. 49-51. © 1992 by The Council for Exceptional Children. Reprinted by permission.

Smith, 1985). Recorded text segments should be kept clear and short. On the tape, a teacher may also provide an overview of the selection before reading begins (Bos & Vaughn, 1988); give clear signals to the reader for page location; and stop periodically in order to summarize important information or ask the student to respond to questions (Salend, 1990). Tapes of textbooks commonly used in content classes are available free of charge, or for a small fee, from organizations such as Recordings for the Blind, 214 East 58th, New York, NY 10022.

Using High-Interest/ Low-Vocabulary Materials

Special educators occasionally must provide students who have extremely poor reading skills with high-interest/low-vocabulary alternatives to their assigned reading selections. Care must be taken to discuss possible alternatives with the regular classroom teacher so that proper content coverage and mastery can be ensured. Excellent lists of commercially available materials can be found in Mercer and Mercer (1989) and Wood (1989).

Altering Instructional Procedures

Many students with learning disabilities can be helped to comprehend textbook materials by relatively minor changes in the teacher's instructional procedures. Usually, these alterations increase the level of teacher-directed instruction and/or the level of active student involvement with the text.

Teaching Textbook Structure

Students must use expository text and organizational structure to find and recall information from their textbooks (Seidenberg, 1989). Unfortunately, this is often problematic for a student with learning disabilities. Therefore, the special educator must directly teach these structures (e.g., "cues" for important information such as headings, subheadings, differing print, or introductory and summary paragraphs), particularly when the information is complex and the textbooks or concepts are new (Carnine et al., 1990). The teacher can focus attention on important features of the text by beginning each reading assignment with a systematic overview of the material. Archer and Gleason (1989) have suggested the following teacher-directed chapter warm-up procedure:

1. Read the chapter title and introduction.
2. Read the headings and subheadings.
3. Read the chapter summary.
4. Read any questions at the end of the chapter.
5. Tell what the chapter will talk about.

Previewing

To preview a reading selection before independent study, the teacher or a peer simply reads aloud the assigned passages (Salend & Nowak, 1988). Previewing is a simple procedure that can readily be combined with other techniques to increase active student involvement during reading. Examples of such techniques are guided questioning by the teacher after short textbook segments are read aloud and reciprocal teaching, in which students take turns assuming the role of teacher (see Palincsar & Brown, 1986).

Providing Advance Organizers

Advance organizers alert students to important information in the reading assignment (Darch & Gersten, 1986). For example, *graphic organizers* are diagrams depicting superordinate and subordinate relationships from the text and can provide students with a visual overview of the reading material before actual reading begins (Horton, Lovitt, & Bergerud, 1990). Similarly, teachers may provide students with a sequential partial outline of critical information, to be completed during the reading process (Bos & Vaughn, 1988). Pairing question numbers from a study guide or from blanks on a partial outline with page numbers on which the information can be found may also help students locate essential information (Wood, 1989).

In order to demonstrate the relationship between textbook questions and the structure of the text, students may be taught to rephrase headings, subheadings, or vocabulary words as questions to be answered during reading. For example, from the heading "The Greek Peninsula," numerous "What," "Where," "How," and "Why" questions might be generated (e.g., "What did the Greek Peninsula look like?"). After students generate their questions, the teacher asks them to state what types of information the answers will contain (e.g., name, date, location, event, cause, etc.). Archer and Gleason (1989) provided a similar technique for helping students understand the relationship between textbook questions and answers:

1. Read each question carefully.
2. Change the question into a part of the answer (e.g., "How did the location of the Greek Peninsula affect the daily lives of its citizens?" becomes "The Greek Peninsula affected the daily lives of its citizens by...").
3. Find the part of the chapter that talks about the topic.
4. Read the section to find the answer.
5. Complete the answer to the question.

Having students generate questions to be answered during reading improves their comprehension of the material (Swicegood & Parsons, 1989; Wong, 1985). Providing them with a structured overview in combination with self-generated questions is even more effective in facilitating comprehension (Billingsley & Wildman, 1988).

Preteaching Critical Vocabulary

Some teachers set up rotating committees of students to seek out and define words that are likely to be troublesome to classmates. Others suggest the use of mnemonic devices to aid students in recalling important vocabulary and concepts (Mastropieri & Scruggs, 1987).

Teaching Textbook Reading Strategies

The following strategies can help students with learning disabilities become active participants in the learning process (Schumaker, Deshler, & Ellis, 1986). Instead of passively reading textbooks, students are taught ways to ask questions, formulate answers, verbally rehearse important information, and monitor their comprehension.

Self-Questioning

Wong, Perry, and Sawatsky (1986, pp. 25–40) described a self-questioning strategy used in social studies by students with learning disabilities. In this strategy, students are taught to ask hemselves the following questions:

. In this paragraph, is there anything I don't understand?

. In this paragraph, what's the main idea sentence? Let me underline it.

. Let me summarize the paragraph. To summarize I rewrite the main idea sentence and add important details.

. Does my summary statement link up with the subheading?

. When I have summary statements for a whole subsection (paragraphs under a subheading):

a. Let me review my summary statements for the whole subsection.

b. Do my summary statements link up with one another?

c. Do they all link up with the subheading?

. At the end of a reading assignment, can I see all the themes here? If yes, let me predict the teacher's test question. If no, go back to step 4 (Wong et al., 1986).

Active Reading

rcher and Gleason (1989) have presented a simple strategy, called *active reading*, to involve students in verbally rehearsing and monitoring their comprehension of textbook passages. During active reading, the student proceeds paragraph by paragraph using the following steps:

. Read a paragraph. Think about the topic and about the important details.

. Cover the material.

. Recite. Tell yourself what you have read. Say the topic and the important details in your own words.

. Check yourself. If you forgot something important, start again.

Study Cards

tudents can place each important new vocabulary word on one side of an index card, with the definition and page number on the reverse (Wood, 1989). The cards are filed by chapter for continuing review and study.

Rooney (1988) detailed an excellent system for producing study cards. tudents are asked to:

. Read the subtitle and the paragraphs under the subtitle. Write on separate index cards all names of people or places, and important numbers or terms.

2. Go back to the subtitle and turn it into a test question. Write the question on one side of an index card and the answer on the other side.

3. Repeat this procedure to produce a set of study cards containing all the main ideas and important details from the reading.

4. Look at each card. Ask yourself, "How are the details related to the material?" Try to answer the main idea questions from memory.

Conclusion

Adapting a textbook does not mean rewriting the text. Altering instructional procedures and/or teaching students strategies to help themselves become more involved participants in the reading process are effective ways to help them use content area textbooks. The following common-sense guidelines can be useful to special educators collaborating with regular classroom teachers in this endeavor:

1. Examine the textbook for vocabulary and concept density and difficulty and for clear organizational structures.

2. Talk to the student regarding his or her perceived difficulties and needs. Ask the student to locate parts of the textbook, to read aloud from the text, and to answer questions about the passage.

3. Talk with the regular classroom teacher regarding his or her perceived needs. Discuss critical knowledge and skills to be mastered.

4. Choose the simplest adaptation that is most likely to meet the needs of both the student and the teacher.

5. Monitor carefully and make changes as necessary.

References

Archer, A., & Gleason, M. (1989). *Skills for school success*. Boston: Curriculum Associates.

Billingsley, B. S., & Wildman, T. M. (1988). The effects of prereading activities on the comprehension monitoring of learning disabled adolescents. *Learning Disabilities Research, 4,* 36-44.

Bos, C. S., & Vaughn, S. (1988). *Strategies for teaching students with learning and behavior problems.* Boston: Allyn and Bacon.

Carnine, D., Silbert, J., & Kameenui, E. J. (1990). *Direct instruction reading* (2nd ed.). Columbus, OH: Merrill.

Darch, C., & Gersten, R. (1986). Direction setting activities in reading comprehension: A comparison of two approaches. *Learning Disability Quarterly, 9,* 235-243.

Hallahan, D. P., & Kauffman, J. M. (1988). *Exceptional children.* Englewood Cliffs, NJ: Prentice-Hall.

Horton, S. V., Lovitt, T. C., & Bergerud, D. (1990). The effectiveness of graphic organizers for three classifications of secondary students in content area classes. *Journal of Learning Disabilities, 23,* 12-22.

Margolis, H., & McGettigan, J. (1988). Managing resistance to instructional modifications in mainstreamed environments. *Remedial and Special Education, 9,* 15-21.

Martens, B. K., Peterson, R. L., Witt, J. C., & Cirone, S. (1986). Teacher perceptions of school-based interventions. *Exceptional Children, 53,* 213-223.

Mastropieri, M. A., & Scruggs, T. E. (1987). *Effective instruction for special education.* Boston: College-Hill.

Mercer, C. D., & Mercer, A. R. (1989). *Teaching students with learning problems* (3rd ed.). Columbus, OH: Merrill.

Palincsar, A., & Brown, A. (1986). Interactive teaching to promote independent learning from text. *The Reading Teacher, 39,* 771-777.

Rooney, K. (1988). *Independent strategies for efficient study.* Richmond, VA: J. R. Enterprises.

Salend, S. J. (1990). *Effective mainstreaming.* New York: Macmillan.

Salend, S. J., & Nowak, M. R. (1988). Effects of peer previewing on LD students oral reading skills. *Learning Disability Quarterly, 11,* 47-54.

Schumaker, J. B., Deshler, D. D., & Ellis, E. S. (1986). Intervention issues related to the education of LD adolescents. In B. K. Wong & J. Torgeson (Eds.), *Psychological and educational perspectives in learning disabilities.* New York: Academic Press.

Seidenberg, P. L. (1989). Relating text-processing research to reading and writing instruction for learning disabled students. *Learning Disabilities Focus, 5,* 4-12.

Smith, G., & Smith, D. (1985). A mainstreaming program that really works. *Journal of Learning Disabilities, 18,* 369-372.

Swicegood, P. R., & Parsons, J. L. (1989). Better questions and answers equal success. *TEACHING Exceptional Children, 21*(3), 4-8.

Wong, B. Y. L. (1985). Self-questioning instructional research: A review. *Review of Educational Research, 55,* 227-268.

Wong, B. Y. L., Wong, R., Perry, N., & Sawatsky, D. (1986). The efficacy of a self-questioning summarization strategy for use by underachievers and learning disabled adolescents in social studies. *Learning Disabilities Focus, 2,* 20-35.

Wood, J. W. (1989). *Mainstreaming: A practical approach for teachers.* Columbus, OH: Merrill.

Children with Mental Retardation

Mental retardation (MR) diagnosis has changed dramatically in recent years. Most notably, the IQ test score necessary for the diagnosis has dropped from one standard deviation below the mean (85) to two standard deviations below the mean (70). The business of IQ testing has become controversial. Early in their history, IQ tests were considered a large step forward in diagnostic procedure. In recent years many persons involved with the assessment of mental retardation have labeled IQ tests a step backward in diagnosis.

The current definition of mental retardation has three criteria: IQ test score of 70 or below; deficits in personal-social adaptive behaviors, and a manifestation during the developmental period (birth to age 18). Only the last criterion is clear-cut. If an individual sustains brain damage that leaves him or her developmentally disabled in adulthood, we do not apply the label mental retardation. The second criterion, deficits in personal-social adaptive behaviors, has gained in importance in assessment procedures since IQ tests have been deemed invalid and unreliable by some professionals. However, adaptive scales measure independence and social behaviors with a simple yes or no (present or absent) rating. The person completing the scale can be biased to report more or less success in personal-social adaptation. The definition of adaptive behavior is unclear. Adaptive scales may also be invalid and unreliable. What, then, is used to determine mental retardation?

A 1979 court case in California concluded that IQ tests were racially and culturally biased because disproportionate numbers of culturally diverse children had been mislabeled as mentally retarded and placed in segregated special classes in violation of PL 94-142. The judge ruled that California children must be assessed for intelligence without the use of existing IQ tests, and any future IQ tests must be approved by the courts before use. While most states still use IQ tests, mental retardation today is usually determined only after multiple assessments of adaptive behavior, cognitive processes, problem-solving strategies, observations of real-life behaviors, and histories of prenatal, neonatal, and early childhood health and development.

Mental retardation diagnosis has also been changed by reducing the use of arbitrary labels such as mild, moderate, severe, and profound based on IQ test scores. There are vast differences between children with mental retardation even if they score exactly the same on an IQ test. For example, one student with an IQ of 50 (formerly considered moderately retarded or "trainable"/not "educable") may learn to read, write, and find a skilled vocational job.

Another student with an IQ of 50 may have difficulty completing even unskilled tasks and may drop out of school at age 16 with functional illiteracy. Mildly retarded individuals can usually profit from academic training and can learn to live alone or semi-independently. Severely retarded individuals can usually profit from training in self-help and communication, but they will probably need custodial care for life.

What causes mental retardation? For the majority of persons with MR, the exact cause(s) cannot be determined. Over one-half of all cases of mental retardation are suspected to be due to some biological factor(s) causing brain damage. Nearly 300 factors have been identified as risks that singly, or in combination, can alter brain functioning or destroy neurons. Prenatally, some risks include drugs, viruses, radiation, chromosomal defects, defective genes, maternal gestational disorders, and inadequate nutrition of mother. Neonatally, some risks include prematurity, low birth weight, trauma, infection, anoxia, metabolic and nutritional factors, and tumors. Early childhood risks include tumors, malnutrition, exposure to drugs or poisons, brain infections, head injuries, physical abuse, and psychiatric disorders. In addition to biological risk factors, some environmental conditions put infants and children at greater risk of developing mental retardation. It is usually impossible to pinpoint exactly what factor(s), singly or in combination, cause each child's unique type and degree of MR.

The Individuals with Disabilities Education Act, PL 94-142, and its amendments, require nondiscriminatory evaluations, zero reject, parental participation, individualized education programs, due process, least restrictive education, and transitional services for persons with mental retardation. As much as possible, everyone involved with the education of MR students should strive to establish the most normal life for them and teach them coping and adapting skills that are culturally appropriate. The earlier that MR infants and preschoolers can be identified and the earlier that they can be brought into special educational services, the easier it is to achieve a measure of "normalization" in their lives.

Early identification and treatment of mental retardation in infants and toddlers (age 0–5) is now mandated by PL 99-457. States are given incentives to establish not only preschool programs for MR children, but also to try to prevent MR through prenatal care, genetic counseling, and improved family planning. Preschool programs for MR children develop Individualized Family Service Plans (IFSPs) and provide parental education as well as early childhood remediation. Diet management, safety, educa-

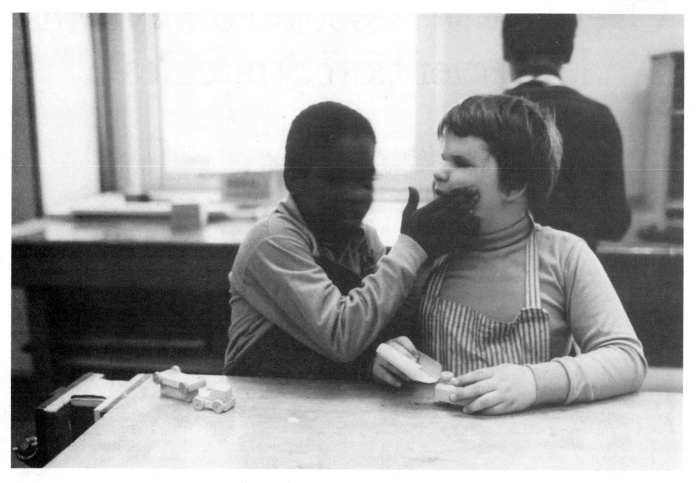

tion, socialization skills, and communication are included in preschool special services. Social services are provided long term for the MR child and his or her family.

Public schools develop Individualized Education Programs (IEPs) for every child with MR and update them annually. In addition to academic skills, the curriculum for MR students usually includes socialization and adaptive behaviors and prevocational and vocational skills. By high school the IEPs for students with MR usually include competitive employment training and community living skills (e.g., travel, personal maintenance, leisure, homemaking).

Transitional services for MR students are now mandated by PL 101-476. Public schools must provide assistance for MR individuals as they move from school to employment and independent living until they reach age 21.

The first article in this unit discusses prevention of, and intervention for, MR caused by drug exposure. Selection two provides strategies for integrating MR students into regular education classes, and it presents both challenges and solutions.

The next article discusses training peer tutors to both help teach transitional skills to MR students in high school and to teach social interaction skills.

Looking Ahead: Challenge Questions

How can poor outcomes such as MR after prenatal drug exposure be avoided? How can the MR caused by drug exposure be ameliorated by intervention?

What solutions have been successfully pursued to meet the challenges of integrating MR students into supported regular classes?

Can social interaction training help peer tutors teach social as well as academic and job-related skills to students with MR?

Prenatal Drug Exposure: An Overview of Associated Problems And Intervention Strategies

Prenatal drug exposure places a child at "high risk" for long-term difficulties. But, as Dr. Tyler makes clear, poor outcomes can be avoided or ameliorated by intervention.

RACHELLE TYLER

RACHELLE TYLER, M.D., is a pediatrician in the Los Angeles area who works with high-risk children in hospitals, outpatient clinics, and schools.

PRENATAL exposure to drugs has been occurring for centuries. In the Bible (Judg. 13:14), Samson's mother was warned against drinking wine or beer during her pregnancy. However, it was not until the latter part of the 20th century that fetal alcohol syndrome was described in this country.

In the 1960s the medical profession began to address the medical complications associated with prenatal drug exposure. These were mainly found to be vomiting, diarrhea, irritability, and poor feeding. These problems caused poor weight gain and fluid loss or imbalance, sometimes leading to shock or even to death.

In the 1960s and 1970s, research projects began to evaluate both the medical and the developmental problems of children with prenatal drug exposure. Most of the research followed up on prenatal exposure to heroin and methadone. The major reasons for this focus were that heroin abusers were presenting themselves for prenatal care in order to receive methadone treatment and thus were the most visible substance abusers. In addition, these infants had higher morbidity and mortality rates than infants who had not been exposed to drugs, and their problems had to be addressed.

Initially, the feeling was that the children would have no long-term problems after their acute medical conditions had been treated. Further study showed that there could be some long-term developmental problems associated with prenatal drug exposure. However, the culprit was felt to be the chaotic postnatal environment: living with parents who continued to use drugs or being placed in a number of different homes. More recent investigations have found some evidence that these children continue to be at risk for developmental or learning problems despite the stabilization of the home environment.

PATTERNS OF DRUG USE

When looking at the problem of prenatal drug exposure, we must include not only illicit drugs, but also alcohol, nicotine, and prescription medicines. The majority of drugs or medications taken by a pregnant woman can cross the placenta and show up in the bloodstream of the fetus. Because the potentially adverse effects of using drugs during pregnancy have been widely trumpeted in the media, a woman who continues to use illicit drugs or alcohol or to abuse prescription drugs during pregnancy almost certainly has a problem with addiction.

When an infant has been exposed to drugs during gestation, there is usually polydrug exposure, because most drug abusers use more than one drug. Although a user may have a drug of choice, when that drug is unavailable a substitute is often found. In other instances, users combine drugs to achieve a particular effect, such as prolonging the "high" or diminishing the "low" after the drug of choice has run its course. Furthermore, illicit drugs are rarely pure; they are usually diluted with other substances to some degree. Since there are no legal restrictions on the manufacture of illicit drugs, most addicts know neither the ac-

From *Phi Delta Kappan*, May 1992, pp. 705-708. Reprinted by permission of *Phi Delta Kappan* and Rachelle Tyler.

> **P**renatal
> drug exposure
> places the fetus
> at risk for a
> number of
> medical problems.

tual dosage they are taking nor the elements used to dilute each dose. Thus the drug history given by the mother may not be particularly revealing. Moreover, a mother may not recall all the substances she took during the course of her pregnancy.

Drug abuse knows no socioeconomic, ethnic, racial, or age limits. The wealthy and the poor, the highly educated and the minimally educated, and all racial and ethnic groups are affected by drug abuse. The problem of drug abuse can begin early and can last a lifetime. Often, drug abuse begins in the preadolescent years with what are called "gateway drugs": alcohol, marijuana, and tobacco. As time goes on, a user may move on to the abuse of other drugs, such as heroin, cocaine, or amphetamines. Children may be introduced to drugs by their peer group or, as is frequently the case, by a family member, either directly or by example. There is strong evidence for an intergenerational component to drug abuse, and this is often a major obstacle in drug treatment.

IDENTIFYING PRENATALLY EXPOSED CHILDREN

A conservative estimate of the incidence of prenatal exposure to illicit substances in the U.S. is 11% of live births. However, this estimate is based on random sampling. Not all infants and mothers are screened at the time of birth and delivery. Before a drug screening occurs for a particular mother/infant pair, there must be some indications of maternal

drug use. These indications include aspects of maternal history, maternal signs and symptoms, or infant signs and symptoms. Only if such indications exist are the mother and baby tested. In addition, maternal histories are often incomplete, and the evaluating health professional must be sensitive to the signs and symptoms of drug exposure.

Urine or blood toxicology screens are used to detect the presence of drugs in the infant's or the mother's system. These tests are not always reliable in revealing the substances to which an infant has been exposed. If there has been no exposure within 72 hours of testing, the screen may be negative despite a history of repeated and prolonged drug use. For this reason, toxicology screens must be combined with a good medical and social history as well as with neurobehavioral evaluation of the infant.

Because not all mothers are screened for drug use during pregnancy, a number of children may escape detection in the newborn period and will not have the opportunity to participate in an early intervention program. These children may show up in school at age 5 or 6 without having had any evaluation since birth. At that point, the most important issue is not to determine whether or not the children have had prenatal drug exposure but rather to assess their functional level, follow their progress, and offer help in the appropriate areas. Drug exposure may be an issue if there is a possibility of postnatal exposure in the home or in the caretaking environment.

MEDICAL COMPLICATIONS

Prenatal drug exposure places the developing fetus at risk for a number of medical problems. Some children may display minimal or undetectable effects, whereas others may exhibit major problems. But exposure to alcohol or illicit drugs during any trimester of pregnancy is detrimental to the developing fetus to some degree. In the first trimester, the developing fetus is most susceptible to malformations of major organs that may be apparent upon inspection or assessment of function.

In the second and third trimesters, the problems brought on by drug exposure can be more subtle and less readily apparent. Fetal growth is often poor, lead-

ing to smaller infants or possibly to miscarriage or premature birth. Premature infants are more likely to have chronic respiratory problems that will require medication during infancy and childhood. They are more likely to suffer from intracranial hemorrhages that place them at risk for cerebral palsy or to have more subtle motor and cognitive problems. They are also at risk for visual and auditory impairments that can affect their functioning in a school setting.

Because of congenital malformations due to early fetal insult or problems related to prematurity, a child may have ongoing medical problems. If these medical problems are significant, recurrent illnesses can lead to frequent school absences. Such problems include recurrent ear infections or a recurrent stuffy nose, particularly if the child has continued to be exposed to drugs in the postnatal environment. And this may be the case if a parent continues to smoke cigarettes or illicit drugs in the presence of the child. Recurrent ear infections interfere with a child's hearing and can have an adverse effect on learning even if the damage is not severe or permanent.

DEVELOPMENTAL COMPLICATIONS

Infants and children with a history of prenatal drug exposure exhibit a variety of signs or symptoms that range from minimal to severe. Major effects can be quite debilitating, whereas minimal effects may have no major impact on the child's school performance or social functioning. In infancy, the baby exposed to drugs may be quite fussy and difficult to soothe, or it may be lethargic for extended periods of time. As the child grows, these behaviors may translate into difficulty with self-regulation. Problems with self-regulation frequently show up as difficulty in sustaining attention or adjusting to transitions during the school day, such as changing from one subject to the next or quieting oneself appropriately after recess.

Infants with prenatal drug exposure often have tremors of their arms and legs. As they progress through childhood, this often translates into motor difficulty of varying degrees, depending on the child and the extent of the exposure. Some children with continued motor difficulty have tremors on a periodic basis, whereas others have problems performing tasks that require motor dexterity, including writing or speaking. It is important to remember that speaking clearly requires a certain amount of motor control. Problems in this area can lead to difficulty in producing understandable speech. If this is combined with intermittent hearing loss caused by recurrent ear infections, then the child is at double the risk for developing speech difficulty. Speech is our primary means of communicating with one another. Major problems in this area make communication difficult and quite frustrating for the child. This frustration may in turn lead to problems with self-esteem and to "acting out" both at home and in the school setting.

As I noted above, infants and children with prenatal drug exposure may spend much of their early life either lethargic or irritable for extended periods of time. They may have few moments of quiet alertness when they are available for social interaction. As they progress through childhood, they acquire, in varying degrees, the ability to quiet themselves and make themselves available for social interaction. Some drug-exposed children can learn to quiet themselves as well as any child who was not exposed to drugs in the womb. Others may continue to have only brief periods of availability, and this must be taken into consideration when the child enters school. The teacher must remember that, through no fault of his or her own, the child may be intermittently unavailable for social interaction or academic work.

Other areas of concern relate to the processing of visual and auditory information and to problems with short-term memory. A drug-exposed child can have difficulty understanding incoming auditory and/or visual information and may require frequent repetitions on the part of the teacher or caretaker. If there are problems with recalling lessons from day to day, the teacher must be patient.

ENVIRONMENTAL INFLUENCES

In addition to the medical and developmental risk factors associated with prenatal drug exposure, environmental issues affect the child as well. The chaotic lifestyle of a drug abuser is not conducive to the healthy development of a child. In such a home, children are rarely exposed to consistently nurturing caretaking, and there is also a possibility of reexposure to drugs. In such cases developmental setbacks can occur that inhibit a child's school performance.

> **The drug-exposed child may be intermittently unavailable for social interaction or academic work.**

Another environmental problem results from the fact that a child who is in the foster care system rarely remains in one placement from birth to adulthood. Although some children experience few changes, most have multiple placements or are forced to live in group homes. Across the country there is a growing shortage of family-style foster homes, and group homes are growing more common. Even if there has been no history of prenatal drug exposure, children who experience multiple foster placements or who reside in group homes are at risk for learning or school problems. The situation is only made worse when the risks associated with prenatal exposure to drugs are added to the equation.

Children who have had only a few foster placements can still be at risk when the court system is fervently working to reunite them with their biological parents. The well-meaning legal system may be placing a child back into a high-risk home with parents who have had but minimal rehabilitation. Even in cases in which parents have received a great deal of help in dealing with their drug abuse, these family reconstructions must be handled carefully. In such cases, the child should have gradually increasing contact with the parents over time, while still remaining legally in foster placement.

For some children, however, the transition from foster placement to parental care is abrupt. In such situations there is minimal time for the child to adjust to a significant change in life, leaving him or her vulnerable to regression both emotionally and academically. Even if the transition is gradual, younger children can become confused and can sometimes be fearful of encounters with parents with whom they are not familiar. Older children may experience feelings of ambivalence toward or fear of their parents. Such uncertainties can lead to "acting out" behaviors, difficulty in attending to work in school, and learning problems.

Still another environmental problem is that caretakers may not always have a working understanding of normal child development, much less know how to deal with the special problems of children who are at high risk. While this is frequently true of the biological parents, it may also be true in well-meaning foster homes.

INTERVENTION

Prenatal drug exposure places a child in what is termed a "high-risk" category. This essentially means that the child is more likely to have long-term difficulties than a child who did not experience such adverse conditions. However, poor outcomes can be avoided or ameliorated by intervention.

Effective intervention entails prevention on all levels, combined with a comprehensive approach. School personnel can be instrumental in prevention on the primary, secondary, and tertiary levels. Primary prevention consists of prevention of the drug abuse altogether. Secondary prevention entails cessation of the drug abuse or drug exposure after it has begun. Tertiary prevention involves intervening after the effects of the drug exposure have been realized.

Primary prevention can take the form of education regarding the risks of drug use, combined with classroom experiences that help build the child's self-esteem. Education regarding the adverse effects of drug abuse is important on one level; however, success in the school setting is also beneficial in helping a child to develop a positive sense of self-esteem. In working toward this end, an individualized approach that takes each child' learning style into account is recommended.

Secondary prevention can take the form of referral to social services that can direct the family toward treatment or family counseling in the event of ongoing drug use in the family or by the child. Tertiary prevention consists of helping the child to work around any possible deficits in order to optimize his or her learning and school performance.

Effective intervention must be comprehensive and interdisciplinary. The major aim must be to stabilize the environment and to provide positive interactions whenever possible. All service providers from all disciplines should be urged to work together to deal with those children who are at high risk. Those involved in the interdisciplinary approach should include teachers, administrators, social workers, physicians, nurses, physical education teachers, psychologists, speech and language specialists, representatives of community resource agencies, and parents or caretakers. It is important that the team work to develop the home/school partnership whenever possible. Sometimes, when parents are not available, there may be family members or community resources in place that can aid in networking to provide services or needed interventions. Each child's social environment must be assessed to determine the major influences in that child's life. For example, those who would intervene on behalf of a child who resides in a home with biological parents and members of an extended family need to determine who has the primary responsibility for decisions involving the child. Without including that individual, all attempts at forming an effective home/school partnership may be in vain.

At times, effective intervention will require the reporting of suspected child abuse or neglect to the appropriate legal authorities. Children may also speak of ongoing drug abuse in the home. And some changes in behavior or school performance may be indications of abuse or neglect. In such cases the teacher is often the first to suspect that there are problems in the home. It is important that each school have a team of staff members who are available to come together in the assessment and reporting of these cases.

A health assessment is important for all children. Poor health can interfere with learning and school performance. Chronic illnesses, such as asthma or skin conditions, should be adequately addressed. Children should have vision and hearing screens every one to two years, and any problems that are discovered should be treated. In order to maintain optimum health, there should also be well-child visits to a physician at the intervals recommended by the American Academy of Pediatrics.

Pharmacological treatment for a child with prenatal drug exposure must be recommended with caution and monitored closely. Before medications are prescribed, there should be a thorough investigation of the child's health, learning difficulties, psychological condition, and social circumstances. After a trial of medication has been conducted, the child must be followed and reevaluated regarding the benefits versus the risks of ongoing pharmacological treatment. Medication alone will not fully address any biochemical or anatomical changes that may have taken place in the central nervous system as a result of prenatal drug exposure. Furthermore, medications are not without problems or side effects themselves and must be taken in appropriately prescribed doses. If a child's home is chaotic, the child may not receive his or her medication regularly or may be overdosed. Teachers and parents must also understand that, although the medication may prolong the child's attention span, learning disorders or retardation must be addressed from a behavioral standpoint.

Classroom strategies must be tailored to the child or children served, whether or not there has been prenatal drug exposure. Ideally, a class should be small, containing 15 students at most, with one teacher and an aide. This allows for more individualized attention with less rigidity in the schedule and makes a second adult available to attend to any child who may be having difficulty during the school day.

In reality, most school districts have large classes of 30 or more children with one teacher and no aide. In such cases schools are forced to work within the constraints of minimal resources. In an effort to provide regularity or consistency in the school experience, the school should make sure that the child has the same teacher throughout the school year. In the case of combined grades in a single classroom, the child should be allowed to remain with the same teacher for a second year. If a child is retained in a grade, every effort should be made to allow that child to remain with the same teacher for a second year if the child/teacher match is reasonably good.

Some schools with large classes do have teacher aides available. And it is important that an aide remain in the same classroom with the same children and teacher in order to minimize environmental changes. Sometimes the aide can be a volunteer who is approved by the school district to act as teacher aide. Retired teachers can be approached and encouraged to become involved, or students' grandparents who have a history of teaching experience may be considered.

It is important that teachers, administrators, social workers, and all others involved in working with children have a basic knowledge of child development as well as of the special problems associated with high-risk children. This knowledge is best acquired through a combination of instruction and experience. Such knowledge increases understanding, and along with understanding come tolerance and patience in dealing with difficult cases.

When working with children who have been exposed to drugs before birth, one must guard against preconceptions regarding outcomes. Drug exposure places children at high risk, but environmental influences play a crucial role in determining long-term outcomes — outcomes that range along a continuum from minimal to severe. Although drug exposure places students at risk, chaotic environmental influences alone can lead to poor outcomes in children's development. Because of the important contribution of environmental influences, the provision of a stable and nurturing environment in all aspects of the child's life is imperative.

When referring to children with prenatal drug exposure, we must remember that each child is an individual first. Terms such as *drug baby* and *crack baby* emphasize the drug exposure first and the child second. They also imply that the child is somehow at fault for his or her adverse prenatal conditions. Deleting such terms from our discussions of children who are at risk is a major first step in early intervention.

INTEGRATING
Elementary Students with Multiple Disabilities into Supported Regular Classes
Challenges and Solutions

Susan Hamre-Nietupski
Jennifer McDonald
John Nietupski

Susan Hamre-Nietupski *(CEC Chapter #88) is an Associate Professor, Division of Curriculum and Instruction/Special Education, The University of Iowa, Iowa City.* **Jennifer McDonald** *is a Special Educator, Adams Elementary School, Des Moines, Iowa.* **John Nietupski** *(CEC Chapter #88) is an Adjunct Associate Professor, Division of Developmental Disabilities and Division of Curriculum and Instruction, The University of Iowa, Iowa City.*

Integrated placement of students with multiple disabilities in regular classes (Strully & Strully, 1989) is being advocated by professionals and parents alike. With this model, assistance is provided in the areas of curriculum modification, participation, and social integration by special education/support teachers, paraprofessionals, integration facilitators (Ruttiman & Forest, 1987), and/or nondisabled peers (Forest & Lusthaus, 1990). Students with disabilities are offered increased opportunities for interactions with nondisabled peers as well as meaningful curricular content (Ford & Davern, 1989; Sailor et al., 1989; York, Vandercook, Caughey, & Heise-Neff, 1990).

The professional literature has described strategies for preparing regular educators and students for positive integration experiences (Certo, Haring, & York, 1984; Gaylord-Ross, 1989; Stainback & Stainback, 1985) and for teaming special educators with regular educators to promote regular class integration (Vandercook, York, & Forest, 1989; York & Vandercook, 1991). One practical concern for teachers is how they can promote both skill gains and social acceptance while involving students in regular class activities.

This article describes four potential challenges to supported education along with solutions that have been effective in meeting those challenges in an elementary school setting. Our observations are based on 4 years of experience in integrating students with multiple disabilities, including students with moderate and severe mental disabilities or autism with accompanying physical, visual, and/or behavior challenges. Our efforts focused on integrating elementary-age students into kindergarten through sixth-grade classes.

Background

The case of Stephanie, a first-grader, illustrates points in each challenge and solution. Stephanie was a student with multiple disabilities, including mental retardation in the moderate to severe range with accompanying physical disabilities and a vision impairment. She attended a 350-student elementary school in a midwestern community of 35,000 people. When Stephanie was kindergarten age, she spent half her day in a regular kindergarten class. The following year, she spent the entire school day in a regular first-grade class.

Challenges and Solutions

Challenge 1: Providing Functional Curriculum in a Regular Class

Instruction on the functional skills necessary to live, work, and participate in recreation activities in integrated community environments is a critical component of an appropriate education for students with multiple disabilities (Falvey, 1989). Since functional skills such as grooming and dressing rarely are taught in regular education, a challenge to supported education is how to teach these skills in the primarily academic environment of a regular class.

Five possible solutions might be considered to address this challenge. First, partial assistance might be provided by a peer in the context of class activities. For example, when Stephanie arrived at school in the winter, she could remove

From *Teaching Exceptional Children*, Vol. 24, No. 3, Spring 1992, pp. 6-9. © 1992 by The Council for Exceptional Children. Reprinted by permission.

her boots easily. However, putting on her shoes was time-consuming, and she often missed out on much of the opening routine. One solution was to have Stephanie remove her boots upon arrival and take her shoes to the opening-group area. There she was taught to ask a nondisabled peer for assistance in putting on and tying her shoes. The peer was shown how to assist Stephanie with the difficult steps while encouraging her independence on the easier steps. This solution resulted in positive interactions between Stephanie and her peers, enabled her to take part in the opening routine, and allowed her to progress in this self-care skill.

A second strategy is to identify the "down times" during the school day in which functional skill instruction could be provided without disrupting the class routine. For example, Stephanie often had a runny nose and had not yet learned to blow her nose independently. The support teacher took her aside at such times as arrival, between academic activities, and prior to and after recess and lunch for brief, unobtrusive instruction. As a result, she missed very little regular class activity and she showed increased independence by the end of the school year.

A third potential solution is to provide parallel instruction on functional skills in the regular classroom while peers participate in their academic work. For example, when the nondisabled students were working on place value in mathematics, part or all of that period could be spent teaching Stephanie functional mathematics skills such as matching coins or other skills. One regular teacher reduced the possible stigma associated with parallel programming by identifying nondisabled students who needed similar instruction and rotating them through the self-care lessons with Stephanie. Since the teacher referred to this as a "health" or "hygiene" unit and involved nondisabled students, Stephanie was not singled out as different from her peers. Nondisabled children can benefit from this functional life skills instruction as well as their peers who have disabilities.

When none of the previously mentioned strategies seems feasible, brief removal of the student from the regular class for specialized instruction might be considered. For example, when nondisabled students receive instruction on academic activities clearly beyond the student's present skill level, instruction

on functional skills such as bathroom use, snack preparation, and street-crossing outside the classroom may be more appropriate.

Finally, to guarantee that instructional time is not sacrificed, districts should ensure that individualized education program (IEP) goals are drawn from an approved curriculum guide (e.g., Falvey, 1989; Ford et al., 1989). Such a guide can provide assurances that important instructional goals will not be overlooked.

Challenge 2: Providing Community-Based Instruction

Another challenge to regular class integration is including community-based instruction within the educational program. Community-based instruction is needed because of the generalization difficulties experienced by students with multiple disabilities. However, little opportunity for such instruction currently is provided to students in regular elementary education.

In addition to following an approved curriculum guide that includes community-based instruction, two strategies might be employed to address this challenge. The first is to bring the community into the classroom. An example of this strategy was implemented in conjunction with a creative writing unit in which students were required to write about turtles. In order to make this unit more meaningful to Stephanie, who had limited exposure to turtles, arrangements were made to borrow a turtle from a local pet store. After the morning visit by the turtle, Stephanie, three of her nondisabled peers, and the support teacher returned the turtle to the pet store. All four students were able to see, touch, and learn about a variety of exotic birds and animals. As Stephanie and two other students looked at the animals, another wrote down the group's favorite pets and their cost. Upon returning to school, the four wrote and shared a story about their trip and sent a thank-you note to the pet store. Thus, all four students had a community experience that was integrally related to the creative writing unit and allowed the nondisabled students to apply their skills to a meaningful situation. While use of community resources may be difficult to achieve on all units, careful consideration of such opportunities can both enhance the regular curriculum

and provide opportunities for community-based instruction.

Another possible strategy involves providing community-based instruction to the student with disabilities in an integrated manner (Ford & Davern, 1989). Small groups of nondisabled students could accompany a peer with disabilities on a rotating basis. The community experiences would allow all students to apply skills being taught in the classroom to real-world settings. For example, integrated instruction in a supermarket could be structured so that a student with multiple disabilities locates various grocery items while peers practice adding costs and comparing prices.

Challenge 3: Scheduling Staff Coverage

Special education staff can support integrated students in many ways, including (a) making adaptations when needed; (b) assisting the classroom teacher in working with a student; (c) coaching nondisabled peers; (d) providing direct instruction; and (e) facilitating positive interactions among students. The scheduling challenge lies in providing this support when it is needed for the student to participate in classroom activities.

One solution in Stephanie's situation was for the regular education and support teachers to determine cooperatively when support was most needed. The support teacher developed a flexible schedule so she could assist Stephanie during activities that were the most challenging for her and/or were most difficult to individualize.

While scheduling support during critical periods is helpful, teachers occasionally need to support several students in several classes simultaneously. In those situations, university students or parent volunteers might provide additional support. With training, these volunteers could assist in regular classrooms when the support teacher is unable to do so.

Another strategy is to empower regular teachers to assume greater instructional responsibility for students with multiple disabilities. Our experience has been that regular teachers can be as effective as special education teachers in meeting the needs of students with disabilities. Encouraging them to do so, involving them in solving instructional problems, demonstrating particular techniques, and reinforcing accomplishments are all strategies for increasing the competence and confidence of regular class teachers.

Another strategy for dealing with the coverage challenge is to work closely with the classroom teacher to identify when and how nondisabled peers might serve in a support role. For example, activities might be designed on the basis of cooperative learning (Johnson & Johnson, 1989), whereby students become responsible for working together and assisting each other.

One additional solution to providing adequate staff coverage is to reduce class size when integrating a student with multiple disabilities. Sailor and colleagues (1989) suggested that this strategy can make support from the regular classroom teacher a more realistic option.

Challenge 4: Promoting Social Integration

The final challenge addressed here is that of promoting social integration and friendships between students with and without disabilities. Strully and Strully (1989) argued that supported education is important because it facilitates the formation of friendships and long-lasting, supportive, personal relationships. Research by Guralnick (1980) has suggested that these relationships do not occur simply through integrated physical placement but must be facilitated.

Administrator Support. Administrators can facilitate friendships in several ways. First, students with multiple disabilities can be assigned to the regular school they would attend if they were not disabled, along with children from their neighborhood, making participation in after-school activities such as parties and school functions more feasible (Brown et al., 1989; Sailor et al., 1989).

Second, administrators can set the tone for integration in a school. In Stephanie's school, the principal strongly believed that all children belonged in regular classes and that promoting positive, cooperative social interactions was an important goal in each classroom. Thus, teachers had a heightened awareness of the social aspects of education and focused on promoting positive relationships among students.

Third, administrators can arrange for after-school social opportunities.

Stephanie's principal was instrumental in developing monthly recreational drop-in programs and summer recreation offerings that allowed all students to socialize.

Teacher Support. Regular class teachers, too, can address the challenge of promoting social interactions and friendships. One well-documented strategy is cooperative learning (Johnson & Johnson, 1989), in which rewards and evaluations are based on the quality of the work and student collaboration.

Regular class teachers also can promote a positive social atmosphere by treating students with multiple disabilities as normally as possible. Stephanie's teacher, for example, placed Stephanie's name on the class roster and assigned her a desk, coathook, and materials space amidst those of the other students. She expected, encouraged, and reinforced adherence to classroom rules for all students, including Stephanie. These actions communicated to all students that Stephanie was as much a member of the class as anyone else.

Finally, regular class teachers can actively promote social relationships (Stainback & Stainback, 1987). Stephanie's teacher did so by pairing children for many activities, modeling and encouraging social interactions, and reinforcing students when positive interactions occurred.

Special educators, support teachers, and integration facilitators can address the challenges of promoting social interaction in several ways. They can model and encourage social interactions. Early in the school year, nondisabled students often would ask the support teacher whether or not Stephanie would like to play and whether or not she enjoyed certain activities. The support teacher would encourage the children to ask Stephanie themselves or show them how to do so. By the end of the year, nondisabled students initiated conversation directly with Stephanie, not through her support teacher.

A second strategy is to develop sensitization sessions that focus on recognizing similarities and differences and getting along with people who are different in some way (Hamre-Nietupski & Nietupski, 1985). In Stephanie's class, her support teacher and the guidance counselor developed a six-session unit on how children are similar and different, how to be friends with those around you, and how to communicate

in different ways. Activities included having all children identify their strengths and weaknesses and likes and dislikes, generate specific ways to be friends with people in the class, and learn how to initiate and respond to social interactions. These activities were carried out in a large group that included Stephanie but did not single her out.

Support teachers can develop circles of friends to promote social interactions (Forest & Lusthaus, 1990). In Stephanie's school, a student with autism was integrated into a regular fifth-grade class. The support teacher, concerned about the lack of social integration, organized a circle of friends with nondisabled volunteer companions. This group identified in- and out-of-school interaction opportunities such as going to the library together and attending the drop-in recreation program, and they socialized with her.

Finally, support teachers can keep parents informed about interaction opportunities and encourage parental support. Stephanie's support teacher regularly kept Stephanie's parents informed about the students she interacted with and upcoming after-school events. On occasion, she even made transportation arrangements so Stephanie could participate with her peers.

Parental Support. Parental support is also necessary to promote social relationships and friendships. Parents can become active in the parent-teacher organization and in school-wide activities. They might encourage their child's participation in extracurricular activities such as Cub Scouts, Brownies, and 4-H or help in initiating play opportunities by having their child invite a nondisabled friend to spend the night or hosting or having their child attend birthday parties. Such activities are extremely important in making and maintaining friendships.

Parents also can promote social relationships through sensitivity to clothing selection and hairstyle. Nondisabled students, even in elementary schools, are keenly aware of "in" clothing. Since this a sensitive and value-laden issue, interventions may need to be quite subtle. For example, when asked, teachers might suggest holiday or birthday gift ideas for students (e.g., "I've noticed that Stephanie really likes Tracy's [name brand] sweatshirts") as a way to assist parents in facilitating social acceptance.

Conclusion

While we are encouraged by the outcomes of the strategies described here, two limitations should be noted. First, the strategies were developed for elementary-age students. Additional research and demonstration are needed to guide teachers serving older students. Second, questions have been raised about how and the degree to which students with profound, multiple disabilities might be integrated into regular classes. At this point, perhaps those questions should remain open—with practitioners and researchers encouraged to examine them through empirical demonstration activities.

Supported regular education for students with multiple disabilities is not without challenges, but potential solutions are beginning to emerge. It is our hope that, through examples such as these, increasing numbers of school systems will be encouraged to integrate elementary-age students with multiple disabilities more fully into regular education classes.

References

Brown, L., Long, E., Udarvi-Solner, A., Davis, L., VanDeventer, P., Algren, C., Johnson, F.,

Gruenewald, L., & Jorgensen, J. (1989). The home school: Why students with severe intellectual disabilities must attend the schools of their brothers, sisters, friends, and neighbors. *Journal of the Association for Persons with Severe Handicaps, 14*, 1-7.

Certo, N., Haring, N., & York, R. (1984). *Public school integration of severely handicapped students.* Baltimore: Paul H. Brookes.

Falvey, M. (1989). *Community-based curriculum: Instructional strategies for students with severe handicaps.* Baltimore: Paul H. Brookes.

Ford, A., & Davern, L. (1989). Moving forward with school integration: Strategies for involving students with severe handicaps in the life of the school. In R. Gaylord-Ross (Ed.), *Integration strategies for students with severe handicaps* (pp. 11-32). Baltimore: Paul H. Brookes.

Ford, A., Schnorr, R., Meyer, L., Davern, L., Black, J., & Dempsey, P. (1989). *The Syracuse community-referenced curriculum guide for students with moderate and severe disabilities.* Baltimore: Paul H. Brookes.

Forest, M., & Lusthaus, E. (1990). Everyone belongs with the MAPS Action Planning System. *TEACHING Exceptional Children, 22*, 32-35.

Gaylord-Ross, R. (Ed.). (1989). *Integration strategies for students with severe handicaps.* Baltimore: Paul H. Brookes.

Guralnick, M. (1980). Social interactions among preschool children. *Exceptional Children, 46,* 248-253.

Hamre-Nietupski, S., & Nietupski, J. (1985). Taking full advantage of interaction opportunities. In S. Stainback & W. Stainback (Eds.), *Integration of students with severe handicaps into regular schools* (pp. 98-112). Reston, VA: The Council for Exceptional Children.

Johnson, D., & Johnson, R. (1989). Cooperative learning and mainstreaming. In R. Gaylord-Ross (Ed.), *Integration strategies for students with handicaps* (pp. 233-248). Baltimore: Paul H. Brookes.

Ruttiman, A., & Forest, M. (1987). With a little help from my friends: The integration facilitator at work. In M. Forest (Ed.), *More education/integration* (pp. 131-142). Downsview, Ontario: Roeher Institute.

Sailor, W., Anderson, J., Halvorsen, A., Doering, K., Filler, J., & Goetz, L. (1989). *The comprehensive local school: Regular education for all students with disabilities.* Baltimore: Paul H. Brookes.

Stainback, S., & Stainback, W. (Eds.). (1985). *Integration of students with severe handicaps into regular schools.* Reston, VA: The Council for Exceptional Children.

Stainback, W., & Stainback, S. (1987). Facilitating friendships. *Education and Training in Mental Retardation, 22,* 10-25.

Strully, J., & Strully, C. (1989). Friendships as an educational goal. In S. Stainback, W. Stainback, & M. Forest (Eds.), *Educating all students in the mainstream of regular education* (pp. 59-68). Baltimore: Paul H. Brookes.

Vandercook, T., York, J., & Forest, M. (1989). The McGill Action Planning System (MAPS): A strategy for building the vision. *Journal of The Association for Persons with Severe Handicaps, 14,* 205-215.

York, J., & Vandercook, T. (1991). Designing an integrated program for learners with severe disabilities. *TEACHING Exceptional Children, 23*(1), 22-28.

York, J., Vandercook, T., Caughey, E., & Heise-Neff, C. (1990, May). Regular class integration: Beyond socialization. *The Association for Persons with Severe Handicaps Newsletter, 16,* p. 3.

The Effects of Social Interaction Training on High School Peer Tutors of Schoolmates with Severe Disabilities

ABSTRACT: This study evaluated the effects of social interaction training on the social interactions directed by high school students without disabilities toward peers with severe disabilities. Eight high school students who were peer tutors in a classroom for students with severe disabilities were matched in pairs and then randomly assigned to interact with and serve as partners for four classmates with severe disabilities. Only one participant in each peer tutor pair received the social interaction training. A statistical analysis indicated that the training increased the frequency of initiations of interactions directed from the students without disabilities toward their partners with severe disabilities. There was also an increase in the proportion of interactions that were social in nature, with a resulting decrease in the frequency of task-related interactions, as well as a significant increase in targeted social behaviors of the participants with severe disabilities.

DEBBIE STAUB

PAM HUNT

DEBBIE STAUB (CEC WA Federation), Project Coordinator, University of Washington, Seattle. PAM HUNT, Research Coordinator, San Francisco State University, California.

☐ In the past decade, many researchers have documented the positive effects of integrated, community-based, instructional models for students with severe disabilities (see Halvorsen & Sailor, 1990). In integrated education, students with and without disabilities have opportunities for interactions, which have many positive benefits for the social abilities of students with disabilities. These benefits include increased rates of social responsiveness (Delquadri, Greenwood, Whorton, Carta, & Hall, 1986; Goldstein & Wickstrom, 1986) and increased numbers of social bids directed toward peers (Brinker & Thorpe, 1986; Strain & Odom, 1986). Similarly, researchers have found such interactions to enhance the communication skills of students with disabilities. These skills include increased rates of conversational initiations (Eichinger, 1990; Gaylord-Ross, Haring, Breen, & Pitts-Conway, 1984; Haring, Roger, Lee, Breen, & Gaylord-Ross, 1986) and increased maintenance of conversations (Gaylord-Ross & Haring, 1987; Hunt, Alwell, Goetz, & Sailor, 1990).

Whereas these studies have documented the positive effects for students with disabilities, results from three recent qualitative studies suggest that integration with peers with severe disabilities may also benefit the social development of students without disabilities. Biklen, Corrigan, and Quick (1989), using data from interviews of students in an integrated program, described the relationships between elementary school students with severe disabilities and their peers without disabilities. The authors found that participation with peers with disabilities enhanced the sensitivity of the students without disabilities toward other people's differences in general. Further, Peck, Donaldson, and Pezzoli (1990) assessed the perceptions of 21 high school students without disabilities regarding the benefits they experienced as a result of developing relationships with peers with moderate or severe disabilities. The authors found that the students without disabilities experienced improvement in self-concept, growth in social cognition, increased tolerance of other people, and reduced fear of human differences. Finally, Murray-Seegert (1989) found that students without disabilities who participated in their high school's peer tutoring program with peers with severe disabilities began spending more time helping others on their own initiative, as their time increased in the peer tutor program.

Although limited in number, these findings suggest that social integration is beneficial for students both with and without disabilities. The nature and frequency of these interactions, however, has not been thoroughly explored. Chadsey-Rusch (1990) found that although high school students with severe disabilities attended an integrated school, very few interactions occurred between them and their peers without disabilities.

From *Exceptional Children*, Vol. 60, No. 1, September 1993, pp. 41-57. © 1993 by The Council for Exceptional Children. Reprinted by permission.

In addition, for students with disabilities at the transition age, the interactions that were observed at school sites, as well as job settings, tended to be task-related rather than social interactions (Chadsey-Rusch, 1990; Chadsey-Rusch & Gonzalez, 1988; Lignugaris/Kraft, Rule, Salzberg, & Stowitscheck, 1986). One potential explanation for this finding, based on a review of social interaction models by Gaylord-Ross and Haring (1987), is that in many programs in schools designed to foster social integration, students without disabilities serve as "tutors" for their peers with disabilities; and tutoring, by virtue of the role, is task oriented. The "circle of friends" program (Forest & Lusthaus, 1989), in which students both with and without disabilities meet for leisure time activities, has been one popular approach to enhancing friendships between both groups of students; but this type of program has not been extended to high school students.

The purpose of this study was to examine the extent to which social interaction training would improve both the frequency and quality (i.e., task vs. socially related interactions) of the interactions between high school students without disabilities and their peers with severe disabilities. We designed this intervention to promote socially related, rather than task-related, interactions. We measured the impact of the intervention on the social behavior of the students without disabilities, as well as the indirect effects on individually targeted social behaviors of the students with severe disabilities.

METHOD

Participants

Students with Disabilities. Four students with severe disabilities participated in this study. They attended a class for students with severe and profound multiple disabilities which was located on a regular high school campus. Students were referred by their classroom teacher for inclusion in the study on the basis of their need for appropriate social interactive behaviors. The four students who were selected to participate displayed a wide range of communication, verbal, and social skills. Two students were female, and two were male. Their ages ranged from 15 to 20 years. The following descriptions of each of the students are based on information from teacher interviews, school records, observations, and other informal assessment procedures.

William was a 15-year-old male with severe mental retardation. He often made loud, extraneous noises and talked to himself in a perseverative manner. He was highly distractible and received medication to control his hyperactive behavior. Because of his poor attention span and frequent self-stimulating behaviors, William seldom reciprocated socially with the peer tutors in

his class who would attempt to interact with him. When William did interact socially with peers, it was often to greet the other person or to say goodbye. These interactions were seldom extended. William was receiving vocational skill training at various job sites and was learning how to prepare food and shop at grocery stores with assistance.

Ben was a 16-year-old male whose primary disability was moderate retardation. Ben was ambulatory, although he was significantly overweight; and his movements appeared to be awkward. Ben used simple, but complete, sentences to express himself. He was shy with his peers and often used a soft, quiet voice. Because of his timid behavior, Ben often had difficulty interacting socially with peers. In particular, he needed practice with turn taking and making conversation. When he did engage socially with peers, however, it was often in an inappropriate manner. For instance, he frequently stood too close to others, blew kisses at others, or engaged in other types of "silly" behavior. Ben was working on vocational skills, domestic skills such as preparing simple recipes, transportation, and community skills such as grocery shopping. Although Ben was not working on academics, he did have sight recognition of 20 words, and he was able to write his name.

Kayse was a 16-year-old young woman with mild retardation and multiple orthopedic disabilities, which required her to use a wheelchair and to seek assistance for bathing, dressing, and eating. Kayse, who came from a home where English was the second language, spoke English at an age-appropriate level but exhibited some articulation problems and her words sounded stilted. Although she was able to effectively initiate conversations with peers, she was often unable to keep the interaction going and often would abruptly end a conversation. Kayse, who read at approximately a second-grade level, participated in some academic activities in English, math, and science provided within the special education classroom. She also received training in domestic skills, recreational skills, and the use of public transportation.

The fourth participant was Megan, a 20-year-old woman with cerebral palsy and moderate retardation. Megan was nonambulatory and used an electric wheelchair. She had limited use of her arms and hands and required total assistance for toileting, dressing, and eating. While she was able to verbalize some words, she relied primarily on a computerized communication system activated by an infrared light attached to a headpiece. Megan was able to understand almost everything said to her. She enjoyed the company of peers and would make noises to express her pleasure when interacting with them. However, Megan seldom used her communication system for social purposes, which severely limited the amount of "social" information that she would express to others. Megan had some academic skills, such as reading simple sentences and adding and subtracting one-digit numbers. She was also working on community, transportation, and domestic skills. In particular, Megan was working on using her communication system in a variety of settings for a variety of purposes.

Students Without Disabilities. The eight students without disabilities who were selected for participation in the study were enrolled in a peer tutor program that was an integral part of the high school's curriculum. Seven of the participants were female; one was male. Three students were sophomores, three were juniors, and two were seniors. All participants had been in the peer tutor program for at least 4 months before the study began. The peer tutors in the program received class credit for their time in the special education classroom. Participants for this study were selected from members of an established peer tutor program because of the convenience of having time already allotted for them to interact with the students in the special education classroom and because of their willingness to participate. Students agreed to participate in the study on a voluntary basis. (These students are referred to as *peer tutors* in the following sections.)

Setting

Baseline and intervention procedures took place within the self-contained classroom of the students with severe disabilities. Because all participants with disabilities were working on community, transportation, vocational, and domestic skills in integrated settings, baseline and intervention data were also collected at various sites outside the school property. Data were collected throughout the school day, 5 days a week.

Social Interaction Training

The independent variable in this study was the social interaction training intervention, which was provided to four of the eight peer tutors who were randomly assigned to receive it. Each of the tutors was randomly assigned to be the partner of one of the four participants with severe disabilities. The training intervention was given for 5 consecutive days for 30 to 40 min per session. The overall training program incorporated techniques of communication and information sharing, behavior strategies, and self-confrontation exercises (Ashmore, 1975; Murray & Beckstead, 1983; Schellenberg, 1970).

The first 2 days of the training focused on ability awareness and information gathering, regarding disabilities in general. Several researchers have suggested that lack of information, social conformity, and certain intrapsychic traits (i.e., feelings and beliefs) may contribute to negative attitudes held by people without disabilities toward those with disabilities (Donaldson, 1980; Gottlieb, 1980; Ogbu, 1978; Pumpian, 1981; Voeltz, 1980). Objectives for the participants for these sessions included (a) using appropriate vocabulary to describe developmental disabilities, (b) identifying ways in which people with disabilities are like and unlike themselves, (c) listing new and old terms used to describe disabilities, and (d) recognizing that people with disabilities are people first and disabled second.

The purpose of the third training session was to increase the participants' understanding of how certain behaviors of peers with severe disabilities might serve as socially oriented communicative messages (Donnellan, La Vigna, Negri-Shoultz, & Fassbender, 1988; Donnellan, Mirenda, Mesaros, & Fassbender, 1984; Schuler & Goetz, 1981). The participants were asked during this session to identify specific behaviors and hypothesize possible communicative functions these behaviors might serve, while thinking of their partners with severe disabilities.

The purpose of the fourth training session was for participants to brainstorm, discuss, and practice the use of techniques designed to enhance and encourage communication with students with severe disabilities, within natural contexts and settings (Carr, 1985; Carr & Durand, 1985; Halle, 1982, 1987). One primary activity for this session included having participants share ways in which they were motivated to interact with others on a social level and then brainstorm ways in which their partner with severe disabilities might be motivated to interact socially. During this session, the participants also practiced ways to initiate social interactions with their partners, and they identified environments and materials that they felt would encourage the social interactions between themselves and their partner.

The final training session focused on having the participants design and discuss ways in which peers without disabilities can enhance and promote the context in which social exchanges take place between themselves and peers with severe disabilities (Haring et al., 1986). The participants identified factors that keep a social interaction "going," topics of communication that would enhance the social interactions with their partners, and ways in which their interactions with their partners were age appropriate and considered to be "normal" for high school students. Using cue cards to stimulate discussion, which highlighted their interests and activities, the participants brainstormed ways in which they might promote conversations or activities with their partners, and then they role-played ways to keep the conversation going.

Dependent Measures

The two dependent variables measured in this

study were the frequency of the social interactive behaviors of the peer tutors toward their partners with severe disabilities and the frequency of the display of targeted social behaviors by the students with disabilities.

Peer Interactions. Measures of peer interactions included the frequency of initiations and expansions and the percentage of both that were either task or socially oriented. *Initiations* were defined as any statements that began a conversation, changed a topic, or provided an instruction to initiate some action. For example, statements such as "Hi," "Good morning," "What do you want to do next?" and "Let's go to the store now" on the part of the peer tutor would have all served as forms of initiations. In addition, initiations could have been nonverbal in nature, such as a handshake or a wave to acknowledge the presence of another.

Expansions were defined as any follow-up statements, questions, or gestures after the occurrence of an initiation which served to continue the social interaction. Verbal statements such as "Go on," "What else did you do?" and "Tell me more," or hand gestures to continue would have been measured as an expansion.

Last, *task-related interactions* were any interactions in which the purpose of the interaction was to accomplish an outcome that went beyond social contact; and *socially related interactions* were those whose major purpose was the interaction itself, and no obvious task was being accomplished other than the social contact.

Targeted Social Behaviors. The targeted social behaviors were measured in this study to determine the extent to which increases in the social interactions between the student with disabilities and his or her partner were associated with increases in specifically targeted social behaviors of the student with disabilities. Each social behavior targeted for measurement was a type of behavior identified by the special education teacher as being needed to enhance the individual participants' social abilities.

The behavior selected for *William* was attending to initiations and expansions that were directed to him. Attending to the interaction was defined for William as having his eyes and body directed toward his peer while not engaging in self-stimulatory behavior during the time of the interaction. The social behavior identified for *Ben* was responding appropriately to the initiations or expansions directed to him from peer partners. Responses were not counted if Ben acted inappropriately, such as talking in "baby talk" or blowing kisses to peers. *Kayse's* target behavior for the study was the use of expansions, defined as any follow-up statements or questions after the occurrence of an initiation that served to

continue a social interaction. Nonverbal behavior such as head nodding or gesturing to go on also served as a form of an expansion. Finally, the target behavior identified for *Megan* was for her to use her communication system to initiate or continue an interaction with a peer. Megan's communication system consisted of a keyboard attached to a tray placed on her wheelchair, which had pictorial symbols as well as the alphabet on it. When the symbols or letters were activated by an infrared light attached to Megan's headpiece, a computerized voice would relay the message communicated by Megan.

Data Collection. We randomly selected 17-min observational periods within the 50-min class periods when peer tutors were present. During these 17-min observations, we measured the peer tutors' interactions and the targeted social behaviors of the participants with severe disabilities. An individual naive to the purpose of the study was hired to collect the data. She was trained by the investigator through field observations until there was 80% or greater agreement between them on collected data over 10 consecutive observational periods.

The data collector wore an earphone that was attached to a small tape recorder that signaled the "observe" and "record" periods within all intervals. There were forty 25-s intervals within the 17-min observational periods. The data collector was directed to observe for 15 s and record for 10 s. If she finished recording before the 10 s had passed, she continued to look down at the data sheet until the tape announced the start of the next "observe" interval. If the data collector was unable to be close enough to the participants to score an interval, she would eliminate that interval from the total count. When observing, the data collector scored only the first initiation and expansion in the interval and then indicated whether the initiation or expansion was task related or socially related and whether the target behavior had occurred for the participant with severe disabilities. Data were summarized at the end of each observation period by dividing the number of initiations, the number of expansions, whether they were social in nature, and the target behavior of the student with severe disabilities, by the total number of intervals observed.

Educational Staff Behavior. An observer rated the behaviors of classroom staff on the average of every fifth to seventh day to ensure that staff behavior relevant to the promotion of social interaction was consistent across all dyads of participants, including the peer tutors who received training and those who did not. The observer took 5-min observational measures on the presence of the following behaviors: (a) staff-directed behaviors toward the peer tutors regarding their social interactions with their partners with severe disabilities, and (b) rate of positive and negative verbal statements directed by the staff toward the peer tutors (both trained and nontrained) during their interactions with their partners with severe disabilities.

Reliability

The investigator and data collector made interobserver reliability checks across baseline and intervention phases for all participants. The reliability checks were randomly selected across the phases of the study for 27% of the total number of observational periods. Interobserver agreement on the occurrence or nonoccurrence of initiations, expansions, the type of interaction (i.e., social or task-related), and the targeted social behaviors of the participants with severe disabilities was calculated by dividing the number of agreements by the number of agreements plus disagreements and multiplying the resulting ratio by 100, to yield a percentage of agreement. An agreement was scored when both observers identified the occurrence of the same types of social behaviors within the same interval.

Procedures

Design. For this study, we used a multiple baseline design (Tawney & Gast, 1984) across four pairs of participants to demonstrate the effectiveness of the social interaction training program on increasing the frequency of the peer tutors' social behaviors toward a partner with severe disabilities. This design was implemented to make the following analyses: (a) comparison across each pair of participants of the social interactive behaviors, across baseline, training, and posttraining phases; (b) comparison within each pair (i.e., the tutor who received training with the tutor who did not receive training) of the social interactive behaviors across baseline, training, and posttraining phases; and (c) the indirect effects of the social interaction intervention on the targeted social behaviors of the participants with severe disabilities.

Baseline. Before the baseline phase began, the eight peer tutors were matched in pairs, according to their grade level and sex. The pairs were also matched so that they were not in the same peer tutoring period together. Each of the four pairs of participants was then randomly assigned to "tutor" one of the four students with severe disabilities. The special education teacher then scheduled each of the eight tutors to participate with his or her assigned partners with severe disabilities on a daily basis.

To ensure that the setting and activities were similar across the two participants in each pair, the special education teacher scheduled activities and environments that were either very similar or identical for each. For example, if Tutor A took

Megan to the grocery store to choose a lunch item, Tutor B would also be scheduled to take Megan to the store to shop for a specific item. The special education teacher was also instructed to continue to set up activities for his peer tutors as he normally had before the study began, with the exception of assigning similar activities for the participants in each pair.

The 17-min observational periods for each participant were randomly selected from the 50-min class time, although the first and last 5 min of the class period were excluded from the random selection. Three days before initiating baseline, the data collector took practice samples during each classroom period to desensitize the students in the classroom to her presence. During baseline and subsequent phases, at the beginning of each period the data collector would put her headset on and begin observing the students, although she was not collecting data at that point. Typically, the data collector sat in the same chair when she was in the classroom observing, and she was approximately 1-3 m (3-10 ft) away from the participants during the observational periods. When the data collector had completed her observational time sample, she continued to keep her headset on until the period ended. If the students went off campus or out of the classroom, the data collector would follow approximately 1.5 m (5 ft) behind.

Training. One peer tutor participant was randomly assigned to receive the social interaction training intervention. The training phase for each participant lasted 5 consecutive days. The other participant continued to receive the same instructions for interacting with the identified peer with severe disabilities as was previously provided during the baseline condition. The data collector continued to measure the dependent variables on all participants during the training phase, including participants receiving training and those not receiving training. The training sessions took place away from the special education classroom, usually outside on the campus grounds. The sessions were conducted for 20 min during the participant's normal peer tutoring period, either at the beginning of the period or at the end. After each session, the participants returned to the classroom or the setting where their partners with severe disabilities could be found, or went on to their next class.

Posttraining. After the social skill training intervention was completed for the selected participant, the dependent variables continued to be measured for both participants (the one who received training as well as the participant who served as the control) during the posttraining phase. At this point, however, the students who had been trained were now identifying the activities that they would participate in with their partner with disabilities. The activity was generally decided on a day before it would occur, and the special education teacher would also schedule a similar activity the next day for the participants who had not received training and their partners with disabilities.

Data Analysis

A statistical analysis was combined with a visual presentation of the data to determine whether there were differences in the frequency of initiations, expansions, the target behaviors of the participants with severe disabilities, and the percentage of initiations or expansions that were social in nature, as a function of the experimental condition (social skills training intervention). Nonparametric randomization tests have been suggested for the analysis of data from small-sample, interrupted time series designs (Edgington, 1967, 1975, 1980a, 1980b, 1980c; Levin, Marascuilo, & Hubert, 1978) and were employed in this study.

A variation of Edgington's (1980b) procedures, which were extended by Marascuilo and Busk (1988) to apply to multiple baseline designs, was used to analyze differences in frequencies for the dependent measures by collapsing the data across the four participants who received training during the baseline and experimental phases. Given the researcher's hypothesis that the training's effects would carry over into the posttraining phases, the training and posttraining data were collapsed. The same analyses were then conducted by collapsing the data across the four participants who served as controls in the study and who did not receive the social skills training intervention.

Edgington's (1980b) procedure is based on the difference in phase means and is given by:

$$\bar{d}_S = \bar{Y}_{AS} - \bar{Y}_{BS}.$$

With four participants, a normal approximation is used to combine the data across participants. For these data:

$$I = \bar{d}_1 + \bar{d}_2 + \bar{d}_3 + \bar{d}_4$$
$$E(I) = E(\bar{d}_1) + E(\bar{d}_2) + E(\bar{d}_3) + E(\bar{d}_4)$$
$$Var(I) = Var(\bar{d}_1) + Var(\bar{d}_2) + Var(\bar{d}_3) + Var(\bar{d}_4); \text{ and}$$
$$Z = [I - E(T) / \sqrt{var\,(7)}].$$

The null hypothesis at $\alpha < .05$ is .05 with the one-tailed alternative at $\mu_A < \mu_B$.

RESULTS

Reliability

There was an average of 92% agreement between the investigator and the data collector across 68 of the 250 (27%) 17-min observational time sam-

ples represented across all phases and participants. The range of agreement was from a low of 80% to a high of 100%.

Educational Staff Behavior

A total of 19 observational checks on staff behaviors were taken across the eight peer tutor participants in the study: two checks on six participants, three checks for one student, and four checks on one student. The range of frequency for physical or verbal prompts of staff-directed behavior toward participants was from 0 to 2 across the 19 validation checks. The range of frequency of positive verbal reinforcement directed by staff to the participants was also from 0 to 2 across the total number of validation checks. The number of prompts and positive reinforcements were consistent across all participants. These data suggest that none of the peer tutor participants was receiving a greater amount of staff attention while interacting with his or her partner with severe disabilities.

Social Interaction Training

The mean frequency of initiations, expansions, the frequency of initiations and/or expansions, (expressed as percentages of intervals) which were measured to be socially related, and the targeted behaviors of the participants with severe disabilities are summarized in Table 1 across baseline, training, and posttraining phases. A total of 23 intervals was omitted from the observational periods because the data collector was not close enough to the participants to score the interval.

Baseline. The frequency of initiations during baseline is shown in Figure 1. During the 17-min observational sessions, the mean percent of intervals in which initiations were coded for the eight peer tutor participants ranged from 5% to 32%. The participants who received the social skills training during the training phase, initiated social interactions with their partners with severe disabilities for 32%, 27%, 5%, and 28% of the time. The participants who did not receive the later training, initiated social interactions with their partners with severe disabilities for 30%, 15%, 17%, and 23% of the time, during baseline sessions, indicating no stable differences between the two groups.

Figure 2 shows the percentage of intervals in which observers coded expansion of social interventions. During the baseline phase, there was a mean percentage range of 2% to 41% of occurrence of expansions among the eight peer tutor participants. The participants selected to receive training expanded their social interactions with their partners with severe disabilities for 27%, 12%, 2%, and 39% of the time. The control participants had a mean frequency of expansions of

TABLE 1
Means for the Four Dependent Measures

Participants	Frequency of Interactions or Behavior Measures (%)		
	Baseline	Training	Posttraining
Initiations of Interactions			
Trained peer tutors			
Carole	32	34	29
Mary	27	38	33
Janna	5	24	14
Celia	28	41	32
Control peer tutors			
Kim	30	24	21
Beth	15	23	9
Mike	17	8	19
Kristy	23	4	24
Expansions of Interactions			
Trained peer tutors			
Carole	27	32	32
Mary	12	34	31
Janna	2	26	13
Celia	39	42	48
Control peer tutors			
Kim	41	17	22
Beth	4	14	7
Mike	17	6	19
Kristy	22	6	20
Initiations and/or Expansions of Interactions That Were Social			
Trained peer tutors			
Carole	33	41	52
Mary	4	35	30
Janna	15	33	45
Celia	27	60	42
Control peer tutors			
Kim	12	17	26
Beth	2	2	8
Mike	38	39	11
Kristy	23	0	16
Targeted Behaviors of Participants with Severe Disabilities			
With trained peer tutor			
Megan with Carole	13	30	33
William with Mary	16	56	63
Ben with Janna	16	66	57
Kayse with Celia	34	47	57
With control peer tutor			
Megan with Kim	28	25	21
William with Beth	40	39	17
Ben with Mike	49	2	47
Kayse with Kristy	16	10	24

Note: Megan, William, Ben, and Kayse were high school students with severe disabilities. Carole, Mary, Janna, Celia, Kim, Beth, Mike, and Kristy were high school students without disabilities who were peer tutor volunteers.

41%, 4%, 17%, and 22% during baseline sessions, again indicating no stable differences between the groups on this variable.

Figure 3 shows the percentage of intervals in which observers recorded initiations and/or expansions that were social in nature. During baseline sessions, trained participants initiated and/or expanded interactions on a social level with their partners with severe disabilities for a mean of 33%, 4%, 15%, and 27% of the time. Control participants had frequencies of initiations and/or expansions on a social level with their partners for a mean of 12%, 2%, 38%, and 23% of the time during baseline sessions. These data indicate no

FIGURE 1
Frequency of Initiation of Social Interactions by Trained and Untrained Peer Tutors with
Partners with Severe Disabilities

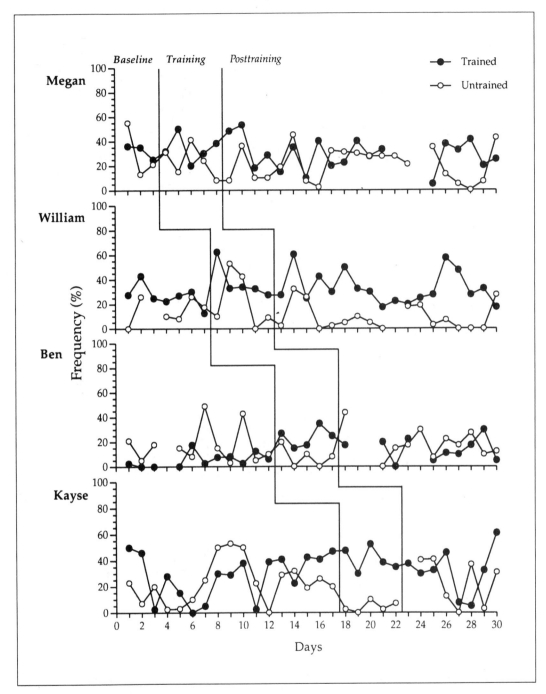

Note: Megan, William, Ben, and Kayse were high school students with severe disabilities. They participated in the peer tutoring program.

stable differences found between the groups on this variable before intervention.

Figure 4 shows the percentage of intervals in which observers coded the occurrence of the targeted behaviors of the participants with severe disabilities. During the 17-min baseline observational sessions for Megan, the mean frequency of responding with her communication system was 13% when she was with her trained partner and 28% when she was with her untrained partner. William had a mean frequency of attending to interactions for 16% when he was paired with his trained partner and 40% when he was paired with his untrained partner during baseline sessions. During baseline sessions for Ben, the mean frequency of responding appropriately to peers was found to be 16% when he interacted with his trained partner and 49% when interacting with

FIGURE 2
Frequency of Expansions of Social Interactions by Trained and Untrained Peer Tutors with Partners with Severe Disabilities

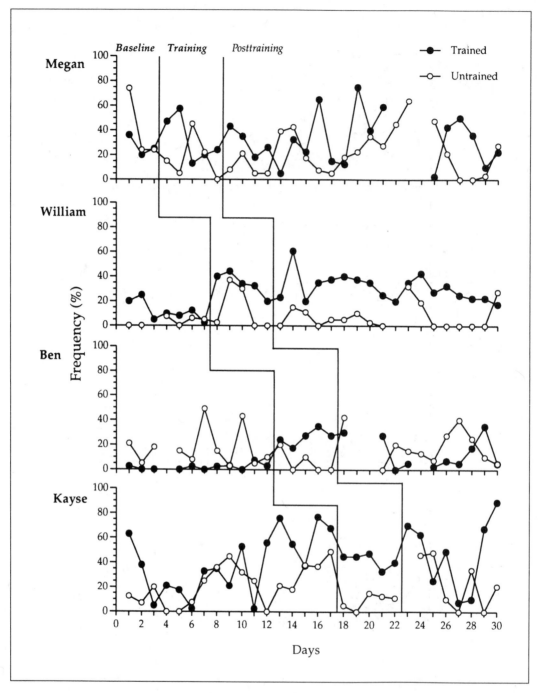

Note: Megan, William, Ben, and Kayse were high school students with severe disabilities. They participated in the peer tutoring program.

his untrained partner. Kayse, whose targeted social behavior was expanding during a social interaction, had a mean frequency of 34% occurrence of expansions when she was paired with her trained partner and 16% occurrence of expansions when she was paired with her untrained partner during baseline sessions. These baselines, though reflecting variability from session to session, were reasonably stable within pairings.

Training. During this period, four peer tutor participants were randomly assigned to receive the social skills training intervention over five sessions. The other four participants, who did not receive training, continued to receive the instructions presented during the baseline phase. During the training sessions, participants who received training experienced an increase in the frequency of *initiations* directed toward their

FIGURE 3
Frequency of Initiations and/or Expansions of a Social Nature by Trained and Untrained Peer Tutors
with Partners with Severe Disabilities

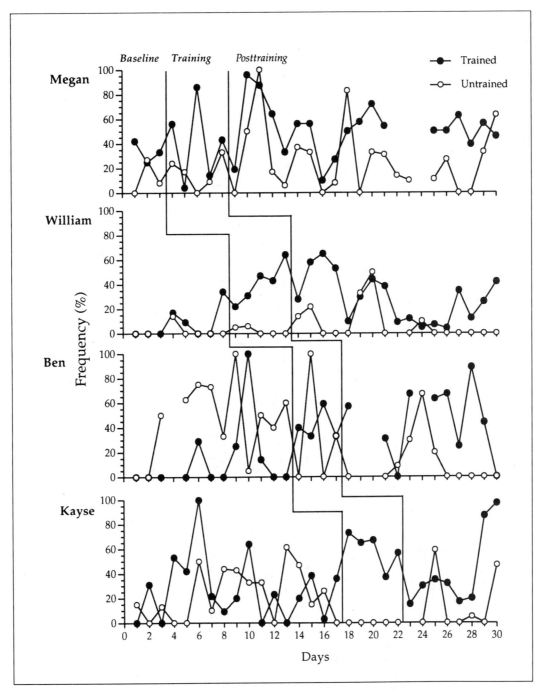

Note: Megan, William, Ben, and Kayse were high school students with severe disabilities. They participated in the peer tutoring program.

partners with severe disabilities (see Figure 1). The participants who did not receive training revealed no systematic pattern in the data from the frequency of initiations toward their partners with severe disabilities.

The mean percentage of intervals of *expansions* (see Figure 2) during the training sessions for the participants who received the training also increased for two of the participants from base-line sessions, but showed no systematic effects for the other two. Three of the participants who did not receive training showed no systematic training effects, and one of them showed a decrease in frequency of expansions.

The mean percentage of intervals of *initiations and/or expansions* that were determined to be social in nature increased for three of the four participants who received the training. During

FIGURE 4
**Frequency of Targeted Behaviors of Participants with Severe Disabilities, When in
Partnership with Trained and Untrained Peer Tutors**

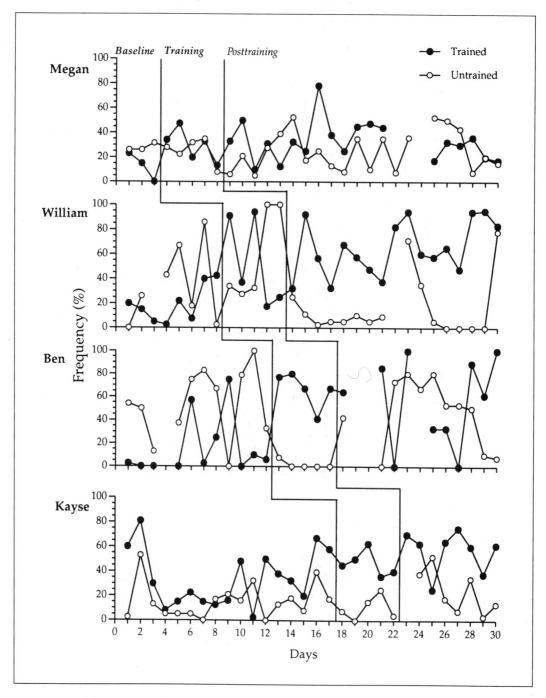

Note: Megan, William, Ben, and Kayse were high school students with severe disabilities. They participated in the peer tutoring program.

training sessions, three of the control participants showed no systematic effects from baseline to training sessions. One participant experienced a decrease in the frequency of social initiations and/or expansions from baseline to training phases.

Finally, Figure 4 shows the frequency of *targeted behaviors* of the participants with severe disabilities, according to the peer tutors (trained or untrained) they were paired with. During the training sessions for Megan, the mean frequency of responding with her communication system increased from baseline sessions when she interacted with her trained partner and decreased slightly from baseline sessions when she interacted with her control partner. William had an increase in the mean frequency of attending to interactions when he was with his trained partner

TABLE 2
Differences Between Baseline and Training Phases for Experimental and Control Participants

Interaction or Behavior Measured	Z	Critical value at α = .05, one tailed	Result
Initiations			
Experimental	−1.69	−1.645	Significant treatment effect
Control	1.04		NS
Expansions			
Experimental	−1.42	−1.645	NS
Control	1.77		NS
Percent of interactions that were social			
Experimental	−1.69	−1.645	Significant treatment effect
Control	−.01		NS
Targeted Social Behavior			
Experimental	−2.60	−1.645	Significant treatment effect
Control	1.60		NS

and a small decrease when he was with his control partner during the training sessions. During training sessions for Ben, the mean frequency of responding appropriately to peers increased when he was paired with his trained partner and decreased dramatically with his control partner. Kayse also experienced an increase in the mean frequency of occurrence of expansions when she interacted with her trained partner and a decrease in expansions with her control partner.

Posttraining. Following the 5 days of training sessions, there was a posttraining phase for each of the groups of peer tutor participants in which there was neither follow-up training nor instructor's feedback provided to any of the participants. For all of the trained and untrained participants, the mean percentage of intervals with initiations (see Figure 1) during these sessions approximated the baseline levels of performance, thus revealing no systematic, long-term, posttraining effects. The mean posttraining percentage of intervals with expansions (see Figure 2) for the trained participants revealed systematic positive effects for two of the participants and no systematic differences for the other two participants. For the control participants, no systematic effects were found from training to posttraining phases.

The percentage of intervals with initiations and/or expansions that were social in nature (see Figure 3) showed a systematic positive effect for one of the trained participants and no systematic effects for the other trained participants. The control participants showed no systematic differences for three of the participants and a systematic decrease in frequency for one of the participants during the posttraining sessions.

During the posttraining sessions, the mean percentage of intervals with targeted social behaviors (Figure 4) showed systematic positive effects for each of the participants with disabilities

in the presence of their trained partners. No systematic effects were found for the mean percentage of targeted social behaviors when the participants with disabilities were in the presence of their control partners, from training to postttraining phases.

Statistical Analyses. Table 2 shows the results of the randomization tests to determine whether there were statistically significant differences between baseline and training phases (collapsing across training and posttraining phase data). Data shown are for the frequency of initiations, expansions, target behaviors of the participants with severe disabilities, and the percentage of initiations and/or expansions that were social in nature (collapsing across the four participants who received training).

Using a one-tailed test, the analyses show that the frequency of initiations, the frequency of the target behaviors of the participants with severe disabilities, and the frequency of initiations and/or expansions that were social in nature, were significantly higher during the treatment phase than during the baseline phase for the peer tutor participants who received social skills training. No statistically significant differences were found between baseline and training phases for the frequency of expansions.

Table 2 also shows the results of the randomization test for the participants who served as controls (collapsing across participants). Using a one-tailed test, the analyses found no significant differences between baseline and training and posttraining phases for the dependent measures across the control group.

DISCUSSION

Four high school students without disabilities, volunteering as peer tutors, were provided with social interaction training, with the intent of facilitating higher frequencies of initiations and expansions of interactions directed toward peers with severe disabilities. In addition, the social interaction training was designed to promote social, rather than task-related, interactions. The possible indirect effect of the training was also evaluated through measurement of targeted social behaviors for each of the participants with severe disabilities. Four other high school students without disabilities, also peer tutors, who did not receive the social interaction training, served as controls.

A nonparametric statistical analysis of the data revealed that the social interaction training significantly increased the frequency of initiations and the proportion of interactions that were social in nature when the data were collapsed across the four peer tutors who received training. In addition, there was a statistically significant increase in the targeted social behaviors of the participants with severe disabilities when they interacted with their trained peer tutor partners. For the control participants, there were no statistically significant differences found among the collapsed data for the four dependent measures between baseline and training phases.

The results suggest that the social interaction training was effective in increasing the frequency of the dependent measures, with the exception of expansions, which were not shown to be statistically significant. Based on these promising findings, continued research in this area appears to be crucial for validating the importance of providing planned opportunities for social interactions between students without disabilities and students with severe disabilities at the high school level. Perhaps the most encouraging finding in the study was the indirect effect of the training on the participants with severe disabilities, who all experienced an increase in their targeted social behaviors when they interacted with their trained partner during the training and posttraining phases. Although it was impossible to pinpoint the variable responsible for this positive side effect, future research in this area should include identification of the interactive behaviors of students without disabilities that promote the social skills of students with disabilities.

Limitations of this study included subject selection and the matching of the pairs of participants. First, the participants without disabilities were students who had previously volunteered for a peer tutoring program. Therefore, they may not have been characteristic of the typical high school student. The data may have revealed different results in interactive behaviors if the training had been provided to students without disabilities who had no experience interacting with peers with disabilities.

Second, although the students without disabilities were matched in pairs by age and sex, the matched students varied considerably on the dependent measures during the baseline phase. By matching students who had similarly low rates of interactive behaviors to begin with, some of the inconsistencies in the data may have been alleviated.

Finally, based on subjective evaluation of the intervention by the trainer, future training of this kind may be even more effective if follow-up sessions after the training were provided to participants to give them an opportunity to review the skills they learned, as well as problem-solve difficulties they were possibly experiencing. In addition, provision of a follow-up training may have alleviated the differences found among groups from the training to posttraining sessions.

Most importantly, the results of this study indicate that planning for reciprocal interactions must be done in a structured way. If we want social interactions to occur between students with and without disabilities, we must provide an effective, efficient training approach for enhancing their occurrence; and we must be prepared to follow through with our efforts.

REFERENCES

Ashmore, R. D. (1975). Background considerations in developing strategies for changing attitudes and behavior toward the mentally retarded. In M. Bega & S. Richardson (Eds.), *The mentally retarded and society: A social science perspective* (pp. 159-174). Baltimore: University Press.

Biklen, D., Corrigan, C., & Quick, D. (1989). Beyond obligation: Students' relations with each other in integrated classes. In D. Lipsky & A. Gartner (Eds.), *Beyond separate education: Quality education for all* (pp. 207-221). Baltimore: Paul H. Brookes.

Brinker, R. P., & Thorpe, M. E. (1986). Features of integrated educational ecologies that predict social behavior among severely mentally retarded and nonretarded students. *American Journal of Mental Deficiency, 91,* 150-159.

Carr, E. G. (1985). Behavioral approaches to language and communication. In E. Schlopler & G. B. Mesibov (Eds.), *Communication problems in autism* (pp. 1-33). New York: Plenum.

Carr, E. G. & Durand, V. M. (1985). The social-communicative basis of severe behavior problems in children. In S. Reiss & R. Boctzin (Eds.), *Theoretical issues in behavior therapy* (pp. 214-254). New York: Academic Press.

Chadsey-Rusch, J. (1990). Social interactions of secondary-aged students with severe handicaps: Implications for facilitating the transition from school to work. *Journal of the Association for Persons with Severe Handicaps, 15,* 69-78.

Chadsey-Rusch, J., & Gonzalez, P. (1988). Social ecology of the workplace: Employers' perceptions versus direct observation. *Research in Developmental Disabilities, 9,* 229-245.

Delquadri, J., Greenwood, C. R., Whorton, D., Carta, J. J., & Hall, V. R. (1986). Classwide peer tutoring. *Exceptional Children, 52,* 535-542.

Donaldson, J. (1980). Changing attitudes toward handicapped persons: A review and analysis of research. *Exceptional Children, 46,* 504-515.

Donnellan, A. M., La Vigna, G. W., Negri-Shoultz, N.,

& Fassbender, L. L. (1988). *Progress without punishment.* New York: Teachers College Press.

Donnellan, A. M., Mirenda, P. L., Mesaros, R. A., & Fassbender, L. L. (1984). Analyzing the communicative functions of aberrant behavior. *Journal of the Association for Persons with Severe Handicaps, 9,* 201-212.

Edgington, E. S. (1967). Statistical inference from $N = 1$ experiments. *The Journal of Psychology, 65,* 195-199.

Edgington, E. S. (1975). Randomization tests for one-subject operant experiments. *The Journal of Psychology, 90,* 57-60.

Edgington, E. S. (1980a). Random assignment and statistical tests for one-subject experiments. *Behavioral Assessment, 2,* 19-28.

Edgington, E. S. (1980b). Validity of randomization tests for one-subject experiments. *Journal of Educational Statistics, 5*(3), 235-251.

Edgington, E. S. (1980c). Overcoming obstacles to single-subject experimentation. *Journal of Educational Statistics, 5*(3), 261-267.

Eichinger, J. (1990). Goal structure effects on social interaction: Nondisabled and disabled elementary students. *Exceptional Children, 56,* 408-416.

Forest, M., & Lusthaus, E. (1989). Promoting educational equality for all students: Circles and maps. In S. Stainback, W. Stainback, & M. Forest (Eds.), *Educating all students in the mainstream of regular education* (pp. 43-57). Baltimore: Paul H. Brookes.

Gaylord-Ross, R. J., & Haring, T. G. (1987). Social interaction research for adolescents with severe handicaps. *Behavioral Disorders, 12*(4), 264-275.

Gaylord-Ross, R. J., Haring, T. G., Breen, C., & Pitts-Conway, V. (1984). The training and generalization of social interaction skills with autistic youth. *Journal of Applied Behavior Analysis, 19,* 209-214.

Goldstein, H., & Wickstrom, S. (1986). Peer intervention effects on communicative interaction among handicapped and nonhandicapped preschoolers. *Journal of Applied Behavior Analysis, 19,* 209-214.

Gottlieb, J. (1980). Improving attitudes toward retarded children by using group discussion. *Exceptional Children, 47,* 106-113.

Halle, J. W. (1982). Teaching functional language to the handicapped: An integrative model of natural environment teaching techniques. *Journal of the Association for Persons with Severe Handicaps, 2,* 29-37.

Halle, J. W. (1987). Teaching language in the natural environment: An analysis of spontaneity. *Journal of the Association for Persons with Severe Handicaps, 12,* 28-37.

Halvorsen, A., & Sailor, W. (1990). Integration of students with severe and profound disabilities: A review of research. In R. Gaylord-Ross (Ed.), *Issues and research in special education* (pp. 111-172). New York: Teachers College Press.

Haring, T. G., Roger, C., Lee, M., Breen, C., & Gaylord-Ross, R. J. (1986). Teaching social language to moderately handicapped students. *Journal of Applied Behavior Analysis, 19,* 159-171.

Hunt, P., Alwell, M., Goetz, L., & Sailor, W. (1990). Generalized effects of conversation skill training. *Journal of the Association for Persons with Severe Handicaps, 15*(4), 240-260.

Levin, J. R., Marascuilo, L. A., & Hubert, L. J. (1978). N = nonparametric randomization tests. In T. R.

Kratochwill (Ed.), *Single subject research: Strategies for evaluating change* (pp. 55-56). New York: Academic Press.

Lignugaris/Kraft, B., Rule, S., Salzberg, C. L., & Stowitscheck, J. J. (1986). Social inter-personal skills of handicapped and nonhandicapped adults at work. *Journal of Employment Counseling, 23,* 20-30.

Marascuilo, L. A., & Busk, P. (1988). Combining statistics for multiple baseline AB and replicated ABAB designs across subjects. *Behavioral Assessment, 10,* 1-28.

Murray, C., & Beckstead, S. (1983). *Awareness and inservice manual (AIM).* San Francisco: San Francisco State University, San Francisco Unified School District. (ERIC Document Reproduction Service No. ED 242182)

Murray-Seegert, C. (1989). *Nasty girls, thugs, and humans like us: Social relations between severely disabled and nondisabled students in high school.* Baltimore: Paul H. Brookes.

Ogbu, J. (1978). School desegregation in racially stratified communities: A problem of congruence. *Anthropology and Education Quarterly, 9*(4), 290-292.

Peck, C. A., Donaldson, J., & Pezzoli, M. (1990). Some benefits nonhandicapped adolescents perceive for themselves from their social relationships with peers who have severe handicaps. *Journal of the Association for Persons with Severe Handicaps, 15,* 241-249.

Pumpian, I. R. (1981). *Variables effecting attitudes toward the employability of severely handicapped adults.* Unpublished doctoral dissertation, University of Wisconsin at Madison.

Schellenberg, J. A. (1970). *An introduction to social psychology.* New York: Random House.

Schuler, A. L., & Goetz, L. (1981). Assessment of severe language disabilities: Communication and cognitive considerations. *Analysis and Intervention of Developmental Disabilities, 1,* 333-346.

Strain, P., & Odom, S. (1986). Peer social initiations: Effective intervention for social skills development of exceptional children. *Exceptional Children, 52,* 543-551.

Tawney, J. W. & Gast, D. L. (1984). *Single subject research in special education.* Columbus, OH: Charles E. Merrill.

Voeltz, L. M. (1980). Children's attitudes toward handicapped peers. *American Journal of Mental Deficiency, 84*(3), 455-464.

This research was supported in part by the U.S. Department of Education Cooperative Agreements #G0087C3056-88 and #H023B00044. The content and opinions expressed herein do not necessarily reflect the position of the U.S. Department of Education, and no official endorsement should be inferred. The authors would like to thank the students at Kennedy High School who participated in the study; their teacher, Rich Perlow; and Chandra Ghosh for her involvement and support.

Manuscript received November 1991; revision accepted August 1992.

Children with Behavioral Disorders and Autism

Professionals do not always agree on the elements that define behavioral disorders. What is "good" behavior? One teacher may enjoy the "all boy" behavior of a child who disrupts the class with funny stories of his gang's shenanigans and who is feisty, sassy, and proud of his delinquency. Another teacher may wish all the students in the class could be as quiet as the "shy girl" who daydreams, has no friends, puts herself down, is unhappy, and talks about death. Both children are probably behaviorally disordered.

To be considered behaviorally disordered, behavior should meet three criteria: severity, chronicity, and adverse effect on learning. However, each of these terms is relative. Another way to define behavioral disorders is to look at the polarities described above: aggressive/acting out/externalizing behaviors versus withdrawn/internalizing behaviors. However, these simple polarities leave out many other disordered behaviors. Four clusters that are typically used to classify atypical behaviors are socialized aggression (e.g., gang membership); conduct disorders (e.g., fighting, temper); immaturity (e.g., short attention, clumsiness); and personality disorders (e.g., avoidant, dependent). Another way to classify atypical behaviors that are relevant to the education of children with behavior disorders is to look at learning—attention, response, order, exploration, social interaction, and mastery. This classification links behaviors to curriculum goals.

Autism and other pervasive developmental disorders of childhood are classified as psychotic disorders by psychiatry. They are considered behavior disorders for educational purposes. Autism is a progressive loss of contact with and interest in the outside world. Children with autism prefer aloneness, insist on sameness, like elaborate routines, and may have some "savant" ability that seems remarkable in light of the apparent retardation of learning in other areas.

A majority of children have occasional episodes of disordered behavior. Assessment of behavior disorders to qualify for special educational services requires marked differences from the behavior of other children and continuation of the severe and typical behavior for a long period of time.

Controversy surrounds the issue of enrolling children with severe behavior disorders in regular education classes. Public Law 94-142 guarantees them the least restrictive environment appropriate for their education. No mention is made of the appropriateness of their enrollment in a class to other children's education or to the teacher's ability to teach. The school system must "show cause" if a child with disordered behavior is moved to a more restrictive setting from a regular classroom.

When a student with a behavior disorder or autism is enrolled in an inclusive education program, the school administration, special education staff, regular teacher, parent(s), and other significant personnel must meet to develop an appropriate IEP (individualized education program) for the student's school progress. Usually some provision is made for pull-out time for supportive psychological counseling services.

Teachers who have children with behavioral disorders or autism in their classrooms need to observe two rules of behavior: (1) empathize, (2) do not condone or reinforce disturbed behaviors. Both types of conduct are very difficult to effect on a consistent basis. They require extreme patience.

Empathy is the ability to project one's own consciousness into another person's being. It is understanding the other's needs, frustrations, stresses, joys, and other social, emotional, and cognitive reasons for behavior. Since nobody can really experience the totality of another person's being, perfect empathy is impossible. A good teacher, however, continually tries to understand the whys and wherefores of the actions of a child with disturbed behaviors.

Understanding why a child misbehaves often leads teachers and other adults to condone, excuse, or pardon disturbed behavior. This is unacceptable. Sympathetic understanding should not lead to tolerance of wrongful acts. All disruptive behavior should be stopped. The child should be helped to learn a different, more acceptable behavior without being ridiculed or condemned. Condemnation leads to resentment. Suggestions of better ways can lead to change. All efforts to alter behavior toward an acceptable standard should be reinforced. If other children observe disturbed behaviors being corrected, they are apt to model the correct behavior. On the other hand, if other children observe disruptive behavior being accepted, they are apt to imitate the misbehavior.

Teachers can often avoid extreme acts of aggression or withdrawal by watching children with behavior disorders or autism very carefully. When and if they see signs of anger, frustration, fear, guilt, or anxiety, teachers can alter their lesson plans. They can provide some form of relief for the child or children who are disturbed. Distractions, rest periods, and other forms of "time-out" can alleviate emotional upheavals.

Teachers of children with behavior disorders or autism can teach self-management skills to both abled and disabled students. Self-monitoring and other self-control procedures not only help regulate the behaviors that occur in the classroom, but they also help each student feel better about the ability to be in control of his or her own life. Self-control and self-esteem go hand in hand and enhance each other.

The first selection in this unit defines and discusses children with autism. The unusual behaviors are described along with some possible explanations for them. The second unit article addresses the problem of students with work inhibition who could learn but do not have any interest in educational performance. Their withdrawal and passivity are put in perspective with suggestions for what teachers can do to alter the behaviors. The next selection discusses the placement of children with behavior disorders or autism in regular education classrooms. Who is severely disturbed? What special services are required? Where should they be provided? When? How should "severe" behavior disorder be assessed? The fourth article discusses discipline from a cultural perspective. Behaviors deemed appropriate or inappropriate vary by culture. Assessment procedures and teaching methods should be sensitive to differences in behavioral patterns in culturally diverse groups.

Looking Ahead: Challenge Questions

What is autism? How can one work with an autistic student?

Why do some students have school work inhibition? How can a teacher empower an inhibited child?

Can public schools fulfill their obligation to serve behaviorally disordered students and also provide appropriate education to nontroubled students simultaneously? Defend your answer.

How can teachers show sensitive discipline for culturally diverse students with behavioral disorders?

Autism

*Autistic individuals suffer from a biological defect.
Although they cannot be cured, much can be done
to make life more hospitable for them*

Uta Frith

UTA FRITH is a senior scientist in the Cognitive Development Unit of the Medical Research Council in London. Born in Germany, she took a degree in psychology in 1964 at the University of the Saarland in Saarbrücken, where she also studied the history of art. Four years later she obtained her Ph.D. in psychology at the University of London. Besides autism, her interests include reading development and dyslexia. She has edited a book in the field of reading development, *Cognitive Processes in Spelling*, and is the author of *Autism: Explaining the Enigma*.

Rodica Prato

CHARACTERISTIC ALONENESS of autistic children has evoked the image of a child in a glass shell

The image often invoked to describe autism is that of a beautiful child imprisoned in a glass shell. For decades, many parents have clung to this view, hoping that one day a means might be found to break the invisible barrier. Cures have been proclaimed, but not one of them has been backed by evidence. The shell remains intact. Perhaps the time has come for the whole image to be shattered. Then at last we might be able to catch a glimpse of what the minds of autistic individuals are truly like.

Psychological and physiological research has shown that autistic people are not living in rich inner worlds but instead are victims of a biological defect that makes their minds very different from those of normal individuals. Happily, however, autistic people are not beyond the reach of emotional contact.

Thus, we can make the world more hospitable for autistic individuals just as we can, say, for the blind. To do so, we need to understand what autism is like—a most challenging task. We can imagine being blind, but autism seems unfathomable. For centuries, we have

known that blindness is often a peripheral defect at the sensory-motor level of the nervous system, but only recently has autism been appreciated as a central defect at the highest level of cognitive processing. Autism, like blindness, persists throughout life, and it responds to special efforts in compensatory education. It can give rise to triumphant feats of coping but can also lead to disastrous secondary consequences—anxiety, panic and depression. Much can be done to prevent problems. Understanding the nature of the handicap must be the first step in any such effort.

Autism existed long before it was described and named by Leo Kanner of the Johns Hopkins Children's Psychiatric Clinic. Kanner published his landmark paper in 1943 after he had observed 11 children who seemed to him to form a recognizable group. All had in common four traits: a preference for aloneness, an insistence on sameness, a liking for elaborate routines and some abilities that seemed

remarkable compared with the deficits.

Concurrently, though quite independently, Hans Asperger of the University Pediatric Clinic in Vienna prepared his doctoral thesis on the same type of child. He also used the term "autism" to refer to the core features of the disorder. Both men borrowed the label from adult psychiatry, where it had been used to refer to the progressive loss of contact with the outside world experienced by schizophrenics. Autistic children seemed to suffer such a lack of contact with the world around them from a very early age.

Kanner's first case, Donald, has long served as a prototype for diagnosis. It had been evident early in life that the boy was different from other children. At two years of age, he could hum and sing tunes accurately from memory. Soon he learned to count to 100 and to recite both the alphabet and the 25 questions and answers of the Presbyterian catechism. Yet he had a mania for making toys and other objects spin. Instead of playing like other toddlers, he arranged beads and other things in groups of different colors or threw them on the floor, delighting in the sounds they made. Words for him had a literal, inflexible meaning.

Donald was first seen by Kanner at age five. Kanner observed that the boy paid no attention to people around him. When someone interfered with his solitary activities, he was never angry with the interfering person but impatiently removed the hand that was in his way. His mother was the only person with whom he had any significant contact, and that seemed attributable mainly to the great effort she made to share activities with him. By the time Donald was about eight years old, his conversation consisted largely of repetitive questions. His relation to people remained limited to his immediate wants and needs, and his attempts at contact stopped as soon as he was told or given what he had asked for.

Autistic Behavior

The traits most characteristic of autistic people are aloneness, an insistence on sameness and a liking for elaborate routines. At the same time, some autistic individuals can perform complicated tasks, provided that the activity does not require them to judge what some other person might be thinking. These traits lead to characteristic forms of behavior, a number of which are portrayed here.

Displays indifference

Indicates needs by using an adult's hand

Parrots words

Laughs and giggles inappropriately

Joins in only if an adult insists and assists

Does not play with other children

Is one-sided in interactions

Talks incessantly about one topic

Behaves in bizarre ways

Handles or spins objects

Does not make eye contact

Does not pretend in playing

Prefers sameness

Yet some do certain things well if the task does not involve social understanding.

Rodica Prato

Some of the other children Kanner described were mute, and he found that even those who spoke did not really communicate but used language in a very odd way. For example, Paul, who was five, would parrot speech verbatim. He would say "You want candy" when he meant "I want candy." He was in the habit of repeating, almost every day, "Don't throw the dog off the balcony," an utterance his mother traced to an earlier incident with a toy dog.

Twenty years after he had first seen them, Kanner reassessed the members of his original group of children. Some of them seemed to have adapted socially much better than others, although their failure to communicate and to form relationships remained, as did their pedantry and single-mindedness. Two prerequisites for better adjustment, though no guarantees of it, were the presence of speech before age five and relatively high intellectual ability.

The brightest autistic individuals had, in their teens, become uneasily aware of their peculiarities and had made conscious efforts to conform. Nevertheless, even the best adapted were rarely able to be self-reliant or to form friendships. The one circumstance that seemed to be helpful in all the cases was an extremely structured environment.

As soon as the work of the pioneers became known, every major clinic began to identify autistic children. It was found that such children, in addition to their social impairments, have substantial intellectual handicaps. Although many of them perform relatively well on certain tests, such as copying mosaic patterns with blocks, even the most able tend to do badly on test questions that can be answered only by the application of common sense.

Autism is rare. According to the strict criteria applied by Kanner, it appears in four of every 10,000 births. With the somewhat wider criteria used in current diagnostic practice, the incidence is much higher: one or two in 1,000 births, about the same as Down's syndrome. Two to four times as many boys as girls are affected.

For many years, autism was thought to be a purely psychological disorder without an organic basis. At first, no obvious neurological problems were found. The autistic children did not necessarily have low intellectual ability, and they often looked physically normal. For these reasons, psychogenic theories were proposed and taken seriously for many years. They focused on the idea that a child could become autistic because of some existentially threatening experience. A lack of maternal bonding or a disastrous experience of rejection, so the theory went, might drive an infant to withdraw into an inner world of fantasy that the outside world never penetrates.

These theories are unsupported by any empirical evidence. They are unlikely to be supported because there are many instances of extreme rejection and deprivation in childhood, none of which have resulted in autism. Unfortunately, therapies vaguely based on such notions are still putting pressure on parents to accept a burden of guilt for the supposedly avoidable and reversible breakdown of interpersonal interactions. In contrast, well-structured behavior modification programs have often helped families in the management of autistic children, especially children with severe behavior problems. Such programs do not claim to reinstate normal development.

The insupportability of the psychogenic explanation of autism led a number of workers to search for a biological cause. Their efforts implicate a defective structure in the brain, but that structure has not yet been identified. The defect is believed to affect the thinking of autistic people, making them unable to evaluate their own thoughts or to perceive clearly what might be going on in someone else's mind.

Autism appears to be closely associated with several other clinical and medical conditions. They include maternal rubella and chromosomal abnormality, as well as early injury to the brain and infantile seizures. Most impressive, perhaps, are studies showing that autism can have a genetic basis. Both identical twins are much more likely to be autistic than are both fraternal twins. Moreover, the likelihood that autism will occur twice in the same family is 50 to 100 times greater than would be expected by chance alone.

Structural abnormalities in the brains of autistic individuals have turned up

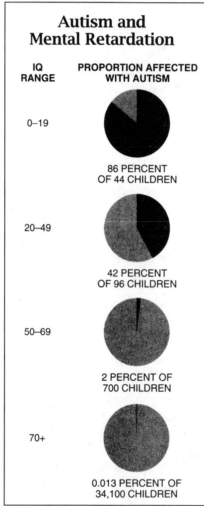

Autism and Mental Retardation

IQ RANGE	PROPORTION AFFECTED WITH AUTISM
0–19	86 PERCENT OF 44 CHILDREN
20–49	42 PERCENT OF 96 CHILDREN
50–69	2 PERCENT OF 700 CHILDREN
70+	0.013 PERCENT OF 34,100 CHILDREN

SOURCE: Lorna Wing, Medical Research Council, London

CLOSE LINK between autism and mental retardation is reflected in this chart. The percentage of children showing the social impairments typical of autism is highest at low levels of intelligence as measured by tests in which an intelligence quotient (IQ) below 70 is subnormal. For example, 86 percent of 44 children in the lowest IQ range showed the social impairments of autism. The data are drawn from a population of about 35,000 children aged under 15 years.

in anatomic studies and brain-imaging procedures. Both epidemiological and neuropsychological studies have demonstrated that autism is strongly correlated with mental retardation, which is itself clearly linked to physiological abnormality. This fact fits well with the idea that autism results from a distinct brain abnormality that is often part of more extensive damage. If the abnormality is pervasive, the mental retardation will be more severe, and the likelihood of damage to the critical brain system will increase. Conversely, it is possible for the critical system alone to be damaged. In such cases, autism is not accompanied by mental retardation.

Neuropsychological testing has also contributed evidence for the existence of a fairly circumscribed brain abnormality. Autistic individuals who are otherwise able show specific and extensive deficits on certain tests that involve planning, initiative and spontaneous generation of new ideas. The same deficits appear in patients who have frontal lobe lesions. Therefore, it seems plausible that whatever the defective brain structure is, the frontal lobes are implicated.

Population studies carried out by Lorna Wing and her colleagues at the Medical Research Council's Social Psychiatry Unit in London reveal that the different symptoms of autism do not occur together simply by coincidence. Three core features in particular—impairments in communication, imagination and socialization—form a distinct triad. The impairment in communication includes such diverse phenomena as muteness and delay in learning to talk, as well as problems in comprehending or using nonverbal body language. Other autistic individuals speak fluently but are overliteral in their understanding of language. The impairment in imagination appears in young autistic children as repetitive play with objects and in some autistic adults as an obsessive interest in facts. The impairment in socialization includes ineptness and inappropriate behavior in a wide range of reciprocal social interactions, such as the ability to make and keep friends. Nevertheless, many autistic individuals prefer to have company and are eager to please.

The question is why these impairments, and only these, occur together. The challenge to psychological theorists was clear: to search for a single cognitive component that would explain the deficits yet still allow for the abilities that autistic people display in certain aspects of interpersonal interactions. My colleagues at the Medical Research Council's Cognitive Development Unit in London and I think we have identified just such a component. It is a cognitive mechanism of a highly complex and abstract nature that could be described in computational terms. As a shorthand, one can refer to this component by one of its main functions, namely the ability to think about thoughts or to imagine another individual's state of mind. We propose that this component is damaged in autism. Furthermore, we suggest that this mental component is innate and has a unique brain substrate. If it were possible to pinpoint that substrate—whether it is an anatomic structure, a physiological system or a chemical pathway—one might be able to identify the biological origin of autism.

The power of this component in normal development becomes obvious very early. From the end of the first year onward, infants begin to participate in what has been called shared attention. For example, a normal child will point to something for no reason other than to share his interest in it with someone else. Autistic children do not show shared attention. Indeed, the absence of this behavior may well be one of the earliest signs of autism. When an autistic child points at an object, it is only because he wants it.

In the second year of life, a particularly dramatic manifestation of the critical component can be seen in normal children: the emergence of pretense, or the ability to engage in fantasy and pretend play. Autistic children cannot understand pretense and do not pretend when they are playing. The difference can be seen in such a typical nursery game as "feeding" a teddy bear or a doll with an empty spoon. The normal child goes through the appropriate motions of feeding and accompanies the action with appropriate slurping noises. The autistic child merely twiddles or flicks the spoon repetitively. It is precisely the absence of early and simple communicative behaviors, such as shared attention and make-believe play, that often creates the first nagging doubts in the minds of the parents about the development of their child. They rightly feel that they cannot engage the child in the emotional to-and-fro of ordinary life.

My colleague Alan M. Leslie devised a theoretical model of the cognitive mechanisms underlying the key abilities of shared attention and pretense. He postulates an innate mechanism whose function is to form and use what we might call second-order representations. The world around us consists not only of visible bodies and events, captured by first-order representations, but also of invisible minds and mental events, which require second-order representation. Both types of representation have to be kept in mind and kept separate from each other.

Second-order representations serve to make sense of otherwise contradictory or incongruous information. Suppose a normal child, Beth, sees her mother holding a banana in such a way as to be pretending that it is a telephone. Beth has in mind facts about bananas and facts about telephones—first-order representations. Nevertheless, Beth is not the least bit confused and will not start eating telephones or talking to bananas. Confusion is avoided because Beth computes from the concept of pretending (a second-order representation) that her mother is engaging simultaneously in an imaginary activity and a real one.

As Leslie describes the mental process, pretending should be understood as computing a three-term relation between an actual situation, an imaginary situation and an agent who does the pretending. The imaginary situation is then not treated as the real situation. Believing can be understood in the same way as pretending. This insight enabled us to predict that autistic children, despite an adequate mental age (above four years or so), would not be able to understand that someone can have a mistaken belief about the world.

Together with our colleague Simon Baron-Cohen, we tested this prediction by adapting an experiment originally devised by two Austrian developmental psychologists, Heinz Wimmer and Josef Perner. The test has become known as the Sally-Anne task. Sally and Anne are playing together. Sally has a marble that she puts in a basket before leaving the room. While she is out, Anne moves the marble to a box. When Sally returns, wanting to retrieve the marble, she of course looks in the basket. If this scenario is presented as, say, a puppet show to normal children who are four years of age or more, they understand that Sally will look in the basket even though they know the marble is not there. In other words, they can represent Sally's erroneous belief as well as the true state of things. Yet in our test, 16 of 20 autistic children with a mean mental age of nine failed the task—answering that Sally would look in the box—in spite of being able to answer correctly a variety of other questions relating to the facts of the episode. They could not conceptualize the possibility that Sally believed something that was not true.

Many comparable experiments have been carried out in other laboratories, which have largely confirmed our prediction: autistic children are specifically impaired in their understanding of mental states. They appear to lack the innate component underlying this ability. This component, when it works normally, has the most far-reaching consequences for higher-order conscious processes. It underpins the special feature of the human mind, the ability to reflect on itself. Thus, the triad of impairments in autism—in communication, imagination and socialization—is explained by the failure of a single cognitive mechanism. In everyday life, even very able autistic individuals find it hard to keep in mind simultaneously a reality and the fact that someone else may hold a misconception of that reality.

The automatic ability of normal people to judge mental states enables us to be, in a sense, mind readers. With sufficient experience we can form and use a theory of mind that allows us to speculate about psychological motives for our behavior and to manipulate other people's opinions, beliefs and attitudes. Autistic individuals lack the automatic ability to represent beliefs, and therefore they also lack a theory of mind. They cannot understand how behavior is caused by mental states or how beliefs and attitudes can be manipulated. Hence, they find it difficult to understand deception. The psychological undercurrents of real life as well as of literature—in short, all that gives spice to social relations—for them remain a closed book. "People talk to each other with their eyes," said one observant autistic youth. "What is it that they are saying?"

Lacking a mechanism for a theory of mind, autistic children develop quite differently from normal ones. Most children acquire more and more sophisticated social and communicative skills as they develop other cognitive abilities. For example, children learn to be aware that there are faked and genuine expressions of feeling. Similarly, they become adept at that essential aspect of human communication, reading between the lines. They learn how to produce and understand humor and irony. In sum, our ability to engage in imaginative ideas, to interpret feelings and to understand intentions beyond the literal content of speech are all accomplishments that depend ultimately on an innate cognitive mechanism. Autistic children find it difficult or impossible to achieve any of these things. We believe this is because the mechanism is faulty.

This cognitive explanation of autism is specific. As a result, it enables us to distinguish the types of situations in which the autistic person will and will not have problems. It does not preclude the existence of special assets and abilities that are independent of the innate mechanism my colleagues and I see as defective. Thus it is that autistic individuals can achieve social skills that do not involve an exchange between two minds. They can learn many useful social routines, even to the extent of sometimes camouflaging their problems. The cognitive deficit we hypothesize is also specific enough not to preclude high achievement by autistic people in such diverse activities as musical performance, artistic drawing, mathematics and memorization of facts.

It remains to be seen how best to explain the coexistence of excellent and abysmal performance by autistic people on abilities that are normally expected to go together. It is still uncertain whether there may be additional damage in emotions that prevents some autistic children from being interested in social stimuli. We have as yet little idea what to make of the single-minded, often obsessive, pursuit of certain activities. With the autistic person, it is as if a powerful integrating force—the effort to seek meaning—were missing.

The old image of the child in the glass shell is misleading in more ways than one. It is incorrect to think that inside the glass shell is a normal individual waiting to emerge, nor is it true that autism is a disorder of childhood only. The motion picture *Rain Man* came at the right time to suggest a new image to a receptive public. Here we see Raymond, a middle-aged man who is unworldly, egocentric in the extreme and all too amenable to manipulation by others. He is incapable of understanding his brother's double-dealing pursuits, transparently obvious though they are to the cinema audience. Through various experiences it becomes possible for the brother to learn from Raymond and to forge an emotional bond with him. This is not a farfetched story. We can learn a great deal about ourselves through the phenomenon of autism.

Yet the illness should not be romanticized. We must see autism as a devastating handicap without a cure. The autistic child has a mind that is unlikely to develop self-consciousness. But we can now begin to identify the particular types of social behavior and emotional responsiveness of which autistic individuals are capable. Autistic people can learn to express their needs and to anticipate the behavior of others when it is regulated by external, observable factors rather than by mental states. They can form emotional attachments to others. They often strive to please and earnestly wish to be instructed in the rules of person-to-person contact. There is no doubt that within the stark limitations a degree of satisfying sociability can be achieved.

Autistic aloneness does not have to mean loneliness. The chilling aloofness experienced by many parents is not a permanent feature of their growing autistic child. In fact, it often gives way to a preference for company. Just as it is possible to engineer the environment toward a blind person's needs or toward people with other special needs, so the environment can be adapted to an autistic person's needs.

On the other hand, one must be realistic about the degree of adaptation that can be made by the limited person. We can hope for some measure of compensation and a modest ability to cope with adversity. We cannot expect autistic individuals to grow out of the unreflecting mind they did not choose to be born with. Autistic people in turn can look for us to be more sympathetic to their plight as we better understand how their minds are different from our own.

FURTHER READING

AUTISM: EXPLAINING THE ENIGMA. Uta Frith. Blackwell Publishers, 1989.

THE COGNITIVE BASIS OF A BIOLOGICAL DISORDER: AUTISM. Uta Frith, John Morton and Alan M. Leslie in *Trends in Neurosciences,* Vol. 14, No. 10, pages 433-438; October 1991.

AUTISM AND ASPERGER SYNDROME. Edited by Uta Frith. Cambridge University Press, 1992.

UNDERSTANDING OTHER MINDS: PERSPECTIVES FROM AUTISM. Edited by Simon Baron-Cohen, Helen Tager-Flusberg and Donald J. Cohen. Oxford University Press, 1993.

THEY CAN BUT THEY DON'T

Helping Students Overcome Work Inhibition

JEROME H. BRUNS

Jerome H. Bruns has more than twenty years of experience as a teacher, counselor, and school psychologist. For a more in-depth treatment of the problem of work-inhibited students, with chapters devoted to what teachers, parents, and counselors can do to help, see his recent book, on which this article is based: They Can But They Don't—Helping Students Overcome Work Inhibition, *published by Viking Penguin.*

A S MANY as 20 percent of American public school students may be work inhibited—that is, they can but they don't do the work of school. They may have the intellectual capability necessary to understand the concepts their teachers present, they may have well-educated parents who want them to do well, and they may have no learning disabilities. Something, however, is blocking them from succeeding. They do not stay on task, do not complete class assignments, do not finish their homework on their own.

Over a period of eight years, in my work as a school psychologist, I conducted a broad series of experimental and empirical studies concerning work inhibition. The impetus for this work came from a series of failed attempts to help teachers and parents by using traditional approaches to make work-inhibited students comply with the demands of school. I observed that the teachers and parents of these students felt defeat and frustration and that it was not unusual for them to go to war with each other over who was responsible for the child's failures.

The term "work inhibition" was coined because the problem is unrelated to abilities, knowledge, or skills. Certain students have no trouble learning; they just have extreme difficulty engaging in the work of school. This condition stirs a range of feelings—from puzzlement to rage—among teachers and parents over generally articulate and able children who do not sustain independent effort to complete school tasks.

Even outstanding teachers have difficulty getting these students to engage in the work of school. One such teacher described her experiences with Jason, a third-grade pupil:

> Jason is never a problem in class or at recess. During oral reading, he enjoys being called on and reads fluently and with meaning. He usually has an appropriate answer or question, and he loves just about any game. His major problem—or maybe it's my problem—is completing assignments.
>
> I always make sure he understands what is required. For example, during math I go to his desk and ask if he understands the directions. If he says, "Yes," I ask him to do the first problem. While I'm kneeling beside him, he invariably completes the problem correctly. I give him an encouraging pat and tell him to continue working. I then go about the room seeing to the other students.
>
> After a period of time, I come back to Jason to see how he is progressing. He usually hasn't completed anything beyond the one problem we began with. I ask him why, and he usually just shrugs or says something like, "I don't know."

When teachers talk about students like Jason, they rarely share tales of success. Rather, they speak of their frustrations getting these children to complete almost any assignment on time or as directed. Since these students are always forgetting, teachers ascribe the behavior to disorganization and memory problems.

"I don't know what else to do. I've tried everything." This teacher spoke of how she kept students in from recess when they hadn't completed their work. She went so far as to make special transportation arrangements for some students to stay after school to finish their assignments. But when 5:00 P.M. arrived and one student had not yet begun to work, it was time to throw in the towel. "I gave up," she said. "There was no way I could make him do the work."

The defeat and frustration teachers often feel is minor compared to what many parents experience. Most parents want their children to be successful, and when they receive negative reports from the school, they usually take it upon themselves to see that their child improves. When efforts fail, their frustration grows and they begin

From *American Educator,* Winter 1992, pp. 38-44. Reprinted by permission of *American Educator,* the quarterly journal of the American Federation of Teachers.

to blame the child and the teachers. Teachers, in turn, frequently believe it is the parents who hold the key, and they expect them to do more to help.

WHO IS WORK INHIBITED?

When I began my studies in 1985, the focus was to discover how many students were work inhibited and if they shared any common traits. Were these children of below-average intelligence? Did they tend to be the students who caused discipline problems in the classroom?

The subjects of the studies resided in Falls Church, Virginia, a small (population 9,500) suburb of Washington, D.C. In general, residents of this city are white middle-class, well-educated professionals.

The community's school system is considered by many to be excellent. A favorable ratio of teachers to pupils enables classes to be small, average scores on national standardized tests are high (in the 70th and 80th percentiles), almost all students are on grade level for reading skills, and less than 1 percent of all students drop out of school.

The first step in my study was to undertake an extensive survey identifying students suffering from work inhibition. To this end, teachers and counselors reviewed the work history of their charges and prepared lists of students in grades three through twelve who routinely submitted significantly less work than typical students. To be considered work inhibited, a student had to have a history of not completing school assignments in all subjects for at least two years. The student's whole record—report cards, notes from parent conferences, plus additional interviews with teachers and parents—was used to analyze the work patterns.

Once identified, further information was sought through student records to determine any distinguishing factors that could explain their work inhibitedness.

The findings surprised parents and teachers alike.

■ Nearly 20 percent of the school population met the definition for work inhibited.

■ Three of every four work-inhibited students were boys.

■ Work inhibition appeared across the continuum of students' abilities and skills (including gifted and learning-disabled). Most of the work-inhibited students not only had good cognitive abilities but had above-average to superior thinking skills, as measured by tests of intellectual ability.

■ Work inhibition did not appear to be a function of socioeconomic class.

■ Work inhibition is not related to birth order.

■ In spite of a history of work inhibition, these students frequently had good academic knowledge and skills. Even for students who hadn't done much work for years, they continued to obtain above-average standardized achievement test scores. The skills most likely to suffer were math computation, spelling, and written composition.

■ The overwhelming majority of work-inhibited students were not disruptive in the classroom. Discipline records revealed that work-inhibited students were sent out of the classroom because of disruptive behavior nearly as often as the general student population.

Demographic studies revealed that the advantages of high socioeconomic status, good solid intellectual abilities, and excellent educational opportunities do not insulate students from becoming work inhibited.

PERSONALITY CHARACTERISTICS

In an effort to develop a descriptive profile, parents and teachers were invited to provide descriptions of work-inhibited students. Other methodologies included case studies, two experimental studies, a correlation study, and clinical interviews.

Dependency

Work-inhibited students will do their work if their teacher is standing or sitting right next to them. Under these circumstances, even chronically work-inhibited students will do their academic assignments.

Teacher after teacher recounted similar experiences at all grade levels. One fourth-grade teacher gave up her daily break to supervise one of her students during recess. Although Philip liked playing with the other students and clearly enjoyed recess, he was kept in almost daily because he failed to complete his morning class assignments.

The teacher was repeatedly amazed, however, at how well Philip worked when they were alone and next to each other; Philip finished each assignment with minimal effort. But on occasions when his teacher was not able to remain in the classroom with him during recess, Philip did not complete his work. He only finished his assignments when his teacher was right next to him.

Self-Esteem

Parents and educators invariably note poor self-esteem as a central characteristic of work-inhibited students. The behaviors associated with dependency are also frequently associated with poor self-esteem.

Work-inhibited students express their poor self-esteem in many ways. Some are obviously self-conscious. They hold back not only in the completion of assignments, but also in opportunities to lead games and discussions. These students are often constricted; they find it difficult to express their feelings and opinions and seem to want to evaporate or disappear from the classroom. When they do interact, they are often silly and immature. Their classmates may laugh at them. Shy, fragile, and preoccupied with feelings of self-doubt, these students often prefer the company of younger children.

Other work-inhibited students express a bravado. They declare that much of their schoolwork is beneath them: "Why bother with this drivel my teacher asks us to do? Who needs it?" "I can do it when I want to. I just have more important things to do!"

In contrast, students who do their work not only share a strong desire to succeed, they also have confidence in their abilities to persevere, solve problems, and complete their work. They have an openness that contrasts with the work-inhibited students' bravado. While these successful students may not all be outgoing, they usually don't appear fragile. They are willing to take risks, do not fear failure, and are confident.

The studies of self-esteem were conducted in a community in which parents placed a high value on education. Failing at endeavors that are most valued by one's parents exacts a great emotional toll. It is possible that parents contribute to a lowered sense of self-worth by reminding their work-inhibited children of their frequent failures to do well. Many of these children feel they are not successful in their relationships with their parents; they report significantly less approval from their family than do students who are successful at school.

Passive Aggression

Another characteristic of many work-inhibited students—and one that is often misunderstood—is the dimension of passive aggression. Passive-aggressive behaviors are subtle, indirect expressions of anger. Passive-aggressive people cannot openly express anger because it frightens them to do so. They may feel it is better to deny the feelings than to allow them to surface.

The paradox is that the passive-aggressive person *does* express anger, but not openly. Passive-aggressive children are not likely to say no or to openly refuse to follow the directions of teachers or parents. Instead, the passive-aggressive student is more likely to smile, say yes, and then "forget."

Passive-aggressive behaviors take many forms; being forgetful is just one of the most common. Some kids play verbal lawyer. They argue any point—often just for the sake of doing so. These children are very good at picking out the exception to almost any rule. Once a teacher spends considerable time explaining complex directions, this verbal lawyer will introduce some highly unlikely, but plausible, exception. After hearing the student's exceptions, the teacher then has to redirect the class before continuing the lesson.

Another powerful weapon in passive-aggressives' battles is withholding. Such children *will* do what is asked, but they take forever doing so. One father called his son "Dilly Dally" since the boy always took so much time to get ready or to do any chore.

Sooner or later the persistent tactics of the passive-aggressive child will result in temper tantrums. But it is not the child who has the tantrum—it's the parent or teacher. When this happens, the child is bewildered and does not really understand why the parent or teacher is so angry. The child is also frightened, because it's scary to see an important adult out of control. Furthermore, the angry response confirms for the passive-aggressive child that feelings of anger are dangerous and should be denied or kept under control.

Some children are maddeningly passive-aggressive; in others the problem may be less severe. It may seem paradoxical that these passive-aggressive children are often likable and engaging, yet these negative behaviors are not to be denied. The passive-aggressive child wants to please, but angry feelings push up to the surface in maladaptive ways. The child is often unaware of the depth of these angry feelings and doesn't understand their cause.

In Perspective

Most parents and teachers believe that most work-inhibited students are not severely emotionally disturbed. Rather, they have emotional conflicts. In spite of their burdens, endearing qualities are often evident. For example, they clearly want to do better. Just ask work-inhibited children or teenagers what they would like to change about their lives. "I'd get better grades. The problem is I don't do the work. I could if I wanted to. It's like I get up and tell myself that I'm going to do it today! And then, I don't know. I put it off and then it's too late."

One parent told of how happy her son was when he did finish a lesson. Others have noted that work-inhibited students relished their occasional good performances. These students want to be successful—just as successful as their parents' dreams for them.

A personality questionnaire given to both work-inhibited and achieving students showed that most personality traits common to work-inhibited students are no different from those of achieving students, with some important exceptions.

As a group, work-inhibited students lack persistence and drive; instead, they are expedient, self-indulgent, and have difficulty in delaying gratification. These students are very insecure. They feel guilty and troubled about their inability to take care of themselves, to do their work, and to live up to their own expectations and those of others. Work-inhibited students are not tough or resilient. In general, they lack the emotional fitness to stay the course when faced with difficult tasks and are unable to assert themselves. They need far more help than most students—not only in doing their work, but also in developing a sense of adequacy.

ETIOLOGY OF WORK INHIBITION

"Why is it so difficult for my son to spend just a few hours a week doing homework? I know he isn't stupid!"

It is clear that the cause of work inhibition is not related to intelligence or to a specific weakness in reading or mathematics. Nor is it due to parental neglect. Most work-inhibited students come from homes where academic success is stressed as an important pursuit, and parents are actively involved in "helping."

Case histories reveal that the beginnings of this problem occur early in children's development. Although the manifestations of work inhibition are not always apparent until the third or fourth grade (the time when the demand for independent academic work becomes substantial), the origins begin during infancy.

Some children come to school secure and ready to be on their own. Others do not. Why do some children have the socially and emotionally adaptive skills to engage in independent schoolwork while these skills are lacking in others?

At the earliest stages of human development, babies are highly dependent upon adults for food, warmth, attention, and affection. Yet very early, infants display an amazing interest in their world and derive satisfaction from exploring their environment.

One of life's major struggles is the quest for independence. Growth toward autonomy becomes particularly evident in the second year of a child's life. The child is motivated to explore, understand, and control its world. The two-year-old's desire to do things in his or her own way is easily remembered by parents: This period is often referred to as the "terrible twos."

The success a young child experiences in becoming psychologically separate from his or her parents is very important to the child's future. A person who has been successful in separating psychologically from parents is equipped to function independently in both play and work.

With work-inhibited students, a breakdown in the independence process appears evident. Something has gone awry to keep these children from developing the social and emotional skills necessary to function well apart from their parents or other significant adults. Perhaps there is something in a child's unique makeup that makes it difficult for him or her to be independent. Perhaps some children receive tacit messages from Mom and Dad that separation from them is not safe—that they won't do well on their own.

Work-inhibited students have not developed the *emotional* skills necessary to do independent schoolwork, which often requires children to be on their own, apart from others, doing a task that is neither easy nor pleasurable. Over time, children who are not autonomous do not develop a healthy sense of self-esteem. The problem evolves into a vicious cycle. As they experience failure to initiate independence successfully, children do not receive the positive reinforcement of a job well done that will, in turn, provide them with the encouragement and good emotional feedback to continue going forth with new tasks.

While standard educational practices are not in themselves the root causes for work inhibition, these practices typically exacerbate the problem. Vulnerable, sensitive, weakly assertive children have difficulty in environments that stress competition rather than cooperation, that are more negative than positive, that reject rather than embrace, that fail rather than encourage, and that blame rather than understand.

As educators begin to understand the dynamics of work inhibition, they will have the opportunity to work in concert with parents to solve this bewildering problem. It certainly would be a relief to parents if positive programs of early intervention existed, so that parents and teachers could join together to help children before undue harm occurred.

HELP FOR WORK-INHIBITED STUDENTS

IDENTIFICATION

Work inhibition is rarely diagnosed as the reason for children's inability to do work; its symptoms are often confused with other educational disabilities. Parents can certainly recognize when their children have difficulty settling down and doing their work, but they rarely know what causes the problem. Even teachers who observe these children daily are often perplexed. At times both parents and teachers suspect that a child's failure to do work is caused by a subtle learning disability, attention-deficit disorder, or perhaps a fine-motor coordination weakness that impairs the ability to write and complete assignments. These questions must be answered if a child is to be helped.

A successful system for evaluating work-inhibited students must accomplish two major objectives. First, educators must identify those students who do not engage in the work of school. Second, educators, working with parents and mental health professionals, must devise and implement a plan to ensure that each of these students is individually understood.

WHAT TEACHERS CAN DO

For work-inhibited students, sitting down and doing schoolwork is painful. It simply is the worst part of their life. They hate it. For many, this problem is of long standing and simple quick fixes are not in the cards. Teachers can, however, make a difference.

Work-inhibited students may be helped in a number of general ways. They benefit from positive relationships with their teachers; they achieve more with supportive help to complete tasks; they benefit when they are actively helped to become independent; and they benefit from opportunities to develop their individual strengths.

Build Nurturing Relationships

In order to grow toward independence, work-inhibited students need friendly, positive, and optimistic relationships with important adults, including teachers. It is reassuring and important to them to feel that their teacher is in their corner.

Most people tend to do better work, or at least enjoy it more, when they work with someone who likes them. Providing work-inhibited students with friendly hellos, greeting them each day with a smile, finding a way to extend unconditional positive regard nurtures a student's sense of well-being.

A teacher's friendliness may be positively disarming to these students. They usually have long histories of negative self-perceptions and do not expect their teachers to be truly interested in them. In response to their teachers' friendly "hello"—away from the classroom, where teachers are not obligated to take notice of them—the students feel a bit better about their teachers and about themselves. Such friendly, inviting greetings in themselves can improve attitudes toward school and pave the way for further positive dialogue.

There is probably no better way to convey interest and nurturance than through listening. Most teacher-student social exchanges are momentary—just a few words and a smile. But sometimes the opportunity presents itself to be with a student in a situation that has nothing to do with schoolwork. Exploit such opportunities to be attentive to remarks about the student's interests. The act of really listening is a tremendous compliment and a powerful tool in building a relationship.

Help Students Develop Stick-to-it-tiveness

Work-inhibited students need help in learning persistence—to stay on task, to withstand failure, and to forge ahead. They need to learn the skills of stick-to-it-tiveness more than academic skills.

Teachers may choose among a variety of strategies to

assist the work-inhibited student to move slowly, incrementally, toward competence. Sometimes an entire class may have the same assignment—which a work-inhibited student may well be able to complete if it is broken down into small incremental steps. As the student completes each part, the teacher gives a pat on the back, a bit of encouragement—an emotional "pick-me-up"—to proceed on to the next step. The teacher tries to extend the student just a little bit.

This method is much like training to run faster. Runners set intervals during which they run hard and fast for a brief period, and then recover. Then they repeat the pattern. The goal is to run faster for short distances and then gradually extend the distance.

Varying the approach helps. Students like novelty. Surprise the child by insisting that only three questions be completed. Set up a challenge to work quickly. Use a timer and ask the student to beat the clock. Highlight or underline certain items and ask the student to finish only those that are so marked.

Maintain a careful record of assignments completed and graph the results. Student and teacher alike may be surprised and positively reinforced by viewing a graph that shows progress.

Do not let the work pile up. At the end of each period, go on to the next activity. If possible, collect any work, both complete and incomplete, and go on. Work-inhibited students easily feel overwhelmed and are unlikely to tackle a tableful of incomplete assignments. They do need to learn to tackle longer and longer assignments, but it is foolish to encourage work-inhibited students to climb a mountain when they are still unable to scale a hill.

Working incrementally means always taking it one day at a time. It means the teacher is pleased to see a work-inhibited student increase effort 100 percent when going from two minutes to four minutes, while most of the other students are able to work independently for half an hour. Bit by bit, focusing on successes, breaking assignments into smaller units, giving assignments that may be completed—this is the direction in which success lies.

Offer Helping Hands

Through positive regard and problem-solving conferences, a work-inhibited student's readiness for accepting help may improve. But a teacher with twenty-five students in a classroom can spend only a fraction of the day being next to and assisting any one individual. Therefore, it may be useful to recruit helpers to assist work-inhibited students. The classmates of work-inhibited students may be a rich resource. Pair classmates and encourage them to assist each other. Older work-inhibited students often welcome the opportunity to tutor younger children with similar weaknesses. It not only adds variety to their day but tutoring also helps them feel important. In high school, members of the National Honor Society, Key Club, or other service organizations may be ready and willing to give tutorial assistance. Each school is filled with helping hands.

Providing positive, effective feedback to students is a powerful tool but not necessarily easy to use. For praise to be effective, certain rules should be remembered.

Reward the action or product, not the person, with positive attention. Comment specifically about what it is the student has accomplished. Comments should not be exaggerated or insincere, but rather true and to the point. "Nineteen out of twenty correct! You really understand!" "Your use of shading in this painting gives the scene perspective and a sense of distance." "Your paragraph included three funny examples of what can happen on the first day of school." "Joe, your speech kept everyone's attention."

Sometimes positive reinforcement does not require words. Just a smile or a pat on the back may keep a student working. What is important is to notice what the student is doing or has accomplished.

Teachers are not the only ones who may give positive reinforcement. Everyone in the class might do it! Encourage classmates to support each other by modeling positive communication. The goal is to create a climate of encouragement.

Empower the Child

Work-inhibited students need all the help they can get in order to bolster their weak egos. These students benefit from opportunities to develop their individual strengths—to feel empowered. Encourage work-inhibited students to participate in extracurricular activities and provide them with opportunities for leadership (safety patrols, office helper).

Another important facet of feeling empowered relates to decision making. In high school, students have opportunities to make important decisions as to what courses they will take and what career paths they may embark on. At all levels, it is important to empower students to make decisions regarding daily activities, including how to accomplish tasks and what is to be studied. Being asked "What do you think?" or "What do you want to do first?" imparts a sense of importance to students and fuels feelings of control and independence. The goal is to promote autonomy so that students may stand on their own and feel a sense of adequacy.

Practices To Avoid

Our schools should not be reluctant to change those practices that are not in the best interests of students. If students are able to demonstrate their acquisition of knowledge and skills without certain homework assignments—give up those assignments. Requiring a child to repeat a grade for failure to complete assignments, punishing children by keeping them in for recess or by denying them access to extracurricular activities are not likely to promote the growth of their interests or their sense of well-being in their school.

In communicating to parents, provide clear descriptions of the student's strengths and weaknesses. Parents need to know that their children have allies in the school. Don't blame. Rather, be objective about the instructional setting and the requirements for success. Parents need to know that school work is not their responsibility. Parents can set the stage by providing a place and establishing a schedule for homework; but they should tell their children that the contract for doing school work is between students and teachers; and then nurture, love, and encourage.

Do Public Schools Have an Obligation to Serve Troubled Children And Youth?

ABSTRACT: *The exclusion of pupils considered socially maladjusted in the Public Law 94-142 definition of seriously emotionally disturbed has led to gaps in services to a population of schoolchildren having significant educational needs. Issues related to this exclusionary clause are discussed in light of current research evidence and school practices. Considerable support exists for the position that the exclusion of these students from special education and related services is neither logical nor valid. A broader perspective is advocated, in which the needs of antisocial students (and their families) are addressed through early intervention for at-risk pupils, as well as in appropriate special education programs.*

C. MICHAEL NELSON

ROBERT B. RUTHERFORD, JR.

DAVID B. CENTER

HILL M. WALKER

C. MICHAEL NELSON (CEC Chapter #83) is a Professor in the Department of Special Education at the University of Kentucky. ROBERT B. RUTHERFORD, JR. (CEC Chapter #455) is a Professor in the Special Education Program at Arizona State University, Tempe. DAVID B. CENTER (CEC Chapter #685) is a Professor in the Department of Special Education at Georgia State University, Atlanta. HILL M. WALKER (CEC Chapter #375) is the Associate Dean of the College of Education at University of Oregon, Eugene.

□ The responsibility of America's schools for providing special services to socially maladjusted pupils has been debated for many years. Much of this debate has focused on the exclusion of youths considered to be socially maladjusted, antisocial, or conduct disordered from services available to those classified as seriously emotionally disturbed (SED). Public Law (P.L.) 94-142 and its recent amendments (P.L. 99-457) specifically excluded "children who are socially maladjusted, unless it is determined that they are seriously emotionally disturbed" (U.S. Department of Health, Education, and Welfare, 1977, p. 42478). However, research, scholarly opinion, and professional practices consistently have indicated that this exclusionary clause is ill founded (Kauffman, 1989). The purpose of this article is to explore problems and issues associated with the exclusion of youth identified as socially maladjusted (SM) from special education programs in the public schools (see Nelson & Rutherford, 1990, for a more extensive discussion).

Although the *Eleventh Annual Report to Congress on the Education of the Handicapped Act* (U.S. Department of Education, 1989) indicated that 9.1% of handicapped students being served in special education programs are SED, this population continues to be significantly underserved. Federal prevalence estimates of SED pupils have ranged between 1.2% and 2.0% of the school population, but 3%-6% is regarded as a more accurate estimate by authorities (Institute of Medicine, 1989). However, less than 1% of public school students have been identified and served in SED programs (Knitzer, Steinberg, & Fleisch, 1990). Aside from the severe shortage of qualified teachers for these pupils, the basis for this serious lack of services appears to be a chain of interrelated circumstances. First, schools are antagonized by and often resist providing services for students whose social behavior deviates considerably from expected norms, especially when their behavior patterns include acts of defiance, aggression, or extreme disruption of the school environment. Second, the exclusionary clause in

P.L. 94-142 provides a rationale for excluding students from special education whose behavior is aversive, unless they also have other identifiable disabilities. As Bower (1982) observed, part of the motivation behind the SM exclusion may have been to minimize the costs of serving the SED population. Third, the *Honig v. Doe* (1988) decision by the U.S. Supreme Court established that pupils with disabilities may not be suspended for over 10 days or expelled for actions that are related to their disabilities. Furthermore, the burden of proof is on the school district to demonstrate that the student's behavior pattern *is not* related to his or her disability when such disciplinary actions are considered (Center & McKittrick, 1987; Yell, 1989). However, if the school district *does not* identify the pupil as having a disability, then suspension and explusion are viable disciplinary options. Thus, given their reluctance to deal positively with social behavior problems considered aversive to others and the court-imposed restriction on their disciplinary options, it may appear in the schools' best interests not to identify and serve students with antisocial, acting-out behavior patterns.

We contend that this exclusionary clause has the effect of denying needed educational and related services to a group of pupils who are seriously disabled by their behavior. Although there is some evidence that antisocial pupils are more often recipients of special education services than other students (Walker, Shinn, O'Neill, & Ramsey, 1987), these actions are reactive (i.e., a response to behavior patterns that have been manifest for some time and are repugnant to school personnel) rather than proactive (i.e., services aimed at preventing the development of extremely deviant behavior patterns). We will support our position through an analysis of (a) definitions of SED and SM populations, (b) the characteristics of persons exhibiting antisocial behavior, (c) identification practices, and (d) the politics of public education.

DEFINITIONS

Seriously Emotionally Disturbed

P.L. 94-142 defines SED as:

> (i) A condition exhibiting one or more of the following characteristics over a long period of time and to a marked degree, which adversely affects educational performance; a. An inability to learn which cannot be explained by intellectual, sensory, or health factors; b. An inability to build or maintain satisfactory interpersonal relationships with peers and teachers; c. Inappropriate types of behavior or feelings under normal circumstances; d. A general pervasive mood of unhappiness or depression; or e. A tendency to develop physical symptoms or fears associated with personal or school problems.

> (ii) The term includes children who are schizophrenic or autistic. The term does not include children who are socially maladjusted, unless it is determined that they are seriously emotionally disturbed (Department of Health, Education, and Welfare, Office of Education, 1977, p. 42478). The federal definition was revised to exclude autistic children. Autism was included in the category "Other Health Impaired" because of lobbying efforts by the National Society for Autistic Citizens.

This federal SED definition has come under widespread attack from the professional community, including criticisms from the author of the original definition that was adopted, with relatively few changes, by the federal government (Bower, 1982). As Bower indicated, section (ii) appears to have been added to his original definition as "a codicil to reassure traditional psychopathologists and budget personnel that schizophrenia and autism are indeed serious emotional disturbances on the one hand, and that just plain bad boys and girls, predelinquents, and sociopaths will not skyrocket the costs on the other hand" (p. 56). Whereas proponents of efforts to separate a population of students whose behavior has a purely emotional basis from those with other disorders (e.g., Clarizio, 1987; Kelly, 1986; Slenkovitch, 1983) have favored an exclusionary definition of SED, others (e.g., Center, 1989a, 1989b; Kauffman, 1989) have pointed out that research has failed to show that disorders having a purely emotional basis can be discriminated from other types of disabilities with behavioral manifestations. Center (1989a, 1989b) argued that the SED label and definition were intended to be inclusive of a wide range of disorders spanning affective, cognitive, functional, and social domains. He noted a logical fallacy inherent in excluding pupils who have problems in the social domain (especially antisocial children and youth) from the larger SED population because "an inability to build or maintain satisfactory interpersonal relationships" is a defining characteristic. Further, such children often have extreme interpersonal problems of a very long duration. Longitudinal research (Kazdin, 1987; Robins, 1966, 1979) has indicated that children with serious antisocial behavior face a greater risk for adult mental problems than any other nonpsychotic population.

Socially Maladjusted

It is noteworthy that over two-thirds of the states fail to mention the exclusion of SM in their state definitions of emotional disturbance or behavioral disorders (Mack, 1985). One factor that may be responsible for the absence of SM exclusionary clauses in state definitions is the lack of a generally accepted definition of social maladjustment. No such definition appears in P.L. 94-142, its amendments, or in the implementing regulations. The term appears to be based on the belief that certain youths are socialized in a deviant cultural group; that is, their behavior and attitudes are shaped by a social context that encourages them to act in ways that violate the standards and mores of the mainstream culture. However, it is assumed that these individuals are not SED because their behavior is in accordance with the norms of their immediate reference group. The behavior patterns considered "normative" of this deviant culture have been termed "delinquent" or "antisocial" by educators, sociologists, psychologists, and criminologists.

Delinquency is a legal term applied by the criminal justice system to indicate that a youth has been adjudicated by the courts and found guilty of criminal behavior or a "status offense" (defined as behavior judged to be deviant in a minor, such as alcohol consumption, which would not be illegal if performed by an adult). On the other hand, *delinquent behavior* is a term used to describe any illegal act, regardless of whether the perpetrator is apprehended, performed by a person under the age of majority (i.e., 18 in most states). The term *antisocial behavior* is less restrictive than delinquency, because it includes behaviors that are norm violating but not necessarily delinquent. Simcha-Fagan, Langner, Gersten, and Eisenberg (1975; cited in Walker et al., 1987, p.7) define antisocial behavior as "the recurrent violation of socially prescribed patterns of action." *Conduct disorder* is another term used to describe students who exhibit antisocial behavior, referring to overt, aggressive, disruptive behavior or covert antisocial acts (Kauffman, 1989). Youths who behave in accordance with the norms of a delinquent peer group appear to be the target of the exclusionary clause in the federal definition of SED (Center, 1989a, 1989b; Cline, 1990). This group has been labeled as *socialized-subcultural delinquents* (Achenbach, 1982; Quay, 1975), and they are characterized as participating in peer-oriented, group delinquent activities, defying adult authority, and having a delinquent value orientation (Quay).

If the exclusionary clause of the federal SED definition was directed at subcultural delinquents, a major issue in defining behavior representative of SM, but not of SED, is whether the norms of the individual's immediate reference group are deviant relative to the mainstream culture. Criteria that may be used to identify SM youth include the standards and values of the peer group, as well as whether the individual is a member of an identifiable, deviant social group, such as a delinquent gang. However, Kerr, Nelson, and Lambert (1987) emphasized that even if the behavior of SM youth conforms to the standards of their deviant reference group, it is difficult to see how they can be logically separated from the population of SED students because their behavior

does violate the norms of the larger social order and is not considered normative or tolerable by the schools. Moreover, a number of factors may be associated with an increased probability that a youth will engage in antisocial or delinquent behavior, including: (a) problems in school; (b) low verbal intelligence; (c) parents who are alcoholic or who have frequent arrests; (d) family reliance on welfare, or poor management of income; (e) homes that are broken, crowded, or chaotic; (f) erratic parental supervision and inadequate discipline; (g) parental and sibling indifference or hostility toward the youth; and (h) substance abuse (Kauffman, 1989). These factors also are strongly associated with SED.

Although the most objective method of defining delinquency and identifying delinquent individuals is in terms of "official" delinquency (commission of more serious crimes that result in arrest or adjudication; Kauffman, 1989), this is a very restrictive definition that fails to identify many youths whose antisocial behavior does not result in arrest. Furthermore, many youths classified as SED for educational purposes engage in delinquent behavior that leads to arrest or incarceration (Knitzer et al., 1990), and nearly 60% of the incarcerated population with disabilities are classified as SED (U.S. Department of Education, 1989). Thus, if separate SED and SM populations exist, they are extremely difficult to discriminate from one another.

CHARACTERISTICS OF ANTISOCIAL BEHAVIOR

Research has established two basic dimensions of disordered behavior: externalizing (overt acting-out behaviors) and internalizing (withdrawn, anxious behaviors) (Walker & Fabré, 1987). Most of the students identified as SED in the public schools are characterized as externalizing. By definition, antisocial behavior involves acting-out behavior patterns. Therefore, it is understandable that researchers studying antisocial youth find considerable overlap between SM and SED populations. Walker and his colleagues have conducted a series of longitudinal investigations of the development of antisocial behavior among middle school boys in school settings (Shinn, Ramsey, Walker, Stieber, & O'Neill, 1987; Walker et al., 1987; Walker, Stieber, & O'Neill, 1990). Pupils in their antisocial cohort exhibited significantly less academic engaged time in instructional settings, initiated and were involved in significantly more negative interactions with peers, were rated by their teachers as substantially less socially competent and adjusted, and had much greater exposure to special education services or placements than students in an at-risk control group. Differences between antisocial youth and control subjects remained consistent across grades 5, 6, and 7. The characteristics of antisocial youth derived from the research literature closely match those of pupils at risk for placement in SED programs—that is, academic deficiencies reflected in low measured achievement, poor grades, and basic skill deficits; little interest in school; careless work; lack of enthusiasm toward academic pursuits; truancy; fighting; theft; temper tantrums; destroying property; and defying or threatening others (Walker et al., 1987).

These behavior patterns bode ill for future adjustment. Walker et al. (1987) have predicted that the continuation of antisocial behavior in school will lead to increased risk of school failure, membership in deviant peer groups, school dropout, and eventual delinquency. Robins' (1966) classic follow-up study of deviant children bears out this prediction. She found that juvenile antisocial behavior was the single most powerful predictor of adult psychiatric status. The extremely high prevalence rates of learning disabilities among incarcerated juvenile offenders (Morgan, 1979; Murphy, 1986; Rutherford, Nelson, & Wolford, 1985) adds further support to the contention that school failure and social acting out are common denominators in the profiles of delinquent youth. Wolf, Braukmann, and Ramp (1987) provided convincing evidence that antisocial behavior, especially when persistent and serious, is a profoundly limiting social disability to those who exhibit it. Furthermore, they argue that long-term supportive environments are a necessary component of treatment for individuals with these behavior patterns.

Research investigating the characteristics and long-term consequences of antisocial behavior thus supports the conclusion that SM is an identifiable disability. Furthermore, antisocial behavior appears to be a frequent characteristic of pupils identified as SED. For example, Wagner (1989) found that nearly 50% of students who had been identified as SED were arrested within 2 years of leaving school. The following discussion explores the question of whether SM and SED pupils can or should be separated for educational purposes.

IDENTIFICATION PRACTICES

Although a number of states are developing standardized, objective procedures and instruments for identifying SED pupils, the final determination regarding whether a pupil is or is not SED, according to the federal definition, rests upon subjective judgment regarding each of the five P.L. 94-142 characteristics, as well as an interpretation as to what constitutes *to a marked degree* and *over a long period of time* (Kauffman, 1989). Likewise, the identification of youths as antisocial is impeded by the lack of objective criteria for defining this condition (Council for Children with Behavioral Dis-

orders, 1990). As we pointed out earlier, because delinquency is defined by actions of the criminal justice system, the tendency exists to use adjudication as a criterion for defining youth considered to be SM. However, even a cursory knowledge of the juvenile justice system will inform one that the identification of individuals as delinquent is neither standardized nor objective. In addition, delinquents constitute a heterogeneous population, with at least three recognized subtypes: socialized-subcultural, unsocialized-psychopathic, and neurotic-disturbed (Achenbach, 1982). Furthermore, far more children engage in antisocial and delinquent behavior than are adjudicated and identified; and even if adjudication were an accurate measure of delinquency, it has no relevance for educational programming.

Attempts to discriminate between SED and SM populations have relied on two sets of procedures: DSM III (American Psychiatric Association, 1980), and child behavior rating scales. (The *Diagnostic and Statistical Manual* (American Psychiatric Association, 1976) has undergone two subsequent revisions: DSM III (1980) and DSM III-R (1987). DSM III constituted a major revision, whereas the majority of changes in DSM III-R involve relatively minor adjustments in terminology.) DSM III-R is a diagnostic and classification system based on a medical model of mental disorders. This was neither designed nor intended for making educational decisions (Center, 1989). Nevertheless, several states and many local education agencies rely on DSM III-R in making SED diagnoses. An attorney has made a career of interpreting the SED definition in terms of diagnostic categories contained in the *Diagnostic and Statistical Manual*. The exclusiveness of her perception of SED is apparent in the following quotation:

> Students may not be placed in special education by virtue of being socially maladjusted, may not be found to be seriously emotionally disturbed because they are antisocial, may not be found to be seriously emotionally disturbed because they have conduct disorders. The law does not allow it. Social maladjustment is not an EHA serious emotional disturbance. (Slenkovitch, 1984, p. 293)

Slenkovitch further asserts that the DSM III diagnostic categories of Conduct Disorder, Antisocial Personality Disorder, and Oppositional Disorder are excluded from the SED definition. According to Slenkovitch, students given one of these diagnoses are not eligible for special education unless they also have been assigned another diagnosis that does qualify them. Through her workshops, Slenkovitch has influenced many school districts and several state education agencies to declare students ineligible for special education services if they do not meet her rigid definition of SED.

Several behavior rating scales have been used to identify both SED and SM pupils. *The Behavior Problem Checklist—Revised* (Quay & Peterson, 1983) contains a socialized aggression scale, and the *Child Behavior Checklist* (Achenbach, 1981) includes a delinquency scale. A third instrument, the *Differential Problem Sorter* (Kelly, 1988) lacks the standardization of the first two checklists, but contains items that, according to the author, discriminate between pupils who are SED ("emotionally disturbed") and SM ("conduct problem"). Rating scales are quick and convenient devices, they usually have face validity, and some (e.g., the *Behavior Problem Checklist—Revised*, the *Child Behavior Checklist*) have been developed through extensive factor analytic studies that established reliable and valid behavioral dimensions. However, behavior rating scales have insufficient breadth and interrater reliability to be used for diagnostic purposes (Salvia & Ysseldyke, 1988). They are useful as *screening* instruments, that is, to identify from a large pool of individuals those who *may* possess characteristics important for making differential educational decisions. They should never be used by themselves to identify or assess pupils (McMahon, 1984). However, some school districts in one state use the *Differential Problem Sorter* to initially classify students as potentially emotionally disturbed or conduct disordered. If an emotional disturbance is indicated a full evaluation is performed, but no further evaluation is conducted if the scale indicates a conduct disorder (Cheney & Sampson, 1990). The use of behavior rating scales for diagnostic classification purposes violates the assumptions upon which these instruments are based. In fact, the American Psychological Association recently adopted a resolution opposing the efforts of some states to exclude conduct-disordered students from special education and related services (Council of Representatives, American Psychological Association, 1989).

The only appropriate procedure for identifying SED and SM pupils is a systematic, comprehensive, multidisciplinary assessment process. This process must include a variety of relevant domains (i.e., cognitive, social, academic, medical, affective, and functional) sampled across the ecological settings and perspectives relevant to the pupil's functioning in school (Wood, Smith, & Grimes, 1985). Reducing decisions regarding whether students are SED or SM down to a matter of which DSM III diagnostic label has been assigned or reliance on scores on a single rating scale is an unacceptable practice. Furthermore, it violates federal law, which requires a multidisciplinary approach to diagnosis.

THE POLITICS OF EDUCATIONAL PROGRAMMING

The evidence we have presented thus far suggests that attempting to exclude SM pupils from special education appears to have no justification that can be attributed to valid distinctions between these populations. The question, then, is why is this done? We have already indicated two possible explanations: the fear that declaring SM pupils eligible for special education will open a floodgate (similar to the phenomenon that occurred when eligibility definitions of learning disabilities based on discrepancies between potential and achievement were established), and avoidance of the suspension/expulsion ban for students protected under *Honig v. Doe* (1988). The expenditure of monies and threats of litigation are powerful disincentives for school districts. Neel and Rutherford (1981) discussed three additional explanations based on prevailing attitudes and practices in the schools, including: (a) SM pupils are not truly disabled; (b) many of these students will be better served under programs for other existing disabilities where the social maladjustment is merely a secondary condition resulting from another, more readily identifiable, disability; and (c) these pupil's needs are better served either in the general school population, with its own treatment and discipline options, or through the juvenile justice system.

The classification of students into categories according to their disabilities is influenced by a host of political, social, and judgmental factors. The identification of a pupil as having a disability is guided by what the school wishes to do with that student and what (if any) special education programs are available. Distinctions between mild, moderate, and severe degrees of some recognized disabilities (e.g., SED) are very hard to make, and school officials have not been trained to recognize antisocial behavior per se as a disability. The absence of clearly articulated identification criteria, as well as the repugnance most educators have for pupils who act out socially, decreases the probability that schools will recognize or provide for their educational needs. As Long (1983, p. 53) observed, "The key issue is not whether all troublesome children should be labeled emotionally disturbed, but rather, whether the schools, and in the final analysis society, would be better served if all children who represent aggressive, disruptive behavior, regardless of how they were labeled, received special attention and help early in their lives."

We believe that efforts to identify, diagnose, or differentiate various categories of pupils in terms of who is and who is not eligible for special education services on the basis of such elusive and unreliable criteria as SED versus SM, conduct disorder, and the like, are misplaced. It is true that not all students should qualify for services that are expensive and in short supply. The right of each pupil to be educated in the least restrictive environment also must be recognized; educators should determine that the regular education program cannot meet pupils' needs before more restrictive placements are considered. However, the practice of sorting students who are disabled by their behavior into one group that receives services and another group that does not is indefensible. It must be recognized that the behavior of antisocial students (i.e., academic deficits, low rates of academic engagement, poor peer relationships, lack of social competence) places them at risk for special education intervention or placement. The needs of at-risk pupils should be addressed, in least-restrictive settings, through prereferral interventions as a prior condition to determining their eligibility for special education programs. Unfortunately, such practices are rare in most public schools, the regular education initiative notwithstanding (Braaten et al., 1988).

The majority of students exhibiting undesirable behavior in school settings generally receive no services, inadequate services under the auspices of regular education programs, or special education services applied piecemeal or too late to be beneficial. If they are unlucky enough to reside in a state or school district in which they have been labeled as antisocial but not disabled, they may be suspended, expelled, or shunted into a variety of "alternative" placements. After years of failure and exclusion, some drop out or are pushed out of school. Others find their way into institutions and programs for delinquents by virtue of their behavior in the community. In either case, schools usually fail to recognize and appropriately meet the special education needs of students with antisocial behavior patterns.

The appalling underidentification of pupils who meet the criteria in the current SED definition is sufficient evidence that the educational system is falling short of its charge to provide a "free and appropriate" education to students who are disabled by their behavior. But we would be remiss in recommending merely that more students be certified and served under the existing definition, given its many inadequacies. In addition to extending special education services to all who need them—regardless of whether they are considered emotionally disturbed, behaviorally disordered, or socially maladjusted—the *process* of identifying and serving students also needs to be changed.

We recommend two major operational changes. First, schools should adopt systematic procedures for screening and identifying pupils who are at risk for emotional or behavioral difficulties early in their school careers. Of course, procedures to identify at-risk students must be accompanied by appropriate interventions if such activities are to be meaningful. The developing technology of early intervention through teacher consultation offers strategies for mobilizing the resources of the regular education system to meet the needs of pupils before more intrusive and stigmatizing special education interventions are considered. Johnson, Pugach, and Hammitte (1988) have observed that special education consultation models have not been widely adopted because such models are incompatible with the use of available school resources. Therefore, the development of teacher assistance teams, comprised of school staff identified with the general education program, may be a more effective strategy (see Fuchs & Fuchs, 1988; Phillips, McCullough, Nelson, & Walker, in press).

The second operational change we recommend is to revise the federal definition of SED. This definition has been widely criticized by the professional community (see our previous discussion). Moreover, the Council for Children with Behavioral Disorders (1987), the professional organization of special educators serving the SED population, has called for a change in both the federal definition and the label SED. The specific changes we suggest include eliminating the exclusion of the socially maladjusted and changing the definition's emphasis on interference with academic performance as a primary criterion. A more accurate conceptualization of the nature of behavioral disorders recognizes it as a condition that interferes with the development and maintenance of appropriate social relationships, regardless of whether academic progress is impaired. It should be noted, however, that the subjectivity inherent in defining behavior that is considered deviant from the norm cannot be eliminated completely. As Kauffman (1989) emphasized, the definition of behavior as disordered is inescapably judgmental, regardless of how objectively the behaviors in question are measured.

Again, we are not suggesting that special education labeling and placement necessarily will solve the problems of SM pupils. The lack of long-term impact of special education on the lives of students with disabilities, particularly those identified as SED, is well documented (Edgar, 1987; Neel, Meadows, Levine, & Edgar, 1988; U.S. Department of Education, 1990). Instead of merely attempting to identify and place more students in special education programs for students with emotional or behavioral disabilities, we should increase our efforts to identify and provide early intervention for students who are at risk due to their antisocial behavior patterns. Systematic school-based screening, identification, and prereferral intervention procedures (McConaughy & Achenbach, 1989; Walker, et al. 1988) must be adopted as routine school practices. Students whose needs cannot be met through this level of intervention should be referred for comprehensive assessments of their eligibility for special education programs. Programming for certified students should be orchestrated through individual educational plans that are multidisciplinary in the sense that each pupil's full range of needs is addressed, not just those needs that exist within school walls. P.L. 99-660 (the Mental Health Services Comprehensive Planning Act) is a step toward the mandate to provide appropriate community-based mental health services to children and adults in need. School and community resources should be coordinated to identify families that are at risk in terms of having at least one child who has a high probability of developing behavioral difficulties in the school or the community. Data from programs that focus on helping parents develop more effective child-rearing practices with preschool children at risk for behavioral disorders demonstrate the wisdom of early family interventions (Johnson, 1988). The national special education/mental health coalition (Forness, 1988) has added impetus to efforts for more comprehensive human services to at-risk populations.

CONCLUSION

The position taken in this article is that similarities in demographic and personal characteristics, the subjectivity inherent in identifying pupils as SED (Benson, Edwards, Rosell, & White, 1986; Kauffman, 1987, 1989), and the absence of any valid evidence or thought which justifies differentiating between SM and SED (Grosenick & Huntze, 1980) invalidate attempts to discriminate between these groups for the purpose of delivering educational services. Thus, the exclusion of SM from the federal definition is unfounded. Further, there are no instruments or methodology that can be used to differentially diagnose SED from SM either validly or reliably. In our view, the problem of delivering effective services to troubled youth supercedes that of differentially diagnosing a student as emotionally disturbed or socially maladjusted. The time spent in such attempts at differential diagnosis seldom results in more effective treatment, and the label resulting from this process may allow school personnel to abrogate responsibility by claiming that SM youth do not qualify for "special" educational provisions or program modifications.

The problem of troubled youth in the schools cannot be addressed in a piecemeal fashion, through services that are fragmented by the several bureaucracies of human service agencies. Differences among agencies in terms of definitions of their service populations and their eligibility criteria have been major factors in the failure to provide effective and cost-efficient services; attempting to make such distinctions within an agency (the public schools) is an invitation to even greater failure. Refusal to provide appropriate services to any pupil is an indictment of the educational system, just as the inability to solve the problem of antisocial behavior is an indictment of our society. The needs of troubled youth and their families across settings and time must be addressed through interdisciplinary planning and intervention, not through exclusionary practices.

REFERENCES

Achenbach, T. M. (1981). *Child Behavior Checklist*. Burlington, VT: University Associates in Psychiatry.

Achenbach, T. M. (1982). *Developmental psychotherapy* (2nd ed.). New York: Ronald Press.

American Psychiatric Association. (1976). *Diagnostic and statistical manual of mental disorders* (2nd ed.). Washington, DC: Author.

American Psychiatric Association. (1980). *Diagnostic and statistical manual of mental disorders* (3rd ed.). Washington, DC: Author.

American Psychiatric Association. (1987). *Diagnostic and statistical manual of mental disorders* (3rd ed., revised). Washington, DC: Author.

Benson, D., Edwards, L., Rosell, J., & White, M. (1986). Inclusion of socially maladjusted children and youth in the legal definition of the behaviorally disordered population: A debate. *Behavioral Disorders, 11*, 213-222.

Bower, E. M. (1982). Defining emotional disturbances: Public policy and research. *Psychology in the Schools, 19*, 55-60.

Braaten, S. R., Kauffman, J. M., Braaten, B., Polsgrove, L., & Nelson, C. M. (1988). The regular education initiative: Patent medicine for behavioral disorders. *Exceptional Children, 55*, 21-27.

Center, D. B. (April 1989a). *Social maladjustment: An interpretation*. Paper presented at the 67th Annual International Convention of the Council for Exceptional Children, San Francisco.

Center, D. B. (1989b). Social maladjustment: Definition, identification, and programing. *Focus on Exceptional Children, 22*(1), 1-12.

Center, D. B., & McKittrick, S. (1987). Disciplinary removal of special education students. *Focus on Exceptional Children, 20*(2), 1-10.

Cheney, C. O., & Sampson, K. (1990). Issues in identification and service delivery for students with conduct disorders: The "Nevada solution." *Behavioral Disorders, 15*, 174-179.

Clarizio, H. (1987). Differentiating emotionally impaired from socially maladjusted students. *Psychology in the Schools, 24*, 237-243.

Cline, D. H. (1990). A legal analysis of policy initiatives to exclude handicapped/disruptive students from special education. *Behavioral Disorders, 15*, 159-173.

Council for Children with Behavioral Disorders. (1987). *Position paper on definition and identification of students with behavioral disorders*. Reston, VA: Author.

Council for Children with Behavioral Disorders. (1990). Position paper on the provision of service to children with conduct disorders. *Behavioral Disorders, 15*, 180-189.

Council of Representatives, American Psychological Association. (1989, August 10). *APA resolution on *special education for children with conduct disorders.* Arlington, VA: Author.

Edgar, E. B. (1987). Secondary programs in special education: Are many of them justifiable? *Exceptional Children, 53*, 555-561.

Forness, S. R. (1988). Planning for the needs of children with serious emotional disturbance: The National Special Education and Mental Health Coalition. *Behavioral Disorders, 13*, 127-132.

Fuchs, D., & Fuchs, L. S. (1988). Mainstream assistance teams to accommodate difficult-to-teach students in general education. In J. L. Graden, J. E. Zins, & M. J. Curtis (Eds.), *Alternative educational delivery systems: Enhancing instructional options for all students* (pp. 49-70). Washington, DC: National Association of School Psychologists.

Grosenick, J. K., & Huntze, S. L. (1980). *National needs analysis in behavior disorders: Severe behavior disorders.* Columbia: University of Missouri.

Honig v. Doe. (1988). 56 S. Ct. 27.

Institute of Medicine. (1989). *Research on children and adolescents with mental, behavioral, and developmental disorders.* Washington, DC: National Academy Press.

Johnson, D. L. (1988). Primary prevention of behavior problems in young children: The Houston parent-child development center. In R. H. Price, E. L. Cowen, R. P. Lorion, & J. Ramos-McKay (Eds.), *Fourteen ounces of prevention: A casebook for practitioners.* (pp.44-52) Washington, DC: American Psychological Association.

Johnson, L. J., Pugach, M. C., & Hammitte, D. J. (1988). Barriers to effective special education consultation. *Remedial and Special Education, 9*(6), 41-47.

Kauffman, J. M. (1987). Social policy issues in special education and related services for emotionally disturbed children and youth. In N. G. Haring (Ed.), *Measuring and managing behavior disorders* (pp. x-xx). Seattle: University of Washington Press.

Kauffman, J. M. (1989). *Characteristics of behavior disorders of children and youth* (4th ed.). Columbus, OH: Merrill.

Kazdin, A. E. (1987). *Conduct disorders in childhood and adolescence.* Beverly Hills, CA: Sage.

Kelly, E. J. (1988). *The Differential Problem Sorter manual: Rationale and procedures distinguishing between conduct problem and emotionally disturbed students and populations.* Las Vegas: University of Nevada—Las Vegas.

Kerr, M. M., Nelson, C. M., & Lambert, D. L. (1987). *Helping adolescents with learning and behavior problems.* Columbus, OH: Merrill.

Knitzer, J., Steinberg, Z., & Fleisch, B. (1990). *At the schoolhouse door: An examination of programs and policies for children with behavioral and emotional problems.* New York: Bank Street College of Education.

Long, K. A. (1983). Emotionally disturbed children as the underdetected and underserved public school population: Reasons and recommendations. *Behavioral Disorders, 9*, 46-54.

Mack, J. H. (1985). An analysis of state definitions of severely emotionally disturbed children. *Policy Options Report.* Reston, VA: Council for Exceptional Children.

McConaughy, S. M., & Achenbach, T. M. (1989). Empirically based assessment of serious emotional disturbance. *Journal of School Psychology, 27*, 91-117.

McMahon, R. J. (1984). Behavioral checklists and rating scales. In T. H. Ollendick & M. Hersen (Eds.), *Child behavioral assessment: Principles and procedures* (pp. 80-105). New York: Pergamon.

Morgan, D. J. (1979). Prevalence and types of handicapped conditions found in juvenile correctional institutions: A national survey. *Journal of Special Education, 13*, 283-295.

Murphy, D. M. (1986). The prevalence of handicapping conditions among juvenile delinquents. *Remedial and Special Education, 7*(3), 7-17.

Neel, R. S., Meadows, N., Levine, P., & Edgar, E. B. (1988). What happens after special education: A statewide follow-up study of secondary students who have behavioral disorders. *Behavioral Disorders, 13*, 209-216.

Neel, R. S., & Rutherford, R. B. (1981). Exclusion of the socially maladjusted from services under P.L. 94-142. In F. H. Wood (Ed.), *Perspectives for a new decade: Education's responsibility for seriously emotionally disturbed and behaviorally disordered youth* (pp. 79-84). Reston, VA: Council for Exceptional Children.

Nelson, C. M., & Rutherford, R. B. (1990). Troubled youth in the public schools: Emotionally disturbed or socially maladjusted? In P. E. Leone (Ed.), *Understanding troubled and troubling youth* (pp. 39-60). Newbury Park, CA: Sage.

Phillips, V., McCullough, L., Nelson, C. M., & Walker, H. M. (in press). Teamwork among teachers: Promoting a statewide agenda for students at risk for school failure. *Special Services in the Schools.*

Quay, H. C. (1975). Classification in the treatment of delinquency and antisocial behavior. In N. Hobbs (Ed.), *Issues in the classification of children* (Vol. l, pp. 377-389). San Francisco: Jossey-Bass.

Quay, H. C., & Peterson, D. R. (1983). *Revised Behavior Problem Checklist.* Coral Gables, FL: University of Miami.

Robins, L. N. (1966). *Deviant children grown up.* Baltimore: Williams and Wilkins.

Robins, L. N. (1979). Follow-up studies. In H. C. Quay & J. S. Werry (Eds.), *Psychopathological disorders of childhood* (2nd ed., pp. 483-513). New York: Wiley.

Rutherford, R. B., Nelson, C. M., & Wolford, B. I. (1985). Special education in the most restrictive environment: Correctional special education. *Journal of Special Education, 19*, 59-71.

Salvia, J., & Ysseldyke, J. E. (1988). *Assessment in special and remedial education* (4th ed.). Boston: Houghton Mifflin.

Shinn, M. R., Ramsey, E., Walker, H. M., Stieber, S., & O'Neill, R. (1987). Antisocial behavior in school settings: Initial differences in an at risk and normal population. *Journal of Special Education, 21*, 69-84.

Simcha-Fagan, O., Langner, T., Gersten, J., & Eisenberg, J. (1975). *Violent and antisocial behavior: A longitudinal study of urban youth.* Unpublished report of the Office of Child Development, OCD-CB-480.

Slenkovitch, J. E. (1983). *P. L. 94-142 as applied to DSM III diagnoses: An analysis of DSM III diagnoses vis-a-vis special education law.* Cupertino, CA: Kinghorn Press.

Slenkovitch, J. E. (1984). *Understanding special education law* (Vol. 1). Cupertino, CA: Kinghorn Press.

U. S. Department of Education, Office of Special Education and Rehabilitative Services. (1989). *Annual report to Congress on the implementation of the Education of the Handicapped Act.* Washington, DC: Author.

U. S. Department of Education, Office of Special Education and Rehabilitative Services. (1990). *Twelfth annual report to Congress on the implementation of the Education of Public Law 94-142.* Washington, DC: U. S. Government Printing Office.

U. S. Department of Health, Education, and Welfare, Office of Education. (1977, Tuesday, 23 August). Education of handicapped children: Implementation of Part B of the Education of the Handicapped Act. *Federal Register, 42,* (163).

Wagner, M. (1989). *The national longitudinal transition study.* Palo Alto, CA: Stanford Research Institute.

Walker, H. M., & Fabré, T. R. (1987). Assessment of behavior disorders in the school setting: Issues, problems, and strategies revisited. In N. G. Haring (Ed.), *Measuring and managing behavior disorders* (pp. 198-243). Seattle: University of Washington Press.

Walker, H. M., Severson, H., Stiller, B., Williams, G., Haring, N. G., Shinn, M. R., & Todis, B. (1988). Systematic screening of pupils in the elementary age range at risk for behavior disorders: Development and trial testing of a multiple gating model. *Remedial and Special Education, 9*(3), 8-14.

Walker, H. M., Shinn, M. R., O'Neill, R. E., & Ramsey, E. (1987). A longitudinal assessment of the development of antisocial behavior in boys: Rationale, methodology, and first year results. *Remedial and Special Education, 8*(4), 7-16.

Walker, H. M., Stieber, S., & O'Neill, R. E. (1990). Middle school behavioral profiles of antisocial and at risk control boys: Descriptive and predictive outcomes. *Exceptionality, 1,* 61-77.

Wolf, M. M., Braukmann, C. J., & Ramp, K. A. (1987). Serious delinquent behavior as part of a significantly handicapping condition: Cures and supportive environments. *Journal of Applied Behavior Analysis, 20,* 347-359.

Wood, F. H., Smith, C. R., & Grimes, J. (Eds.). (1985). *The Iowa assessment model in behavioral disorders: A training manual.* Des Moines, IA: Department of Public Instruction.

Yell, M. L. (1989). *Honig v. Doe*: The suspension and expulsion of handicapped students. *Exceptional Children, 56,* 60-69.

The Culturally Sensitive Disciplinarian

Thomas McIntyre

Thomas McIntyre, Professor, Department of Special Education, Hunter College of City University of New York, 695 Park Avenue, New York, New York 10021

ABSTRACT

Given the increasing cultural diversity of the schoolage population, teachers must become more aware of cultural differences in behavior. This article addresses some of these differences and recommends behavior management modifications.

Since their inception, our schools have changed from predominantly white institutions to multicultural environments. While the 25 largest school systems have a student population comprised mostly of minority students (National Information Center for Children and Youth with Handicaps, 1988), nonurban areas are also seeing such developments (Alston, cited in Armstrong, 1991). By the year 2000, one-third (Grossman, 1990) to one-half (Wilson, 1988) of America's school students will be from a minority group.

At present, 92% of the teaching force is from the white majority culture. This figure will increase to 95% by the turn of the century (Henry, 1990). The contrast in cultural background between teachers and students applies to an even greater extent in special education where minority youth are overrepresented in various programs for the disabled including those for pupils with emotional or behavioral disorders (Chinn & Hughes, 1987; Viadero, 1992). Much of this phenomenon may be attributable to the mismatch between the expectations present in the students' homes and those of the school environments (Almanza & Moseley, 1980; Grossman, 1990).

Behavioral patterns and actions considered to be abnormal vary by culture (Light & Martin, 1985; Toth, 1990). When educators and their charges come from different backgrounds, it can be expected that each will often display behaviors different from those in the other's culture. Given that most individuals truly understand only their own culture and find it difficult to appreciate behavior culturally different from their own (Garcia, 1978; Grossman, 1990; McIntyre, 1992), there is a strong chance that teachers will misinterpret their pupils' culturally-based behavior as requiring a referral for special education or at least disciplinary action (Foster, 1986; Grossman, 1990; Hanna, 1988). Indeed, children who display culturally diverse behaviors, especially recent immigrants (Sugai, 1988), are particularly susceptible to diagnosis for behavioral disorders (Hanna, 1988; Sugai & Maheady, 1988).

CULTURAL DIFFERENCES IN BEHAVIOR

A lack of appreciation and tolerance for cultural differences is often found among educators. These teachers expect their students to adopt majority culture behaviors overnight, denying the validity of centuries of cultural practice. "The teacher's expectation is that the student should be compliant, docile, and responsive to authority. The student is expected to conform to a standard of behavior that the teacher is familiar with, the compliant child standard that was indicative of the teacher's upbringing" (Dent, 1976, p. 178). These teachers are at risk for reacting to culturally determined behavior in ways that are insensitive, inappropriate, counterproductive, or offensive to students and their culture.

As an example of culturally disrespectful intervention, consider that in the majority American culture a child is expected to look at the authority figure when being disciplined. Lowered eyes are associated with deceit or inattention (Armstrong, 1991; Grossman, 1990). To gain eye contact, the instructor may lift the student's chin and say, "Look at me when I'm talking to you." The educator may not realize that in many Asian, African-American, and Hispanic homes, children are taught to lower their eyes when being disciplined as a sign of respect and submission (Armstrong, 1991; Grossman, 1990; Nine-Curt, 1976). *Assertive Discipline* (Canter & Canter, 1976) and other behavior management systems that recommend gaining eye contact while disciplining unknowingly fail to respect the behavior promoted in the student's home environment. Additionally, the teacher probably fails to realize that direct eye contact by these students during disciplinary situations typically indicates defiance rather than respect (Grossman, 1990; Hanna, 1988). The educator may also not realize that many culturally diverse children smile during disciplinary situations, not to express defiance, but rather, due to anxiety, appeasement attempts or confusion as to why the instructor is confronting them (Henkin & Nguyen, 1981; Nine-Curt, 1976).

Minority students are often penalized by teaching methods which contrast with their culturally based preferred style of learning (Blackorby & Edgar, 1990). Consider, for example, the individualistic and competitive environment of the typical classroom which works against the more cooperative learning style common among Hispanics, African-Americans, and Native Americans (Brendtro, Brokenleg, & Van Bockern, 1991; "CASSP national workshop," 1988; Grossman, 1990). While displaying their culture's helpfulness, brotherhood, or generosity, students may assist their peers or allow them to copy their answers, not considering this to be "cheating" (Grossman, 1984). If criticized for doing this in front of their peers or made to compete against their will, these pupils may rebel against such treatment or withdraw from further attempts to succeed in school or relate to their teachers (Grossman, 1990). Majority culture educators may then use their own culturally based disciplinary behavior: removing affection (Grossman, 1984). However, this reaction is less commonly found in the students' culture and may not gain the desired results (Grossman, 1984).

Other traditional methods of promoting positive classroom behavior such as checks, gold stars, sweets, and prizes may also be less effective with Hispanic and other learners. The reason, explains Grossman (1984, pp. 37 and 40), is that "Hispanics tend to be more interested in and dependent on the approval of others than Anglos who are more likely to be receptive to more impersonal and materialistic forms of recognition." Instead, teachers should use praise, hugs, pats on the back, and other personal contact. They should also stress that Hispanic students' families will be proud of them and share the honor of their accomplishments. This particular strategy might also be useful in motivating Arab and Asian students who wish to bring pride to their families (Nydel, 1987; Wei, 1984).

While touch is often recommended as a reinforcement procedure, especially for cultural groups that use a great deal of bodily contact, it may be contra-indicated for some Asian students. Those whose heritage was influenced by Confucianism view the body as being more sacred as one approaches the area of the head where the soul is believed to reside (Kaczor, 1988). Given this wide body spacing and the lack of touch between Asian individuals (Yao, 1980), teachers should avoid certain actions that are used to motivate and reinforce Hispanic, Arabian, and African-American students (e.g., hair mussing, placing hands on the shoulder, back slapping).

While the majority culture places great emphasis on promptness and working diligently on task (Althen, 1988), most other groups have a more flexible view of time (Nine-Curt, 1976; Sung, 1987). As a result, minority students may be late to school or might not complete classroom work as quickly as their majority culture peers. They may be viewed as being "off task" and tersely told to "get to work." When rushed, or told to stop working before completion of that assignment in order to begin the next task with their peers, the students may resist, appearing to misbehave (Grossman, 1984).

Other groups may also be negatively affected by the demands of the traditional school setting. A teacher's expectations for quiet, nonactive student behavior would be in opposition to the more active and emotionally outspoken contributory styles of Arabian students (Nydel, 1987). This can result in the students' behavior being viewed as inappropriate. A similar learning style is frequently evident among African-American pupils who show attention and cognitive involvement with vocal responses, exuberance, and physical movement (Gay, 1975; Ogbu, 1988). Teachers oftentimes consider these students to be inattentive, restless, disruptive, or hostile (Gay, 1975), and evidencing "an attitude" (Gilmore, 1985). They may impose disciplinary procedures rather than incorporating spontaneity, performance, and audience reaction into their lessons.

Another common misunderstanding involves a teacher who explains a task to an Asian student and then asks if the directions are understood. Although the student says "yes", upon later review the teacher finds that the instructions were not comprehended. He or she is perplexed by the apparent dishonesty of the student, unaware that the pupil may have been attempting to "save face" (Woo, 1985). Among the Asian cultures there is a commonly held belief that one should avoid conflict or public embarrassment which would shame not only the individuals involved, but by extension, their families (Henkin & Nguyen, 1981; Leung, 1988; Wei, 1984). The student in the testing situation may have been trying to prevent the dishonor or humiliation of admitting that he or she was incapable of understanding the directions (Woo, 1985), or perhaps the pupil was trying to avoid humiliating the teacher for not having done a good job of explaining the task (Wei, 1984). These students may also fail to volunteer answers during class discussions for fear of giving an incorrect response (Henkin & Nguyen, 1981; Woo, 1985).

The same applies to the "pow-wow" (Hobbs, 1966) in which a student's report on whether he or she has achieved preselected goals is followed by peer commentary as to whether they agree. This could be quite uncomfortable for Asian students as they might publicly "lose face" if goals have not been attained.

Therefore, teachers should not assume that the less direct and more subdued behavior common in the Asian cultures is indicative of "sneakiness" or noncompliance. While penalizing the student for this behavior is inappropriate, any shame and embarrassment is compounded when public reprimands such as those in the warning system recommended in *Assertive Discipline* (Canter & Canter, 1976) are used (Jones, 1991). Listing the student's name, followed by checkmarks indicating recurring misbehavior, may cause Asian students (and many Arabian students whose families also place great emphasis on family honor) to "lose face." A private rather than public critique of behavior is the intervention of choice.

Contrary to the facesaving behavior promoted by certain cultures, other groups provide an upbringing which may increase the likelihood of teacher-student conflict. For example, in the Hispanic culture which tends to be male dominant (Arredondo, 1991; Devore & Schlesinger, 1987), adolescent boys may resist complying with commands from female educators (Grossman, 1984). With these students, cooperation is best gained through nonauthoritative methods which request rather than demand compliance (Grossman, 1984).

Defiance may also be demonstrated to a great extent by low income urban African-American youth whose parents often teach them to fight to avoid being victimized in their tough neighborhoods (Hanna, 1988; McIntyre, 1991, in press). Growing up in these areas is more likely to produce traits that impede success in school (e.g., a more physical style of action, a greater approval of the use of violence, less disguised aggression, lack of subtlety in verbiage, and ridiculing of others; Hanna, 1988; McIntyre, 1991, in press). These behaviors and the previously mentioned learning style differences may explain why African-American youth receive one-third of the corporal punishments (Quality Education for Minorities,

1990), are twice as likely as whites to be suspended (Gibbs, 1988), and are suspended for longer periods than whites (Gibbs, 1988).

Few teachers realize that African-American, Mexican-American, Native Hawaiian, and Native American youth are often under great pressure from their peers *not* to achieve in school (Gollnick & Chinn, 1990; Hanna, 1988; Ogbu, 1990). Individual success in schooling or professions is viewed as inappropriate if the group does not also advance (Fordham, 1988; Ogbu, 1990). For many students merely attending school is viewed as evidence of rejection of their culture (Fordham, 1988; Ogbu, 1990). For others, misbehavior is a strategy of resistance to being pressured to think and act "white" in the schools (Fordham, 1988; Gibson, 1988; Ogbu, 1988, 1990; Quality Education for Minorities, 1990). Because of the peer pressure, those who strive for academic excellence may feel the need to camouflage their academic efforts (Fordham, 1988).

This rejection of schooling may result in disciplinary action or referral for behavior disorders services. Teachers can best assist and support these students by using private disciplinary action (and even allowing usually compliant students to misbehave at times), modifying instruction to better match their culturally determined learning styles, allowing them to downplay accomplishments, and avoiding public recognition unless approved by them (McIntyre, in press). Teachers can expect that these students might not respond well to public praise and rewards for actions which may be perceived as "acting white."

Even devoid of racial influences, defiant and aggressive behaviors occur more often in the lower socioeconomic stratum (McIntyre, in press; Strom, 1965). As a result of harsh and inconsistent home discipline (Hanna, 1988; Horton & Hunt, 1976), low income urban pupils may have developed an escape and avoidance reaction style to discipline, or come to view physical punishment as a sign of caring (Rosenfeld, 1971; Silverstein & Krate, 1975). They may be confused by the subtle and supportive behavior management practices of middle-class teachers (Hanna, 1988; Harrison-Ross & Wyden, 1973).

While some educators support corporal punishment in the belief that these students are best disciplined by a style to which they are accustomed (Bauer, Du-

banoski, Yamauchi, & Honbo, 1990), most middle-class oriented educators believe in permissiveness and an appeal to reason. The first group's methods are ineffective because schools cannot offer aversive consequences as severe as those at home. The second group fails to realize that lower-class youth have a different frame of reference regarding discipline that involves physicalness and toughness (Foster, 1986; McIntyre, in press). These youth "test" teachers to see if they can "make" the youth behave (Foster, 1986) and come to view whites and middle-class minorities as passive and weak if they cannot do so (Hanna, 1988). Implementing a structured behavior management approach in which predetermined penalties are consistently administered for violations of clearly stated rules gives one "clout" and influence. However, this should still be blended with reinforcement for appropriate behavior in order to promote a positive classroom climate.

The emphasis on positiveness also applies to working with Native American students. The imposition of authority in a demanding or demeaning manner typically results in passive resistance and withdrawal on the part of these pupils (Hurlburt, Gade, & McLaughlin, 1990; Kleinfeld, 1972). An appeal to their good nature and the use of appropriate reinforcement is more productive than coercive or confrontational strategies (Brendtro et al., 1991).

The same principle applies for Arabian-American students. As in the Hispanic and Native American cultures, frank criticism may be perceived as a personal insult (Nine-Curt, 1976). Best practice includes indirect criticism mixed with encouragement and praise regarding any positive points or expectations that were met (Nydel, 1987).

RECOMMENDATIONS

It is imperative that educators practice respect for culturally different behavior. Instead of viewing behavior as *right* or *wrong,* it is best judged by how well it is suited to the demands of the educational environment (although schools must also assess how well they are meeting the needs of their culturally diverse populations). To better serve their charges, educational personnel need to develop an awareness of how cultural background affects the way one behaves, and con-

versely, how one perceives and judges the behaviors of those not like oneself.

As Light and Martin (1985, p. 43) point out, "An understanding of cultural expectations and roles can contribute to the development of child management techniques specifically designed to eliminate value differences between a child's family, the school system, and the larger society." By working *with* rather than *against* a culture, any student resentment about having to behave differently in school can be managed (Grossman, 1990). One recommendation regarding discipline which pertains to all groups is to be positive rather than negative or confrontational. A skilled, culturally sensitive behavior manager entices rather than coerces students into proper behavior (Bauer et al., 1990).

For students from African-American, Hispanic, Native American, and Arabian cultures which place greater emphasis on socializing and bodily contact than the white and Asian cultures (Kleinfeld, 1972; Nine-Curt, 1976; Nydel, 1987), teachers can increase their effectiveness by displaying more "warmth" (Kleinfeld, 1972). This involves reinforcing students via the use of touch, hugs, smiles, and closer body spacing. When discipline is necessary, because of their desire to socialize with peers, timeout may be especially effective with these pupils (Hanna, 1988).

In order for our schools to become more culturally sensitive in their disciplinary practice, changes will need to be implemented at each educational stratum (McIntyre, 1992). Teacher training institutions must assume the larger share of the burden of imparting cultural information. At this level, it can be assured that future teachers will study this information and be guided in its use in practicum settings. Generally, however, university programs in education are not presenting this information (Garcia, 1978; Yates, 1988). Before teacher trainers can impart information regarding cultural characteristics, instructional modifications, and culturally sensitive behavior management practices, they must first educate themselves in this area.

Schools can promote cultural understanding in a number of ways ranging from conducting inservice sessions with national level consultants or local civic leaders of particular cultures to hiring individuals from minority groups who are able to communicate information across cultures (Armstrong, 1991). Additionally, schools might provide services to culturally diverse students to assist them in becoming *cultural chameleons* capable of displaying *school behavior* if their culturally-based actions interfere with educational achievement or interaction with others. This is not an easy decision for educators and the community at large who must wrestle with the issue of whether to promote and/or teach majority culture behaviors to the student population. Caught in the horns of a cultural dilemma, they must decide whether to chance making one culture look preferable to another or hazard impairing students' future employability by failing to expose them to the expectations of the typical workplace.

If it is deemed necessary to teach white behavior, this can be accomplished via specially designed lessons perhaps utilizing activities from published social skills curricula. Students would then role-play common situations. Career education lessons that focus on the benefits of being able to display office behavior might also be planned.

Paramount at the classroom level, however, is the creation of an atmosphere of cultural tolerance and acceptance. Students of all ethnic cultures need to feel valued, respected, and psychologically and physically safe. This is accomplished by proactively adapting one's classroom management study to the students' culturally-based characteristics (Grossman, 1990).

Finally, it is imperative that professional organizations concerned with cultural diversity and behavioral disorders focus more on culturally-based differences in behavior and culturally sensitive behavior management practices in their publications and conference planning.

CONCLUSIONS

Teachers oftentimes create much of the misbehavior about which they complain. Via modification of traditional behavior management procedures one can create a productive classroom environment that values the culture of one's students (Jones, 1991). When educators are knowledgeable of and able to critically examine differences in culturally-based behavior, they can be more confident that all students are being treated fairly and respectfully.

REFERENCES

Althen, G. (1988). *American ways.* Yarmouth, ME: Intercultural Press.

Almanza, H., & Moseley, W. (1980). Curriculum adaptions and modification for culturally diverse handicapped children. *Exceptional Children, 46,* 608–614.

Armstrong, L. (1991, March 20). Census confirms remarkable shifts in ethnic makeup. *Education Week,* pp. 1, 16.

Arredondo, P. (1991). Counseling Latinas. In C. Lee & B. Richardson (Eds.), *Multicultural issues in counseling: New approaches to diversity* (pp. 143–156). Alexandria, VA: American Association for Counseling and Development.

Bauer, G. B., Dubanoski, R., Yamauchi, L. A., & Honbo, K. M. (1990). Corporal punishment and the schools. *Education and Urban Society, 22,* 285–299.

Blackorby, J., & Edgar, E. (1990). A third of our youth? A look at the problem of high school dropout among mildly handicapped students. *Journal of Special Education, 24,* 508–510.

Brendtro, L. K., Brokenleg, M., & Van Bockern, S. (1991). The circle of courage. *Beyond Behavior, 2*(1), 5–12.

CASSP national workshop identifies culturally specific needs of minority children with emotional handicaps. *Focal Point, 3*(1), 5–6.

Canter, L., & Canter, M. (1976). *Assertive discipline: A take-charge approach for today's educator.* Los Angeles: Canter & Assoc.

Chinn, P., & Hughes, S. (1987). Representation of minority students in special education classes. *Remedial and Special Education, 8*(4), 41–46.

Dent, H. L. (1976). Assessing Black children for mainstream placement. In R. L. Jones (Ed.), *Mainstreaming and the minority child* (pp. 77–91). Reston, VA: The Council for Exceptional Children.

Devore, W., & Schlesinger, E. G. (1987). *Ethnic-sensitive social work practice* (2nd ed.). Columbus, OH: Merrill.

Fordham, S. (1988). Racelessness as a factor in Black students' school success: Pragmatic strategy or pyrrhic victory? *Harvard Educational Review, 58*(1), 54–84.

Foster, H. (1986). *Ribbin', jivin', and playin' the dozens.* New York: Ballantine.

Garcia, R. (1978). *Fostering a pluralistic society through multi-ethnic education.* Bloomington, IN: Phi Delta Kappa.

Gay, G. (1975, October). Cultural differences important in the education of Black children. *Momentum,* pp. 30–33.

Gibbs, J. B. (Ed.). (1988). *Young, Black, and male in America: An endangered species.* New York: Auburn House.

Gibson, M. (1988). *Accommodation without assimilation: Sikh immigrants in an American high school.* Ithaca, NY: Cornell University Press.

Gilmore, P. (1985). Gimme room: School resistance, attitude, and access to literacy. *Journal of Education, 167,* 111–128.

Gollnick, D., & Chinn, P. (1990). *Multicultural education in a pluralistic society.* Columbus, OH: Merrill.

Grossman, H. (1984). *Educating Hispanic students: Cultural implications for instruction, classroom management, counseling, and assessment.* Springfield, IL: C. C. Thomas.

Grossman, H. (1990). *Trouble-free teaching: Solutions to behavior problems in the classroom.* Mountain View, CA: Mayfield.

Hanna, J. (1988). *Disruptive school behavior: Class, race, and culture.* New York: Holmes & Meier.

Harrison-Ross, P., & Wyden, B. (1973). *The Black child.* Berkeley, CA: Medallion.

Henkin, A., & Nguyen, L. (1981). *Between two cultures: The Vietnamese in America.* Saratoga, CA: Rand.

Henry, W. (1990, April 9). Beyond the melting pot. *Time,* p. 28.

Hobbs, N. (1966). Helping disturbed children: Psychological and ecological strategies. *American Psychologist, 21,* 1105–1115.

Horton, P., & Hunt, C. (1976). *Sociology* (2nd ed.). New York: McGraw-Hill.

Hurlburt, G., Gade, E., & McLaughlin, J. (1990, May). Teaching attitudes and study attitudes of Indian education students. *Journal of American Indian Education,* pp. 12–18.

Jones, V. (1991). Responding to students' behavior problems. *Beyond Behavior, 2*(1), 13–16.

Kaczor, B. (1988, December 20). Military course helps avoid cross-cultural clashes, gaffs. *Saint Petersburg Times,* p. 6B.

Kleinfeld, J. (1972). *Effective teachers of Indian and Eskimo high school students.* Anchorage: University of Alaska, Institute of Social, Economic, and Government Research.

Leung, E. (1988). Cultural and acculturational commonalities and diversities among Asian Americans: Identification and programming considerations. In A. Ortiz & B. Ramirez (Eds.), *Schools and culturally diverse exceptional students* (pp. 86–95). Reston, VA: The Council for Exceptional Children.

Light, H., & Martin, R. (1985). Guidance of American Indian children. *Journal of American Indian Education, 25*(1), 42–46.

McIntyre, T. (1991). Understanding and defusing the streetcorner behavior of urban Black socially maladjusted youth. In R. B. Rutherford, Jr., S. A. DiGangi, & S. R. Mathur (Eds.), *Severe behavior disorders of children and youth* (Vol. 14, pp. 85–97). Reston, VA: Council for Children with Behavioral Disorders.

McIntyre, T. (1992). A primer on cultural diversity for educators. *Multicultural Forum, 1,* 6, 13.

McIntyre, T. (in press). Teaching urban behavior disordered youth. In R. Peterson & S. Ishii-Jordan (Eds.), *Behavior disorders in the context of culture and community.* Boston, MA: Brookline.

National Information Center for Children and Youth with Handicaps. (1988). *Minority issues in special education: A portrait of the future.* Washington, DC: Author.

Nine-Curt, C. (1976). *Nonverbal communication in Puerto Rico.* Cambridge, MA: National Assessment and Dissemination Center for Bilingual/Bicultural Education.

Nydel, M. (1987). *Understanding Arabs.* Yarmouth, ME: Intercultural Press.

Ogbu, J. (1988). Class stratification, racial stratification, and schooling. In L. Weiss (Ed.), *Class, race, and gender in American education* (pp. 163–180). Albany, NY: State University of New York Press.

Ogbu, J. (1990). Minority education in comparative perspective. *Journal of Negro Education, 1,* 45–57.

Quality Education for Minorities. (1990). *Education that works: An action plan for the education of minorities.* Cambridge, MA: Massachusetts Institute of Technology.

Rosenfeld, G. (1971). *Shut those thick lips! A study of slum school failure.* New York: Holt.

Silverstein, B., & Krate, R. (1975). *Children of the dark ghetto: A developmental psychology.* New York: Praeger.

Strom, R. (1965). *Teaching in the slum school.* Columbus, OH: Merrill.

Sugai, G. (1988). Educational assessment of culturally diverse and behavior disordered students: An examination of critical effect. In A. Ortiz & B. Ramirez (Eds.), *Schools and culturally diverse exceptional students* (pp. 63–75). Reston, VA: The Council for Exceptional Children.

Sugai, G., & Maheady, L. (1988, Fall). Cultural diversity and individual assessment for behavior disorders. *Teaching Exceptional Children,* pp. 27–31.

Sung, B. (1987). *The adjustment experience of Chinese immigrant children in New York City.* Staten Island, NY: Center for Migration Studies.

Toth, M. K. (1990). *Understanding and treating conduct disorders.* Austin, TX: Pro-Ed.

Viadero, D. (1992, April 29). New definition of 'emotionally disturbed' sought. *Education Week,* p. 24.

Wei, T. (1984). *Vietnamese refugee students: A handbook for school personnel.* Cambridge, MA: Lesley College (EDAC).

Wilson, R. (1988, May 4). Bennett notes improvement of schools in past 5 years but paints bleak portrait of U.S. education in report. *Chronicle of Higher Education,* p. A29.

Woo, J. (1985). *The Chinese-speaking student: A composite profile.* New York: Hunter College, Bilingual Education Multifunctional Support Center.

Yao, E. (1980). Implications of biculturalism for the learning process of middle-class Asian children in the United States. *Journal of Education, 61*(4), 61–72.

Yates, J. (1988). Demography as it affects special education. In A. Ortiz & B. Ramirez (Eds.), *Schools and culturally diverse exceptional students* (pp. 1–5). Reston, VA: The Council for Exceptional Children.

Children with Communication Disorders

Communication that calls attention to itself, and/or interferes with relaying a message, and/or distresses either the speaker or the listener is considered disordered. Communication is defined as the transmission of information. Language is the set of symbols used to represent the message being transmitted. Speech, a subsystem of language, is the physical process involved in producing the sound symbols of the language. Both communication and language can be nonverbal. Speech is oral.

Communication disorders can take two forms: delays and disorders. Delays are quite common and are usually resolved easily with proper treatment. Delays in language have the highest cure rate and the shortest time in need of special services of any of the conditions of exceptionality. Delays are often due to lack of language stimulation, bilingual or multilingual stimulation, or hearing impairments.

A disordered form of language is less common than a language delay and usually requires more treatment. Many language disorders are complicated by other areas of exceptionality (e.g., disorders of behavior, mentation, learning, audition, physical coordination). Language disorders may involve aphasia (no language) or dysphasia (difficulty with language). Language disorders may be due to disordered mentation or to anatomical defects such as cleft lip and/or palate, damaged vocal cords, defects of the lips, teeth, or tongue, or may be acquired after injuries—including brain injuries. Language disorders may involve receptive disorders (difficulty in understanding language) and/or expressive disorders (difficulty in expressing oneself through language). The American Speech-Language-Hearing Association (ASLHA) has identified three underlying problems in language disorders: the form the language takes (involving rules and structural principles); the content of the language (involving semantic meanings); and the function of the language in communication (involving practical, pragmatic usage).

Speech, the subsystem of language involving oral production of sound, may be disordered in one or more of three forms: articulation, voice, or fluency.

Articulation involves the functioning of muscles and nerves, of the tongue, lips, teeth, and mouth to produce recognizable speech sounds. Four possible ways in which articulation can be disordered are substitution of sounds, distortion of sounds, omission of sounds, or the addition of extra sounds.

Voice involves respiration by the lungs, phonation by the larynx and vocal cords, and resonance through the air passages of the nose to control sound quality. Two possible ways in which voice can be disordered are phonation (breathy, strained, husky, hoarse, no sounds) and resonance (hypernasality, hyponasality).

Fluency involves appropriate pauses and hesitations to keep speech natural, smooth, and understandable. Two possible ways in which fluency can be disordered are by cluttering (very rapid speech with extra sounds) and by stuttering (verbal blocks, and/or repetitions of sounds, especially at the beginning of words).

Each child can be expected to have his or her own unique differences in language reception and production and speech coordination. In addition, each child will communicate differently, depending on personality factors, information-processing factors, and motivational factors. Assessment of when language and/or speech is delayed or disordered is, therefore, very difficult.

Speech-language pathologists are therapists who are prepared to help alleviate all the problems of language and speech. When a child is assessed as having a communication disorder, PL 94-142, and its amendment PL 99-457, entitle that child to free and appropriate speech-language therapy in the least restrictive environment. Public Law 99-457 ensures services for infants, toddlers, and their families if a speech-language disorder is diagnosed early (e.g., cleft palate speech). Whenever a child receives special services for a communication disorder, the therapy is more successful and shorter when there is parental involvement and transdisciplinary cooperation. Individualized family service plans (IFSPs) and individualized education programs (IEPs) need to be annually updated to reflect the effectiveness of prior therapy, the new short-term and long-term goals, the changing nature of the communication disorder, and the special services required. Children with communication problems make up the second largest group of children in the United States receiving special educational services, after children with learning disabilities. The earlier each child begins therapy, the better the prognosis.

Therapy and transdisciplinary approaches to remediation of communication disorders are the most common forms of intervention. However, for some children, speech-language therapy and family-school cooperation cannot cure or substantially alleviate the problem. For some children, intervention takes the form of augmented communication or facilitated communication. There are many new forms of augmentative and facilitated communications. These include sign language, keyboards for typing words, computers with synthetic voices, talking picture boards, and talking beams. Which forms of augmented or

facilitated communication are used with each child are ideally determined by a transdisciplinary team including parent, child (if old enough), teacher, and speech-language pathologist.

Dialects should not be assessed as communication disorders in and of themselves. It is possible, however, for a child with a communication disorder to have it complicated by a speech dialect. Special care must be made when assessing linguistically different students for inclusion in special educational services. To be communication disordered, the child should have difficulty in his or her mother tongue, not merely in English. Bilingual special education may provide remediation in both the mother tongue and English. Transitional programs help non-English-speaking children learn the English language sufficiently for instruction to take place in English.

The first article selected for this unit addresses techniques that work to promote language in early childhood. The second article defines programs and services for culturally and linguistically diverse learners in special education. The next article discusses nonverbal symbols that are used as a means of communicating thoughts and emotions. Nonverbal language is often used by school children in place of speech. The final article focuses on one of many forms of augmentative communication: a picture task analysis.

Looking Ahead: Challenge Questions

How can early childhood educators promote appropriate speech and language?

How can the learning environment be enhanced for culturally and linguistically diverse learners?

Can teachers understand the language of nonverbal behavior?

How can picture tasks be used to augment speech?

Preschool Classroom Environments That Promote Communication

Michaelene M. Ostrosky

Ann P. Kaiser

Michaelene M. Ostrosky *(CEC Chapter #46) is a Doctoral Student and* **Ann P. Kaiser** *(CEC Chapter #69) is Professor, Department of Special Education, Peabody College of Vanderbilt University, Nashville, Tennessee.*

Children learn what language *is* by learning what language can *do* (Bates, 1976; Hart, 1985). The function of language depends upon it's effects on the environment. An environment that contains few reinforcers and few objects of interest or meets children's needs without requiring language is *not* a functional environment for learning or teaching language.

Recent research suggests that environmental arrangement is an important strategy for teachers who want to promote communication in classrooms (Alpert, Kaiser, Ostrosky, & Hemmeter, 1987; Haring, Neetz, Lovinger, Peck, & Semmell, 1987). To encourage use of language, classrooms should be arranged so that there are materials and activities of interest to the children. In addition, teachers must mediate the environment by presenting materials in response to children's requests and other uses of language (Hart & Rogers-Warren, 1978). Creating such opportunities and consequences for language use through environmental arrangement can play a critical role in a child's language acquisition (Hart, 1985).

Both social and physical aspects of the environment set the occasion for communication (Rogers-Warren, Warren, & Baer, 1983). The physical environment includes the selection and arrangement of materials, the arrangement of the setting to encourage children's engagement, and scheduling of activities to enhance children's participation and appropriate behavior. The social environment includes the presence of responsive adults and children and the verbal and nonverbal social interactions that occur among the people in the environment. In addition, contingencies for language use, the availability of a communication partner, the degree to which adults preempt children's communicative attempts, and the affective style of the listener have an impact on children's language acquisition and production (Hemmeter, 1988).

As shown in Figure 1, the social and physical aspects of the environment are linked to communication when an adult mediates the physical environment in response to children's use of language. The adult links the child's language to the environment by ensuring that the child's communication attempts are functional and reinforced. As a mediator, the adult can use an incidental teaching process to model and prompt elaborated language in order to expand the child's current skills (Hart, 1985).

Environmental arrangement can encourage children to initiate language as a means of gaining access to materials and getting help. By providing the materials requested by a child, the adult serves the important function of specifically reinforcing that child's use of language. In addition, the environmental arrangement supports the adult in attending to the child's interest and communication attempts, thereby increasing the likelihood that the adult will respond to the child's interest and provide materials contingently (Haring et al., 1987).

Seven Strategies for Arranging the Environment

The basic goal of environmental arrangement is to increase children's interest in the environment as an occasion for communication. The environment is managed and arranged to promote requests and comments by children and to support language teaching efforts by adults. Using the environment to prompt language includes the following steps:

1. Focusing on making language a part of children's routines.
2. Providing access to interesting materials and activities.
3. Providing adult and peer models who will encourage children to use

From *Teaching Exceptional Children*, Vol. 23, No. 4, Summer 1991, pp. 6-10. © 1991 by The Council for Exceptional Children. Reprinted by permission.

language and respond to their attempts to do so.

4. Establishing a contingent relationship between access to materials or assistance and use of language.

The seven environmental strategies described here are designed to (a) increase the likelihood that children will show an interest in the environment and make communicative attempts and (b) increase the likelihood that the adult will prompt the use of language about things of interest to the children by providing clear and obvious *nonverbal* prompts for them to communicate. When the environment is arranged in this way, attractive materials and activities function as both discriminative stimuli and reinforcers for language use.

Interesting Materials

Materials and activities that children enjoy should be available in the environment. Young children are most likely to initiate communication about the things that interest them. Thus, increasing the likelihood of children's interest

in the environment increases the opportunities for language use and teaching. Teachers usually know which toys and materials individual children prefer. However, a simple inventory of preferences can be taken at staff meetings or by systematically observing children's choices during free play. Parents often can provide information regarding their children's preferred toys and activities. Once toy preference has been determined, teachers can enhance interest in the environment by making such toys or materials available. For example, if a child enjoys bead stringing, various shaped and colored beads, noodles, and sewing spools could be made available. Identifying preferred activities and materials is especially important for a young child with severe disabilities. Variations in activities and materials must be carefully monitored to ensure that the child remains interested. For example, a child with severe disabilities who likes squeak toys may enjoy a variety of these toys but not like a Jack-in-the-box that makes a similar sound. Rotating the toys available at any given time is also a good way to make old toys more interesting; when they reappear they seem brand new!

Out of Reach

Placing *some* desirable materials within view but out of reach will prompt children to make requests in order to secure the materials. Materials may be placed on the shelves, in clear plastic bins, or simply across the table during a group activity to increase the likelihood that the children will request access to them either verbally or nonverbally. These requests create opportunities for language teaching, since when children request a specific material they are also specifying their reinforcers (Hart & Rogers-Warren, 1978). Thus, a teacher who prompts language and provides the requested material contingent on the child's response effectively reinforces that response. The effectiveness of this strategy can be enhanced by showing the children materials, naming the materials, and then waiting attentively for the children to make requests. During snack time or before a cooking activity, a teacher can prompt children to make requests by placing the cooking materials across the table from them. Children with severe disabilities might gain access to these materials by point-

Figure 1. Social and physical aspects of the environment set the occasion for communication as the adult serves as the mediator in response to children's use of language.

ing or eye gazing, whereas more skilled children might be encouraged to use signs, words, or even complete sentences. Teachers must be careful not to frustrate students by placing too many communicative demands on them. A balance of requesting materials and playing independently is important in every activity.

3 Inadequate Portions

Providing small or inadequate portions of preferred materials such as blocks, crayons, or crackers is another way to arrange the environment to promote communication. During an activity the children enjoy, an adult can control the amount of materials available so that the children have only some of the parts that are needed to complete the activity. When the children use the materials initially provided, they are likely to request more. Providing inadequate portions of an interesting and desirable material creates a situation in which children are encouraged by the arrangement of the physical environment to communicate their needs for additional materials. For example, during snack time, an adult can encourage requests by presenting small servings of juice or pieces of a cookie rather than a whole cookie. A child who enjoys watching the teacher blow bubbles can be encouraged to make requests if the teacher blows one or two bubbles and then waits for the child to request more.

When children initiate language with requests for more, the teacher has the opportunity to model and prompt more elaborate language as well as to provide functional consequences for the children's communicative attempts. For example:
Teacher: (Blows two bubbles and stops.)
Child: "More"
Teacher: "Blow more bubbles?"
Child: "Blow more."
Teacher: (Blows more bubbles)

4 Choice Making

There are many occasions when two or more options for activities or materials can be presented to children. In order to encourage children to initiate language, the choice should be presented nonverbally. Children may be most encouraged to make a choice when one of the items is preferred and the other is disliked. For example, the adult may hold two different toys (e.g., a big yellow dump truck and a small red block) and wait for the child to make a verbal or nonverbal request. If the child requests nonverbally, the adult has the option of prompting the child to verbalize ("Tell me what you want") or simply modeling a response for the child ("Yellow truck"). Children's verbal requests can be followed with expansions of their language ("You wanted the yellow truck") or models of alternative forms for requesting ("Yellow truck, please").

5 Assistance

Creating a situation in which children are likely to need assistance increases the likelihood that they will communicate about that need. The presence of attractive materials that require assistance to operate may encourage children to request help from adults or peers. A wind-up toy, a swing that a child needs help getting into, or an unopened bottle of bubbles are all examples of materials that can provide a nonverbal prompt to ask for help.

6 Sabotage

Setting up a "sabotage" by not providing all of the materials the children will need to complete a task (e.g., paints and water but no paintbrush following an instruction to paint), or by otherwise preventing them from carrying out an instruction, also will encourage them to make requests. This environmental strategy requires children to problem solve and indicate that something is wrong or missing. They must first determine what is needed, and this initial discovery may require prompts from an adult. The missing materials are cues for the children to communicate that something is not right or that additional materials are needed. Sabotage is an effective prompt for language when the cues are obvious and children's cognitive skills are sufficiently developed to make detection of the missing material easy and rapid. Sabotage should be carried out in a warm, engaging manner by the teacher; the episode should be brief and never frustrating to the child.

7 Silly Situations

The final environmental strategy is to create a need for children to communicate by setting up absurd or silly situations that violate their expectations. For example, an adult who playfully attempts to put a child's shoes on the adult's feet may encourage the child to comment on the absurd situation. During snack time, an adult can set up an absurd situation by placing a large piece of modeling clay or a colored block on a child's plate instead of a cracker, then waiting expectantly for the child to initiate a verbal or nonverbal request.

Children develop expectations for the ways things should be in everyday environments. They learn routines and expect that things will happen in a particular order. When something unexpected happens, they may be prompted to communicate. Of course, children must *have* expectations before the expectations can be violated. Thus, use of this strategy must be tailored to the individual skills of the children and to their familiar routines. For example, a child who always stores articles of clothing and materials in a specific "cubbie" will probably notice when an adult places a silly picture over it; a child who does not consistently use a specified "cubbie" would be unlikely to notice and respond to such a change in the environment.

Making the Strategies Effective

To make these seven environmental strategies work, the teacher must follow the student's lead. The teacher must notice what the child is interested in, establish joint attention on the topic of interest, and encourage the child to make communicative attempts. By monitoring the child's interest and identifying which materials and activities the child enjoys, an adult can select the ones that will best serve as reinforcers for language.

The nonverbal cues that accompany the environmental arrangement strategies should be faded over time so the child is responding more to things of interest in the environment and less to the adult's cues (Halle, Marshall, & Spradlin, 1979). For example, it may be necessary at first for teachers to shrug their shoulders, raise their eyebrows, and tilt their heads, while extending their hands containing different toys, in order to direct children's attention to the environment and to the opportunity for choice making. As children become more skilled at initiating requests, fewer and less obvious nonverbal prompts should be given.

The use of environmental strategies must be tailored to each child's cognitive level and responsiveness to the environment. For example, putting a coat on a child backward and waiting for the child to communicate that something is wrong may require additional prompts if the child is unable to problem solve at this level. For environmental strategies to be effective, they must be geared to each child's level and they must cue communicative responses that are emergent in the child's repertoire.

Conclusion

How adults respond to children's communication attempts when they are elicited by environmental arrangement is extremely important. Immediate feedback and access to the desired material or requested assistance, as well as a positive affective response, are essential consequences for communication attempts. As in all applications of naturalistic teaching processes, these episodes should be brief, positive, successful for the children, and designed to reinforce the children's use of language and their social engagement with adults (Hart & Rogers-Warren, 1978).

References

Alpert, C. L., Kaiser, A. P., Ostrosky, M. M., & Hemmeter, M. L. (1987, November). *Using environmental arrangement and milieu language teaching as interventions for improving the communication skills of nonvocal preschool children.* Paper presented at the National Early Childhood Conference on Children with Special Needs, Denver, CO.

Bates, E. (1976). Pragmatics and sociolinguistics in child language. In O. M. Moorehead & A. E. Moorehead (Eds.), *Normal and deficient child language* (pp. 411–463). Baltimore: University Park Press.

Halle, J., Marshall, A., & Spradlin, J. (1979). Time delay: A technique to increase language use and facilitate generalization in retarded children. *Journal of Applied Behavior Analysis, 12,* 431–439.

Haring, T. G., Neetz, J. A., Lovinger, L., Peck, C., & Semmell, M. I. (1987). Effects of four modified incidental teaching procedures to create opportunities for communication. *The Journal of the Association for Persons with Severe Handicaps, 12,*(3), 218–226.

Hart, B. M. (1985). Naturalistic language training strategies. In S. F. Warren & A. Rogers-Warren (Eds.), *Teaching functional language.* Baltimore: University Park Press.

Hart, B. M., & Rogers-Warren, A. K. (1978). Milieu language training. In R. L. Schiefelbusch (Ed.), *Language intervention strategies* (Vol. 2, pp. 193–235). Baltimore: University Park Press.

Hemmeter, M. L. (1988). *The effect of environmental arrangement on parent-child language interactions.* Unpublished master's thesis, Vanderbilt University, Nashville, TN.

Rogers-Warren, A. K., Warren, S. F., & Baer, D. M. (1983). Interactional bases of language learning. In K. Kernan, M. Begab, & R. Edgarton (Eds.), *Environments and behavior: The adaptation of mentally retarded persons.* Baltimore: University Park Press.

The development and dissemination of this paper were partially supported by Grant No. G008400663 from the Office of Special Education and Grant No. G008720107 from the National Institute for Disability and Rehabilitation Research. The authors are grateful to Cathy Alpert and Mary Louise Hemmeter for their contributions in the development of these environmental arrangement strategies.

Toward Defining Programs and Services for Culturally and Linguistically Diverse Learners in Special Education

Shernaz B. García and Diana H. Malkin

Shernaz B. García *(CEC Chapter # 101), Lecturer and Associate Director, Bilingual Education Program and* **Diana H. Malkin** *(CEC Chapter # 101), recently completed a máster's degree, Department of Special Education, The University of Texas at Austin.*

Effective program design for services for students from culturally and linguistically diverse (CLD) backgrounds who also have disabilities is based on the same principles and purposes of multicultural education that create supportive learning environments in general education. In the absence of appropriate programs in regular and special education, these students are at higher risk of being misidentified as having disabilities, and their educational experiences may not take into account the reality that linguistic and cultural characteristics coexist and interact with disability-related factors. For example, a girl with a learning disability may also have limited English proficiency (LEP), be living in poverty, and come from a family of migrant farm workers. Special education programs for this student must address the interacting influence of these variables. How will bilingual education and English as a second language (ESL) in-

struction be modified for this child? How do the family and larger community respond to her disability? How does the presence of an impairment influence the family's goals and expectations for their daughter? Would these differ if the child were male? How? Do her language characteristics—in the native language and in English—reflect linguistic differences, or do they, instead, result from socioeconomic factors? Failure to consider such issues may result in inadequate student progress or dropping out of school.

Special education services must be culturally and linguistically appropriate if they are to be truly inclusive. To meet the needs of CLD students with exceptionalities, special educators need knowledge and skills in four specific areas: (1) information about the language characteristics of learners with disabilities who are bilingual or have limited English proficiency that will assist in the development of a language use plan (Ortiz & García, 1990; Ortiz & Yates, 1989); (2) information about cultural factors that influence educational planning and services; (3) characteristics of instructional strategies and materials that are culturally and linguistically appropriate; and (4) characteristics of a learning environment that promotes success for all students.

Addressing Language Characteristics

Several aspects of the individualized education program (IEP) are influenced by students' language characteristics. Even when students are proficient in English, their cultural backgrounds may influence language use in academic settings. Dialectal differences, different patterns of language use and function among varied language communities, and nonverbal communication style differences among cultures can have a significant impact on student performance.

Gathering Essential Language Information

An accurate description of the language characteristics of students from language minority backgrounds, obtained from many sources, is necessary before decisions can be made regarding the language(s) of instruction as well as type(s) of language intervention to be provided in special education. For each language spoken by the student, several aspects of language proficiency and use should be considered, including information about the student's (a) language dominance and proficiency; (b) acquisition of the surface structures (grammar, syntax, vocabulary, phonology, etc.), as well as functional language use (pragmatics); and, (c) receptive and expressive language skills. Language information should be current to ensure that educational planning is reponsive to language shifts that may have occurred since any previous testing. (Readers interested in a more detailed discussion of language profiling are referred to Ortiz & García, 1990.)

Developing the Language Use Plan

When educators assume that students with disabilities who have limited English proficiency will be confused by two languages, or that services for their disability-related difficulties should receive priority over services for their language needs, they are likely to remove students from language programs, or they may fail to realize the importance of coordinating services across bilingual and special education settings. However, students with LEP are entitled to bilingual and ESL instruction and should receive both to ensure that goals and strategies are pedagogically appropriate for their disability, as well as their language status. Foremost in the IEP should be a language use plan that specifies the language(s) of instruction for each goal and related objectives, the person(s) responsible for instruction in the targeted language(s), and the type of language intervention recommended (Ortiz & Yates, 1989).

In all instances except ESL instruction, ways of providing native language or bilingual instruction to these students should be explored, even if such services are not readily available. Alternatives may include the use of bilingual paraprofessionals, parent and community tutors in the native language(s), bilingual peer tutoring, collaboration with the student's bilingual/ESL teacher, and any other resources available in the district. Even when students do not qualify for bilingual education and ESL programs or have recently exited from these programs, some may

still need language support to succeed in academic tasks that demand greater English proficiency than they possess. Unless teachers understand that the English performance of students from language minority backgrounds may reflect language status rather than cognitive ability, instruction may be geared to the former rather than the latter. These students need instruction that accommodates their language level while teaching concepts that are at the appropriate cognitive level. The learning environment should support the language of instruction in a variety of contextualized, nonverbal, multisensory ways.

The Influence of Cultural Factors

In the most general sense, culture provides a world view that influences our ways of perceiving the world around us. It defines desirable attitudes, values, and behaviors, and influences how we evaluate our needs. As a result, the culture and subcultures of the school are likely to impact what and how children should be taught, as well as when and how successfully it is taught (Lynch, 1992). These culturally conditioned influences on educational programs and curriculum development are more difficult to perceive if educators do not have adequate cultural self-awareness and an understanding of other cultures. In order to truly understand how culture mediates school experiences, it is important to go beyond the "tourist" curriculum that focuses on external characteristics such as food, music, holidays, and dress (Derman-Sparks, 1989). An awareness of the internal (values, thoughts, cognitive orientations) and hidden (unspoken rules, norms) aspects of culture is also needed. For instance, it is helpful to understand the influence of culture on the size and structure of the family; standards for acceptable behavior (decorum and discipline); language and communication patterns (including rules for adult, adult-child, child-child communication); religious influences on roles, expectations and/or diet; and

traditions and history (e.g., reason for immigration, contact with homeland) (Saville-Troike, 1978).

Influences on Childrearing Practices

Enculturation is the part of the socialization process through which children acquire the language and characteristics of their culture (Gollnick & Chinn, 1986). For example, the community's values and orientation toward dependence-independence-interdependence will influence parents' goals for their son or daughter from infancy through adulthood. How the roles and status of children in the family and community are defined influences acceptance or rejection of specific behavior in a range of situations, including child-child, child-adult, family-school, and family-community interactions. In the case of students with disabilities, it is also helpful to know how parents' expectations and goals for their child have been influenced by cultural values, beliefs, and expectations for individuals with disabilities. Cultures vary in their definition of *family*; consequently, "the term…must be defined in a way that is relevant to the targeted cultural groups; otherwise, a very important resource for classroom learning and motivation may be overlooked" (Briscoe, 1991, p. 17). Failure to do this can lead to false assumptions about the role of parents in the care and education of their children and the extent to which parents or other primary caregivers should be involved in formal schooling activities, as well as the beliefs of school personnel that minority parents do not value education.

Finally, how children acquire strategies for learning and which patterns of thinking and learning are reinforced by the family have also been shown to vary across cultural contexts (Philips, 1983; Ramirez & Castaneda, 1974). When the culture of the classroom values behaviors such as independent seatwork, self-direction, and competition, or when success is defined primarily in academic terms, students whose families value interdependent behavior, or those for whom family well-being supersedes individual success, may have difficulty in school and are at risk of being mislabeled as "overly dependent," seeking "excessive" adult approval, or lacking the ability to become independent learners.

Influences on Communication Styles

Effective cross-cultural communication requires a knowledge of the cultural referents as well as individual and situational factors that influence how students use language in conversational and academic contexts. Examples include pragmatic variables such as turntaking behavior, greeting conventions, proximity, and rules of conversation—including unspoken rules (Cheng, 1987). In addition, cultural values and orientations are influential in defining the norms, rules, roles, and communication networks that govern interpersonal and intercultural communication. How students process information (their cognitive style); how they deal with conflict; and which strategies they prefer during negotiation, persuasion, or other types of communication may be influenced by the cultural context in which they are raised. Their self-concept and social identity (the influence of group membership on self-concept) are also affected by their membership in a particular cultural community (Gudykunst & Ting-Toomey, 1988). Given the "hidden" nature of many of these rules, norms, roles, and expectations, our awareness of their existence may develop only when they are violated and we attempt to identify the source of the misunderstanding.

Variations in communication styles also exist as a function of gender, socioeconomic status, and/or ethnicity (e.g., Heath, 1986; Hecht, Collier, & Ribeau, 1993), and they are present in any language, including native English-speaking communities. For example, African-American students, Appalachian children, or individuals from rural or low-income environments whose language does not reflect the language

and language uses valued at school may experience some of the same difficulties as speakers of other languages if they are not accustomed to the way language is used by teachers and in textbooks and other materials. In fact, class differences may negatively influence teacher responses, even when teachers and students are members of the same ethnic community. In such instances, teachers using an inclusive approach would

acknowledge and respect the language a child brings to school while focusing on building and broadening the child's repertoire of language varieties to include Standard English.

Instructional goals and strategies should be instrumental in helping students experience academic success, provide opportunities for them to try new learning situations, and increase the range of learning environments in

Table 1. Cultural and Linguistic Considerations Related to IEP Development

Selection of IEP Goals and Objectives

Considerations for IEP Development	Classroom Implications
IEP goals and objectives accommodate the student's current level of performance.	• At the student's instructional level • Instructional level based on student's cognitive level, not the language proficiency level • Focus on development of higher level cognitive skills as well as basic skills
Goals and objectives are responsive to cultural and linguistic variables.	• Accommodates goals and expectations of the family • Is sensitive to culturally based response to the disability • Includes a language use plan • Addresses language development and ESL needs

Selection of Instructional Strategies

Considerations for IEP Development	Classroom Implications
Interventions provide adequate exposure to curriculum.	• Instruction in student's dominant language • Responsiveness to learning and communication styles • Sufficient practice to achieve mastery
IEP provides for curricular/instructional accommodation of learning styles and locus of control.	• Accommodates perceptual style differences (e.g., visual vs. auditory) • Accommodates cognitive style differences (e.g., inductive vs. deductive) • Accommodates preferred style of participation (e.g., teacher- vs. student-directed, small vs. large group) • Reduces feelings of learned helplessness
Selected strategies are likely to be effective for language minority students.	• Native language and ESL instruction • Teacher as facilitator of learning (vs. transmission) • Genuine dialogue with students • Contextualized instruction • Collaborative learning • Self-regulated learning • Learning-to-learn strategies
English as a second language (ESL) strategies are used.	• Modifications to address the student's disability • Use of current ESL approaches • Focus on meaningful communication
Strategies for literacy are included.	• Holistic approaches to literacy development • Language teaching that is integrated across the curriculum • Thematic literature units • Language experience approach • Journals

which they can be successful. When parents' goals and expectations for their child are not consistent with the school's definition of success, attempts to "re-educate" the family should be avoided in favor of working collaboratively to determine mutually acceptable goals and helping parents in the decision-making process by sharing pertinent information.

Selection of Appropriate Instructional Strategies

Given the high frequency with which IEPs focus on instructional goals related to reading and language arts, this section addresses language and literacy development. However, many of the principles of effective literacy instruction are appropriate for use in other subject areas. In general, teaching/learning strategies and materials should be selected that facilitate high levels of academic content. Recent literature examining the instructional processes that foster literacy for students with disabilities (Cummins, 1984; Englert & Palincsar, 1991; García, Ortiz, & Bergman, 1990; Goldman & Rueda, 1988; Graves, 1985; Ruiz, 1989; Willig & Ortiz, 1991) emphasize the role of interactive learning environments. A critical assumption is that culture determines how literacy is defined, instructed, and evaluated. From this perspective, literacy is developed in environments that engage students and teachers in meaningful dialogue through activities that are authentic, holistic, and relevant (Cummins, 1984; Englert & Palincsar, 1991). Specifically:

1. Language and dialogue are essential to learning because they scaffold cognitive growth and mediate new learning for students.

2. Instructional goals should focus on student ownership of the literacy process to the extent that students can transform what they have learned into authentic writing activities.

3. Instruction cannot be transmitted or totally scripted by teachers, because learning occurs through student-

Table 2. Checklist for Selecting and Evaluating Materials

☐ Are the perspectives and contributions of people from diverse cultural and linguistic groups—both men and women, as well as people with disabilities—included in the curriculum?

☐ Are there activities in the curriculum that will assist students in analyzing the various forms of the mass media for ethnocentrism, sexism, "handicapism," and stereotyping?

☐ Are men and women, diverse cultural/racial groups, and people with varying abilities shown in both active and passive roles?

☐ Are men and women, diverse cultural/racial groups, and people with disabilities shown in positions of power (i.e., the materials do not rely on the mainstream culture's character to achieve goals)?

☐ Do the materials identify strengths possessed by so-called "underachieving" diverse populations? Do they diminish the attention given to deficits, to reinforce positive behaviors that are desired and valued?

☐ Are members of diverse racial/cultural groups, men and women, and people with disabilities shown engaged in a broad range of social and professional activities?

☐ Are members of a particular culture or group depicted as having a range of physical features (e.g., hair color, hair texture, variations in facial characteristics and body build)?

☐ Do the materials represent historical events from the perspectives of the various groups involved or solely from the male, middle-class, and/or Western European perspective?

☐ Are the materials free of ethnocentric or sexist language patterns that may make implications about persons or groups based solely on their culture, race, gender, or disability?

☐ Will students from different ethnic and cultural backgrounds find the materials personally meaningful to their life experiences?

☐ Are a wide variety of culturally different examples, situations, scenarios, and anecdotes used throughout the curriculum design to illustrate major intellectual concepts and principles?

☐ Are culturally diverse content, examples, and experiences comparable in kind, significance, magnitude, and function to those selected from mainstream culture?

teacher dialogue and classroom interactions that connect what students need to know to their current knowledge and experiences.

4. Teachers must view errors as a source of information regarding the emergence of new literacy skills rather than as student deficits or undesired behaviors.

5. Student difficulties should be interpreted as areas in which teachers need to provide greater mediation, rather than problems that reside in the student.

Table 1 summarizes key variables to be considered when selecting instructional strategies for students with disabilities who are also culturally and/or linguistically different and suggests approaches that are more likely to be responsive to issues of student diversity.

Creating Supportive Learning Environments

Achievement of IEP goals and objectives depends on the context in which teaching and learning occur. A supportive classroom culture is part of the larger "psychological environment" of the school, and it can increase student motivation and attitudes toward learning (Maehr, 1990). Three ways in which the learning environment can be enhanced are by careful selection and evaluation of instructional materials, incorporation of students' language and culture, and involvement of parents and community.

Selecting and Evaluating Instructional Materials

Careful selection of instructional materials that promote high interest, motivation, and relevance to their sociocultural, linguistic, and experiential backgrounds increases the likelihood that students will respond to them positively. Materials published after the early 1970s are more likely to give attention to issues of diversity (Derman-Sparks, 1989). When using older instructional materials, teachers should develop and use relevant guidelines to determine whether they can be adapted and will be useful in increasing students' awareness of issues such as stereotyping, prejudice, and discrimination or it would be better to replace them. This is not meant to imply that classical literature that reflects gender or racial bias, for example, should be totally eliminated from the curriculum. Rather, in addition to appreciating the literary value of these materials, students can develop a better understanding of the historical contexts in which oppression occurs and can learn to identify ways in which discrimination against people, including individuals with disabilities, can be reduced or eliminated. Table 2 lists guidelines to assist special educators in developing their own criteria for evaluating materials they currently have available.

Incorporating Students' Language and Culture

Bilingual education programs are designed not only to provide native language instruction and ESL development, but also to enhance cognitive and affective development and provide cultural enrichment (Baca & Cervantes, 1989). Even in schools and communities where bilingual programs are not available and in situations where educators do not speak the students' language, it is possible to communicate a positive attitude toward students' backgrounds and heritage (Cummins, 1989). The following strategies are examples of ways in which classrooms and materials can reflect the diversity of backgrounds that is present in many schools and in the larger society (Cummins, 1989; Derman-Sparks, 1989).

1. Students are encouraged to use their first language around the school in various ways, even when they are not receiving native language instruction. For example, books are provided in several languages in each classroom and in the library for use by students and parents; bulletin boards, signs, and greetings employ various languages; and students are encouraged to use their native language to provide peer tutoring support.

2. Pictures and other visual displays show people from various backgrounds and communities, including individuals with varying abilities, elderly people, and men and women in blue-collar and white-collar roles. Images accurately depict people's contemporary daily lives—at work as well as in recreational activities.

3. Units developed for reading and language arts include literature from a variety of linguistic and cultural backgrounds and reflect the diversity in U.S. society across race, religion, language, class, gender, and ability. In addition to making children aware of a range of lifestyles, values, and characteristics of diverse groups, literature can reflect their struggles, achievements, and other experiences. Reflecting on such accounts, fictional as well as biographical, may also help some students understand and deal with their own struggles and difficulties.

4. Teachers and other school personnel understand that their interactions and behaviors, even if inadvertent and unintentional, may teach their students gender, racial, and other biases. This is reflected in educators' attention to their own verbal and nonverbal behaviors; avoidance of sexist or ethnocentric language; and parallel expectations for academic performance for girls, students with varying abilities, children from low-income environments, and so on.

5. The seating arrangement and organization of the classroom reflect consideration of learning style differences and encourage students to try new ways of interacting and learning.

Involving Parents and Families

As diversity in the student population increases, alternative models of parent involvement will have to be developed (Harry, 1992). Historically, many parents from language minority groups have had to overcome barriers to their effective participation in the regular and special education process, including educators' perceptions about these parents and their communities; their values regarding educational, linguistic, and cultural differences; and socioeconomic factors. Rather than being part of the problem, parents from culturally and linguistically diverse backgrounds can be effective advocates for their children. They represent a largely untapped resource to assist educators in responding effectively to multicultural issues (Briscoe, 1991).

Implementing Multicultural Special Education

Developing Intercultural Competence

Intercultural competence is an essential ingredient in teachers' ability to implement multicultural special education. Educators who possess such competence can feel comfortable and effective in their interactions with people from a variety of cultures, and they can help students and families feel comfortable as well. Finally, these skills are necessary to accomplish IEP goals. Acquisition of these skills is a gradual process, progressing through several stages. The following elements are helpful in this process (Lynch, 1992):

1. Developing an understanding and appreciation of one's own culture. This process of self-awareness and introspection allows us to examine our own assumptions and values, particularly those that may have been taken for granted because they are so much a part of our own family and community systems.

2. Gathering information about the other target cultures and analysis of this information with respect to individual students and families who reside within the community. Through our interactions with each family, we can determine the extent to which the family and its individual members share the cultural characteristics of their ethnic group. (Ethnic identity is determined by the individual and should not be assigned by others based on their observation of external traits.)

3. Discovering the parent's (or other primary caregiver's) orientation to childrearing issues, values, and orientations, including the family's goals and aspirations for their child with special needs.

4. Applying this knowledge to the development of cross-cultural skills. This results in interventions and interactions that are successful with students from diverse cultures.

Strategies for Enhancing Intercultural Understanding

The following questions may arise as special educators explore implications of multicultural education for their own programs.

While it sounds good, how can I, as one teacher, respond to so many diverse characteristics without being overwhelmed? How long will it take? Where do I start? Focusing on the cultures included at your school and within your community can be a good start, because this allows you to identify materials and strategies that are inclusive of the students you teach on a regular basis. It is a good idea to review your needs periodically—perhaps once at the beginning of each school year—to make sure that the information is updated. Which cultures are represented among your students? Does the information include any new families recently arrived in the community? Once a profile has been developed, you can reflect on your own knowledge of these cultural groups. How much do you know about each one? Which one is the most familiar? The least? This information will be useful as you evaluate what you feel comfortable about and identify areas in which you want to learn more.

How accurate is my current knowledge? What were my sources? Think about what you already know. How did you acquire this information? How extensive is your contact with the communities this knowledge presents? Is this information based on the students' country of origin, or does it encompass the experiences of the group in the United States (e.g., Mexican vs. Mexican American)? Is it based on traditional or contemporary

life-styles? Pitfalls to avoid include information that is stereotypic; sources that fail to acknowledge within-group differences based on class, gender, language, religion, ethnicity, and geographic region; and information and experiences that are limited to a "tourist curriculum" (music, food, dress, holidays, etc.), which fail to highlight aspects of culture such as historical experiences related to the group's arrival in the United States, reasons for migration, accomplishments in various fields, values and belief systems, and communication patterns.

Where can I get more information? There are many ways of learning more about cultures, including formal study, reading, workshops, travel, and audiovisual materials. In addition, activities that allow students to share their experiences and the participation of parents and other community members in the school (e.g., speaking to the class about their language, culture, or religion) will make this information a part of the ongoing routine of school activities, and it will be acquired in a natural context. The following are some strategies to consider:

• As you prepare the demographic profile of your own classroom, school, or community, ask parents whether they would be willing to speak to the students about their cultural heritage, their own accomplishments, and any barriers they have overcome. Develop a resource directory that can support other curriculum development and planning efforts as well.

• Identify community organizations and groups that can provide access to audiovisual materials and other resources for personal study as well as instructional use.

• Identify print materials, journals, and other professional publications that highlight model programs, instructional strategies and curricula, and resources for multicultural education.

What if my classes do not reflect much cultural or linguistic diversity? Even in schools where students from diverse cultural and linguistic backgrounds are represented in very small numbers, or in predominantly middle-class communities, the larger culture is made up of

subcultures from different religious, gender, and geographic backgrounds. White students also represent diverse ethnic backgrounds, and even when they may perceive their identity as "American," several cultures are represented in their ethnic heritage (Boutte & McCormick, 1992). Family histories and other activities can offer opportunities for them to explore and appreciate their unique characteristics. Finally, it is important to examine the influence of gender on teacher expectations, career counseling, and referral to special education.

A related, and equally important, issue for all students, regardless of color, gender, religion, or other differences, is the development of cross-cultural competence. As the diversity in U.S. society continues to increase, students must be prepared to become members of a workforce that is much more heterogeneous. Multicultural education can help *all* students increase their appreciation of diversity; develop positive self-concepts; respect individuals' civil and human rights; understand the historical context in which prejudice, oppression, and stereotyping occur; and ultimately fulfill their own potential while resisting and challenging stereotyping and barriers to success that exist in the society (Sleeter, 1992).

Conclusion

Efforts to implement multicultural special education services are more likely to succeed when teachers' individual efforts are supported by a school- or district-wide orientation toward improving academic achievement for all students from culturally and linguistically diverse backgrounds. Ensuring that all educators possess the necessary knowledge and skills is a long-term process. Ongoing staff development efforts must supplement preservice teacher preparation programs. In addition, effective instruction in multicultural special education requires greater collaboration between special educators and general educators, including bilingual educators, ESL specialists, migrant educators, Chapter I teachers, and other individuals who serve CLD students with disabilities. The school's multicultural resources can be considerably enhanced when collaborative efforts also involve parents and the community in meaningful ways. Effective services for a multicultural student population in general and special education requires a comprehensive, multidimensional approach that is capable of accommodating the diverse needs of students. We must develop a more effective interface with the programs that have traditionally served these children.

References

Baca, L. M., & Cervantes, H. T. (Eds.) (1989). *The bilingual special education interface* (2nd ed.). Columbus, OH: Merrill.

Briscoe, D. B. (1991). Designing for diversity in school success: Capitalizing on culture. *Preventing School Failure, 36*(1), 13-18.

Boutte, G. S., & McCormick, C. B. (1992). Avoiding pseudomulticulturalism: Authentic multicultural activities. *Childhood Education, 68*(3), 140-144.

Cheng, L. L. (1987). *Assessing Asian language performance: Guidelines for evaluating limited-English-proficient students.* Rockville, MD: Aspen.

Cummins, J. (1984). *Bilingualism and special education: Issues in assessment and pedagogy.* Clevedon, Avon, England: Multilingual Matters.

Cummins, J. (1989). A theoretical framework for bilingual special education. *Exceptional Children, 56,* 111-119.

Derman-Sparks, L. (1989). *Anti-bias curriculum: Tools for empowering young children.* Washington, DC: National Association for the Education of Young Children.

Englert, C. S., & Palincsar, A. S. (1991). Reconsidering instructional research in literacy from a sociocultural perspective. *Learning Disabilities Research and Practice, 6*(4), 225-229.

García, S. B., Ortiz, A. A., & Bergman, A. H. (1990, April). *A comparison of writing skills of Hispanic students by language proficiency and handicapping condition.* Paper presented at the annual conference of the American Educational Research Association, Boston, MA.

Goldman, S., & Rueda, R. (1988). Developing writing skills in bilingual exceptional children. *Exceptional Children, 54,* 543-551.

Gollnick, D. M., & Chinn, P. C. (1986). *Multicultural education in a pluralistic society* (2nd ed.). Columbus, OH: Merrill.

Graves, D. (1985). All children can write. *Learning Disability Focus, 1*(1), 36-43.

Gudykunst, W. B., & Ting-Toomey, S. (1988). *Cultural and interpersonal communication.* Newbury Park, CA: Sage.

Harry, B. (1992). Restructuring the participation of African-American parents in special education. *Exceptional Children, 59,* 123-131.

Heath, S. B. (1986). Sociocultural contexts of language development. In *Beyond language: Social and cultural factors in schooling language minority students* (pp. 143-186). Los Angeles: Evaluation, Dissemination and Assessment Center, California State University.

Hecht, M. L., Collier, M. J., & Ribeau, S. A. (1993). *African American communication: Ethnic identify and cultural interpretation.* Newbury Park, CA: Sage

Lynch, J. (1992). *Education for citizenship in a multicultural society.* New York: Cassell.

Maehr, M. (1990, April). *The psychological environment of the school: A focus for school leadership.* Paper presented at the annual meeting of the American Educational Research Association, Boston, MA.

Ortiz, A. A., & García, S. B. (1990). Using language assessment data for language and instructional planning for exceptional bilingual students. In A. L. Carrasquillo & R. E. Baecher (Eds.), *Teaching the bilingual special education student* (pp. 25-47). Norwood, NJ: Ablex.

Ortiz, A. A., & Yates, J. R. (1989). Staffing and the development of individualized educational programs for the bilingual exceptional student. In L. M. Baca & H. T. Cervantes (Eds.), *The bilingual special education interface* (pp. 183-203). Columbus, OH: Merrill.

Philips, S. U. (1983). *The invisible culture: Communication in classroom and community on the Warm Springs Indian reservation.* New York: Longman.

Ramírez, M. III, & Castañeda, A. (1974). *Cultural democracy: Bicognitive development and education.* New York: Academic Press.

Ruiz, N. (1989). An optimal learning environment for Rosemary. *Exceptional Children, 56,* 130-144.

Saville-Troike, M. (1978). *A guide to culture in the classroom.* Rosslyn, VA: National Clearinghouse for Bilingual Education.

Sleeter, C. (1992). *Keepers of the American dream: A study of staff development and multicultural education.* Bristol, PA: Palmer.

Willig, A. C., & Ortiz, A. A. (1991). The nonbiased individualized education program: Linking assessment to instruction. In E. V. Hamayan & J. S. Damico (Eds.), *Limiting bias in the assessment of bilingual students* (pp. 281-302). Austin, TX: Pro-Ed.

DO YOU SEE WHAT I MEAN?

BODY LANGUAGE IN CLASSROOM INTERACTIONS

Mary M. Banbury
Constance R. Hebert

Mary M. Banbury (CEC Chapter #514) is Associate Professor, Department of Special Education and Habilitative Services, University of New Orleans, Louisiana. **Constance R. Hebert** is Psychiatric Social Worker, Orleans Parish School System, New Orleans.

Photographs by Russ Thames.

The teacher uttering the mixed metaphor "Don't look at me in that tone of voice" to a student is intuitively aware of the impact of the student's nonverbal message. All teachers should be aware of nonverbal communication in the classroom in order to enhance their ability to (a) receive students' messages more accurately; (b) send congruent and positive signals to denote expectations, convey attitudes, regulate interactions, and reinforce learning; and (c) avoid incongruent and negative cues that confuse students and stifle learning (Miller, 1986; Woolfolk & Brooks, 1985). Nonverbal communication plays a significant role in all classroom interactions. According to Smith (1979), "Whether teachers are talking or not, they are always communicating" (p. 633). In fact, studies have revealed that 82% of teacher messages are nonverbal; only 18% are verbal (Grant & Hennings, 1971). Several studies have shown that the nonverbal component of classroom communication is more influential than the verbal component (Keith, Tornatzky, & Pettigrew, 1974; Woolfolk & Brooks, 1985).

In recent years investigators have examined commonly used nonverbal signals in educational settings. They have studied frequency and intensity of direct eye contact (Brooks, 1984), interpersonal distance (Brooks & Wilson, 1978), teacher-approval gestures (Nafpaktitis, Mayer, & Butterworth, 1985), and nonverbal criticisms (Simpson & Erickson, 1983). While teachers know about these nonverbal communication indexes, many are unaware of the influential role of nonverbal behaviors. They need to realize, for instance, that if there is incongruity or discrepancy between words and body language, the nonverbal message will dominate (Miller, 1986).

This article explains how teachers can analyze their own communication styles so that there is harmony between what they say and how they say it and they can learn to interpret selected nonverbal signals frequently used by students. In particular, it focuses on *proximics*, a person's use and perception of space, and *kinesics*, a person's facial and body cues. It should be noted that individual nonverbal behaviors do not have implicit meaning; they should be considered in context. As Bates, Johnson, and Blaker (1982) stated, "Nonverbal messages cannot be read with certainty. To suggest that they can is irresponsible, but to ignore them is equally irresponsible" (p. 129).

Physical Distance and Personal Space

The amount of space people maintain between themselves and others provides information about relationships, regulates interactions, and affects the impressions they develop about each other. According to Hall (1966), space tolerances range from the intimate zone,

Scenario 1

Susan, a 16-year-old with mild learning and behavior problems, is sitting in the back of the room putting on makeup during her mainstreamed English class. Her teacher considers this to be unacceptable behavior and decides to correct her. He gives the assertive verbal message, "When you put makeup on during class discussion, I feel frustrated because my time is wasted while I wait for you to participate."

Don't

Figure 1. Hostile Body Language. *The teacher has clearly invaded the student's personal zone. His body positioning signals confrontation since his shoulders are squared with those of the student. He is using his height to dominate and possibly to intimidate. Finally, the pen pointing is not only a further intrusion into her space, but also a threatening and intimidating gesture. These aggressive nonverbal signals defeat the purpose of an assertive message.*

Figure 2. Passive Body Language. *Equally ineffective is the opposite approach pictured above. Here the teacher appears to be intimidated and fearful of confrontation. He approaches from the rear and does not enter the student's personal distance zone. His arms are drawn up over his chest in a protective manner. His chin is retracted inwardly and hidden behind his fists. His lips are taut, and there is no eye contact. With such submissive body language, it is unlikely that his message will be taken seriously.*

Do

Figure 3. Assertive Body Language. *The teacher gives himself a chance for a successful intervention by considering space, positioning, and body language. In this case he has approached the student from a nonthreatening lateral position, near enough to be effective but not invasive. His hands and arms are in a "open" position; his facial expression is relaxed, and his eyes are gazing at the student. Since his verbal message is congruent with his nonverbal one, he has increased the likelihood that the student will put away her makeup.*

with actual physical contact, to "personal distance," (approximately 1.5-3 feet), to "social or public distance" (more than 3 feet). Typically, people tend to get closer to those they like. They maintain more distance from those they dislike or fear; they also stand farther away from people who have disabilities or who are from different racial backgrounds (Miller, 1986).

By adjusting the distance at which they position themselves, teachers and students suggest desired levels of involvement and convey impressions about whether they are intimate, aloof, intrusive, or neutral. In certain situations a person may use close physical proximity to influence, intimidate, or warn another person. Generally, however, teachers and students use closeness to signal acceptance, concern, and approval (Richey & Richey, 1978). Conversely, they employ distance to indicate indifference, rejection, and disapproval (Brooks & Wilson, 1978).

The meaning of a given distance depends on the situation, the intentions of the individual, and the congruency between the verbal and nonverbal messages. For example, an assertive teacher sets limits by combining touch with a verbal message, eye contact, and the student's name (Canter & Canter, 1976). Likewise, a teacher who wants to increase positive communications and reinforce acceptable behaviors in the classroom says, "I like what you are doing," while making a conscious effort to move within the personal space zone of all the students, not only the favorite ones or high achievers (Miller, 1986).

Eye Contact and Facial Expressions

Eyes transmit the most expressive nonverbal messages (Marsh, 1988). They indicate mood, emotion, and feelings; they can also warn, challenge, or reassure. Although there are exceptions, most students associate wide open eyes, raised brows, and frequency of eye contact with approval, acceptance, and concern. Research demonstrates that direct and frequent teacher eye contact can improve attention, intensify participation, increase the amount of information students retain, and boost self-esteem (Woolfolk & Brooks, 1985).

Direct teacher eye contact can also express domination, disapproval, or dis-

like. Prolonged neutral eye contact with raised eyebrows serves as a powerful restraining or corrective measure. Students commonly refer to this as the "evil eye" or the "teacher look." Richey and Richey (1978) have warned teachers to keep their stares passive to avoid sending a message of dislike. Lowered eyebrows and eyes that squint or glare evoke feelings of antagonism, aggression, or denunciation.

Teachers can also use their eyes to guide discussions, promote or reward student participation, and regulate and monitor verbal exchanges. Open eyes and lifted brows signal the beginning of an activity or a request for an explanation; the brief glance serves as a conversational signal or a comprehension check. The actual amount of eye contact controls listening and speaking roles and signals information about personality, status, and culture (Marsh, 1988).

Other facial features combine with the eyes to communicate basic emotions. For example, smiles coupled with wrinkles around the eyes best predict happiness and transmit feelings of approval. (A smile is the teacher's most powerful social reinforcer; some refer to it as a "visual hug.") Lowered eyes and a downturned mouth reveal sadness or disappointment. Indicators of anger or disapproval include pursed or tightly closed lips, clenched teeth, and frowns or scowls (Hargrave, 1988).

Not all students are adept at discriminating facial affect or using social perceptual cues. In particular, students who have developmental delays, learning disabilities, or cultural differences or are inexperienced may have difficulty in describing affective states, judging nonverbal reactions, inferring information, and using body language (Wiig & Harris, 1974; Woolfolk & Brooks, 1985). Exacerbating this problem, some people may voluntarily control their facial expressions because of social dictates or cultural teachings. Therefore, the context in which they occur, as well as the accompanying verbal messages, play important roles in determining the meaning of nonverbal behaviors.

Gestures and Body Movements

Body motions or positions do not have specific meanings in and of themselves. The accompanying verbal message must be considered, as well as the individual's kinesic motions. Even then, there are times when the verbal message is not congruent with the nonverbal one. This occurs when an individual is purposely trying to mislead his or her audience or is actually unaware of the underlying emotion. For example, a young female may deny that she is angry while tightly clenching her teeth and rapidly tapping her foot; a teenage male with listless posture, overall passivity, and general drooping may refuse to acknowledge that he is depressed or, perhaps, suicidal; a teacher with fists clenched, arms crossed, and lips pursed may profess to be open to differences of opinions or other perspectives.

There are no universal clear-cut rules for interpreting body language. While it is relatively easy to read individual expressions, gestures, and movements, definitive conclusions should not be based on the observation of isolated kinetic movements. Since each element of body language can be controlled, simulated, amplified, or suppressed, it is important to observe the composite picture: the clusters of facial expressions and body movements and the congruency of verbal and nonverbal messages.

Table 1

Congruency of Verbal and Nonverbal Messages

	Approving/ Accepting	Disapproving/ Critical	Assertive/ Confident	Passive/ Indifferent
Verbal message	"I like what you are doing."	"I don't like what you are doing."	"I mean what I say."	"I don't care."
Physical distance	Sit or stand in close proximity to other person.	Distance self from other person; encroach uninvited into other's personal space.	Physically elevate self; move slowly into personal space of other person.	Distance self from other person.
Facial expressions	Engage in frequent eye contact; open eyes wide; raise brows; smile.	Engage in too much or too little eye contact; open eyes wide in fixed, frozen expression; squint or glare; turn corners of eyebrows down; purse or tightly close lips; frown; tighten jaw muscle.	Engage in prolonged, neutral eye contact; lift eyebrows; drop head and raise eyebrow.	Avert gaze; stare blankly; cast eyes down or let them wander; let eyes droop.
Body movements	Nod affirmatively; "open" posture; uncross arms/legs; place arms at side; show palms; lean forward; lean head and trunk to one side; orient body toward other person; grasp or pat shoulder or arm; place hand to chest.	Shake head slowly; "close" posture; fold arms across chest; lean away from person; hold head/trunk straight; square shoulders; thrust chin out; use gestures of negation, e.g., finger shaking, hand held up like a stop signal.	Place hands on hips; lean forward; touch shoulder; tap on desk; drop hand on desk; join fingers at tips and make a steeple.	Lean away from other person; place head in palm of hand; fold hands behind back or upward in front; drum fingers on table; tap with feet; swing crossed leg or foot; sit with leg over chair.

Table 1 is designed to assist teachers in interpreting and conveying congruent nonverbal messages; it depicts selected behavioral indexes and their verbal and nonverbal behavioral correlates. Classroom teachers who are able to recognize nonverbal signals can enhance their management techniques by curbing hostile or passive gestures and movements, matching verbal and nonverbal messages, and providing reliable and effective cues to their students.

Analysis of Nonverbal Behaviors

Teachers should examine the photographs shown here, analyze the nonverbal interactions of the teacher and the students, and match their interpretations with those of the authors. Since behavior is related to its context, there

may be more than one way to interpret the nonverbal behaviors. The purpose of this activity is to heighten teachers' awareness of nonverbal interactions during specific management and instructional activities. Scenario 1 shows how a teacher's body language can detract from or enhance his or her verbal language. Scenario 2 describes two students' nonverbal signals and suggests teacher responses.

Conclusion

The distance at which individuals position themselves, their eye focusing, facial expressions, gestures, and body movements all consciously or unconsciously complement, supplement, or supplant verbal communication. The individual significance of isolated nonverbal cues, however, is subject to as many

Scenario 2

John and Carol spend a portion of each day in a resource room for students with behavior disorders. They have been instructed to work on an in-class assignment.

Figure 4. John is exhibiting a nonreceptive posture. His intense gaze suggests that he would like to engage in the "stare-down" game. His crossed arms and legs, indicative of a "closed" position, could be a sign of insecurity or defensiveness. This student, however, does not appear to be intimidated. His body position, in general, is one of reclining. A person interested in protecting himself generally does not recline. The shoulders are squared, not rounded, and he is turned away from his desk, not "hiding" behind it. In this case there may even be an unconscious attempt to hold back from physical aggression. This student is actually holding his left arm tightly into his chest rather than simply crossing his arms in resistance.

A person who was aware of nonverbal signals would not openly confront this student. There should be no prolonged looks, sudden moves, aggressive gestures, or threatening comments. With arms at his or her side, a teacher would approach the student slowly from a lateral position, using nonthreatening comments to open a dialogue.

Figure 5. At first glance, Carol, the student pictured above appears to be bored or uninterested. Upon closer examination, however, she is exhibiting several body signals for depression. Her shoulders are drooped and rounded; her torso is retracted; and her affect is flat. Her eyes are downcast; her jaw is slack and lowered; and her lower lip is in a pouting position. The twisting of the lock of hair, especially if it is done incessantly, could be a sign of anxiety. If her teacher observes a pattern or ongoing series of symptoms such as these, the student should be referred for further assessment.

interpretations and intentions as there are people who receive or send messages. Therefore, observers of body language should concentrate on interpreting the total congruent picture, including context, verbal and nonverbal behaviors, and prior and subsequent events, before they reach conclusions based on observation and comprehension of isolated signals. Likewise, people who desire to use proximics and kinesics to enhance their communication style should verify that their body language is indeed communicating their intended messages and their nonverbal behaviors are congruent with their verbal ones.

To improve their communication styles, teachers could videotape their classroom performance, identify intended messages, and solicit structured feedback regarding the congruency of their verbal and nonverbal behaviors from students or colleagues by using a chart, checklist, or rating sheet. They could role play selected events or simulate interactions with peers to assure that they are sending congruent messages while responding to the expected defensiveness of certain students and parents. To develop and enhance their ability to interpret the nonverbal messages of other people, teachers could set aside 10 minutes a day to consciously notice and interpret proximic and kinesic signals sent by students, friends, and family members. They could focus on academic or social interactions, using a videotape without the audio portion to read the body language and replaying the scene with sound to check their perceptions. Alternatively, they could examine photographs, especially family albums, paying particular attention to the body language and what it indicates about personal and interpersonal relationships, attitudes, and emotions. Taking the time to study ways of interpreting and conveying nonverbal messages can help teachers enhance the teaching and learning process.

References

Bates, M., Johnson, C., & Blaker, K. E. (1982). *Group leadership: A manual for group counseling leaders.* Denver: Love.

Brooks, D. M. (1984, April). *Communicating competence: Junior high teacher behavioral expression during the first day of school.* Paper presented at the annual meeting of the American Educational Research Association, New Orleans.

Brookes, D. M., & Wilson, B. J. (1978). Teacher verbal and nonverbal expression toward selected students. *Journal of Educational Psychology, 70,* 147-153.

Canter, L., & Canter, M. (1976). *Assertive discipline: A take charge approach for today's educator.* Los Angeles: Lee Canter.

Grant, B. W., & Hennings, D. G. (1971). *The teacher moves: An analysis of nonverbal activity.* New York: Teachers College Press.

Hall, E. T. (1966). *The hidden dimension.* Garden City, NY: Doubleday.

Hargrave, J. (1988, March). Actions speak louder than words. *OEA Communique,* pp. 28-31.

Keith, L. T., Tornatzky, L. G., & Pettigrew, L. E. (1974). An analysis of verbal and nonverbal classroom teaching behaviors. *Journal of Experimental Education, 42,* 30-38.

Marsh, P. (Ed.). (1988). *Eye to eye: How people interact.* Topsfield, MA: Salem House.

Miller, P. W. (1986). *Nonverbal communication* (2nd ed.). Washington, DC: National Education Association.

Nafpaktitis, M., Mayer, G. R., & Butterworth, T. (1985). Natural rates of teacher approval and disapproval and their relation to student behavior in intermediate school classrooms. *Journal of Educational Psychology, 77,* 362-367.

Richey, H. W., & Richey, M. H. (1978). Nonverbal behavior in the classroom. *Psychology in the Schools, 15,* 571-576.

Simpson, A. W., & Erickson, M. T. (1983). Nonverbal communication patterns as a function of teacher race, student gender, and student race. *American Educational Research Journal, 20,* 183-189.

Smith, H. (1979). Nonverbal communication in teaching. *Review of Educational Research, 49,* 631-672.

Wiig, E., & Harris, S. (1974). Perception and interpretation of nonverbally expressed emotions by adolescents with learning disabilities. *Perceptual and Motor Skills, 38,* 239-245.

Woolfolk, A. E., & Brooks, D. M. (1985). The influence of teachers' nonverbal behaviors on students' perceptions and performance. *The Elementary School Journal, 85,* 513-528.

Using a Picture Task Analysis

to Teach Students
with Multiple Disabilities

Wynelle H. Roberson

Jane S. Gravel

Gregory C. Valcante

Ralph G. Maurer

Wynelle H. Roberson *is Lead Teacher at the Multi-disciplinary Training Project Diagnostic Classroom;* **Jane S. Gravel** *is formerly with the Department of Psychiatry, College of Medicine;* **Gregory C. Valcante** *(CEC Chapter #1024) is Special Educator at the Children's Mental Health Unit, Department of Psychiatry, College of Medicine; and* **Ralph G. Maurer** *is Chief, Children's Mental Health Unit, Department of Psychiatry, College of Medicine, University of Florida, Gainesville.*

The task analysis approach to teaching multiple-step skills to students with disabilities has been used for many years (Brown, 1987). Teachers of students with moderate and severe disabilities provide instruction across domains by (a) breaking the skill into component steps; (b) prompting students through forward, backward, or total task chains; and (c) recording step-by-step progress toward skill acquisition. Likewise, the use of pictures to augment communication for persons with speech and language disabilities now is commonplace (ASHA, 1981). In addition to this use as a method of expressive communication, pictorial symbols are used in advertising, transportation, and public facilities.

Increasingly, educators and researchers have combined task analysis and augmentative communication procedures to produce sequences of pictures that represent the steps an individual must perform to carry out domestic, community, vocational, and leisure tasks. A *picture task analysis* is a pictorial representation of the critical steps in a task analysis sequenced and displayed for the learner to follow. Picture task analyses enable learners with moderate and severe disabilities to gain meaningful skills that previously were beyond their grasp.

Benefits of Picture Task Analyses

One of the earliest studies of sequenced pictures (Robinson-Wilson, 1977) was conducted with picture recipes based on previously published cookbooks. Since then, the use of sequenced pictures has been validated for instruction in cooking (Johnson & Cuvo, 1981), grooming (Thinesen & Bryan, 1981), and vocational skills (Connis, 1979; Wilson, Schepis, & Mason-Main, 1987). Wiggins and Behrmann (1988) used sequenced pictures for community instruction in grocery stores and restaurants. In fact, picture task analyses can be used to teach any skill that can be analyzed into component steps (e.g., operating a tape player, using a calculator, making coffee, emptying trash).

All of the advantages of using traditional task analytic instructional strategies (e.g., size and number of steps tailored to student ability levels) are maintained with the picture task analysis format. Furthermore, picture task analyses may be integrated into existing educational methods. For example, they may be used in conjunction with other prompting strategies for students who need more than just the visual cue, and a time delay procedure may be incorporated if desired. Picture task analyses

By use of a picture task analysis, this student is shown a skill broken down into component steps.

enhance receptive communication, serve as a memory aid, and are cost and time efficient.

Receptive Communication Strategy

Effective communication between teacher and student is essential for effective teaching. One of the limitations of a traditional task analysis is its accessibility. A task analysis typically is written by the teacher for a student with little, if any, reading ability. The teacher must then communicate these steps to the learner, usually by modeling and by employing numerous verbal, physical, and gestural prompts. The picture task analysis provides additional input and increases the likelihood that the message will be understood. The pictures communicate that the task to be performed

requires a sequence of steps to be carried out and that there are specific starting and stopping points.

Memory Aid

While verbal prompts and cues last only momentarily, the visual format of the picture task analysis endures to serve as a constant reminder of the steps to be completed. Students may refer back to the pictures as often as necessary to ensure that they are performing the steps accurately. This enduring nature of the pictorial representation holds a great advantage over other prompting and cueing strategies.

The ultimate goal of a picture task analysis is to enable the student to perform meaningful tasks independently. However, in some cases, complete independence may not be possible due to the nature of the individual's disabilities or the complexity of the task. In these

cases, a picture task analysis can serve as an adaptive device or memory aid, allowing the student to progress from partial participation to further levels of independence.

Efficiency

An additional benefit of picture task analyses is their time and cost effectiveness. They are easy to develop and implement. They are portable and allow other personnel (e.g., job supervisors, paraprofessionals, volunteers) to supervise or aid in instruction. Although modeling provides a living, three-dimensional cue, it does not endure over time like the picture task analysis does, and it requires the instructor's presence. The visual representation of the picture task analysis, on the other hand, allows the instructor to spend time with other students and to fade direct supervision. Once created, all or part of a picture task analysis may be used for several students if it is appropriate to their individual needs and ability levels. It lends itself not only to teacher data recording but also to students' producing data-based documentation of their own progress (Connis, 1979).

At the University of Florida, we have used picture task analyses with students who have multiple disabilities, including moderate and severe intellectual disabilities, language impairments, and behavior problems. This article presents an easy method of constructing picture task analyses and steps for integrating their use into community environments based on our experience.

Developing and Implementing a Picture Task Analysis

Our procedure for constructing picture task analyses requires only (a) photographs (which may be taken with an instant camera and film); (b) manila folders, posterboard, or another medium on which to mount the photo; (c) glue; and (d) clear contact paper or lamination to protect the photographs. The following steps are taken:

1. An appropriate skill is selected from the student's individualized education program (IEP) and broken down into component steps suitable for the student's abilities.

2. A symbol system is selected. At the

University of Florida, instant photographs are used to represent component steps. Line drawings or other symbols may be appropriate for other students.

3. The necessary materials are gathered.
4. A photograph is taken of each step in the task analysis.
5. The photos are arranged in sequential order on a manila folder and secured with glue.
6. Numbers depicting the sequence of steps are written beneath the photos and arrows are drawn to direct the learner's attention from one step to the next step in the sequence.
7. A description of the behavior in each photograph is written below the photograph.
8. The picture task analysis is laminated to preserve the photographs.

Instructional Procedure

The instructional procedure follows five steps. The duration of each step depends on the abilities, disabilities, and learning patterns of individual students.

1. The teacher presents the picture task analysis and reviews it with the student by pointing to each photo and reading the sentence accompanying it.
2. The teacher models the behaviors while the student watches and follows along with the picture task analysis. Students who read should read the description of each step as the teacher performs it.
3. The student guides the teacher through the task using the picture task analysis as a guide. The teacher may prompt the student by asking "What do I do next?" Students with reading ability read the description of each step aloud. Nonreaders and nonverbal students may respond by pointing to the appropriate photograph.
4. The student begins performing parts of the task one step or group of steps at a time, using the picture task analysis as a guide. The teacher completes the steps not yet attempted by the student and provides feedback and supervision. The number of steps attempted at one time depends on the student, the difficulty of the task, and whether a forward chaining, backward chaining, or total task procedure is used.
5. The teacher gradually fades his or her presence so that the student eventually performs the task, using the picture task analysis as a guide without direct supervision.

A Collaboration Success Story

In one of our classes, an adolescent with multiple disabilities was taught to make coffee using a standard automatic coffeemaker. Initially, the teacher consulted with the speech/language pathologist to determine the appropriateness of photographs as symbols for the student and the skill of coffeemaking. The speech/language pathologist then wrote the task analysis and provided written descriptions of the steps for making coffee in language appropriate for the student's ability level. An audiovisual technician took photographs of the teacher performing each step, and the teacher prepared the picture task analysis. After demonstrating the use of the folder and modeling the correct performance of coffeemaking, the teacher assisted and supervised the student as she began to prepare coffee.

The acquisition phase of the 13-step task began on October 5, with a paraprofessional implementing the instruction following the instructional procedure just outlined. The following chronology illustrates this student's progress, the fading of prompts, and the fading of the instructor as supervisor:

- October 14: Performed one step without referring to pictures.
- October 21: Performed three steps without referring to pictures.
- November 5: Corrected own mistake.
- November 17: Checked own work using pictures.
- November 21: Performed four steps without referring to pictures.
- December 8: Began by saying "Wash hands," the directions for step one.
- January 14: Only one prompt (verbal) given.
- January 20: Paraprofessional proximity faded to outside the office door.
- February 18: Performed with only natural job supervisor.

As can be seen from this chronology, within the first month and a half this adolescent began performing some steps without referring to the picture task analysis. Furthermore, after 3½ months the student was able to prepare coffee without any teacher supervision. The picture task analysis facilitated this student's learning and allowed her to gain independence more quickly than if she had to rely on teacher prompts. An additional benefit of this learning experience was seen in April, when a revised picture task analysis was introduced briefly for the student to learn to prepare coffee in a different environment, with a different coffeemaker, as part of her vocational program. As expected, she used the picture task analysis to learn the new steps required with different equipment and quickly progressed from teacher supervision to natural job-site supervision.

Conclusion

Picture task analyses are adaptive devices that are easily constructed by classroom teachers. They may be used in a variety of natural community and vocational environments. As a supplement to other instructional strategies, picture task analyses can provide access to independence from teacher supervision for learners with severe disabilities.

References

American Speech-Language-Hearing Association (ASHA). (1981). Position statement on nonspeech communication. *Asha, 23,* 577-581.

Brown, F. (1987). Meaningful assessment of people with severe and profound handicaps. In M. E. Snell (Ed.), *Systematic instruction of persons with severe handicaps* (pp. 39-63). Columbus, OH: Merrill.

Connis, R. T. (1979). The effects of sequential pictorial cues, self-recording, and praise on the job task sequencing of retarded adults. *Journal of Applied Behavior Analysis, 12,* 355-361.

Johnson, B. F., & Cuvo, A. J. (1981). Teaching mentally retarded adults to cook. *Behavior Modification, 5,* 187-202.

Robinson-Wilson, M. A. (1977). Picture recipe cards as an approach to teaching severely and profoundly retarded adults to cook. *Education and Training of the Mentally Retarded, 12,* 69-73.

Thinesen, P. J., & Bryan, J. A. (1981). The use of sequential picture cues in the initiation and maintenance of grooming behaviors with mentally retarded adults. *Mental Retardation, 19,* 246-250.

Wiggins, S. B., & Behrmann, M. M. (1988). Increasing independence through community learning. *TEACHING Exceptional Children, 21*(1), 20-24.

Wilson, P. G., Schepis, M. M. & Mason-Main, M. (1987). In vivo use of picture prompt training to increase independent work at a restaurant. *Journal of the Association for Persons with Severe Handicaps, 12,* 145-150.

Children with Hearing Impairments

Deaf children are disabled to the extent that they cannot hear speech through the ear, even with some form of amplification. They are dependent on vision for language and communication. Hard-of-hearing children can hear speech through the ear, but they need some form of amplification to make it more understandable. Hard-of-hearing children far outnumber deaf children. Most of them can be enrolled in inclusive education programs, with some modifications to the classroom and to their ears. While 8 to 10 percent of school children have some loss of hearing, only about 1 percent qualify for special educational services for their hearing impairments.

The assessment of hearing impairments is usually accomplished by identifying and measuring the decibel levels (loudness) of sounds, which the child can hear. These units can be generated on an audiometer. The child holds up a finger and points to the ear in which he or she hears a sound. An audiogram shows the results of an audiometric test. Children should be able to discern the pitch of sounds from 500 to 2,000 hertz, the range for spoken language. They normally can hear between 0–25 decibels (dB). A hearing loss from 26–40 dB is slight, loss from 41–55 dB is mild, loss from 56–70 dB is moderate, loss from 71–90 dB is severe, and a loss of more than 90 dB is deaf in each ear.

If an infant is born with a hearing impairment, he or she has a congenital hearing impairment. If the hearing loss is acquired later in life, it is an adventitious hearing impairment. If a hearing loss is present in both ears, it is bilateral. If it is present in only one ear, it is unilateral. If the loss of hearing occurs before a child learns language, it is prelinguistic. If it occurs after a child learns language it is postlinguistic. In terms of special adaptations required in education programs, the child with the former of each of these terms (congenital, bilateral, prelinguistic) usually needs more help. These forms of losses can occur in many combinations.

Two additional terms are very important in the assessment of hearing impairments: sensorineural hearing loss and conductive hearing loss. A sensorineural loss is usually more serious and requires more education adaptations than a conductive loss. Sensorineural hearing impairments involve defects or disorders of the auditory nerve or portions of the inner ear. They are difficult or impossible (depending on the problem) to correct with surgery, medicine, or sound amplification. Conductive hearing impairments involve defects or disorders of the outer or middle ear. Depending on the problem, they are often correctable with surgery, medicine, or sound amplification.

The causes of hearing impairments are not always easy to determine. In about 1/3 of all cases, the cause is unknown. Congenital losses may be inherited or caused by something during the mother's pregnancy and delivery, such as viral infections, drugs, prematurity, or low birth weight. Adventitious hearing losses may be due to injuries or diseases such as encephalitis, meningitis, or otitis media.

It is very important to assess hearing in infancy. PL 99-457 mandates comprehensive multidisciplinary services for infants and toddlers and their families. Once a hearing impairment is assessed, services should begin immediately. If the loss is conductive, the infant or toddler should be fitted with a sound amplification device (hearing aid). If the loss is sensorineural, the infant or toddler and the parents should begin learning sign language. Special educational services should also begin. Both receptive language (understanding what is said) and expressive language (speaking) are fostered with the earliest possible intervention. Cognitive processes and socialization processes are also dependent on early comprehension of some form of language.

Children who are deaf or hearing impaired are frequently enrolled in regular education classes for elementary, middle, and/or high school. Decisions about where to place them depend on many factors: age of onset of hearing loss, degree of hearing loss, language ability, cognitive factors, social factors, parental factors, and presence or absence of other educational disabilities. Individualized education programs must be annually updated. Sometimes the best environment (least restrictive) for a hearing impaired child is regular class for a portion of time and special class for another length of time. The nature of the child's problem determines the long- and short-term goals and the criteria for gauging the effectiveness of each special educational modification.

Teachers who have children who are hard of hearing in their classrooms should learn to read their audiograms, help them benefit from any residual hearing, and learn to use any kind of amplification system provided. These may include FM auditory training devices, microphones, or hearing aids. If a deaf child is enrolled in a regular education classroom, the teacher should make provisions for an interpreter, a notetaker, and/or captioned films and videos. If the child reads lips, the teacher must keep mouth movements visible. Speech reading (also called lipreading) is difficult for the child. The teacher should remember that the average speechreader only grasps about 5 percent of what is being said. If a computer is provided for the hearing impaired student, the teacher should be aware of software needs and appropriateness. Many deaf students are taught oral speech. It may be difficult to understand. A regular education teacher should work to comprehend it as much as possible. Since speech is important to the integration of deaf individuals to a hearing society, they are discouraged from using gestures, pointing, or written messages instead of speech.

Each child with a hearing loss should be motivated to do all he or she is capable of doing in both the educational and in the social activities of the school. The teacher has a major responsibility to help the nonhearing impaired peers understand the special needs of the child with a hearing loss. Teachers, peers, and all ancillary school personnel should encourage the child to participate to the fullest extent possible. The hearing impairment should not be allowed to become an excuse for nonparticipation. Children with hearing losses should be reinforced for their efforts but not praised for inaction. Understimulation and/or pity are detrimental both to educational progress and to socialization and self-esteem.

The first article selected for this unit provides information about the uses of the frequency modulation (FM) auditory training device in a regular class. FM devices are increasingly being used by children with hearing losses in inclusive education classes. The second article provides information about the presence of an educational interpreter in a regular classroom to assist children who are deaf. The interpreter may translate spoken language into sign language or may silently mouth the message in an oral form that is easier to speechread. The third selection addresses the controversy of providing special services to deaf and hard-of-hearing children who choose a private school over a public school education. The final article selected for this unit emphasizes the nonacademic lessons that deaf and hard-of-hearing students need to learn: independence and responsible transitional behaviors for success in life.

Looking Ahead: Challenge Questions

What is a FM (frequency modulation) auditory training device? What must a classroom teacher know about

wearing a microphone and checking the receiver worn by the student?

When an interpreter accompanies a deaf child to class, what should a teacher do? What role, if any, will the interpreter have with other students, other school personnel, or parents?

Should tax dollars pay for an interpreter for a deaf student who attends a private school? Why, or why not?

What skills should be taught to adolescents with hearing impairments to help them make a successful transition to adulthood?

HEARING FOR Success IN THE
C·L·A·S·S·R·O·O·M

JoAnn C. Ireland
Denise Wray
Carol Flexer

JoAnn C. Ireland is Communication Specialist/ Audiologist, Special Education Regional Resource Center, Cuyahoga Falls, Ohio. **Denise Wray** *is Assistant Professor of Speech Pathology, Department of Communicative Disorders, University of Akron, Ohio.* **Carol Flexer** *is Associate Professor of Audiology, Department of Communicative Disorders, University of Akron, Ohio.*

■Increasing numbers of hearing-impaired children are being mainstreamed, causing educators to express legitimate and realistic concerns. Many of these concerns are in regard to the assistive listening devices needed by hearing-impaired children. Although this equipment can be intimidating, it is essential; hearing-impaired children cannot function in the classroom setting without it (Berg, 1986; Ross, Brackett, & Maxon, 1982). This article answers questions that are typically asked about the technology necessary for children with any degree of hearing loss, from mild to profound, to participate actively in *any* educational environment.

A Prerequisite for Achievement

Hearing is pivotal to academic achievement. Hearing loss is an initial step in a detrimental progression of cause and effect. Loss of hearing sensitivity acts as an acoustic filter that hinders a child's normal language development due to inappropriate sensory input (Ling, 1976). The hearing loss subsequently impacts expressive language as well as reading, writing, attending skills, social interaction, and, ultimately, overall academic achievement (Ross, Brackett, & Maxon, 1982). Since reading and writing are built on verbal language skills, they suffer as a direct result of hearing loss. Until the problem of auditory reception is addressed, the pervasive effects of hearing loss will persist and escalate. Therefore, anything that can be done to maximize hearing will have a positive impact on the child's academic performance.

Hearing aids are typically worn to augment auditory reception. Unfortunately, however, the problems of distance, room reverberation, and background noise can greatly interfere with the wearer's ability to discriminate a preferred auditory signal such as a teacher's voice (Berg, 1986; Bess & McConnell, 1981). In fact, speech discrimination is significantly reduced, even when the child is only 1 foot away. A signal must be 10 times louder than the background noise in order to have a signal-to-noise ratio that will allow for intelligibility of speech (Hawkins, 1984; Ross & Giolas, 1978). A typical classroom could not possibly provide a preference signal (teacher's voice) that is loud enough to be intelligible over the background noise (Berg, 1986).

When the signal-to-noise ratio is poor, an auditory signal may be audible to a hearing-impaired child, but not necessarily "intelligible" (Boothroyd, 1978). In other words, the child may respond in a seemingly appropriate way but not really understand what he or she has heard. The child may actually be responding only to intonation patterns and not truly comprehending the specifics of the utterance.

Lipreading is an ineffective substitute for hearing, because visual cues do not provide enough information for identifying the many homophenous words in the English language, for example, "pan," "man," and "ban" (Jeffers & Barley, 1971). These words look alike on the lips and cannot be discriminated without the addition of some auditory information. Therefore, lipreading is considered important, but only as a complement to auditory reception (Boothroyd, 1978).

Preferential seating, even with the use of hearing aids, is not enough! Neither lipreading skills nor hearing aids can substitute for a learning strategy that incorporates the use of an optimal auditory signal.

FM Assistive Listening Devices

Frequency Modulation (FM) auditory training devices are one of the many systems available as personal listening devices. According to Zelski and Zelski (1985), assistive listening devices are products designed to solve the problems of noise, distance, and reverberation that cannot be solved with a hearing aid alone. They do not replace hearing aids, but augment them to more fully meet the needs of hearing-impaired individuals in group listening situations.

From *Teaching Exceptional Children*, Winter 1988, pp. 15-17. © 1988 by The Council for Exceptional Children. Reprinted by permission.

An FM auditory trainer is comprised of a microphone, which is placed near the desired sound source (e.g., teacher, loudspeaker, etc.), and a receiver worn by the listener, who can be situated anywhere within approximately 200 feet. These devices can often be coupled to the child's own hearing aid for appropriate individual amplification. There are many models of FM equipment on the market (Van-Tasell, Mallinger, & Crump, 1986). It is important to obtain a model that can be worn by both the teacher and the child in an inconspicuous fashion (Flexer & Wood, 1984). The multiple FM fitting and setting options require visits to the audiologist for appropriate selection and adjustments.

The FM device creates a listening situation that is comparable to the teacher's being only 6 inches away from the child's ear at all times. Ideally, if the unit is fitted and adjusted correctly by an audiologist, its use promotes speech intelligibility and not simply audibility. For example, a child might hear the teacher's voice through a hearing aid alone, but might not be able to distinguish the differences between words such as "wade/wait," "can't/can," "invitation/vacation," and "kite/kites." Such confusions are detrimental to the child's concept and vocabulary development, and they influence the child's potential for success in a regular classroom.

Unfortunately, the FM system is not a panacea for classroom management of hearing-impaired students (Ross, Brackett, & Maxon, 1982). One successful supplement to the regular class curriculum with FM use is to provide tutoring, which can be offered on a pre- and postlesson basis. Teachers can also employ other facilitating strategies such as repeating and rephrasing information and using the cue word "listen" prior to presenting instructions.

Incorporating FM into the Classroom

The Ling Five Sound Test offers a quick and easy way to check, on a daily basis, whether or not a hearing-impaired child can detect the necessary speech sounds (Ling, 1976). This information is vital for instruction. The test can be administered with the child at the far end of the classroom, wearing the FM device and facing away from the teacher. The child repeats each sound as the teacher says it 6 inches from the microphone. The sounds used are /a/, /oo/, /e/, /sh/, and /s/ and are representative of the speech energy contained in every English phoneme. If the child can detect these five sounds, he or she can detect every English speech sound (Ling, 1976). Responding to the sounds may take some practice for children who have not been encouraged to use their residual hearing to its fullest extent.

If the Ling Five Sound Test reveals absent or abnormal FM function, the teacher should always check the battery first. Some 90% of breakdowns reportedly are due to problems with the battery (Ross, 1981). The charge should be checked with a battery tester, because even a new battery or one that has been plugged in may not be fully charged. The teacher should make sure the battery is in the compartment properly and check to see that the poles match. A contact person should be available to take care of quick repairs. Many repairs such as replacing cords or receivers can be done inhouse by an audiologist, speech-language pathologist, or other trained personnel.

As soon as a hearing-impaired child enters any kind of classroom situation, even preschool, an FM device is necessary and appropriate. The child will need to wear the FM unit throughout the school day, since it provides vital assistance any time instructions or information are presented (e.g. gym rules, art, lunch, speech therapy, etc.).

Children never outgrow their need for FM units; even college students find them invaluable. Hearing-impaired people use the devices any time they wish to hear in public or group situations such as lectures, movies, or church services (Leavitt, 1985).

Summary

It is evident that FM auditory trainers are an integral part of educating hearing-impaired students. These units improve speech intelligibility by reducing the effects of background noise and reverberation and providing an adequate signal-to-noise ratio. There are no substitutes for the efficient use of residual hearing. Therefore, all hearing-impaired children mainstreamed into regular classrooms need FM units. If such a device is not provided, both teacher and child are made to function at an unnecessary disadvantage. The classroom teacher may need to serve as the child's advocate in order to maximize his or her potential for academic success and minimize the frustration often encountered when hearing-impaired pupils are mainstreamed.

References

Berg, F. S. (1986). Classroom acoustics and signal transmission. In F. J. Berg, K. C. Blair, S. H. Viehweg, & J. A. Wilson-Vlotman (Eds.), *Educational audiology for the hard of hearing child* (pp. 157-180). New York: Grune & Stratton.

Bess, F. H., & McConnell, F. E. (1981). *Audiology, education, and the hearing-impaired child.* St. Louis: C. V. Mosby.

Boothroyd, A. (1978). Speech perception and severe hearing loss. In M. Ross & T. G. Giolas (Eds.), *Auditory management of hearing-impaired children* (pp. 117-144). Baltimore: University Park Press.

Flexer, C., & Wood, L. A. (1984). The hearing aid: Facilitator or inhibitor of auditory interaction? *Volta Review, 86,* 354-355.

Hawkins, D. B. (1984). Comparisons of speech recognition in noise by mildly-to-moderately hearing-impaired children using hearing aids and FM systems. *Journal of Speech and Hearing Disorders, 49,* 409-418.

Jeffers, J., & Barley, M. (1971). *Speechreading (lipreading).* Springfield, IL: Charles C Thomas.

Leavitt, R. (1985). Counseling to encourage use of SNR enhancing systems. *Hearing Instruments, 36,* 8-9.

Ling, D. (1976). *Speech and the hearing-impaired child: Theory and practice.* Washington, DC: The Alexander Graham Bell Association for the Deaf.

Ross, M. (1981). Classroom amplification. In W. R. Hodgson and R. H. Skinna (Eds.), *Hearing aid assessment and use in audiologic habilitation* (2nd ed., pp. 234-257). Baltimore: Williams & Wilkins.

Ross, M., Brackett, D., & Maxon, A. (1982). *Hard-of-hearing children in regular schools.* Englewood Cliffs, NJ: Prentice-Hall.

Ross, M. & Giolas, T. G. (1978). *Auditory management of hearing-impaired children.* Baltimore: University Park Press.

VanTasell, D. J., Mallinger, C. A., & Crump, E. S. (1986). Functional gain and speech recognition with two types of FM amplification. *Language, Speech and Hearing Services in Schools, 17,* 28-37.

Zelski, R. F. K., & Zelski, T. (1985). What are assistive devices? *Hearing Instruments, 36,* 12.

THE ROLES OF THE EDUCATIONAL INTERPRETER IN MAINSTREAMING

Spencer J. Salend • Maureen Longo

Spencer J. Salend *(CEC Chapter #615), Professor, State University of New York at New Paltz.* **Maureen Longo***, Educational Interpreter, Florida School for the Deaf and Blind, St. Augustine.*

As a result of Public Law 94-142, the Individuals with Disabilities Education Act (formerly known as the Education for All Handicapped Children Act of 1975), many students with hearing impairments are being educated in regular education settings with their hearing peers. Data from the *Fifteenth Annual Report to Congress on the Implementation of the Individuals with Disabilities Education Act* (U.S. Department of Education, 1993) indicate that approximately 47% of students with hearing impairments are taught in inclusive settings. These students need a variety of services to enhance their academic performance and social adjustment in such settings.

One essential service that many students with hearing impairments attending regular classes may need is an educational interpreter (Commission on

The authors would like to thank Ruth McLachlan for her valuable assistance in preparing this article.

the Education of the Deaf, 1988; Rittenhouse, Rahn, & Morreau, 1989). The National Task Force on Educational Interpreting (1989) has estimated that approximately 4,000 interpreters are needed to serve students with hearing impairments in school settings. An educational interpreter, sometimes referred to as an *educational transliterator,* facilitates the transmission of information between individuals who do not communicate with a common language or code (Massachusetts Commission for the Deaf and Hard of Hearing, 1988). Additionally, an educational interpreter can work with parents and professionals to guide the delivery of appropriate educational services to students with hearing impairments.

Since the preferred mode of communication of students with hearing impairments may vary, there is a variety of educational interpreting methods. A *signed system interpreter* translates spoken language directed toward a student

with a hearing impairment into a signed system such as American Sign Language (ASL), Conceptually Accurate Signed English (CASE), Manually Coded English (MCE), or Signs in English Word Order. An *oral interpreter* facilitates the hearing impaired student's understanding of verbal messages by silently mouthing the complete verbal message or its paraphrased equivalent (Castle, 1988). In either of these methods of interpreting, the interpreter employs voice interpretation if the student needs assistance in converting his or her responses into the preferred mode of understanding of the individual communicating with the student. Other students with hearing impairments may benefit from the services of a cued speech facilitator (Kipila & Williams-Scott, 1988).

Several states (e.g., Florida, Massachusetts, North Carolina, Virginia, and New York) and national groups (i.e., The Commission on the Education of the Deaf, the National Task Force on Educational Interpreting) have begun to establish procedures to guide the development and delivery of educational services. In light of the uniqueness and newness of the use of interpreters in inclusive settings, their roles need to be clearly specified to avoid possible role confusion, facilitate collaborative interactions, and promote the independence of students with hearing impairments (National Task Force on Educational Interpreting, 1989).

This article offers guidelines and suggestions related to the interpreter's relationship with students with hearing impairments, teachers, the student's peers and parents, supportive service personnel, and administrators. Educators and interpreters should tailor the guidelines to the unique circumstances of their educational settings.

INTERACTING WITH STUDENTS WITH HEARING IMPAIRMENTS

The interpreter and the student should meet prior to the beginning of the school year to become acquainted and establish clear guidelines concerning their interactions. A sample agenda for the meeting is provided in Figure 1. The interpreter and student should discuss the roles the interpreter will perform to assist the student as well as instances when it would not be appropriate for the interpreter to intervene. While the language level used to convey information may vary depending on the age of the student, the interpreter and the student should discuss the following questions:

1. What method of communication should be used?
2. Will the interpreter be responsible for speaking for the student? (Some students may prefer to verbalize for themselves.)
3. What will be the interpreter's role with peers?
4. Will the interpreter be available to foster communication with teachers and peers after class?
5. At what times will the interpreter be available to translate for teachers and

students in tutoring sessions and when working on homework?
6. How will the interpreter maintain confidentiality and deal with personal information about the student?

In delineating roles, the student and the interpreter should examine each role with respect to its impact on the student's independence. Independence should follow a pattern of growth from dependence to independence, and the interpreter's role will vary depending on the student's level. For example, the interpreter and the student may agree to work toward an arrangement whereby (a) the student will direct all classroom communication to the teacher and peers; (b) the interpreter will not redirect the student's attention during class; and (c) the interpreter will only assist the student with peers outside the classroom when the student requests assistance.

At the end of the meeting, the interpreter and the student should exchange telephone numbers or determine an appropriate procedure for notifying each other when one will not be in school. Since perspectives change and new problems may arise, the interpreter and the student should meet periodi-

Figure 1. Sample Agenda for Interpreter/Student Conference

1. Introduce the interpreter and the student.
2. Review the purpose of the meeting.
3. Discuss the rationale for the use of an interpreter.
4. Discuss the roles of the interpreter from the interpreter's and the student's perspectives, including:
   Roles with teachers.
   Roles with students.
   Roles with parents.
   Roles with others.
5. Establish a consensus on roles.
6. Discuss time availability for out-of-class interactions.
7. Agree on policies regarding absences.
8. Summarize and review the results of the meeting.
9. Determine an appropriate date for the next meeting.

cally to evaluate their progress, identify their successes, and discuss and resolve their problems.

INTERACTING WITH TEACHERS

An educational interpreter can facilitate the academic performance of a student with a hearing impairment in the regular class setting by translating directions, content, and assignments presented orally by teachers and the comments of peers, as well as sharing the student's responses and questions with teachers and peers. However, interpreters can function most effectively as an instructional resource in the classroom only when they carefully coordinate their efforts with teachers.

Early in the school year, the teacher and the interpreter should agree upon the roles each will play in working with the student. They should come to a consensus concerning their responsibilities with respect to such issues as grading, contacting parents, working with other students, assigning and assisting with homework and other assignments, designing and administering tests, arranging for peer note takers, communicating with other professionals, using media, and disciplining students. Generally, roles should be defined so that the teacher has primary responsibility and the interpreter serves in a supportive role. For example, if a student is having difficulty with homework, the teacher, rather than the interpreter, should correct the homework and meet with the student to deliver remedial instruction. However, the interpreter should be present to facilitate the remedial process. To help schedule out-of-class activities, the teacher and the interpreter should exchange schedules and try to identify mutually convenient times.

Since the interpreter may not have prior exposure to the content and instructional strategies employed in the classroom, it would be helpful if the teacher provided him or her with an orientation to the curriculum. At the beginning of the school year or semester, the teacher could furnish the interpreter with curriculum guides, textbooks, and

The student may choose not to use an interpreter outside the classroom.

other relevant instructional materials and review them with the interpreter if necessary. A knowledge of class routines, projects, and long-term assignments can assist the interpreter in helping students with hearing impairments understand and prepare for these assignments. Additionally, the interpreter should be informed of the dates, times, and content of special assemblies and class trips (Florida State Education Department, 1986).

Throughout the school year, the teacher and the interpreter should meet to review curriculum and discuss their efforts to work collaboratively. When a unit of particularly difficult material is to be covered that includes new technical vocabulary and material that is hard to explain in alternative forms of communication, the teacher and the interpreter may want to meet on a more frequent basis. For example, when

teaching a unit about the geological history of the earth, the teacher might provide the interpreter with a list of key terms and a copy of lesson plans so that the interpreter can plan in advance how to translate and explain such terms as *Paleozoic era, Oligocene epoch,* and *the Jurassic period.*

An important factor for the teacher and the interpreter to examine is the location of the interpreter in the classroom. Whenever possible, the interpreter should be seated in a glare-free, well-lit location with a solid-colored background free of visual and auditory distractions (Hurwitz & Witter, 1979). Waldron, Diebold, and Rose (1985) have provided guidelines for interpreters to coordinate the visual and auditory messages associated with class presentations. They have suggested that the interpreter sit slightly in front of the student without blocking the view of the

chalkboard, overhead, or teacher; focus the student's attention by pointing with one hand to the visuals as the teacher refers to them; and use the other hand to communicate the dialogue of the teacher or the other students. Since many teachers move around when they present content to the class, they should understand that interpreters and students with hearing impairments may need to leave their seats to watch them.

The positioning of the interpreter also depends on the nature of the instructional activity (Florida State Department of Education, 1986). When the teacher is using a lecture format, it may be desirable for the interpreter to stand or sit to the side and slightly in front of the teacher, with the student's desk located 3 to 5 feet from the interpreter. In a one-to-one instruction setting, the interpreter should be placed next to the hearing individual and facing the student from a distance of about 4 to 6 feet. During group activities, the group should be seated in a circular fashion with the interpreter located across from the student. Additional guidelines are available for locating an interpreter who is interpreting for several students in a class or for oral students (Florida State Department of Education, 1986).

Procedures for maximizing the effectiveness of the interpreter and facilitating the process also should be discussed. The interpreter may need to sensitize the teacher to the processing time delays that are associated with interpreting (Hurwitz & Witter, 1979). The teacher should be told to talk to the student and not to the interpreter. The teacher should avoid directing comments or questions to the interpreter during class time and should discuss them after class (Frishberg, 1986). Similarly, the interpreter and the student should not engage in extended conversations in class. When communication problems arise during class that affect the translation process, such as the teacher talking too rapidly, or a peer speaking inaudibly, the interpreter should ask for clarification. For example, if an interpreter did not understand a peer's comment, he or she could say, "I'm sorry, I didn't understand that. Could you please repeat it?" If professionals notice recurrent behavior problems exhibited by students with hearing impairments—for example, two students talking to each other using sign language during a class lecture—they may want to signal each other or discuss their concerns at the next class break or after the class is completed.

Occasionally, the teacher may use media such as videocassettes and audiocassettes to convey information to students. These types of media can cause special problems for the interpreter and the student with a hearing impairment. When using such media, the teacher can reduce problems by providing the interpreter with a script, locating the interpreter near the screen, stopping periodically to paraphrase the content presented and check student comprehension, and asking the interpreter to bring an interpreter's lamp or a flashlight. Students with hearing impairments also may benefit from the opportunity to view media such as videocassettes privately with their interpreters so that they can review and discuss key points (R. C. McLachlan, personal communication, July 14, 1990).

INTERACTING WITH OTHER STUDENTS

The interpreter also may be called upon to interact with hearing students in the class. Since most hearing students will not have encountered an interpreter previously, the teacher should first introduce the student with a hearing impairment and the interpreter to the class. If the student feels comfortable, the student and the interpreter can discuss the student's needs and the role of the interpreter with the other class members. If the student uses a hearing aid, he or she can explain the parts and maintenance of the aid and allow other students to use it for a brief period of time. Similarly the teacher may ask the interpreter to introduce students to alternative communication systems by (a) teaching students the manual alphabet and having them practice their spelling words manually; (b) presenting math problems using hand signs for numbers; and (c) using basic signs to give directions (Salend, 1994).

The initial orientation also should provide hearing students with guidelines for interacting with the interpreter. Students should be informed that the interpreter is there to facilitate communication with the student with a hearing impairment and is not available to assist with assignments and tests or to tutor students. Similarly, students should be told not to ask the interpreter for permission to leave the room or assistance in resolving disputes. Students also should be cautioned that if the interpreter is asked by school personnel about inappropriate behaviors and negative comments, he or she may be required to report all observations.

Because they cannot read signs and write at the same time, students with hearing impairments may need a note taker. Therefore, the need for and role of a note taker also should be reviewed with the student's peers. Following this discussion, peer note takers should be solicited (Frishberg, 1986). Peer note takers should demonstrate mastery of the class content, skill in taking notes, sensitivity to students with disabilities, and an ability to work independently. Since peer note takers may be absent periodically, it also is necessary to identify backup note takers (R. C. McLachlan, personal communication, July 14, 1990). The note-taking process can be facilitated by offering training in note-taking skills to peers and providing the note takers with special carbonless paper (Wilson, 1981).

INTERACTING WITH PARENTS

The extent to which the interpreter will interact with the student's parents depends upon the hearing acuity of the parents. If the parents have hearing impairments, the interpreter may be asked to interpret in order to facilitate communication between them and school personnel. However, if the parents do not have hearing impairments, their interactions with the interpreter may be limited to meetings with professionals at which the student is present. While parents may look to the interpreter to serve as a liaison with teachers and school staff, they should be encouraged to interact directly with these professionals (Florida State Education Department, 1986). For example, rather than asking the interpreter about their child's progress in classes, parents should be asked to direct these questions to the appropriate school personnel. However, the educational interpreter may be a resource for parents concerning information about the efficacy of the communication methodology that the interpreter and student are using.

INTERACTING WITH SUPPORTIVE SERVICE PERSONNEL

In addition to teachers, the interpreter will interact with ancillary service personnel. Because the interpreter spends a large amount of time with students in a variety of instructional and social settings, he or she will have a unique perspective on the student's needs that can be helpful to the multidisciplinary planning team. Therefore, in evaluating and planning services for the student, the multidisciplinary team may want to solicit information from the interpreter. However, since confidentiality is an important aspect of the interpreter-student relationship, educational interpreters should follow the school district's policies and use discretion when sharing information that is essential to the student's safety, welfare, and educational program (National Task Force on Educational Interpreting, 1989). To facilitate the interpreter's ability to interact with others at multidisci-

plinary team meetings, many school districts are hiring another educational interpreter to interpret for the student during these meetings (R. C. McLachlan, personal communication, July 14, 1990).

The interpreter also may work closely with speech and language therapists. Speech and language therapists can provide information concerning the extent to which students with hearing impairments should verbalize. Although the interpreter can provide speech and language therapists with information regarding the student's communication skills, he or she is not trained to evaluate the student's speech skills and should not be asked to do so. However, while the multidisciplinary

team will determine the modes of communication used by the student and the interpreter, the educational interpreter can provide useful information regarding the success of these communication methodologies in increasing the student's ability to acquire instructional content and interact with others (National Task Force on Educational Interpreting, 1989).

INTERACTING WITH SCHOOL ADMINISTRATORS

School administrators are usually responsible for coordinating the delivery of services to students with disabilities. When the need for an interpreter is identified, the school administrator, in consultation with others, should develop a job description that meets local needs and specifications (National Task Force on Educational Interpreting, 1989). The job description should identify the roles and responsibilities of the educational interpreter and include statements about the educational levels of the students and the mode(s) of communication to be used in interpreting. The job description also should specify (a) the job title, (b) the qualifications and skills required, (c) the supervisory arrangement, (d) nonclassroom interpreting activities, (e) professional development opportunities, and (f) salary and benefits (Florida State Education Department, 1986). To promote collaboration with others and an understanding of the roles of the educational interpreter, the job description should be shared with parents and professionals. Sample job descriptions are available (Massachusetts Commission for the Deaf and Hard of Hearing, 1988; National Task Force on Educational Interpreting, 1989).

When the multidisciplinary placement team determines that a student needs the services of an interpreter, the administrator should inform regular classroom teachers that the student will be included in their classes and will be receiving the services of an interpreter. Additionally, the administrator should introduce the interpreter to the teachers and review districtwide policies regard-

During an interpreter/student conference, they evaluate progress, identify successes, and discuss and solve problems.

ing the delivery of services by an interpreter. For example, the district may have a policy prohibiting the interpreter from being asked to watch or teach a class while the teacher cannot be in the room. Similarly, districtwide policies regarding communication modes should be reviewed. Administrators may be called upon to resolve disagreements between the interpreter and other school personnel, such as a teacher refusing to use the services of an interpreter. Administrators also should attempt to allay any fears that teachers may have about having another adult in the classroom and promote positive attitudes toward the student, the interpreter, and the process of inclusion.

If the interpreter is new to the school, a school administrator should provide an orientation including (a) a tour of the building; (b) an introduction of key school personnel; (c) an explanation of the need for and the rules relating to confidentiality; (d) a review of school dress codes and other standards of decorum; (e) an identification of out-of-class interpreting activities; and (f) a discussion of school schedules, calendars, and procedures relating to absences and emergencies.

The orientation also should include a discussion of the educational interpreter's schedule. This schedule should be carefully planned to promote the continued effectiveness of the interpreter. To facilitate collaborative interactions with teachers, parents, and other professionals, the schedule should provide time for the interpreter to meet with others and plan for interpreting activities. Additionally, to lessen the likelihood of fatigue or injuries associated with repetitive movements (e.g., carpal tunnel syndrome), the interpreter's schedule should include a break after each hour of continuous interpreting (National Task Force on Educational Interpreting, 1989).

Administrators also may be responsible for supervising the educational interpreter and coordinating the multidisciplinary team's evaluation of the services provided to the student. The interpreter's technical skills should be evaluated periodically. Since school administrators often are not trained as interpreters, qualified consultants can be hired to evaluate the interpreter's technical skills. For example, the Massachusetts Commission for the Deaf and Hard of Hearing offers the services of a staff member to perform evaluations of educational interpreters. The evaluation also should examine the effectiveness of and satisfaction with the services the interpreter provides from the perspectives of those who interact with the interpreter. Feedback from the interpreter also should be collected, including self-evaluation data. All involved individuals should be surveyed to identify potential solutions to problem areas as well as changes that need to be made in order to promote the independence of students with hearing impairments. Sample evaluation questions may include the following:

1. Are teachers and the interpreter working cooperatively to deliver instruction to students?

2. In what ways is the present system assisting students to become independent?

3. What are the impacts of the interpreter on the student's peers and the social interactions between students with hearing impairments and their peers?

4. Has the interpreter aided professionals in communicating with parents who have hearing impairments?

5. Are administrative policies regarding the use of the interpreter appropriate?

Many states will hire only educational interpreters who have been certified by the Registry of Interpreters for the Deaf (RID). RID-certified interpreters must pass a test that includes both a written and a performance portion. The written portion assesses mastery of content related to the field of interpreting, including the history and ethics of the profession, sociological and cultural factors associated with hearing impairments, language development, and linguistics. The performance section examines the interpreter's skills in a variety of interpreting situations. While the RID has served as a national certifying agency for professional interpreters, it currently does not offer a specific certification for educational interpreters (Commission on Education of the Deaf, 1988). However, the RID is now working with the Council for the Education of the Deaf (CED) to develop standards and procedures to certify educational interpreters (R. C. McLachlan, personal communication, July 14, 1990). Additional guidelines regarding certification for oral interpreters and cued speech facilitators are available from the Alexander Graham Bell Association for the Deaf and the National Cued Speech Association, respectively.

As with other professionals, the school administrator should assist educational interpreters in their professional development (National Task Force on Educational Interpreting, 1989). The school administrator or other professionals can work with individual interpreters to plan a series of appropriate professional development activities that address the interpreter's unique needs, interests, and job functions. For example, North Carolina has established a professional development model whereby trainers of interpreters work with interpreters to design inservice activities (R. C. McLachlan, personal communication, July 14, 1990). Professional development activities can include reading books and articles, viewing media, attending workshops and conferences, enrolling in courses, and visiting model programs. As part of the interpreter's professional development, it may be appropriate to offer inservice training sessions to teachers, ancillary support personnel, and parents to introduce them to the roles and responsibilities of the educational interpreter.

CONCLUSION

The primary goal of the educational interpreter is to facilitate communication between two parties who use different communication systems. To achieve this goal and to aid in the inclusion of students with hearing impairments, the interpreter must fulfill many roles that require interaction with a variety of individuals. These roles should be identified and discussed with the student with a hearing impairment, school personnel, parents, and peers so that all are working to further the academic and social independence of students with hearing impairments.

REFERENCES

Castle, D. (1988). *Oral interpreting: Selections from papers by Kirsten Gonzalez.* Washington, DC: Alexander Graham Bell Association for the Deaf.

Commission on the Education of the Deaf. (1988). *Toward equality: Education of the deaf. A report to the President and the Congress of the United States.* Washington, DC: U.S. Government Printing Office.

Florida State Education Department. (1986). *Interpreting in the educational setting.* Tallahassee: Author.

Frishberg, N. (1986). *Interpreting: An introduction.* Rockville, MD: Registry of Interpreters for the Deaf.

Hurwitz, T. A., & Witter, A. B. (1979). Principles of interpreting in an educational environment. In M. E. Bishop (Ed.), *Mainstreaming: Practical ideas for educating hearing impaired students* (pp. 138–140). Washington, DC: Alexander Graham Bell Association for the Deaf.

Kipila, E., & Williams-Scott, B. (1988). Cued speech and speech reading. *Volta Review, 90,* 179–192.

Massachusetts Commission for the Deaf and Hard of Hearing. (1988). *An information guide related to standards for educational interpreting for deaf and severely hard of hearing students in elementary and secondary schools.* Boston: Author.

National Task Force on Educational Interpreting. (1989). *Educational interpreting for deaf students.* Rochester, NY: National Technical Institute for the Deaf, Rochester Institute of Technology.

Rittenhouse, R. K., Rahn, C. H., & Morreau, L. E. (1989). Educational interpreter services for hearing impaired students: Provider and consumer disagreements. *Journal of the American Deafness and Rehabilitation Association, 22,* 57–63.

Salend, S. J. (1994). *Effective mainstreaming: Creating inclusive classrooms* (2nd ed.). New York: Macmillan.

U. S. Department of Education. (1993). *Fifteenth annual report to Congress on the implementation of the Individuals with Disabilities Education Act.* Washington, DC: Author.

Waldron, M. B., Diebold, T. J., & Rose, S. (1985). Hearing-impaired students in regular classrooms: A cognitive model for educational services. *Exceptional Children, 52,* 39–43.

Wilson, J. J. (1981). Notetaking: A necessary support service for hearing-impaired students. *TEACHING Exceptional Children, 14,* 38–40.

Public Aid for Handicapped and
Educationally Deprived Students

The Establishment Clause As Antiremedy

Steven Huefner

STEVEN HUEFNER is a judicial clerk for Justice Christine M. Durham of the Supreme Court of Utah, Salt Lake City.

Mr. Huefner critiques the reasoning in Aguilar v. Felton *and in a later case involving Jimmy Zobrest, a deaf student — and he proposes some alternative means of addressing similar issues in the future.*

SCHOOLS, a fundamental institution of American culture and society, have historically failed to meet the needs of significant groups of students, including students with disabilities, minorities, and impoverished youths. In recent decades the U.S. Congress has sought to remedy some of these failures by establishing various assistance programs targeted at specific groups. Predictably, however, many obstacles stand in the way of the full success of such programs. For instance, the Education for All Handicapped Children Act (P.L. 94-142) and

its successor require all public school districts in the United States to provide appropriate educational services to all special education students within their district boundaries.[1] Yet, although this requirement extends to *all* special education students, whether or not they are enrolled in a public school, the establishment clause of the First Amendment to the Constitution prevents the government from providing many sorts of assistance to sectarian institutions. Thus when a deaf student who attends a parochial school seeks, under P.L. 94-142, to obtain from the local public school district the services of a sign language interpreter, the establishment clause may preclude the desired injunctive relief. But should it?

Precisely this controversy arose in a federal district court case brought in Arizona in 1989 by deaf student Jimmy Zobrest. Using Jimmy's case as a means of framing the issues, I will examine the broader relationship of the establishment clause to supplementary educational programs that may have an incidental impact on sectarian institutions. First, I will examine the background and central issues of Jimmy's case — issues that resemble

those in the much more widely reported 1985 Supreme Court decision, *Aguilar v. Felton*.[2] Next I discuss the decisions in both Jimmy's case and in *Felton*, considering how their implications for the remedial goals of supplementary education may lead us to view them as instances of "antiremedy" — a term coined by Kellis Parker of Columbia University. I then offer a final critique of the reasoning in these cases and propose some alternative means of addressing similar issues in the future.

P.L. 94-142

Congress passed P.L. 94-142 in the wake of growing concern over the treatment that students with disabilities were receiving in the public schools. Sometimes these students were relegated to "special" programs, in which all they really learned was to withdraw further from their nondisabled peers; at other times they were left in the regular classroom entirely unassisted.[3] P.L. 94-142 sought to improve the education of students with disabilities by keeping them in the regular classroom when appropriate while providing them with whatever support services they needed, such as wheelchair ramps,[4] braille texts and other instructional materials,[5] sign language interpreters, or other special tutors. P.L. 94-142 also stipulated that any state receiving federal education funds had to show that all of its school districts were providing "all handicapped children the right to a free appropriate public education" in the least restrictive environment.[6] Theoretically, states can refuse to comply and thereby simply lose their federal funding, but the states are currently too dependent on federal aid to do so. Hence, the statute is effectively compulsory.

Although P.L. 94-142 required little in the way of specific progams, its broad mandate to the states required them to demonstrate that, "to the maximum extent appropriate, handicapped children, including children in public or private institutions or other care facilities, are educated with children who are not handicapped, and that . . . removal . . . from the regular classroom occurs only when . . . education in regular classes with the use of supplementary aides and services cannot be achieved satisfactorily."[7] Subsequent court decisions have established that schools are required to enable students with disabilities to receive special education instruction in the regular classroom to the maximum extent appropriate, using whatever related services may be required in the process — a form of "mainstreaming."

THE *LEMON* TEST

Jimmy Zobrest was a deaf high school student who required "the services of a sign language interpreter" to assist him in his schooling.[8] He resides within the Catalina Foothills public school district in Arizona, and, had he wished to attend the local public high school, he would have been entitled to the assistance of a sign language interpreter at school at public expense, according to the provisions of P.L. 94-142. But Jimmy wished to attend a religiously affiliated school, the Salpointe Catholic High School, where his entitlement to an interpreter under P.L. 94-142 was less certain. In the summer of 1989 Jimmy and his father brought suit against the Catalina Foothills School District, seeking an injunction mandating that the school district provide a sign language interpreter for him at Salpointe.[9]

At first blush it may seem hard to imagine how a court could compel a public school district to provide support for the educational programs of *any* private school. Yet this aspect of Jimmy's case is not an issue. P.L. 94-142 requires each state to establish procedures that will ensure that all children with disabilities who are in need of special education have access to appropriate special educational services, even if they attend private schools.[10] The Supreme Court has held that publicly employed teachers may provide instruction in special programs at private schools if instruction comparable to that which public school students are receiving is not otherwise available.[11] School districts already routinely include private and parochial school students in many of their programs, although this mixing is most easily accomplished when the supplemental programs occur on public (or at least nonsectarian) property. Therefore, Jimmy's problem was not that he wished to attend a private school and still obtain a state-sponsored interpreter. Rather, his problem was that the private school he desired to attend was a *religiously affiliated* school and that the assistance he needed had to be provided on the school grounds. He thus encountered problems with the establishment clause.

The establishment clause is of primary importance whenever the relationship between government and sectarian schools is at issue; any public aid granted to a private institution having a religious affiliation is likely to receive careful scrutiny to ensure that it does not constitute "an establishment of religion." The principal judicial standard used today for assessing whether an educational program violates the establishment clause is the test articulated by the Supreme Court in 1971 in *Lemon* v. *Kurtzman*.[12] This three-part "*Lemon* test" structures the analysis of a congressional or state statute with respect to the establishment clause as follows:

> First, the statute must have a secular legislative purpose; second, its principal or primary effect must be one that neither advances nor inhibits religion; finally, the statute must not foster "an excessive government entanglement with religion."[13]

When Jimmy sought to have an interpreter from the public schools assist him at Salpointe as part of his entitlement to "a free appropriate public education," the second and third parts of this test stood in his way. The first part of the test was easily satisfied: the statute's clear and singular purpose was to provide better education for *all* students with disabilities. But satisfying the second and third parts of the test — neither advancing or inhibiting religion nor fostering excessive government entanglement — was much harder.

Central to Jimmy's difficulty was the district court's reliance on the 1985 Supreme Court decision in *Aguilar* v. *Felton*. This case involved a challenge to New York City's administration of a congressional program designed to provide supplemental education in local schools to "educationally deprived children" from low-income families.[14] The program, now part of Chapter 1 of the Education Consolidation and Improvement Act of 1981, sought to improve the education of *all* children whose opportunities had been limited by their economic background. It mandated that students attending private schools also receive supplemental educational services comparable to those they would receive if they were in a public school. Some 13% of the students eligible for the assistance in New York City in 1982 were enrolled in parochial schools, and federal funds were being used to pay public employees to work at these parochial schools, where they taught courses in remedial reading, reading skills, remedial mathematics, and English as a second language.

In *Felton*, six taxpayers had successfully challenged these expenditures as a violation of the establishment clause, thus creating a precedent that boded unfavorably for Jimmy.

ANTIREMEDY RULES THE DAY

In *Zobrest* v. *Catalina Foothills School District*, the U.S. District Court for the District of Arizona, following *Felton* with almost no discussion, denied Jimmy the interpreter he needed.[15] Although superficially the reasoning in *Felton* — and by extension in Jimmy's case — is well within the normal bounds of establishment clause reasoning and thus seems to advance the legitimate ends of separation of church and state, the apparent logic of the analysis only masks the deeper remedial failures that it causes.

In *Zobrest* the district court stated that the interpreter would "act as a conduit for the religious inculcation of James — thereby, promoting James's religious development at government expense." Such entanglement of church and state is not allowed, the court said, citing *Aguilar* v.

Felton. The majority opinion in *Felton* first considered the religious character of the schools in question, noting that their substantial purpose was "the inculcation of religious values." Although New York City carefully supervised the Chapter 1 remedial classes being taught in the schools to ensure that no inculcation of religious beliefs actually occurred in these special courses, the Court determined that this day-to-day supervision created an excessive entanglement between "pervasively sectarian" institutions and the state. Although the classes all took place in classrooms free of any religious icons and were taught by public school personnel who had complete control over both the curriculum and the students in their classes and who used only materials provided by the government, the Court was still troubled by the symbolic link between government and religion.[16]

Implicit in the *Felton* and *Zobrest* analyses is a concern for the purpose of the Court's recent establishment clause reasoning, which has been to preserve religious freedom and independence. This important end must not be overlooked. Fearing that state-supported indoctrination of religious beliefs "would have devastating effects on the right of each individual voluntarily to determine what to believe (and what not to believe) free of any coercive pressures from the State,"[17] the Court has nullified a wide variety of practices deemed to constitute state support of religion.

In terms of the theory of judicial remedies, such decisions have usually served both a declaratory function (delineating the acceptable scope of state/church behavior) and an expectation function (ensuring citizens that their religious protections are being safeguarded). Yet an overly cautious decision under the establishment clause may go beyond what is needed either to create legitimate expectations regarding these protections or to declare their proper scope. Meanwhile, such caution may abrogate other legitimate interests. Such a result could properly be labeled an *antiremedy.*

Antiremedy refers to the result that occurs when the success of one "remedy" actually creates or exacerbates another problem, sometimes leaving everyone worse off or even destroying "the possibility of a better future."[18] Antiremedy is almost always present to some extent in every legal controversy, since the prevailing party's remedy will be an anti-

remedy to the losing party. But the concept of antiremedy takes on added meaning when it is used to describe a remedy gone wrong, a form of relief no longer functioning as it should. A misapplication of the establishment clause in a way that fails to advance its intended remedial end will thus be antiremedy to society at large — and doubly so if, in the process, it also frustrates important remedial aims of other statutes. In addition, even a proper invocation of the establishment clause will function as antiremedy to those particular individuals who are challenging its invocation.

The *Felton* opinion describes the intended end of the establishment clause as preventing the government from "promot[ing] or hinder[ing] a particular faith or faith generally."[19] Whether the decisions in these cases actually advanced this end will depend on how "promote" or "hinder" are interpreted, but the interpretation implicit in *Felton* is hard to defend. If, as *Felton* holds, the teaching of secular material by public employees is a promotion of religion when it occurs at a parochial school, then the fire marshal's visit to instruct students about fire safety or a public health nurse's visit to advise students about hygiene would also be a promotion of religion. Yet these are matters of routine. We expect public employees to become "entangled" with parochial institutions to a certain extent, to ensure that legitimate secular ends are also being advanced in the sectarian setting. Therefore, preventing remedial education teachers from fulfilling their secular role in a sectarian setting can be seen as an anomalous result — an antiremedy to the community they serve.

A sign language interpreter is arguably different from a fire marshal or a remedial education teacher, however, because in a parochial school the interpreter will actually be conveying religious content to the student. Yet the interpreter is merely a tool of communication, much as eyeglasses or hearing aids are tools that facilitate communication. It would be absurd to think that public funds could not be used to purchase glasses or hearing aids for needy students who intended to use them in a parochial school on the theory that providing such devices would "further the religious inculcation" of the students. Rather, establishment clause problems would arise only if this assistance were being provided *exclusively* to parochial students.

Similarly, if P.L. 94-142 provided in-

terpreters only for deaf students attending parochial schools, it would immediately violate the establishment clause. But the services are available to all students who need them to receive an appropriate education, in whatever educational setting they have chosen. The only proper restriction on the availability of these educational services should be that they be used in a setting approved by the state as providing an appropriate education. When the state accredits an educational setting — be it a private, parochial, or home school — the state expresses its conclusion that the school provides a satisfactory alternative to the public schools. When Congress then asks states to provide special services to all students with disabilities, the aid should be available to students in all such accredited schools, just as hearing aids might be provided to all hearing-impaired students. Yet because Jimmy's needs could not be satisfied by a simple mechanical tool, the district court denied him access to public assistance as long as he remains a parochial school student.

Thus, to Jimmy Zobrest, the establishment clause must surely feel like antiremedy. Paradoxically, it has operated to constrain his religious freedom, which is explicitly protected by the free exercise clause of the First Amendment, because he is effectively being told that, in exercising his religious freedom by attending his parochial school, he will become ineligible for a government benefit, the sign language interpreter. Although the statute frames this entitlement as a benefit available to all students with disabilities, in fact, Jimmy must forsake his religious education if he is to qualify for this service.

Likewise, the hundreds of thousands of students across the country who were adversely affected by the *Felton* decision initially had to choose between remaining in their parochial schools or obtaining access to government-sponsored remedial education; they could not do both. As a result, immediately after *Felton*, participation of private school students in Chapter 1 programs dropped 98% in Los Angeles and dropped significantly in all other urban areas as well.[20] Surely, to the thousands of students no longer receiving the supplementary services, as well as to the sponsors of the remedial programs of Chapter 1, this invocation of the establishment clause was an antiremedy.

Slowly, however, the states have come up with alternative ways of providing remedial educational services to parochial students. The most common means has been to purchase portable classrooms, place them on property leased from the parochial schools or on adjoining land, and use them for the remedial instruction. Alternatively, some districts have begun to make extensive use of computer-assisted instruction.

Yet participation is still well below the pre-*Felton* levels. More important, these "solutions" adopted by the school districts to circumvent the *Felton* decision have only increased the cost of the remedial programs, while not furthering the goals of the establishment clause. When a publicly employed teacher conducts remedial instruction in a mobile trailer parked next to a parochial school, the risk that religion is thereby being impermissibly promoted or that the state is thereby excessively entangled with a sectarian institution is practically the same as if the instruction took place within the school under carefully controlled conditions. Even admitting that there could be some small difference, this marginal difference comes at great cost: the expense and inconvenience of using a fleet of trailers and leased land rather than freely available space. Thus, even to the taxpayers who brought the suit, the decision in *Felton* may be an antiremedy.

The four dissenting opinions in *Felton* also support the idea that in cases like *Felton* and *Zobrest* the establishment clause has become an antiremedy, with one dissenter, Justice Byron White, claiming that such decisions are even "contrary to the long-range interests of the country."[21] Besides arguing that no legitimate establishment clause interest was served, Chief Justice Warren Burger's dissenting opinion expressed dismay about the significant educational needs that were being frustrated: "Under the guise of protecting Americans from the evils of an Established Church such as those of the 18th century and earlier times, today's decision will deny countless schoolchildren desperately needed remedial teaching services funded under [Chapter 1]."[22]

The establishment clause is a critical protection in our pluralistic society, but it can be misconstrued. Both P.L. 94-142 and Chapter 1 also have important goals. When a true conflict arises between the establishment clause and one of these statutory programs, the establishment clause must prevail. But courts should not go out of their way to find such conflicts

when no legitimate infraction of the establishment clause needs to be remedied. In the two supplemental educational programs considered above, the establishment clause was invoked to deny the relief Congress intended to provide, without furthering any of the proper concerns of separation of church and state.

MAKING *LEMONADE*

How to make the best of this bad situation will depend on who one is. Jimmy Zobrest has very different concerns from those of a U.S. senator worried about the undermining of congressional intent, though both suffer from the same antiremedy problem: overzealous use of the establishment clause to limit supplementary educational programs. Possible responses may come at the individual, local, or national levels and may be directed at the schools, the legislatures, or the courts.

Jimmy must face some immediate problems. He has three obvious options: struggle on at Salpointe without an interpreter, perhaps making little educational progress but enjoying the social and spiritual community there; transfer to the public high school, where he will have to foreclose his religious training and adjust to a new environment (a particularly difficult task for a student with a disability); or use his family's funds to pay for a private interpreter to assist him at Salpointe. This last option may seem most attractive, but a full-time private interpreter is costly. The fact that Jimmy attends a private school reveals little about his family's financial status, since parochial schools frequently provide very low-cost education to members of their faith. Jimmy may simply be unable to afford an interpreter.

A less obvious possibility would be for Jimmy to negotiate with the school district — and also with other concerned students and parents — to develop some intermediate level of assistance. Perhaps computers or other technologies could be put to use to create some sort of compromise program. If a feasible alternative were to be found, the district would be required to provide it. But it is much harder to find an intermediate solution to meet the needs of a disabled student like Jimmy, who requires assistance in his total educational program, than to find a compromise to meet the need for remedial instruction created in the wake of *Felton*, because students who require Chap-

ter 1 services could receive them anywhere, for only a few hours a day.

Hence it seems that Jimmy may have a hard time doing anything to improve his antiremedial position by himself. He did, however, appeal the decision to the Ninth Circuit, where, as this was being written, it was still pending.[23] Although it is doubtful that the appeals court will feel any freer than did the district court to distinguish Jimmy's case from *Felton*, his case is slightly different because it involves the interests of so few students. One concern in *Felton* was that the monitoring necessary to supervise the work of dozens of teachers who were instructing hundreds of students would involve excessive government "entanglement." But in Jimmy's case a school district could monitor the work of a single interpreter without much entanglement at all. On the other hand, Jimmy's interpreter would be heavily involved in the transmission of religious material, and this was another sort of "entanglement" equally disdained by *Felton*. Thus Jimmy seems to stand little chance of succeeding at the appellate level as long as *Felton* is good law.

Also worth thinking about, however, is an ultimate petition to the Supreme Court, urging a reversal of *Felton*. Several intervening events since *Felton* suggest that such a petition could prove successful. First, the experiment with mobile trailers following the decision may have shown the Court the arbitrary nature of the way in which it has been drawing the "excessive entanglement" line. Second, in 1986 the Court itself, in *Witters* v. *Washington Department of Services for the Blind*, concluded that state aid available through a vocational rehabilitation program could be used to finance one student's preparation for the ministry at a Bible college without violating the establishment clause.[24] If rehabilitation funds may be used to support religious instruction, thus allowing a student who would not otherwise even be in the sectarian environment to receive such instruction, it seems arbitrary to prevent funds for the education of students with disabilities from being used to help a deaf student receive an appropriate education in a sectarian setting *in which he is already enrolled*.[25] The final intervening event is that Justices Antonin Scalia, Anthony Kennedy, and David Souter are now on the bench, and what had been a 5-4 decision could be ripe for reversal.

Furthermore, the reasoning within the

Felton decision is widely recognized as weak. Hence it deserves to be reconsidered. The decision's treatment of the second and third parts of the *Lemon* test curiously turned them into a sort of Catch-22. *Felton* first held that extensive monitoring would be necessary to ensure that the New York City Chapter 1 program did not violate the second part of the *Lemon* test by impermissibly advancing religion. But then the Court held that any such monitoring sufficient to prevent the impermissible advancement of religion would inevitably involve the state in "excessive government entanglement" with the sectarian schools, thus creating a violation of the third part of the *Lemon* test.[26] The school districts were stuck, unable to satisfy both parts. This kind of reasoning from the *Lemon* test makes it worthy of its sour name.

The problem lies in the entanglement component of the *Lemon* test. The Court now makes an entanglement inquiry regardless of whether or not it has identified any real threat to religious liberty.[27] Dissenters in *Felton* made it clear that they were ready to abandon this use of the entanglement component and to rely only on the first two parts of the *Lemon* test in most circumstances. The Court has never attempted to eliminate all contact between church and state; indeed, it has approved such indirect aid to parochial schools as subsidizing bus fares and providing textbooks. As a result, the Court must continually face the vague question of what constitutes excessive entanglement. Answering this question as a separate inquiry, independent of what direct impact on religious institutions is likely to occur, produces antiremedies by disqualifying programs that have only an incidental impact on the religious institution.

Thus there are several reasons why a reversal of *Felton* is conceivable. Nevertheless, waiting and hoping for this to happen is not a particularly promising response to the problem created by the *Felton* and *Zobrest* decisions. Unfortunately, none of the other responses yet discussed is particularly promising either. However, one alternative holds potential: basing the provision of various supplemental educational services on a system of vouchers.

A voucher system would first identify the types of services to be provided, e.g., sign language interpretation for deaf students or remedial reading for impoverished students performing below grade

level. Vouchers entitling the bearer to procure such services at government expense would then be prepared, and individuals who qualified for the vouchers would be identified. The identified students would be given the vouchers, in appropriate quantity. Individuals and their families would make their own determination about where to use the aid, redeeming the vouchers at their pleasure for government-funded instruction or assistance. The assistance could be "purchased" for use at any educational institution, just as a tutor could be hired with private funds for tutoring at any location.

No impermissible entanglement is deemed to have occurred when the choice of where to use the aid is a private one, just as no impermissible entanglement was involved when a vocational rehabilitation participant made an independent decision to use the rehabilitation benefits to pursue religious studies. Under this system, the vouchers authorize payment, while individuals determine where to use them. Such a system could be adopted either on a national level or on a local level, but either would require significant lobbying of legislators.

That the current interpretation of the establishment clause could be circumvented by something like a voucher system further demonstrates the arbitrariness of the Court's currently strict application of the excessive entanglement component of the *Lemon* test.

Both *Zobrest* and *Felton* saw the establishment clause trump important congressional programs because of perceived "entanglement." Yet, as the federal government becomes more involved in public education generally, it also inevitably becomes more entangled with private and parochial schools. According to former Justice Lewis Powell, such schools provide "an educational alternative . . . , afford wholesome competition with our public schools; and in some States they relieve substantially the tax burden incident to the operation of public schools."[28] Hence the government must be able to deal with these schools as well as with the public schools in order to accomplish its educational objectives. Unfortunately, the vague notion of "entanglement" has proved to be an antiremedy in this area, increasing the cost and complexity required to achieve the public goals.

When life gives you lemons, make lemonade. The best response here would be to rethink (and abandon) the "entan-

glement" criterion of establishment clause jurisprudence as articulated in the *Lemon* test — at least for cases like *Zobrest*. In the meantime, school districts and students will need to employ a little creativity in applying federal programs, and legislators may be able to make use of a voucher system to further many of the same desirable ends.

1. Codified at 20 U.S.C. Sections 1232, 1401-2, 1405, 1406, 1411-20, 1453 (1988). (In 1990 the Education for All Handicapped Children Act became the Individuals with Disabilities Education Act.)

2. 473 U.S. 402 (1985).

3. See S. Rept. 168, 94th Cong., 1st sess., 8 (1975).

4. 20 U.S.C. Section 1406 (1988).

5. Ibid. at Sections 1452-53.

6. Ibid. at Section 1412(1).

7. Ibid. at Section 1412(5). P.L. 94-142 also authorized an administrative agency to oversee the statute, which predictably produced extensive interpretive regulations.

8. *Zobrest* v. *Catalina Foothills School District*, No. Civ.-88-516-TUC-RMB, at 1 (D. Ariz. 18 July 1989).

9. Ibid.

10. 20 U.S.C. Section 1413(a)(4)(A)(1988).

11. See *Wheeler* v. *Barrera*, 417 U.S. 402, 420-21 (1974).

12. 403 U.S. 602 (1971).

13. Ibid. at 612-13.

14. 473 U.S. 402, 404 (1985).

15. The complete opinion (cited above) is barely over one page long.

16. See *Grand Rapids School District* v. *Ball*, 473 U.S. 373, 385 (1985). (This was the companion case to *Felton*.)

17. Ibid. at 385.

18. Kellis Parker, "Remodeling Remedies," unpublished paper, 1990.

19. 473 U.S. at 414.

20. Mark Walsh, "Study Finds *Felton* Led to a Drop in Private Students in Chapter 1," *Education Week*, 11 October 1989, p. 7.

21. *Felton*, 473 U.S. 402, at 400 (Justice White, dissenting in both *Ball* and *Felton* in single opinion reported with the majority opinion in *Ball*).

22. *Felton*, 473 U.S. at 419 (Chief Justice Burger, dissenting).

23. In a case with very similar facts, the Fourth Circuit recently ruled that aid could not be provided for the student without violating the establishment clause. *Goodall* v. *Stafford County School Board*, 17 EHLR 745 (4th Cir. 1991). However, in 1990 the Office of Special Education and Rehabilitative Services reaffirmed the position of former Secretary of Education William Bennett that the Department of Education would not interpret *Felton* to preclude the provision of services to students in parochial schools under statutes such as P.L. 94-142.

24. 474 U.S. 481 (1986).

25. *Witters* is distinguishable, however, in that it concerned a higher education setting, while *Zobrest* involved secondary education. But this distinction may prove more form than substance.

26. 473 U.S. at 412-14.

27. Ibid. at 419 (Chief Justice Burger, dissenting).

28. 473 U.S. at 415 (Justice Powell, concurring).

Developing Independent and Responsible Behaviors

in Students Who Are Deaf or Hard of Hearing

John Luckner

John Luckner *(CEC Chapter #381), Associate Professor of Special Education, Division of Special Education, University of Northern Colorado, Greeley.*

For some students who are deaf or hard of hearing, the development of responsibility and the steps toward independence are relatively smooth. They receive support from family, school, and friends. They mature emotionally and socially so that they are able to manage adult financial and interpersonal responsibilities. However, many other deaf or hard-of-hearing individuals have difficulty moving out on their own. They get jobs and leave them after a few weeks or they go off to postsecondary programs only to return before the end of the semester (Commission on Education of the Deaf, 1988; Frisina, 1981; Rayson, 1987).

Prior to graduation, students who experience difficulty in making the transition from school to the "real" world have typically exhibited behaviors indicating that they might have a less than smooth path ahead. They have had problems getting work completed on time, maintaining a positive attitude while engaging in difficult tasks, accepting feedback, solving problems on their own, taking care of personal belongings, taking turns when working in a group, being able to work independently, controlling anger, showing respect for other individuals' property, and/or following school rules. As a result, many of the skills and behaviors necessary for success in the world of work or postsecondary education have not been developed or mastered during the students' elementary or secondary education program.

Responsibility means being able to distinguish between right and wrong, think and act rationally, and be accountable for one's behavior (*Webster's New World Dictionary,* 1987). Responsible self-direction does not "just happen"; therefore, it is important for students who are deaf or hard of hearing to have support and well-planned assistance in school and at home. Teachers of students who are deaf or hard of hearing cannot make them become responsible people. However, teachers can set up environments that promote the development of responsibility, and they can recognize and reinforce responsibility when it occurs. Simultaneously, they can learn to refrain from rewarding dependent behaviors. For example, teachers often help out when students forget books, homework, lunch money, or permission slips. The result is that students learn quickly that they can count on others rather than accept responsibility for their own actions. Teachers need to ask themselves, "Am I really helping? Is the assistance I am giving helping students to cope more effectively with the world that they will be living in after graduation? Or is it better to let them experience the real consequences of their behavior?"

In addition to monitoring the manner in which teachers interact with students, there are some specific interventions that can be implemented in order to help students develop responsibility. They include providing formal instruction in the area of decision making and responsibility, helping students understand and articulate their personal values, teaching goal setting, and working with students' families.

Instruction in Decision Making and Responsibility

Young people of today are asked to make many more decisions than were previous generations. Every day, people encounter life situations requiring thought, decision making, and action. Teachers can help students develop an awareness of how they make decisions and teach them the following six-step procedure for making and acting on decisions (Beyer, 1987):

1. Define the goal.
2. Identify the alternatives.
3. Analyze the alternatives.
4. Rank the alternatives.
5. Judge the highest-ranked alternatives.
6. Choose the best alternative.

Using these steps as a blueprint, teachers can model their own thought processes as they make decisions on a daily basis (e.g., "What will I eat for lunch?; what should I do when my car won't start?; what do I plan to do over the weekend?"). It is also helpful to give the class a true problem or a hypothetical situation and have the students generate responses to each of the steps in an effort to make a decision. Helping students learn to think ahead, make decisions, and be able to answer the question "What would you do if…?" is a valuable intervention. The following are some decision-making situations that can be used for discussion purposes:

1. You found another student's wallet or purse.

From *Teaching Exceptional Children,* Vol. 26, No. 2, Winter 1994, pp. 13-17. © 1994 by The Council for Exceptional Children.
Reprinted by permission.

2. You saw a small boy or girl being beaten up by some of your classmates.
3. Your friend asked you to smoke behind the school.
4. You want to buy a telecommunication device for the deaf (TDD).
5. Your friend told the teacher about something that you did and you got in trouble.
6. Someone was making fun of you because of your hearing aids and/or use of sign language.
7. You want to go to camp this summer with other kids who are deaf or hard of hearing.

To make things more personally relevant to the students you work with, have them develop their own list of problems or situations that occur at school or at home. As a group, they can analyze each situation for choices and consequences and discuss how and why they would make the decision they choose.

In addition to providing instruction and opportunities for discussion about decision making, you can teach a unit on responsibility. When teachers help students learn responsibility, they are focusing on three subgoals: teaching students to care about themselves, teaching them to care about others, and teaching them to care about the world around them (Pendergrass, 1982). Begin by helping the students understand what responsibility is and why it is something people hold in high regard. Provide clear examples of what is responsible behavior, as opposed to irresponsible behavior. Reinforce the students when they demonstrate responsible behaviors.

Figure 1 is an example of an activity sheet that has been adapted from Borba (1989) and Reasoner (1982). It can be used for discussion purposes and for having students evaluate themselves. It could also be used as a stimulus for goal setting, which is discussed later.

Develop a Sense of Purpose

A value is something that is desirable in and of itself. Without values, self-management becomes little more than choosing from an array of equally wor-

thy or unworthy activities. Without values, it is easy to become motivated by objects and events that are immediate and easy, rather than those that are most meaningful. One of the ways to help students develop responsibility is to provide them with some different stimuli for thought and discussion to increase their awareness of the beliefs and behaviors that shape their decisions (see Figure 2, which has been adapted from Borba [1989] and Reasoner [1982]). After students have developed an awareness of their values, they can use this information to write personal goals.

Goal Setting

Responsible people set goals and establish steps to achieve the goals. Our goals lend direction to our lives. Without them we often flounder, uncertain of who we are and what we want to become. Teachers can help students develop an essential life skill by talking about goals and helping them learn to set and strive for achievable personal goals. These goals should (a) be concrete and specific; (b) be realistic; (c) be measurable in some quantitative and/or qualitative way; (d) include deadlines; (e) be anchored in personal values; and (f) be written. Figure 3 is an example of an activity sheet that can be used to help students establish and evaluate their goal-setting behavior.

While providing instruction in the area of goal setting, invite students to read stories or read stories to them about people who have set and achieved goals. *Great Deaf Americans* (Panara & Panara, n.d.), *I'm Deaf Too* (Bowe, 1973), *Hometown Heroes: Successful Deaf Youth in America* (Robinette, 1990), *Courageous Deaf Adults* (Toole, 1980), and *Successful Deaf Americans* (Toole, 1981) are excellent resources. You can also invite successful adults who are deaf or hard of hearing from the community to share their life experiences with your students.

Teach Skills for Independent Learning

Many students who are deaf or hard of hearing have difficulty acquiring the

"WHAT WOULD YOU DO IF...?"

You found another student's wallet or purse.

Your friend asked you to smoke behind the school.

You want to go to camp this summer with other kids who are deaf or hard of hearing.

skills to become active, independent learners (Schlesinger, 1988). Yet, lifelong learning is becoming a necessity for survival in an information-based society. Certain skills are essential for success in school and for continued learning after leaving formal education. Teachers can help students learn those skills by directly teaching them and establishing opportunities to use them. For example, managing time and materials, knowing how to study, and taking tests are critical to school success (Archer & Gleason, 1989). Students should learn to organize their time by learning to use an assignment calendar or notebook to keep track of work that needs to be completed. They can get prepared to complete homework by discussing where to work, the materials they will need, when to do the homework, and how to check their assignments before turning them in. Learning how to read and understand directions in workbooks is another skill necessary for school success. These skills should be introduced to students in the early grades and systematically reinforced throughout their educational careers. Additional skills that can be taught to help students become independent learners include the following:

- How to study.
- How to manage time.
- How to ask questions when you don't understand something.
- How to take notes.
- How to answer questions at the end of a textbook chapter.
- How to use a telecommunication device for the deaf (TDD) and relay services.
- How to proofread your work.
- How to take a multiple-choice, true-false, or essay test.
- How to use an interpreter.
- How to locate community support services.
- How to cope with stress.
- How to resolve conflicts.

Work with Students' Families

To help students become responsible and independent, teachers should work with students' families to establish carryover from what goes on in the

school setting to what occurs at home. Inform parents that teaching independence and responsibility are essential educational goals. Share with them the desire to work together to reinforce the development of specific behaviors. Suggest to parents—during a conference or through a short letter—that you would like them to refrain from acting as rescuers for their children. Explain that when their children forget books, homework, hearing aids, permission slips, or lunch money they should experience the consequences of their behavior rather than having adults reinforce unwanted behaviors. Additional interventions to consider sharing with parents include asking them to:

- Give their child opportunities to make decisions for himself or herself.
- Invite their child to write future goals.
- Reinforce their child at home when he or she demonstrates responsible behavior.
- Discuss with their child how to establish plans in order to finish important work.
- Design a weekly schedule for recreation and TV viewing. Help their child learn to limit the amount of television and choose in advance the programs preferred.
- Teach their child different ways to write reminders about important materials, projects, or dates.
- Teach their child household organizational skills such as where to place important materials at night and in the morning so they will not be forgotten.
- Encourage their child to work independently on assignments.
- Demonstrate enthusiasm over high-quality completed work.
- Invite their child to be responsible by asking him or her to select

---

Figure 1. Personal Responsibilities

List five responsibilities that you have at home and five responsibilities that you have at school. Rate yourself on each responsibility to show how successful you are. Use the following numbers to rate yourself:

1 = Excellent   3 = Fair
2 = Good   4 = Poor

Home Responsibilities	Rating
Example: Taking out the garbage	3
1. _____	_____
2. _____	_____
3. _____	_____
4. _____	_____
5. _____	_____

School Responsibilities	Rating
Example: Handing in my homework	2
1. _____	_____
2. _____	_____
3. _____	_____
4. _____	_____
5. _____	_____

Note. From *Building self-esteem: Teacher's guide and classroom materials* by R. W. Reasoner, 1982, p. 87. Copyright 1982 by Consulting Psychologists Press. Adapted by permission.

chores to complete and budget money.

Figure 2. Personal Values

Read each statement. Decide how important it is to you and check the appropriate box.

———— Value ————	———— Importance ————		
	Very Important	Important	Not Important
Being healthy	☐	☐	☐
Getting good grades	☐	☐	☐
Playing well in games and sports	☐	☐	☐
Having a good friend	☐	☐	☐
Being with my family	☐	☐	☐
Having lots of friends	☐	☐	☐
Reading books and magazines	☐	☐	☐
Having money to spend	☐	☐	☐
Being good at making friends	☐	☐	☐
Being liked by teachers	☐	☐	☐
Watching television	☐	☐	☐
Being by myself	☐	☐	☐
Wearing nice clothes	☐	☐	☐
Eating good food	☐	☐	☐
Going to parties	☐	☐	☐
Going on vacations	☐	☐	☐

Note. From Building self-esteem: Teacher's guide and classroom materials by R. W. Reasoner, 1982, p. 227. Copyright 1982 by Consulting Psychologists Press. Adapted by permission.

Figure 3. Daily Goal Setting

Write a goal that you would like to accomplish each day. At the end of the day or the next morning, mark how well you feel you achieved your goal.

	Goal	Achieved	Partially Achieved
Monday:	_____	_____	_____
Tuesday:	_____	_____	_____
Wednesday:	_____	_____	_____
Thursday:	_____	_____	_____
Friday:	_____	_____	_____

Note. From Building self-esteem: Teacher's guide and classroom materials by R. W. Reasoner, 1982, p. 333. Copyright 1982 by Consulting Psychologists Press. Adapted by permission.

Conclusion

For students to become independent and responsible, they need environments that support their initiatives and allow them to make choices. Teachers cannot make students become responsible persons. They can, however, teach about responsibility and how to make decisions; assist them in developing an awareness of their values and how to develop and achieve personal goals; teach them the skills they need to continue to learn independently; work with their families; and reinforce them when they exhibit responsible behaviors.

References

Archer, A., & Gleason, M. (1989). *Skills for school success.* North Billerica, MA: Curriculum Associates.

Borba, M. (1989). *Esteem builders: A K-8 self-esteem curriculum for improving student achievement, behavior, and school climate.* Rolling Hills Estates, CA: Jalmar Press.

Bowe, F. (1973). *I'm deaf too.* Silver Spring, MD: National Association of the Deaf.

Commission on Education of the Deaf. (1988). *Toward equality: Education of the deaf.* Washington, DC: U.S. Government Printing Office.

Frisina, D. R. (1981). A perspective on the mental health of young deaf adults in modern society. In A. M. Mulholland (Ed.), *Oral education today and tomorrow* (pp. 485-494). Washington, DC: The Alexander Graham Bell Association for the Deaf.

Panara, R., & Panara, J. (n.d.). *Great deaf Americans.* Silver Spring, MD: T. J. Publishers.

Pendergrass, R. H. (1982). A "thinking" approach to teaching responsibility. *The Clearing House, 56* (2), 90-92.

Rayson, B. (1987). Emotional illness and deafness. In E. D. Mindel & M. Vernon (Eds.), *They grow in silence: Understanding deaf children and adults* (pp. 65-101). Boston: College-Hill.

Reasoner, R. W. (1982). *Building self-esteem: Teacher's guide and classroom materials.* Palo Alto, CA: Consulting Psychologists Press, Inc.

Robinette, D. (1990). *Hometown heroes: Successful deaf youth in America.* Washington, DC: Kendall Green Publications.

Schlesinger, H. (1988). Questions and answers in the development of deaf children. In M. Strong (Ed.), *Language learning and deafness* (pp. 261-291). Cambridge, England: Cambridge University Press.

Toole, D. (1980). *Courageous deaf adults.* Beaverton, OR: Dormac.

Toole, D. (1981). *Successful deaf Americans.* Beaverton, OR: Dormac.

Webster's new world dictionary of the American language. (1987). New York: World.

Children with Visual Impairments

Students with visual impairments are one of the smallest groups of students being served by special educational services in the public schools. However, they are increasingly being served in public schools rather than special schools. Their numbers in public schools increased from about 10 percent to almost 90 percent between 1950 and 1990.

The definitions of legal blindness and low vision are based on measures of visual acuity and field of vision. Low vision is defined as acuity from 20/70 to 20/180 in the best eye after correction and a field vision from 20 to 180 degrees. Legal blindness is defined as 20/200 acuity or less in the best eye after correction and/or a field of vision restricted to an area of 20 degrees or less (tunnel vision).

These definitions are useful for assessment of needs for special services. They do not specify actual vision. One must consider the amount of vision in the worst eye, the perception of light, the actual field of vision (if it is between 20 and 180 degrees), and visual efficiency and functional vision. These last two terms are used to describe how well a person uses whatever vision is available.

Visual impairments may be separated into the categories of blind or low vision based on visual efficiency and functional vision. A child with so little functional vision that he or she learns primarily through the other senses is assessed as blind. A child with enough functional vision to learn primarily through the visual channel is assessed as having low vision. About 80 percent of the visually impaired students who attend public schools are assessed as having low vision rather than blindness. Children with refractive errors (nearsightedness, farsightedness, and astigmatism) are rarely assessed as low vision students in need of special services. This is because refractive errors can usually be corrected with glasses.

The causes of legal blindness and low vision are not always easy to determine. About 15 percent of blindness is due to unknown factors. Heredity and prenatal factors (maternal illness, drugs, prematurity, low birth weight) are believed to contribute to more than one-half of all visual impairments. Other known causes of blindness or low vision are diseases, injuries, poisonings, and tumors.

Depending on the nature and the degree of the visual impairment, a teacher may need to become acquainted with a wide variety of special services used to assist in appropriate education for blind or low vision students.

Most children who are blind are taught to read using their sense of touch. Braille is a form of writing using raised dots that are "read" with the fingers. It takes many years to learn to read braille. Most braille readers read considerably slower than print readers. Their individualized education programs (IEPs) may include braille books and braille reading, and writing braille with a slate and stylus or brailler (six-keyed device like a typewriter). Most children who are blind also use Optacon scanners, talking books (books on tape), speech plus talking hand-held calculators, closed-circuit television, typewriters, and/or personal computers with special software. IEPs are specifically designed and annually updated to meet the unique and changing needs of each child who is blind.

Most children with low vision are taught to read using their residual vision. Their IEPs usually include the goals of using low vision aids and large type to read print. They also may use felt tip pens, wide-lined paper, or typewriters for writing, and personal computers with special software for both reading and writing.

Children who are blind or have low vision need to learn to use their other senses to provide information they miss through their eyes. Listening skills are especially important. Blind children are not born with better hearing. Their hearing may be normal, below normal, or they may be hearing impaired or deaf. If they have any hearing ability, they need to learn to use it as efficiently as possible. IEPs usually include the goal of teaching discrimination of near-far, loud-soft, high-low, and of ignoring distracting background noises.

Children who are blind or have low vision usually have more difficulty with orientation of their bodies in space and movement in their spatial environments than normal vision children. Most teachers need to include lessons in orientation and mobility (O&M) to the IEPs of visually-impaired students. These lessons are usually given by trained O&M instructors in conjunction with regular education teachers. The long cane used in O&M both serves as a probe and bumper for its user, and also signals sighted persons that its user is visually impaired. Only a very small percentage of visually-impaired students use guide dogs. If a student has a guide dog, the teacher and sighted student must learn to treat the dog as a working guide, not as a pet. Most persons with visual impairments occasionally use sighted persons as guides. Teachers and sighted students need to learn how to guide their blind or low vision friends with a few simple dos and don'ts.

Each child with low vision needs to feel accepted by his or her more visually abled peers. The teacher plays a major role in encouraging positive interactions between children with and without visual impairments. The teacher should discuss each child's special visual needs with the class. Having one's very own personal computer, television, talking calculator, or other intriguing piece of techno-

logical equipment may be viewed as favoritism. The need for the equipment should be explained fully at the beginning of the school year and whenever questioned during the remainder of the school year. With each new school year, and with each technological change, more explanations are required to help children without visual impairments understand the special child's needs.

The first article selected for this unit examines the efficacy of classroom special services for low vision students. In most classrooms, the use of technological equipment lags behind the students' needs. The next article suggests an efficient way for public schools with blind or low vision students in regular classrooms to utilize the services of schools for the blind. Residential schools can provide a wide range of services to mainstreamed children on an intermittent basis. The last article in this unit addresses the education of children who have hearing impairments in addition to visual impairments. Children who are deaf-blind have many special needs. This selection is concerned with teaching students who are deaf-blind to make choices and develop independence.

Looking Ahead: Challenge Questions

How many low vision students who qualify for special educational services are actually receiving them, according to the article "Efficacy of Low Vision Services for Visually Impaired Children"?

Is it possible for public schools and residential schools for the blind to collaborate? Can children in inclusive education programs be pulled out to residential schools for occasional hands-on instruction?

How can choice making be taught to students who are deaf-blind?

Efficacy of Low Vision Services for Visually Impaired Children

Abstract: Though it is known that visually impaired children can be helped by low vision aids, little research has been done on the use of such aids by children. In this study of 137 children, subjects were screened for visual capacity. Where appropriate, recommendations were made that they be examined further, in most cases by low vision specialists and in others by general optometrists. Follow-up was made on many of the children who received aids as a result of these examinations to determine whether the aids were being used effectively.

H.W Hofstetter

Henry W Hofstetter, O.D., Ph.D., professor emeritus of optometry, Indiana University, 2615 Windermere Woods Drive, Bloomington, IN 47401.

Several studies of adults classified as visually impaired have demonstrated that a majority, whether or not they routinely receive conventional vision care services, can be significantly helped by specialized ophthalmic analyses, low vision aids, and supportive rehabilitation services (Mayer, 1927; Feinbloom, 1935; Freeman, 1954; IHB Optical Aids Survey, 1957). However, the studies included few if any children, because the frequency of visual impairments uncorrectable by conventional eyewear is highly correlated with aging.

In addition to the lack of studies, a well-known physiological factor points to the need for a separate study of children who are visually impaired. It is the phenomenon of accommodation: the ability of the normal or optically corrected eye to focus clearly on objects at various distances. This physiological function is greatest in infancy and gradually declines to zero by about age 58. In contrast, an 18-year-old can normally see clearly from infinity to within 5 inches of the face, and a 6-year-old can see clearly up to about 3 inches.

This ability enables the school-age child to get an image on his or her retina that is double, triple, or even quadruple its normal size, merely by holding an object extremely close to the face. Therefore, a child is less likely than an older person to utilize a low vision aid for reading, even though it might have been recommended. Differences in the frequency of successful utilization by children and adults justify a separate investigation of children.

Another reason study is needed is to determine how schools follow up with low vision children. It has been too readily assumed that because a child has been certified as visually impaired, there is continuous follow-up with rehabilitation measures that will enable him or her to utilize residual vision more effectively (Hofstetter, 1983). On the contrary, there seems to be an "abandoning attitude," held by general eye professionals as well as others, that the low vision child should simply be taught how best to live with the handicap. Study is essential to clarify the attitudes and presumptions of adults.

Final considerations for undertaking the study are the explosion in low vision aid technology and the emergence of low vision care as a professional specialty. These developments raise the question of whether the successes reported in the earlier surveys indicate the rehabilitative potentials today.

The study described here and elsewhere (Hofstetter 1985, 1988) was designed to screen a sample of low vision children from all grade levels, determine their visual capability, prescribe the most effective low vision aids, and in cooperation with teachers, evaluate the degree of successful utilization of aids.

Procedure

This study was carried out from 1985 to 1988. Personnel included a coordinator from the Indiana Department of Education, seven optometrist members of the Indiana Low Vision Rehabilitation Society, teachers of the visually impaired, and directors of special education. The low vision children were identified by interdisciplinary committees (administrative, teaching, nursing, and/or medical personnel) as having visual defects which, even with conventional eyewear, necessitated special education. The interdisciplinary committee relied on information provided by whatever local optometrist or ophthalmologist each child had consulted, plus whatever other criteria might have indicated the advisability of special teaching procedures.

Team members contacted teachers of the visually impaired to enlist their cooperation in identifying eligible children and in arranging for screening dates and working space. The parents or guardians of 137 children—almost all of whom were invited to let their visually impaired children participate—signed the consent form. Although three of the children did not show up for screening, all 137, approximately 25 percent of Indiana students classified as visually impaired, were included in the study.

Geographically, the participants represented communities in 15 counties. No single school provided more than 13 percent of the participants, and no single low vision examiner was clinically involved with more than 28 percent of them.

As described in the original report (Hofstetter, 1985), the screening procedure was an abridgment of the complex examining procedures employed by low vision specialists, but it included several trials with optical magnifiers for distant and near viewing. After processing, the records for each child included information provided by the child's responses, the parent or guardian, the teacher, the optometrist performing the tests, and in cases referred for clinical evaluation, by the optometrist or an associate low vision specialist. With input from so many sources, there were numerous omissions in isolated categories of data, necessitating selective analyses of data to include for each inference only the paired correlation factors for which reliable entries had been made. For example, in several instances funds were unavailable to purchase prescribed low vision aids, so utilization could not be computed.

One particular shortcoming of the procedure was the lack of rehabilitative services as a follow-up to the prescription of low vision aids. To some extent, the children who had teachers of the visually impaired may have had some rehabilitative services, but such services were not formally programmed into this study. Thus, the success rates obtained in utilization may be considered statistically conservative.

Traits of the sample

Sex

Figure 1 shows the number of males and females at each age level. There is a rather puzzling mean ratio of three males to two females, with the males predominating in all but 3 of the 16 age groups represented. A statistical evaluation of the male minus the female frequencies for each age shows a mean value significantly different from zero at the chance probability of only 0.003.

There was a similar imbalance in the first of the two research reports (Hofstetter, 1985) from which this article is adapted. In that report, the names of the 60 screened children indicated 40 males and only 14 females. Six names were undifferentiable in terms of sex. Males predominated in all but one of the 13 age levels, and the statistical evaluation of male minus female frequencies at each age showed a mean value even more significantly different from zero than that of the present group. It is not known whether these lopsided ratios are the result of biology or a social bias in designating participants for study.

of 132 of the subjects with the conventional correction each was wearing at the time of screening and the best attainable acuity for the better eye of 116.

Table 1. Frequency distribution of visual acuities of the better eye.

Snellen acuity of the better eye	As previously corrected N=132	Best attainable N=116
20/20 to 20/49	17.4%	23.3%
20/50 to 20/124	35.6%	32.7%
20/125 to 20/319	22.7%	25.9%
20/320 to 20/799	15.2%	9.5%
20/800 to 20/1999	3.0%	2.6%
20/2000 to under	6.1%	6.0%

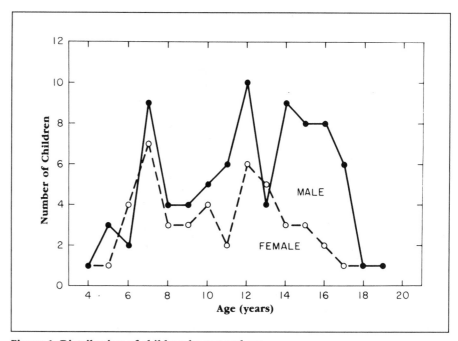

Figure 1. Distribution of children by sex and age.

Causes of low vision

Classifying the 137 children according to their most impairing etiology, 62 percent had receptor system or muscular control defects, 10 percent had opacities in the media, 22 percent had optical or refractive deformities, and 6 percent had undetermined etiologies. The proportions of defects were almost identical for both sexes and did not differ significantly from the proportions in the prior study (Hofstetter, 1985).

Vision correction

Although loss of Snellen visual acuity, which relates to the perception of small details, is only one type of visual impairment, it is the single most frequently used criterion of reference. Table 1 shows the habitual acuity recorded for the better eye

(The fact that the table shows only a modest improvement with the best possible spectacle correction points up the relatively greater significance of magnification, brightness, contrast, illumination, field enhancement, and color in the application of special aids for the visually impaired.)

The table also makes it clear that virtually all the children had been examined earlier and when substantial refractive errors were found, conventional corrective glasses had been appropriately prescribed.

Of the 137 subjects, three (2%) wore contact lenses and 82 (60%) wore glasses. The latter percentage is at least four times greater than that of the general school population.

Fifty-one of the 82 pairs of glasses were

evaluated. Forty-two were judged to be in satisfactory physical condition and only nine (18%) in poor condition (e.g., damaged or undersized frames, scratched lenses). The low percentage of glasses in poor condition indicates that most were new as compared with those of other children, since children outgrow frames and scratch lenses at a fast rate.

Academic standing

Teachers were asked to indicate on a checklist whether the student's academic progress was average, above average, or below average. Of the 110 youngsters for whom these evaluations were made, 52

ophthalmologists or optometrists to obtain new lenses, update their eyewear, or receive other services. The remaining 31 (23%) were deemed to have received or to be receiving all the ophthalmic services that could currently be of benefit.

The actions, dispositions, and evaluations that followed the screening are listed in Table 2.

The first column of figures in Table 2 relates to the 82 children for whom comprehensive clinical evaluations were recommended. For reasons such as limited funding, the unavailability of transportation, parental neglect, or unwillingness on the part of the child, 23

indicated successful utilization. No follow-up information was pursued for the other child who received an aid or for the 19 who had routine optometric services.

The third column of figures in Table 2 shows that 1 of the 31 children who had not been referred for vision care was brought to one of the low vision specialists by his parents for the full evaluation. A special visual aid was provided and a subsequent report indicated that it was being utilized moderately.

One more point on utilization: Some of the children who were given special aids didn't use them for near visual tasks. This may mean that they preferred to bring the visual task extremely close to the eye for retinal magnification, as many young children do.

Table 2. Interrelated results of screening and subsequent examinations.

	Low vision examination recommended for 82 children	General optometric examination recommended for 21 children	Referral not indicated for 31 children
Low vision examination not made	23	19	30
Special low vision aid not recommended	1	0	0
Special low vision aid recommended	58	2	1
Prescribed aids were not ordered	3	0	0
Prescribed aids were provided	56	2	1
Prescribed aids not used	5	0	0
Moderate success indicated by subsequent use	13	0	1
Significant success indicated by subsequent use	30	1	0
Follow-up information lacking	34	20	30

(47.3%) were rated average, 19 (17.3%) above average, and 39 (35.4%) below average.

That so few of the visually impaired children were below average is even more remarkable when one realizes that quite a few were also additionally handicapped. For example, 14 percent were partially or totally immobilized without physical assistance. Another 12 percent were unable to read print at all and 11 percent could read only with difficulty. Sixty-two percent were utilizing no other low vision aids than conventional eyewear. It seems reasonable to conclude that the visually impaired students had all the academic potential of the general school population.

Clinical evaluations

Of the 134 children screened in school by the low vision specialists, it was recommended that 82 (61%) have comprehensive clinical evaluations in an adequately equipped office or clinic. An additional 21 (16%) were advised to contact their

subjects were not clinically examined. Of the 59 who were, 56 were provided with low vision aids. (One was advised that aids were not presently justified and two others, for whom aids were prescribed, declined to accept them for cosmetic reasons.)

Follow-up information on 48 of the 56 children who received aids was obtained from visitations and from teachers' reports. It was learned that five (10%) were neglecting to use their aids, 13 (27%) were using them less than they should have for maximum benefit, and 30 (63%) were utilizing them successfully. No follow-up information was sought for the 23 children referred for clinical evaluations who did not receive them.

In Table 2, the second column of figures, which reports on the 21 children who had been referred only for routine optometric services, shows that two were given full low vision evaluations anyway, at the request of their parents. Both were provided with special low vision aids. Follow-up information on one of the two

Summary

Screening by specialists indicated that 61 percent of the children studied could benefit significantly from low vision care by specially qualified eye practitioners and another 16 percent could benefit from services generally available in the community. Follow-up showed high confirmation of the screening accuracy, with clinical evaluations determining that 60 percent of the children could benefit from special services and 14 percent from general care.

Subsequent surveillance showed that the recommendations were satisfactorily utilized by 53 percent of the children classified as needing low vision services and 13 percent of the children classified as needing general ophthalmic care. Thus, 66 percent benefited appreciably from appropriately applied vision care.

Even allowing for test reliability limitations, one can safely conclude that a majority of the impaired vision children in Indiana could be made more competent by the vision care now available.

A number of additional observations emerged from the study:

• A predominance of frequency of males over females at all age levels suggests a sexually related difference in visual impairment or that there was a social bias in the identification of participants.

• More than three-fourths of the children had attainable central visual acuity of only 20/50 or less in the better eye.

• Central visual acuity without magnification aids was only moderately improved by changes of conventional eyewear, but even modest improvements are extremely important for low vision persons.

• Sixty percent of the children were wearing glasses at the time of screening and 82 percent of the glasses were rated to be in satisfactory condition.

• Academic progress ratings of the visually impaired children by their teachers showed 47 percent to be average, 35 percent below average, and 18 percent above average.

• The fact that visually impaired children are officially classified for special education does not seem to provide any added incentive to seek or provide appropriate, periodically needed vision care.

Further research is needed to explore the implications of these suggestions.

References

Feinbloom, W. (1935). Report of 500 cases of sub-normal vision. *American Journal of Optometry,* **12**(6) 238–249.

Freeman, E. (1954). Optometric rehabilitation of the partially blind: A report of 175 cases. *American Journal of Optometry and Archives of American Academy of Optometry,* **31**(5) 230–239.

Hofstetter, H.W (1983). *Unmet vision care needs in Indiana.* Indianapolis: Indiana Chapter of the American Academy of Optometry, Suite 1920, 201 N. Illinois Street, Indianapolis, IN 46204.

Hofstetter, H.W (1985). *The unmet vision care needs of the visually handicapped of Indiana.* Indianapolis: Indiana Chapter of the American Academy of Optometry, Suite 1920, 201 N. Illinois Street, Indianapolis, IN 46204.

Hofstetter, H.W (1988). *Efficacy of low vision services for visually impaired children.* Indianapolis: Indiana Chapter of the American Academy of Optometry, Suite 1920, 201 N. Illinois Street, Indianapolis, IN 46204.

IHB optical aids service survey (1957). Brooklyn, New York: The Industrial Home for the Blind.

Mayer, L. (1927). Visual results with telescopic spectacles. *American Journal of Ophthalmology,* **10**, 256–260.

A Direct Service Program for Mainstreamed Students by a Residential School

P. J. Cronin

Peter J. Cronin, head of community services, Burwood Education Centre for Blind Children, 333 Burwood Highway, Burwood, Melbourne, Victoria 3125, Australia.

Abstract: Residential schools are appropriately placed to provide a wide range of direct services to mainstreamed children with visual impairments. One of these services can be occasional withdrawal to the residential school for teaching skills that are unique to visual impairment, but that are not specifically included in the regular education program.

A survey of 45 American residential schools by Harley and English (1989) presented a comprehensive overview of the services these schools provide to students who are mainstreamed into local public schools. The most frequently used services were professional development services, summer school programs, the provision of materials, and assessment. Direct services to students were provided much less frequently and included mainly orientation and mobility, career education, independent living skills, personal care, and recreational and leisure education.

The Burwood Educational Centre for Blind Children, Melbourne, Australia, the children's services department of the Royal Victorian Institute for the Blind, (RVIB), has taken a much more active position in the provision of direct services to children in mainstream settings. Since the 1970s, the center has provided a range of interrelated on-site and off-site services through which many mainstreamed children with visual impairments can move freely as their educational needs alter. As an independent organization that receives a combination of governmental subsidies and privately raised funds, it is well placed to do so. It also maintains a complementary relationship with another support service, the Victorian State Ministry of Education, Visiting Teacher Service.

The direction taken by the Burwood center is in line with Hatlen and Curry's (1987) warnings about polarized integrated and segregated settings and observations on mainstreamed children who developed academic proficiency but were left with poor self-sufficiency skills. These observations confirmed for the Burwood Center the notion that students in main-stream settings need complementary skill-development programs and direct teaching from trained educators to meet their "unique needs" that are not covered by regular school programs. However, the center expanded on Hatlen and Curry's list of needs (concept development, communication skills, social and recreational skills, career education, independent living skills, and orientation and mobility) to include computer education, physiotherapy, sports, tactile awareness training, braille music, and speech therapy. Hatlen's 1990 article was a timely confirmation for Burwood of the inadequacy of exclusively consultation-oriented peripatetic services and of the necessity for students to receive "hands-on" instruction by trained teachers of visually impaired students. This article outlines one aspect of the center's direct services program—the Friday Program, in which mainstreamed students attend the Burwood center for a once-a-month skills-development day.

The Friday Program

Eighteen students who attend Burwood for one full day each month are placed in one of four groups according to their age and ability. The aim of the day, which is always a Friday, is to provide skills training in areas in which the children do not receive services in the regular education setting.

The majority of students are totally blind, and braille is a major communication medium for all but one. Seven students have always been educated in mainstream settings, and 10 of the remaining 11 spent one to four primary-school years in reverse-integration groups at Burwood before they were mainstreamed. (Reverse integration classes contain a mixture of students with visual impairments and local sighted children who attend the center for one full year of schooling. The ratio of students in these classes is usually about 3 or 4 with visual impairments to 5 or 6 sighted students.)

The Friday Program is staffed by on-site specialists and by visiting teachers. Most students begin the program at about age 9 and continue for the next five or six years. Students do not attend in the last three or four years of secondary school, by which time most of their skills have been established and they are free to tackle the academic demands of their final years.

All the students are supported, in the school of their parents' choice, by visiting teachers, employed either by RVIB or by the Victorian Ministry of Education (four students), for periods of 3–6 hours per week. Sixteen students are also assisted by integration aides who are employed by the Victorian government for periods of 2–20 hours per week.

The priorities of the program are decided through team meetings, which may include the student's visiting teacher, the Friday Program teacher, the parents, and the teacher's aide. The following sections briefly describe the range of skill-development areas in which the students may be placed. The rationale and mode of service delivery is outlined for each area.

Physical development

Even in the absence of other impairments, severe visual impairment or total blindness may have an impact on a child's physical development. Therefore, students may have difficulty in the areas of strength, balance, posture, gait, fine-motor skills, and sensory development (Palazesi, 1986; Wyatt, 1989).

Seven students require continuing physiotherapy treatment or surveillance. Two adventitiously blind children have hemiplegia. The other five students have a range of physical problems, including congenital hypotonia, reduced strength, poor kinesthesia, abnormal or reduced sensation, abducted gait, kyphosis, poor static muscle control, and sensory difficulties in the tactile-vestibular and proprioceptive areas. All these problems are either attributed to or compounded by the lack of vision.

Given the philosophy of integration, these students could be receiving treatment from community physiotherapists. However, experience has led the Burwood staff to believe that students are best treated by therapists who are experienced in the area of visual impairment and who have a thorough knowledge of the possible affects of visual loss on physical development. Community physiotherapists cannot be relied on or expected to have this knowledge, since training courses for physiotherapists may not offer adequate information on the diagnosis and treatment of conditions related to blindness. The degree course for physiotherapists in Melbourne, for example, devotes one hour to blindness in a four-year course and about 5 percent of the content to pediatric conditions. Newly appointed physiotherapists at the Burwood center know little about blindness and require extensive training and supervision from a senior physiotherapist who is experienced in this area.

In the Friday Program, physiotherapists screen all students when they begin the program; students with needs are treated at each visit, and developmental exercise programs are devised that are then supervised at home by the parents or at school by the teacher's aide, visiting teacher, or physical education teacher. The physical status of the students improves only minimally from monthly treatment, but, as physiotherapists at the center have found, students who are motivated to exercise regularly (even daily) have improved significantly, particularly in the areas of strength, balance, and proprioception. Attaining success in the program, students develop confidence and become more motivated and willing to take risks with more difficult gross motor tasks. At each treatment session, the physiotherapist assesses the student's progress and extends the program to provide added challenges to him or her.

Sports

Jones (1987) noted that in integrated settings students with visual impairments may not have their physical-development needs met and may have reduced physical competencies, well below those of their sighted peers. Fewer opportunities for active play and for inclusion in the physical education program may compound this problem.

Physical education and sports can be an area of difficulty for students with visual impairments. The majority of team sports involve the pursuit of one student by another or of balls traveling through the air. Visually impaired students are often relegated to the role of scorers or are placed in useful but isolating individual physical programs. Although schools cannot be expected to change the rules of traditional games like football, soccer, or basketball, the visiting teacher or the residential school can be a source of adapted or invented games that blind and sighted students can enjoy together and compete in on an equal basis (Pfisterer, 1983). Furthermore, if students with visual impairments are trained in a range of specific sports skills, they will be more readily included in physical education lessons and adapted games.

In the Friday Program, students are checked by the physical education teacher against a list of skills that relate to swimming; gymnastics; running with and chasing a partner; training in the location of sounds; rope skipping with a partner; the use of bats and racquets; and throwing, catching, and kicking balls. Areas of difficulty are isolated and recommendations for training are made to parents, teacher's aides, and the physical education teacher in the regular school. Burwood's physical education teacher also travels to the regular schools to provide ongoing consultation and to observe and record the skills that need to be consolidated when a child attends the Friday Program.

Computer training

Students with visual impairments use individually assigned computers or classroom computers to complete a wide range of academic tasks. Most students complement this use with brailler and braille 'n' print usage, and some students use computers almost exclusively for general work output and examinations.

It is possible for students with visual impairments to be trained in the use of computers by regular education teachers. However, there are a number of factors that suggest that specialists who are trained in visual impairments also need to be extensively involved:

1. The QWERTY keyboard, which is a prerequisite for the use of computers, can be mastered using commercially available taped programs, but programs devised by trained teachers of visually impaired students (English, 1989) seem most effective.

2. Many of the commands and terms (such as "center the heading," "tabulate the columns," "insert a space," "move to the end of the line," "set for double spacing," and "align the paragraph") that students need to learn are based on visually or spatially oriented concepts and re-

quire careful verbal description. Educators of visually impaired students are experienced in providing such explanations.

3. To lead a braille-using student with little or no vision to an understanding of a print readout, the instructor should also know braille, so he or she can explain the differences between the two processes. Furthermore, it is important for the instructor to realize that many of the commands for initiating print on a screen, such as "bold," "overwrite," "insert," "block," "string search," and "underline," may be well outside the student's experience.

4. Equipment that is adapted for students with visual impairments usually emanates from the agencies that support the students and differs significantly from equipment for sighted students. The selection of braille embossers, voice synthesizers, braille input devices, and software that is specific to visual impairment is often heavily reliant on advice from educators of visually impaired students and specially trained technicians who have the clearest idea of which equipment is most appropriate for the students' needs. Many adapted programs like Wordtalk and B.E.X. also have commands that are specific to visual impairments and can be most efficiently taught to students by those who are familiar with them.

5. It takes significant amounts of one-to-one instruction for students to be trained, not just in computer usage, but in the organization and coordination of work materials for computer-orientated tasks that may include the following steps:

1. Read brailled version of assignment.
2. Collect appropriate text in braille and taped form.
3. Read materials.
4. Engage computer and insert software.
5. Key in the answer to the assignment; refer to brailled and taped materials as required.

6. Print assignment in braille and in print.
7. Staple print answer sheet to print question sheet; set aside for the teacher.
8. Staple braille answer sheet to brailled question sheet.
9. Locate the appropriate subject folder and store.
10. Return the disc, braille texts, and taped texts to the material storage system.

The staff at Burwood have observed that even the most willing regular education teachers cannot always allot this amount of time to training a visually impaired student while dealing thoroughly with the educational needs of their other students.

In the Friday Program, the students are trained or reinforced in the operation of computers. They bring in an assignment from their schools and are trained in the organization of materials. The instructors also teach the students braille-to-print and print-to-braille modes and travel to schools to maintain the equipment and to offer advice on the selection and use of equipment.

Training in tactile graphics

Within the past 20 years, educators of visually impaired students and braille transcribers have increasingly presented students whose major communication medium is braille with thermoformed or stereocopied tactile representations of pictorial or graphic forms. These representations include tactile versions of simple geometric forms, letters of the alphabet, graphs, maps, diagrams, and simple two-dimensional drawings.

However, the interpretation of tactile materials has not always been taught with the same degree of systematic methodology and enthusiasm as has the development of residual vision, braille literacy, and listening skills. The situation is complex for students who have been mainstreamed from an early age who require systematic training in this area. Incidental, "as the need arises" approaches to teaching these skills are inadequate for mainstreamed students who are not in constant contact with adults who are trained in the appropriate methodology.

In the Friday Program, each student is given tactile-awareness training and is shown how to approach tactile representation methodically and to recognize a hierarchy of tactile representations from the most basic to a degree of complexity that is consistent with the child's academic level. The teacher is also the major consultant for the standardization of all tactile materials produced at Burwood. Therefore, one bonus of the program has been the opportunity for the on-site braille transcribers to observe first hand the tactile skills of the students for whom they are brailling.

Braille music

In the large residential schools of the past, music was seen as a vital part of the curriculum and a means of providing creative and vocational opportunities for students with visual impairments. Many students, who were taught by totally blind music instructors, attained a high standard of musical achievement and became performing artists, music teachers, composers, accompanists, or allied professionals like piano tuners.

With the move toward integration, the teaching of music has been transferred to community or mainstreamed music teachers who are sighted. Since these teachers and the visiting teachers do not know the braille music code and the visually impaired students cannot sight-read printed codes, the teachers rely on memory-based methods of teaching that do not develop the full musical potential of the students or teach them to use musical scores in the same way as sighted musicians do. Thus, the visually impaired students have difficulty playing in bands or orchestras

or participating in class lessons involving music notation.

In the Friday Program, students receive instruction in the braille music code from a qualified visually impaired music teacher who uses the students' level of ability in instrument playing as the basis for teaching music notation. The majority of students learn an instrument or singing from a community teacher, who consults with the Burwood teacher, by phone or in person, on each student's progress; the Burwood teacher advises the community teacher about the methodology that is appropriate to each student. Homework in braille music may be monitored by the student's parents, the teacher's aide, or the visiting teacher. The Burwood music teacher is also responsible for the braille transcription of all individual and class music lessons and assignments and all scores to be used in music examinations.

Home-crafts and living skills

Because of the lack of experience, the delayed conceptual and gross-motor development, and the inability to imitate and practice from a visual model, children with visual impairments and no other impairments may be at risk in a number of fine-motor areas. These areas include delayed bilateral and unilateral hand-finger dexterity, delayed development of a range of grips, reduced hand and upper-arm strength, reduced wrist flexibility, poor understanding of finger-hand pressure, reduced tactile sensation, poor manipulative abilities, and reduced spatial understanding when attempting object-to-object tasks (Fullwood, 1990).

Many students need systematic instruction to compensate for these potential risks and some need extensive support from adults to establish a range of self-organizational, fine-motor, and self-care skills, such as tying shoelaces, putting toothpaste on a toothbrush, placing a pillow in a pil-

low case, and packing a suitcase, that sighted children acquire with minimal or no adult intervention. Furthermore, unlike sighted children, visually impaired children have not established a repertoire of cutting, slicing, peeling, mixing, and pouring skills by the time they are ready to take a home economics course in the late-primary or early secondary-school years.

In the classroom, visiting teachers, regular education teachers, therapists, and teacher's aides can help the children attain fine-motor and organizational skills that are related to the content of the educational program. However, it would be an inappropriate and sterile activity for them to run an individual home economics/living skills program that is parallel to the academic program of the classroom. Although parents could be the sole teachers of these skills, many find it a burden to provide anything more than incidental instruction to their children. This burden can also be shared by the children, who do not enjoy their parents acting as teachers.

In the Friday Program, a living skills teacher and an orientation and mobility instructor provide instruction in basic home-craft and self-sufficiency skills and use the lunchtime meal to develop eating and social skills. Skills are checklisted, and parents are given an ongoing record of those that have been mastered and can be consolidated at home. A brailled book of modified recipes and a text on living skills (Fullwood, 1988) is also made available to parents.

Speech therapy

Four students require ongoing treatment and surveillance from a speech pathologist. One student has articulation problems that are unrelated to visual impairment and could be treated by a speech pathologist in the community, but the method required to provide articulation therapy with students with visual impairments is often not within the experience of these professionals. The usual methods of articulation therapy that are used with sighted children are highly visual. However the speech pathologist who works with a student with visual impairments must rely on the techniques of verbal description, tactile cueing, and the encouragement of accurate listening. All these instructional methods are, of course, familiar to experienced speech pathologists and teachers of visually impaired students.

Three children in the Friday Program have language difficulties that are related to or compounded by severe or total visual impairment, including problems in abstract thinking and expression, difficulty initiating contact with others, an inadequate understanding of conversational procedures (questioning, responding, commenting, and so on), and reduced reasoning abilities.

In the Friday Program, the speech pathologist diagnoses the problems and provides individual or group treatment, which involves a parent, the visiting teacher, the teacher's aide, or sometimes another student. Ongoing exercises are prescribed and are followed up at home or in the regular school.

Additional social benefits

Students in the Friday Program are likely to be the only child with a visual impairment in their local schools and frequently miss contact with other students who are encountering identical or similar experiences or problems; some have never even met another child with visual impairments. These students enjoy the opportunity to discuss issues related to having a visual impairment and often arrange to maintain friendships via telephone or visits to each other's homes.

The students' parents also have the opportunity to share informally their opinions of the perils and benefits of mainstream education. They can freely exchange the experiences they have encountered in dealing with regular education teachers, specialists, parents of sighted children, and members of the community. For some, it has been their first contact with another parent of a child in a mainstream setting.

Discussion

The challenge for residential schools is to offer a flexible range of service delivery options that provide for the diverse needs of students and complement community resources. The Friday Program is but one aspect of the Burwood center's response to this challenge.

The purpose of this article has not been to suggest that this approach is the most appropriate means for children with visual impairments to acquire their "unique" skills. The Friday Program has emerged not solely because of the center's philosophical commitment, but because of a number of historical, geographic, and legislative factors that are specific to Burwood and to the State of Victoria.

However, irrespective of the type of full- or part-time support service offered to mainstream students and whether the student is placed in a resource base attached to a school or is the only child with a visual impairment in a regular school, five basic philosophical tenets need to be considered when an agency is planning to establish a mode of service delivery.

• Students with visual impairments require direct instruction from teachers and therapists who are trained in areas of skill development that are related to or compounded by severe visual loss. Contact time is also needed for the diagnosis of needs whose fulfillment can form the basis of programs that other people carry out. Such program planning cannot be conducted by visiting teachers, who are restricted by time and legislation to the role of general consultants.

• It is unnecessary and impractical for regular education teachers and other professionals in the community to be expert in the same skills as are teachers of visually impaired students. They do not have to have complete mastery of braille or all types of adapted software or know how to develop long-cane techniques or remedy fine- and gross-motor deficits, for example. However, with the help of professionals from residential schools and other experts, regular education teachers should have a general knowledge of visual impairments that allows them to develop teaching strategies that will be effective with students with visual impairments. If all the needs of these students are to be met, both the general skills of the regular education teachers and the specific skills of the trained support specialists are essential.

• The "unique" needs of students with severe visual impairments need to be addressed in ongoing programs that are part of or parallel to the students' general academic programs. This approach is preferable to programs (such as the rehabilitative "Living Skills" programs, offered to postsecondary students on completion of their academic education) that strive to remediate or fill in what has been omitted in the students' education. If the aim of schooling is to prepare students for life, then "rehabilitation" should not be necessary. If students with visual impairments complete their education with well-developed academic skills but poorly developed self-sufficiency skills, then the educational structures that supported the students can be blamed for the student's deficits.

• The content of any direct service that involves the withdrawal of students with visual impairments from the mainstream must be generalized to the students' homes and regular classrooms. The Friday Program would be an ineffective exercise if it remained at the level of monthly attendance without feedback, joint case planning, ongoing consultation, and the planning of programs to be carried out by parents, visiting teachers, regular education teachers, integration aides, and professionals in the community.

• In a time of social and educational change, residential schools should not need to struggle to maintain a positive image. They should be centers of excellence, uniquely poised to provide a flexible range of placements, direct services, and types of consultation that directly enhance the educational and lifetime options for students who are blind or visually impaired.

References

English, D. (1989). *Keyboarding by touch and tape*. Melbourne: Royal Victorian Institute for the Blind.

Fullwood, D. (1988). *A start to independence for your visually impaired child*. Melbourne: Royal Victorian Institute for the Blind.

Fullwood, D. (1990). *The impact of vision impairment on fine motor development*. Paper presented at conference on therapy, Burwood Educational Centre, Melbourne.

Harley, R. K. & English, W. H. (1989). Support services for visually impaired children in local day schools: Residential schools as a resource. *Journal of Visual Impairment & Blindness, 83*, 403–406.

Hatlen, P. H. & Curry, S. A. (1987). In support of specialized programs for blind and visually impaired children: The impact of vision loss on learning. *Journal of Visual Impairment & Blindness, 81*, 7–13.

Hatlen, P. H. (1990). Meeting unique needs of pupils with visual impairments. *Re view 22*(2), 79–82.

Jones, G. (1987). *Learning to live with self: The child/youth and body*. Proceedings of the Eighth Quenquennial International Conference on Education of the Visually Handicapped, Wurzburg, Germany.

Palazesi, M. A. (1986). The need for motor development: Programs for visually impaired preschoolers. *Journal of Visual Impairment & Blindness, 80*, 573–576.

Pfisterer, U. (1989). *Games for all of us*. Melbourne: Royal Victorian Institute for the Blind.

Wyatt, L. (1989). *Possible effects of visual impairment on physical development*. Melbourne: Royal Victorian Institute for the Blind.

TEACHING CHOICE-MAKING SKILLS TO STUDENTS WHO ARE DEAF-BLIND

Carole R. Gothelf, Daniel B. Crimmins, Caren A. Mercer, and Patricia A. Finocchiaro

Carole R. Gothelf (CEC Chapter #45), *Director, Education Services, The Jewish Guild for the Blind, New York, New York.* **Daniel B. Crimmins,** *Director, Department of Psychology, Westchester Institute for Human Development/University Affiliated Program, Valhalla, New York.* **Caren**

A. Mercer (CEC Chapter #45), *Principal, Guild School, The Jewish Guild for the Blind, New York, New York.* **Patricia A. Finocchiaro,** *Coordinator, Day Treatment Program, The Jewish Guild for the Blind, New York, New York.*

The ability to make choices is an essential part of functioning independently and with dignity (Guess, Benson, & Siegel-Causey, 1985). Providing choice-making opportunities for students with the most severe disabilities (e.g., students who are deaf-blind with cognitive disabilities), who often do not communicate independently, presents a major challenge to educators. For example, Shevin and Klein (1984) have stressed that choice-making should be a "teaching target" (p. 60), yet there are few guidelines available for educators on

TABLE 1. CHOICE-MAKING INSTRUCTION

	STEP 1	STEP 2	STEP 3
PRINCIPLE	People typically make choices in the environments in which the outcomes of their choice are available.	The boundaries in which the choice-making activity takes place should be defined through the use of appropriate aids and cues. Providing boundaries minimizes the visual/motor and cognitive requirements of orienting and reaching.	Individual preferences play an important role in enhancing motivation for the activity.
PROCEDURE	Choosing what to eat should take place where the student normally eats. Teaching choice-making in an artificial environment removes many of the naturally occurring cues to the event.	A dycem placement can be used to secure a cafeteria tray on a table or on the lap tray of a student's wheelchair. A second dycem mat can be used to secure the plates and glasses on the tray. (Dycem is a nonslip plastic that is helpful in stabilizing objects on surfaces. It comes in reels or sheets that can be cut to size. It is portable, easily cleaned, inexpensive, and available from adaptive aids catalogs.)	The student is presented with two entree samples, one at a time. The items from which the student is choosing should be two foods that he or she is likely to want to eat.
SPECIAL CONSIDERATIONS	Administrative policies and procedures should ensure that the choice-making process can take place. This may involve working with the cafeteria staff or revising lunchtime schedules.	If cafeteria trays are not available or necessary, the plates of food can be placed on a dycem mat directly on a table. For students with vision, the color of the dycem should be selected to provide contrast with the tray or table and the plates.	Administrators should work with cafeteria staff to ensure that appropriate alternatives are made available. (E.g., if two hot meals are not available, a choice between a hot meal and sandwich or between two sandwiches should be substituted.) Staff should be aware that food preferences are influenced by a student's cultural and family background.

(table continues on next page)

From *Teaching Exceptional Children*, Vol. 26, No. 4, Summer 1994, pp. 32-35. © 1994 by The Council for Exceptional Children. Reprinted by permission.

(United Nations/O. Monsen)

When children have multiple disabilities, it is important to teach them about making choices.

	STEP 4	STEP 5	STEP 6	STEP 7
PRINCIPLE	Choices should be presented consistently in order in reinforce the physical structure within which choosing occurs. Placing the choices in the same locations in relation to the student's body each time helps the student to anticipate where the sample is likely to be.	The student is made aware of the food through tactile/kinesthetic cues (guided or paired movements between the teacher and the student) and/or visual, verbal, gestural, and object cues. The teacher must assess the conditions that facilitate comprehension (e.g., with gestures, without gestures, etc.)	Establishing routines within instructional sequences enables the student to anticipate the next step and encourages self-initiated choice-making. A pause or time delay in a sequence (hands in the lap) may serve as a prompt to the student to initiate an interaction or make a selection (Siegel-Causey & Ernst, 1989).	Reliable communication of preference depends upon a foundation of consistent responses to the student's nonverbal behaviors. Nonverbal behaviors need to be acknowledged by the teacher on the assumption that the individual is attempting to communicate meaningful dialog. This provides a basis for communicating shared meanings (Guess, et al., 1985; Williams, 1991).
PROCEDURE	The first sample is presented on the student's left, tasted with the left hand, and then removed. The second sample is then presented on the student's right, tasted with the right hand, and then removed. Care must be taken to ensure that the individual is not always choosing the sample on the right or the sample on the left.	For each sample of food, the student is guided through touching the plate, touching the food, smelling the food, and tasting the food. A staff member says the name of the food, signs it, and shapes the student's hands to sign the name of the food.	Both samples are then presented to the student. The student touches the left plate with the left hand and the right plate with the right hand. As the student touches each sample, he or she is reminded of its name. The student is then directed to place both hands in his or her lap (using verbal and/or physical prompting as needed). The student is then instructed, "It is time to pick what you want for lunch." Language input should be provided at a level and in a mode that the student can comprehend.	The student chooses the desired food by touching one of the samples, looking or making facial gestures, starting to eat, making vocal sounds and/or body movements, signing, or in any other way that indicates his or her preference.
SPECIAL CONSIDERATIONS	The student's ability to reach, grasp, and manipulate utensils or the food itself may be influenced by poor muscle tone, stability, or coordination, as well as limited visual functioning. Generally, proper postural alignment can be attained through the use of adaptive positioning equipment. Grasping and manipulating utensils can be assisted through the use of adaptive aids such as special spoons, plates with lips, or slant trays.	The student's receptive vocabulary may be limited. Natural routines should be maintained within the normal context of mealtime in order to help the student comprehend the expectancies for his or her behavior.	If the student does not respond when the question is repeated, the teacher says, "That's OK. If you don't want the meat or the rice, I'll ask you again soon." The teacher should always return and provide the student with another opportunity and additional prompting if necessary.	If the student reaches for both or neither, the teacher must repeat the previous procedure and reinforce that the student must choose one sample. The teacher must acknowledge any form of communication. If the student repeatedly reaches for both, he or she should be given some of each for lunch.

(table continues on next page)

how to do this. As a result, the systematic instruction necessary to teach students with severe disabilities how to make meaningful choices remains largely absent from the curricular content and daily routines of these students' educational programs.

PROGRAM DESCRIPTION

This article offers a set of principles, procedures, and special considerations for teaching students who are deaf-blind with cognitive disabilities to make their own choices during mealtimes. It is intended to show teachers how a typical daily activity can be used to teach choice-making and how this skill can be increased in complexity as the student progresses.

Mealtime is ideal for such instruction because it naturally occurs on a consistent, daily basis in school, at home, and in community environments. The act of choosing what to eat or drink results in natural consequences that are generally self-reinforcing. Instruction centers on providing the student with structured opportunities for selecting foods, by offering a series of choices among familiar, meaningful, and disparate options.

The instructional principles and procedures are described in Table 1.

The procedures were field tested by classroom teachers, teacher assistants, administrative personnel, and parents of students from 7 to 14 years of age who are deaf-blind with cognitive and physical disabilities. Once the procedures were found to work, they were structured to make them understandable to virtually anyone who might be called on to offer a meal to a student, including his or her parent(s) and group home staff. As a follow up, the procedures were replicated and fine-tuned by the instructional staff of a day-treatment program serving adults with cognitive disabilities who are visually impaired or who are deaf-blind.

STEP 8	STEP 9	STEP 10
Components of everyday routines should be employed to establish correspondence between words and their meanings. Routines enable students to take an active part in the activity and to communicate with the teacher.	In addition to establishing correspondence between words and their meanings, the process of systematically using routines in the choice-making process must be established.	Contingent communicative behavior is reinforced by getting the requested item. The student communicates through an action or a signal to indicate his or her preference.
The staff signs "Finished" for the undesired plate, guides the student through the sign for "Finished," and prompts the student to move the plate away.	The teacher signs "Eat" and the name of the desired food and prompts the student to do the same. This procedure must follow the previous one.	The student is served a full portion of the food that was selected.
Initially, the student may require the teacher to move the hands for him or her. Subsequently, the teacher and the student should move their hands together cooperatively, the student's hands riding on top of the teacher's. The teacher should pause in the pushing action, and allow the student to communicate a desire to continue by moving the teacher's hands.	The teacher may choose other ways to communicate the same message, such as signing the student's name followed by the signs for "Wants to eat" and the name of the food. Language input should be provided at a level and in a mode that the student can comprehend.	The student must join the cafeteria line to obtain the full portion of food.

IMPLICATIONS

The instructional procedures teach students about making choices and give them increased opportunity for control over one portion of their day. This provides several potential benefits. First, choice-making instruction allows students to take control of an aspect of their environment that is meaningful and motivating to them. This is significant in itself, because these students often have few opportunities for exerting such control. Second, there is evidence that student-selected tasks and reinforcers yield better performance than teacher-selected ones (Meyer & Evans, 1989; Parsons, Reid, Reynolds, & Bumgarner, 1990). Third, this finding has also been observed for challenging behaviors, with fewer challenging behaviors occurring when students select their activities than when the teacher assigns the activity (Crimmins & Gothelf, in press; Durand, 1990; Dyer, Dunlap, & Winterling, 1990).

A curricular approach that encourages students to exercise their own initiative requires both systematic teaching of choice-making and provision of opportunities to practice choosing. While this article provides examples of choice-making during mealtime, similar opportunities can be built into a variety of daily routines that promote the use of this skill. Teachers are encouraged to provide choices in the context of natural routines that can be made increasingly more complex.

■ REFERENCES

Crimmins, D. B., & Gothelf, C. R., (in press). Examining the communicative purpose of behavior. In *American Foundation for the Blind: Deaf-Blind Project.* New York: AFB.

Durand, V. M. (1990). *Severe behavior problems: A functional communication training approach.* New York: Guilford.

Dyer, K., Dunlap, G., & Winterling, V. (1990). Effects of choice-making on the serious problem behaviors of students with severe handicaps. *Journal of Applied Behavior Analysis, 23,* 515–524.

Guess, D., Benson, H. A., & Siegel-Causey, E. (1985). Concepts and issues related to choice-making and autonomy among persons with severe disabilities. *The Journal of the Association for Persons with Severe Handicaps, 10,* 79–86.

Meyer, L. H., & Evans, I. M. (1989). *Nonaversive intervention for behavior problems: A manual for home and community.* Baltimore: Paul H. Brookes.

Parsons, M. B., & Reid, D. H. (1990). Assessing food preferences among persons with profound mental retardation: Providing opportunities to make choices. *Journal of Applied Behavior Analysis, 23,* 183–195.

Parsons, M. B., Reid, D. H., Reynolds, J., & Bumgarner, M. (1990). Effects of chosen versus assigned jobs on the work performance of persons with severe handicaps. *Journal of Applied Behavior Analysis, 23,* 253–258.

Shevin, M., & Klein, N. K. (1984). The importance of choice-making skills for students with severe disabilities. *The Journal of the Association for Persons with Severe Handicaps, 9,* 159–166.

Siegel-Causey, E., & Ernst, B. (1989). Theoretical orientation and research in nonsymbolic development. In E. Siegel-Causey & D. Guess (Eds.), *Enhancing nonsymbolic communication interactions among learners with severe disabilities* (pp. 17–51). Baltimore: Paul H. Brookes.

The preparation of this manuscript was supported in part by a grant from the New York State Department of Education (NYSED), Office for Special Education, Title VI-C. The information does not necessarily represent the policy of NYSED, and no official endorsement should be inferred.

Children with Physical and Health Impairments

A physical impairment is a condition that interferes with a person's ability to move, use, feel, or control one or more parts of the body. A health impairment is a condition that requires some form of medical treatment. Children may be physically impaired, health impaired, have both physical and health impairments simultaneously, or may be multiple handicapped (e.g., the addition of a learning disability, mental retardation, behavioral disorder, communication disorder, or other disorder). Physical impairments are classified as mild, moderate, or severe, depending on the extent to which children can use their bodies. If a child can walk alone, he or she is usually considered only mildly impaired. If a child needs crutches or other aids to walk, the impairment is usually moderate. Children in wheelchairs are usually considered severely physically impaired.

Physically impaired children may have a body part disabled by either a neurological cause or an orthopedic cause. A neurological impairment involves an injury or dysfunction in a part of the brain or spinal cord resulting in a loss of some bodily movements. An orthopedic impairment involves an injury or dysfunction in a part of the skeletal system resulting in a loss of some bodily movements. The difficulties in body movement, sensation, perception, or control may be identical with either neurological or orthopedic causations. Prefixes such as mono (one), di (two), tri (three), or quadri (four) are often placed before plegia (paralysis) to designate the number of limbs (arms and legs) that are affected. Hemiplegia is used to designate the loss of movement of one side of the body. Paraplegia is often used to designate the loss of movement of both legs.

Children with health impairments must have some form of medicine or medical attention in order to attend school. Health impairments are classified as mild, moderate, or severe, depending on duration (temporary or chronic) and limitations to activity (normal stamina or debilitated and weak). Most of the health impairments that qualify for special educational services under PL 94-142 are chronic and/or debilitating illnesses. Some examples are cancer, diabetes, epilepsy, sickle cell anemia, asthma, AIDS, heart defects, eating disorders, and pregnancy.

Intervention for children with physical or health problems should begin as soon as the impairment is diagnosed. Special educational services, as well as medical services, may be initiated at birth. Preschools now provide multidisciplinary services to children with physical or health impairments. Public schools must supply equal opportunities for children with disabilities to participate in school activities, transitional services, and free and appropriate education. The reforms and restructuring of special education, mandated by the courts, have opened public school doors to many physically and/or health-impaired children who were formerly taught at home, in hospitals, in residential institutions, or in special schools.

The age at which a child acquires a physical or health impairment is an important area to consider when developing the individualized education program (IEP). A child who is born with a disability usually has permanent, severe limitations but has grown up adjusting to the restrictions imposed by immobility or medical attentions. A child who acquires the impairment later in childhood may have a greater chance of partial or complete recovery. However, this child has had no time to learn to cope with the disability. Children who have just developed physical or health impairments may go through periods of denial, mourning, and depression before they accept the limitations imposed by their conditions. Their IEPs should include short-term goals for helping them adjust. They usually need to be motivated to comply with physical or occupational therapy, or medicines and medical procedures. Medical social workers often participate in the development of individualized family service plans (IFSPs) or IEPs with suggestions for special services aimed at helping the students and their families adjust to the impairments.

The visibility of the physical or health impairment is another important consideration when developing short- and long-term goals for children who are debilitated. Children with very obvious disabilities not only look different but also feel different because of all the attention their handicap receives. They may have to struggle to develop positive self-images and self-esteem. Children with less obvious impairments (e.g., diabetes, sickle cell anemia, asthma, epilepsy) may be asked to participate in more activities than they can handle, or in forbidden activities. They have to constantly explain that they are different, even if they do not look different. They may be accused of being lazy or hypochondriacal.

Teachers have a responsibility to help establish positive interactions between children with disabilities and their abled peers. It is important that teachers and other school personnel become acquainted with the special situations of each physically or health-impaired child. They should understand limitations, needs, treatments, and/or medications. In addition, they should discuss each child's condition openly with his or her classmates. Peers are more willing to accept special arrangements or time given to children with physical or health impairments if the need for them has been made clear from the beginning.

Teachers of children with physical or health impairments may be called on to do some extraordinary pro-

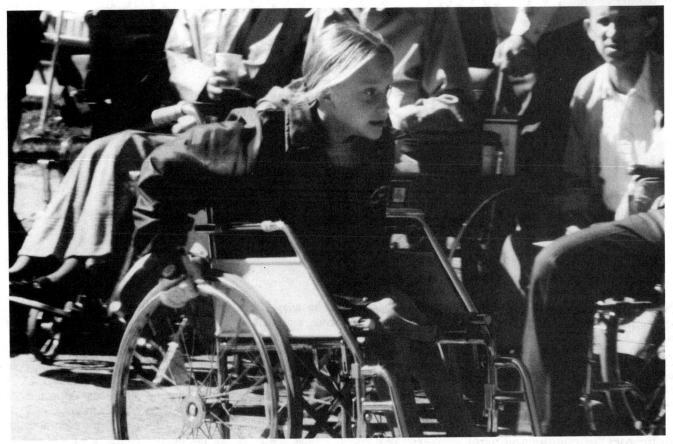

cedures. Judicial rulings have established life support services as legitimate duties of schools with regular education classes. For example, if a child needs urinary catheterization during the school day, the school staff must provide this service. If a school nurse is not available, a teacher may be asked. Teachers may be asked to supervise ambulatory kidney dialysis, oxygen administration, intravenous feedings, or ventilators. They may need to learn how to handle diabetic shock, asthmatic attacks, and epileptic seizures. In addition to medical special services, the teacher must also educate the children appropriately and challenge them to work up to their highest levels of ability. Sympathy assignments, or sympathy grades, are detrimental to all children.

The first article in this unit discusses three health impairments: cancer, medical fragility, and at-risk birth status. Special services should be initiated as soon as the conditions are diagnosed. The second article presents the danger that some physically and health-impaired children face: child abuse. Teachers need to be aware of the implications of the research in this area. The next selec-

tion addresses the question of the appropriateness of enrolling students with physical or health impairments in regular classes. Both the "up"side and the "down"side are presented along with a discussion of supplementary aids and services. The last article provides a summary of educational adaptations for children with physical and health impairments in inclusive classrooms. The tips in the article are designed both to help teachers and to raise their awareness of the positive aspects of inclusion.

Looking Ahead: Challenge Questions

What modifications of school curriculum should be made for children who survive life-threatening illnesses?

How can we help prevent the abuse of children with physical or health impairments? How can we help support their families?

Is inclusion appropriate for children with physical and health impairments?

What can teachers do to make inclusion of physically impaired children a more pleasant, nonthreatening experience?

Medical Treatment and Educational Problems In Children

NETTIE R. BARTEL AND
S. KENNETH THURMAN

NETTIE R. BARTEL (Temple University Chapter) and S. KENNETH THURMAN are professors in the Special Education Program, Department of Psychological Studies in Education, Temple University, Philadelphia.

Educators, in conjunction with the medical profession and parents, must respond to the special physical and cognitive needs of children who are alive today only because of advances in medical technology, Ms. Bartel and Mr. Thurman suggest.

JANET IS a 13-year-old who attends a junior high school. She is shorter and heavier than most of her classmates, and her physical development seems more suited to an elementary school. Although she is well-motivated and has two supportive parents, Janet is barely getting by in her school program. In elementary school, she was labeled "learning disabled" and received assistance in arithmetic and reading comprehension in a resource room. Her homeroom teacher describes Janet as industrious and earnest but indecisive and easily discouraged. Her mother states that Janet needs a structured home environment to enable her to function successfully in such everyday situations as getting herself ready for the school bus in the morning or completing her homework and household chores in the evening.

Janet's functioning is like that of many other students with learning disabilities. But there is one major difference. Janet was once precocious and lively. At age 5 she suddenly became anemic and sickly. Her pediatrician administered some blood tests and diagnosed her as having acute lymphocytic leukemia. She was taken to a major children's hospital in a nearby city and given treatment that saved her life. That treatment included cranial radiation.

Janet is one of thousands of children whose lives have been saved by aggressive medical treatment. Only later was it discovered that the very treatment that saved their lives also reduced the quality of their lives. These children provide poignant evidence that the miracles of modern medical technology sometimes come with unanticipated costs — costs that often must be borne by the very children whose lives are saved. These costs include the educational difficulties that can result from treatment.

We will consider the educational implications for three groups of children whose health conditions are such that they would not survive without medical intervention. Some of these children are like Janet: after a period of normal, healthy life, they contract a disease (often cancer) that would be fatal without medical treatment; yet the side effects of the treatment may cause school problems.

Other children seem normal at conception and during fetal development but have difficulties that can be attributed to the fact that they were born "too soon" or "too small." That is, they were born prematurely or born with low birth weight. Years ago, these babies would simply have died; today, many survive, sometimes with significant developmental problems.

A third group of children are those whose difficulties apparently go back to the prenatal period. These children (sometimes referred to as "medically fragile") are born with complex medical needs and remain alive only because of intensive medical care that often continues throughout their lives. A few years ago, these children, too, would not have survived. But today they are found in significant numbers in our infant, preschool, and school programs.

CHILDREN TREATED FOR CANCER

There are a number of potentially lethal childhood diseases. However, because of their prevalence and the success with which they are being treated, we will concern ourselves here only with childhood cancers.

Nature of the condition. Cancer is a disease in which one or more cells of the body divide more rapidly than is healthy. The most common childhood cancer, acute lymphocytic leukemia (also known as acute lymphoblastic leukemia) is a cancer of the blood-forming organs of the body, including the bone marrow, the spleen, and the lymph nodes. Eighty percent of all cases of acute lymphocytic leukemia are seen in children, where it accounts for approximately one-third of total childhood cancers. In this disease, the body produces a large number of immature white blood cells that are unable to develop into normally functioning parts of the immune system. These immature cells proliferate rapidly, crowding out and interfering with the manufacture of other crucial blood cells, including red cells and platelets.

Taken together, leukemias and malignancies of the brain and nervous system account for more than half of all childhood cancers. Current statistics indicate that at least one child in 800 to 1,000 is a cancer survivor. This suggests that most schools have at least one survivor of childhood cancer in the student body.

The causes of these cancers are not known. As with other cancers, a number of factors appear to trigger the disease — including viruses, a genetic propensity, and exposure to radiation or other environmental factors.

The early symptoms of cancer in children are vague and frequently include headache, fatigue, a low-grade fever, easy bruising, and pallor. Bleeding, irritability, frequent infections, lowered resistance to infections, loss of appetite, weight loss, and facial puffiness are also seen. Diagnosis of acute lymphocytic

> Overall, children who survive leukemia or brain tumors show a decline in cognitive functioning.

leukemia is made by a complete blood count and an examination of a blood marrow sample. In the case of brain tumors, diagnostic imaging techniques — including x-rays, CAT scans, and NMRI (nuclear magnetic resonance imaging) — are often used.

Nature of the treatment. The treatment goal for acute lymphocytic leukemia is to eliminate all leukemic cells and to induce a remission. This goal is achieved by various combinations of radiation, chemotherapy, and systemic drug therapy. Treatments are given at the time of diagnosis and as a prophylaxis following initial treatment. Cranial radiation is also given prophylactically in an effort to prevent central nervous system disease later.

Treatment for brain tumors usually includes a combination of surgery, radiation, and chemotherapy. The use of cranial radiation has been suspected as a major cause of cognitive dysfunction. Because brain-tumor therapy requires much higher doses of radiation than does leukemia therapy, children with brain tumors may be at higher risk for subsequent learning problems than children with leukemia.

As recently as the 1950s a child diagnosed as having leukemia had an average life expectancy of three months. Today, almost 90% of such children achieve initial remission, and almost 80% are symptom-free five years after diagnosis. Patients with a poorer prognosis — boys, blacks, those younger than age 2 or older than age 10, and those with complications — require more aggressive treatment. The survival rate for brain cancer

and nervous system cancer is not as high, hovering just above 50%.

Families of children with cancer frequently experience a roller coaster of emotions in which the initial shock of the diagnosis of a life-threatening disease is followed by relief at the apparently successful medical treatment. In cases in which the diagnosis calls for cranial radiation, this feeling may be followed by increasing concern on the part of the family as it becomes apparent that the child is manifesting learning difficulties that were not present previously. Many parents, in an attempt to avoid having the child stigmatized, may try to minimize the seriousness of the child's condition to school personnel. Yet, when learning problems become more pronounced, families and schools need to work closely together to address the special learning needs of the child.

Educational implications. Overall, children who survive leukemia or brain tumors show a decline in cognitive functioning and academic ability, with more severe problems evidenced by the latter group. While it is believed that acute lymphocytic leukemia does not in and of itself cause learning problems, the situation is more complicated in the case of brain tumors. It is difficult to separate the effects of the tumors themselves from the effects of the treatment. Recent studies have attempted to delineate the exact nature, severity, and possible cause or causes of adverse aftereffects of childhood cancers. It has been proposed that children treated at an early age (4 or younger) are more vulnerable to serious effects than are children treated when they are older. This suggestion is based in part on the theory that, because it is rapidly developing, the immature brain is more susceptible to adverse influences than the mature brain.

One major study reported intellectual and neuropsychological dysfunction over time in a group of children whose acute lymphocytic leukemia had been treated with cranial radiation.[1] This study is especially significant because it evaluated children both at the time of diagnosis and every six months for three years afterward. Three years after being treated with radiation and methotrexate, this group's average I.Q. score was 89, as compared to 109 at their first evaluation. The researchers concluded that the cognitive decline was not apparent until at least three years after treatment, that the children who were younger at diagnosis suffered greater adverse effects, and that children who received radiation experienced more adverse effects than children treated with methotrexate in the absence of radiation. The results of this study are typical of a number of similar studies, most of which have found an I.Q. decline of 12 to 20 points, with specific types of intellectual and academic deficits most frequently seen.

Between one-half and two-thirds of children who survive acute lymphocytic leukemia have been found to require some kind of special academic help, as compared to 15% of their siblings (about average for the school population as a whole). Teachers and parents report that these survivors take longer to complete tasks, have difficulty following multiple commands, and learn more slowly. They also describe them as less active, less expressive, and less able to concentrate.

A higher percentage of leukemia survivors than of the general student population attend special education classes or receive some form of specialized instruction; a higher than usual percentage of these children repeat grades. The reports of teachers and parents suggest that the specific areas in which these children experience the greatest difficulties include attention/concentration, mathematics, motor speed, visual/motor integration, timed performance, comprehension, spelling, planning ability, fine motor skills, and abstract thinking.

Of children successfully treated for brain tumors, about two-thirds are found in special education programs, while many of the rest require some specialized school help. Declines of 25 I.Q. points are common, and the school achievement of children who survive brain tumors is markedly below that of the general population. Learning disabilities are common. In one study in which none of the children with brain tumors had been in special education prior to diagnosis, at six months after treatment 50% of those under age 6 and 11% of those over age 6 were in special classes.

The specific learning problems of children who have been treated for brain tumors include attention deficits, problems with arithmetic, difficulty in self-organization, and reduced speed and dexterity. In addition to cognitive dysfunction and problems with school achievement, children treated for brain tumors often exhibit problems with emotional adjustment, shortened stature, and poor peer relations that stem from hair loss and

> The ultimate prognosis for low birth weight and premature infants is most clearly mediated by environment.

otherwise feeling "different." Factors that seem to affect cognitive and academic functioning include amount of radiation, pre- and postoperative mental status, postoperative central nervous system infection, and how much of the head is irradiated.

Current treatment protocols for children with acute lymphocytic leukemia emphasize reducing or eliminating the use of cranial radiation whenever possible without reducing the child's survival chances. And fewer children with leukemia are receiving cranial radiation today than five years ago. Nevertheless, a significant number of such children still need this treatment if they are to have a chance of surviving. This means that educators will continue to see children with the specific cognitive deficits described above. The very success of treatment for these two most common childhood cancers is creating a population of children at risk academically and is presenting educators with the unique challenge of developing and implementing interventions that may spare these children from failure in school. Improved medical interventions in the future will no doubt increase the rate of survival even more and result in the presence of more cancer survivors in our nation's schools.

LOW BIRTH WEIGHT AND PREMATURITY

Nature of the condition. Low birth weight is defined as weighing less than 2,500 grams or 5.5 pounds at birth. Very low birth weight refers to infants who weigh less than 1,500 grams or 3.3

pounds at birth, and extremely low birth weight is defined by a weight of 1,000 grams (or 2.2 pounds) or less at birth. In 1986 the National Center for Health Statistics reported that 6.8% of all infants born were classified as low birth weight. Given that there are between 3.5 and four million births each year in the U. S., this means that every year about 255,000 infants are born who can be classified as low birth weight. Sixty percent of all neonatal deaths (i.e., death within the first 28 days of life) can be accounted for by low birth weight, and 20% of babies who die in the first year of life were low weight at birth.

Typically, low birth weight is the result of premature birth or of intrauterine growth retardation. Birth is deemed premature when an infant is born after less than 37 weeks of gestation. Prematurity occurs in about 11% of all births, according to 1986 data from the National Center for Health Statistics. This means that about 412,000 infants are born prematurely each year. A number of factors are related to increased risk of premature birth, including adolescent pregnancy, maternal age greater than 35 years, poverty, poor nutrition, poor prenatal care, and drug use.

Retarded intrauterine growth is the other major contributor to low birth weight. This condition often results from decreased blood flow to the fetus that may be related to incomplete placental development, the effects of drugs, high altitude, or multiple births. It may also be related to certain chromosomal abnormalities. Babies whose growth was retarded in utero are referred to as small for gestational age. Unlike babies who are premature, babies who are small for gestational age are most often carried to full term. However, babies who are born prematurely may also be considered small for gestational age if their birth weight is more than 90% below the weight that would be expected for their particular gestational age.

Both low birth weight and prematurity place infants at increased risk of poor development. Examining the literature since the early 1970s reveals an improving prognosis for low birth weight infants, especially those weighing less than 1,500 grams. In the early 1970s only about 20% of infants weighing less than 1,000 grams survived. By the early 1980s about 40% of these infants were surviving. A recent study also suggests that these infants are surviving with a lower incidence of developmental problems.[2] The data indicate that, by age 5, 80% of children who weighed 1,000 grams or less at birth showed either slight or only minor neurodevelopmental difficulties.

The prognosis for a low birth weight or premature infant can be influenced by a number of factors. The treatment of these infants in neonatal intensive care units may require physicians to deal with such complications as brain hemorrhages, lung damage, infections, and damage to sensory systems. Multiple complications may affect one infant, while another of equal birth weight or gestational age goes unaffected. Unfortunately, there is no way to tell at the onset which infant is more likely to experience such complications and to need extraordinary treatment.

The ultimate prognosis for these infants is most clearly mediated by environment. Studies have consistently demonstrated that infants of low birth weight and premature infants who are reared in enriched environments fare better than their counterparts who are reared in poverty or without the proper types of nurturance and stimulation from caregivers.

The birth and subsequent hospitalization of a premature or low birth weight infant can have significant impact on a family. The uncertainty experienced by the family during hospitalization can create stress. As one mother recalled:

> After I got over the initial shock of Julia's appearance it got easier to visit her. . . . I couldn't feel comfortable in the NICU [neonatal intensive care unit]. . . . Hospitals are intimidating; NICUs are even more so. I felt I had no control; I was just a bystander. Meanwhile, my poor husband was run ragged. [He] would work all day, and then drive to the hospital, which was a three hour round trip. [He] was also assembling furniture, painting her room, and scouting around for very tiny baby clothes.[3]

Once the infant has been brought home, the family remains under stress since the baby's course of development is not yet clear. In addition, prematurity alters the patterns of interaction between infants and their caregivers. Premature infants tend to be more irritable, less regular in their sleeping and eating patterns, and more ambiguous in the social cues that they emit. As a result, parents of these infants may tend to feel frustrated and less than competent.

Educational implications. Infants who survive low birth weight or prematurity need early intervention. At a minimum, these infants should be evaluated periodically to help make certain that they are developing properly. Early intervention should stress cognitive, language, and motor development and should focus on providing the necessary supports to the family to reduce stress and maximize the development of the child. The passage and implementation of P.L. 99-457 and its recent reauthorization with the passage of the Individuals with Disabilities Education Act Amendments (P.L. 102-119) provide the framework within which this early intervention can take place.

The need for special education services for these children as they get older is very much a function of the individual child. It is important to keep in mind that the largest percentage of children who experience low birth weight or who are premature function well within normal limits by the time they reach school age. Thus, while many children who begin life in neonatal intensive care units do manifest developmental and learning problems when they reach school age, it would be unwise to conclude that any child whose life begins under these trying circumstances is predestined to require special educational services.

THE MEDICALLY FRAGILE

Nature of the condition. The term *medically fragile* refers to children whose medical needs are complex and encompasses a wide range of conditions that affect the health and subsequent education and development of the children. Most often, the problems experienced by these children are chronic and require ongoing — frequently daily — treatment and monitoring (sometimes in a hospital setting) if the children are to survive. These children have conditions that are "extremely disabling or life-threatening. Usually such [children] are dependent on life-support equipment such as ventilators, feeding tubes, or apnea (i.e., breathing) monitors for survival."[4] However, children with such conditions as diabetes, sickle-cell anemia, cystic fibrosis, and hemophilia may also on occasion manifest acute symptoms and have medical needs that significantly interfere with their education.

It is difficult to determine the incidence and prevalence of medically fragile chil-

dren because the term is rather broad and because those children with multiple disabilities can end up being classified under some other label. The U.S. Department of Education estimates that, during the 1988-89 school year, there were 50,349 children between the ages of 6 and 21 who were classified as health-impaired and who were being served in special education programs across the nation.[5] Keep in mind that this low figure does not include any children who fall into another classification.

Because their conditions vary greatly, the exact prognosis of children with complex medical needs is difficult to determine. Many have decreased life expectancies. Some children with complex medical needs can experience relatively long periods of stability, though constant monitoring of their conditions remains necessary. For example, a child who has a tracheostomy and is dependent on a ventilator for assistance with breathing may be able to function reasonably well from day to day with proper suctioning, cleaning, and maintenance of the tubes that connect him or her to the ventilator. However, that situation may change rapidly if the child acquires an upper respiratory infection.

Families of medically fragile children often experience stresses that go beyond those of other families. They must adapt to the special needs of their child and often must learn how to maintain the equipment and use specialized devices and therapeutic techniques. Moreover, they must cope with the uncertainty of when their child's condition may suddenly become acute, requiring emergency treatment or hospitalization. At the same time, they may need to provide additional emotional support to help the child cope more easily with the medical condition. The constant care required by children who have complex medical needs can lead to parental fatigue and can create the potential for burnout. Such effects can adversely affect the relationships in the family.

Educational implications. Children with complex medical needs can be unique challenges to the education system. On occasion, these children will require homebound or hospital-based instruction. When they are attending school, these children may tire more easily and thus need periods of rest or inactivity between instructional sessions.

Nor is it uncommon for these children to require the services of a nurse or of a physical or occupational therapist in order to render treatment or to help them gain the most benefit from their learning experiences. Frequent or prolonged periods of hospitalization can further disrupt the educational process and frustrate the teacher, the child, and the family. Finally, it may be necessary to modify classroom space and routines in order to accommodate the equipment to maintain a child with complex medical needs. The effective education of these children depends on a flexible, interdisciplinary approach that can be equally responsive to their medical, psychological, and educational needs.

Educators, in conjunction with the medical profession and parents, must respond to the issues raised by the presence in our schools of children who are alive today only because of advances in medical technology. As we learn more about the physical and cognitive needs of these children and as their numbers increase with the use of new medical procedures, we must work to see that the quality of their lives remains at the highest possible level. Only as parents and educators are trained to help children overcome the cognitive problems brought about by their medical conditions and treatments can this goal be achieved.

1. Ann T. Meadows et al., "Declines in I.Q. Scores and Cognitive Dysfunction in Children with Acute Lymphocytic Leukemia," *Lancet*, vol. 2, 1981, pp. 1015-18.

2. William H. Kitchen et al., "Children of Birth Weight <1,000 Grams: Changing Outcome Between Ages 2 and 5 Years," *Pediatrics*, vol. 110, 1987, pp. 283-88.

3. Jean D. Rapacki, "The Neonatal Intensive Care Experience," *Children's Health Care*, vol. 20, 1991, p. 16.

4. Beverly A. Fraser, Robert N. Hensinger, and Judith A. Phelps, *Physical Management of Multiple Handicaps: A Professional's Guide*, 2nd ed. (Baltimore: Paul H. Brookes, 1990), p. 5.

5. *Thirteenth Annual Report to Congress on the Implementation of the Individuals with Disabilities Education Act* (Washington, D.C.: Office of Special Education and Rehabilitative Services, U.S Department of Education, 1991).

PHYSICAL ABUSE:
Are Children with Disabilities at Greater Risk?

A look at the facts.

Thomas J. Zirpoli

Thomas J. Zirpoli, PhD, is currently an assistant professor and program director for special education at the College of St. Thomas in St. Paul, Minnesota. Address: Thomas J. Zirpoli, Mail #5017, College of St. Thomas, St. Paul, MN 55105.

Child abuse, a generic term, is used to describe emotional or psychological injury, negligence, non-accidental physical injury, and sexual molestation of children by caregivers. Nonaccidental injury, or physical abuse of children with disabilities by caregivers, will be the focus of this article.

One of the more tragic elements regarding the abuse of our nation's children is the lack of accurate data concerning the scope of the problem. Estimates of the prevalence of child abuse in the United States are limited to the number of reports recorded by local agencies. Local data are submitted to national agencies where they are totaled and reported back to the public. As of 1987, the American Association for Protecting Children reported over 2 million cases of child abuse nationally. This compares to 1 million cases reported in 1980 and .5 million cases reported in 1976.

It is unclear whether the amount of child abuse is actually increasing or if the increase in documented cases reflects a greater public awareness of the problem and a greater willingness to report suspected cases (Hoffman, 1981). As previously stated, these numbers reflect only *reported* cases. It is important to keep in mind that much abuse remains unreported; some professionals believe that the number of actual cases is at least twice the number of reported cases (Straus, Gelles, & Steinmetz, 1980).

Child Abuse and Neglect Reported by Year (1976–1987)

Year	Reported Cases
1976	669,000
1977	838,000
1978	836,000
1979	988,000
1980	1,154,000
1981	1,225,000
1982	1,262,000
1983	1,477,000
1984	1,727,000
1985	1,928,000
1986	2,086,112
1987	2,178,384

Source: American Association for Protecting Children, Personal Communication, 1/16/90.

Understanding the Variables Associated with Abuse

Before discussing the issue of abuse of children with disabilities, it is important to understand the variables associated with child abuse in general. Child abuse is the result of an interaction of many variables. These variables include the characteristics of the caregiver, environmental and sociocultural factors, and the characteristics of the child or victim of abusive behavior. Each of these will be briefly discussed below.

Characteristics of the Abusive Caregiver

Child abuse research has historically focused on the characteristics of the abusive caregiver, with relatively little attention on other variables frequently associated with abusive behavior. This focus was based upon the belief that most abusive caregivers were mentally ill and that early discovery and treatment of caregiver dysfunction was the key to prevention (Gelles, 1973). Current theories of child abuse, however, view the caregiver role as a single, although significant, variable, within a model of many interacting variables that cannot be separated and understood in isolation (Pianta, Egeland, & Erickson, 1989).

From *Intervention in School and Clinic*, Vol. 26, No. 1, September 1990, pp. 6-11. © 1990 by PRO-ED, Inc. Reprinted by permission.

Johnson and Showers (1985) found that the median age of abusers in their study was 25 years. Rogers (1978) reported 26 years and 30 years as the mean age of female and male abusers, respectively. These studies do not take into account recent significant increases in teenage pregnancies leading to adolescent parents with little or no knowledge of child development, poor parenting skills, and unrealistic expectations of child behavior. These adolescent parents frequently live within dysfunctional families, in addition to the hardships of other disadvantageous environmental circumstances (outlined below). When combined with their own immaturity and the lack of appropriate social support, adolescent parents may not be able to cope with the responsibilities of parenthood, and their children may be considered at risk for maltreatment (Meier, 1985).

Caregivers who abuse their children often are victims of abusive behavior themselves (Straus, 1983). In addition, they may have witnessed other forms of domestic violence between parents or other family members. Many abusive caregivers have only their abusive parents from whom to model and learn the skills of caring for children and how caregivers and children should interact. Egeland, Jacobvitz, and Papatola (1984) followed 47 women who had been physically abused as children and found that 70% were maltreating their children at 2 years of age.

Straus, Gelles, and Steinmetz (1980) found that many abusive caregivers believed physical punishment of children and slapping a spouse were appropriate behaviors. Female caregivers who were victims of spouse abuse tended to be more violent toward their children (Straus, 1983), and males were likely to abuse their own spouse and children after having lived in a home where spouse abuse existed (Rosenbaum & O'Leary, 1981). Unless this cycle is broken, and as long as other environmental and sociocultural factors continue to exist, the cycle of abuse is likely to continue.

Environmental Factors
Environmental conditions are frequently thought of as trigger variables in child abuse. That is, abusive behaviors are likely to occur under certain conditions that, given an already dysfunctional caregiver-child relationship, trigger inappropriate caregiver behavior. These conditions may include unemployment, household poverty, frustration, and a dysfunctional family structure (Straus, 1983).

The absence of a support system tends to aggravate the effects of the other environmental conditions. For example, extended family members may be able to assist a single caregiver who has recently become unemployed. Neighborhood support groups, social agencies, and other community organizations may also provide assistance to caregivers and reduce the burden to a tolerable level. Garbarino (1982) talked about the importance of social support systems for healthy families, and noted that, as society becomes more mobile, many couples find themselves separated from the natural support systems of their extended families and longtime friendships.

Sociocultural Factors
One cannot begin to understand the problem of child abuse without reviewing the significant sociocultural factors that foster abusive environments. Straus (1983) has referred to the culturally sanctioned violence within families where spouse abuse and child abuse are learned and acceptable forms of interaction. Zigler (1979) reviewed the acceptance of physical punishment of children within our homes and schools and stated that the willingness of caregivers to employ physical punishment is the most significant determinant of child abuse in America.

Even the United States Supreme Court, in the case of *Ingraham v. Wright* (1977), found that children are not protected from cruel and unusual punishment. This decision followed the case of a student who was severely spanked with a 2-foot paddle by three school teachers. Rose (1983) found that the majority of school administrators reported using physical punishment with students with disabilities. Violence seems to be embedded in our society, and this social acceptance of violence, found within families, on television shows, and in our schools, is directly related to the high prevalence of child abuse in America (Zirpoli, 1986).

Characteristics of the Abused Child
Abused children should never be blamed for the maltreatment they receive from caregivers. It is helpful to understand the child-variables that may place children at greater risk for abusive treatment, however.

The idea that children affect caregivers' behavior (known as *child effects*) has received considerable attention during the past two decades, beginning with Bell's (1968) review of the parent-child relationship as a *reciprocal* relationship. As professionals have begun to realize the significant contribution children make toward caregiver-child interactions, interest in the characteristics of children abused by caregivers has increased considerably (Rusch, Hall, & Griffin, 1986; Zirpoli, 1986; Zirpoli, Snell, & Loyd, 1987).

Many researchers believe that younger children are at greater risk for abusive behavior than older children. In fact, premature infants, representing less than 10% of all births, have been reported to represent up to half the cases of child abuse (Fontana, 1971). Pianta, Egeland, and Erickson (1989) reported that "there appears to be a greater chance of a maltreated woman to maltreat her toddler age child than there is for her to maltreat her school age child" (p. 203). However, in a study by Gill (1970), over three-quarters of the abused children were over 2 years of age. Rusch, Hall, and Griffin (1986) stated that there does not appear to be a consensus on the impact of age on child abuse.

Premature infants present an ex-

Factors Associated with Physical Child Abuse

Caregiver Characteristics
** Victim of child abuse, victim of spouse abuse
** Low self-esteem and feelings of isolation
** Youthful marriages and unwanted pregnancies
** Unrealistic expectations & general lack of understanding about the nature and behavior of young children
** High vulnerability to caregiving stress with little or no understanding of basic child management.
** Infrequent use of reinforcement or other positive methods of behavior management
** Frequent use of physical punishment as the primary method of behavior management

Environmental Influences
** Household poverty and general family disorganization or dysfunction
** Lack of extended family or inadequate community social support systems
** Conflict between spouses or among other family members within the home
** Conflict between caregiver and child
** Unemployment & economic hardship
** Substance abuse, especially alcohol abuse

Sociocultural Factors
** Widespread social acceptance of physical punishment
** Children not provided adequate constitutional protection

** Inadequa
vices and
** Low prio
issues at
cal levels
** Vague and varied child abuse laws and guidelines

Victim Characteristics
** Prematurity and dysmaturity (low birth weight)
** Difficult temperament, irritable, frequent crying, poor sleeping & eating habits
** General unresponsiveness to caregiver expectations & demands
** Require special and additional caregiving and attention
** Emotional/behavioral disabilities
** Developmental disabilities

---

cellent example of the theory of child effects. These infants are prone to colic, irritability, and restlessness. They have irregular sleeping and eating patterns, and may be difficult to feed. The premature infant may have an annoying and irritating cry, and usually requires additional parental care and attention. Combined with some of the caregiver, environmental, and sociocultural factors outlined above, one can easily understand how the premature infant may be at greater risk for maltreatment by caregivers who are already stressed by other family and environmental challenges.

There is some debate concerning the extent or degree of child effects on adult behavior; specifically concerning the role of child effects in child abuse. Some professionals believe that child effects are short term and situational, and that child effects do not account for the quality of caregiving over time (Patterson, 1983; Starr, 1982). It is generally agreed, however, that some child characteristics have been associated with maltreatment, but that these characteristics

alone are not enough to predict future child abuse. Again, if we are to understand child abuse, we must understand the interaction of a multiple of variables. The following statement reinforces this point.

> To the extent that the child with extreme individual differences is placed in a family which may not be ready to parent, characteristics of that child may exacerbate an already difficult situation. This child may become the victim of maltreatment, not because of its own behavior, but because the child places added burdens upon an already stressed or incapable family system, resulting in a breakdown in the processes of good parenting. (Pianta et al., 1987, p. 203)

Maltreatment of Persons with Disabilities

There is documented evidence of the maltreatment of children with disabilities throughout history (Sakemiller, 1986). A review of early history outlined the legalized killing of infants born with disabilities, and

the selling of these children for slave labor and prostitution (Rogers, 1978). During the late 1800s and early 1900s, concern regarding the hereditary transmission of disabilities was followed by mass institutionalization, sterilization, and castration of persons with disabilities. As stated so well by Cranefield (cited in MacMillian, 1982) "Seldom in the history of medicine have so many intelligent and well-meaning men embarked on so vicious and brutal a program with so little scientific foundation for their actions" (p. 13).

But the general maltreatment and physical abuse of persons with disabilities continued and by the mid- and late 1900s, many investigations concerning persons in institutional settings had exposed hundreds of cases of abuse (Sakemiller, 1986). The maltreatment of persons with disabilities has not been limited to institutional settings. Zirpoli (1990) has outlined his concerns of the maltreatment of persons with disabilities in community settings where appropriate support systems are not in place, where direct care staff are in-

Child Abuse Organizations

American Humane Association
725 East Hampden Ave.
Denver, CO 80231-4919
303/695-0811

American Association for Protecting Children
Same as American Humane Association

C. Henry Kempe National Center for the Prevention and Treatment of Child Abuse and Neglect
1205 Oneida St.
Denver, CO 80220
303/321-3963

International Society for the Prevention of Child Abuse and Neglect
Same as C. Henry Kempe National Center

National Association of Counsel for Children
Same as C. Henry Kempe National Center

National Center on Child Abuse and Neglect
Children's Bureau
Administration for Children, Youth and Families

U. S. Department of Health and Human Services
PO Box 1182
Washington, DC 20013
202/245-2840

National Child Abuse and Neglect Clinical Resource Center
University of Colorado Health Sciences Center
Same as C. Henry Kempe National Center

National Child Abuse Coalition
1125 15th St., NW
Suite 300
Washington, DC 20005
202/293-7550

National Child Abuse Hotline
800/422-4453

National Clearing House for Child Abuse and Neglect
PO Box 1182
Washington, DC 20013
703/821-2086

National Committee for Prevention of Child Abuse
332 S. Michigan Ave.
Suite 950
Chicago, IL 60604-4357
312/663-3520

National Resource Center on Child Abuse
Same as American Humane Association
800/227-5242
303/695-0811

National Resource Center for Child Sexual Abuse
11141 Georgia Ave.
Suite 310
Wheaton, MD 20902
301/949-5000 (Maryland)
205/533-KIDS (Alabama)
800/KIDS-006 (toll free)

Parents Anonymous 22330 Hawthorne Blvd.
Suite 208
Torrence, Ca 90505
800/421-0353 (outside California)
800/352-0386 (inside California)

St. Joseph Center for Abused Handicapped Children 1835 K. St., NW
Suite 700
Washington, DC 20006
202/634-9821

Source: Clearinghouse on Child Abuse and Neglect Information

---

adequately prepared, and where profit seems to be a greater priority than quality of life.

Disabilities as Antecedents to Abusive Treatment

As the debate regarding the general characteristics of children as antecedents to child abuse continues, so does the debate regarding the association between specific disabilities and abusive treatment. It is generally accepted, however, that although many caregivers cope very well with children who have disabilities (Dunlap & Hollingsworth, 1977), having a child with disabilities, in combination with environmental variables

previously outlined, may induce a greater level of stress than a caregiver can manage.

Many studies have found relationships between specific disabilities and disproportionate incidents of abuse. Martin (1972) found that 33% of the 42 physically abused children he studied had an IQ less than 80. Sandgrund, Gaines, and Green (1974) studied 120 children (60 abused, 30 neglected, and 30 nonabused). They reported that 25% of the abused group were found to be mentally retarded compared to 20% of the neglected group and 3% of the nonabused group. In a study of all (430) students referred for evaluation of learning problems from Oahu, Hawaii, during a 1-year period, it

was found that 6.7% of them had been reported as abuse victims (Frisch & Rhoads, 1982). This was 3.5 times higher than the rate of child abuse reported for all other children from Oahu during the same time period.

Bousha and Twentyman (1984) found that children who were victims of abusive behavior were significantly more aggressive than control subjects. Lorber, Felton, and Reid (1984) also found that abuse victims were more disruptive and aggressive. The research on children with physical handicaps is mixed. A study by Diamond and Jaudes (1983) found that 20% of 86 children with cerebral palsy (CP) were victims of physical abuse. However, Martin, Beezley, Conway, and Kempe (1974) found no physical disabilities among 58 abused children.

Abused Versus Nonabused Comparisons

Whether a child's disability is directly or indirectly related to abusive treatment will probably be an ongoing topic for future research. Meanwhile, two studies have explored this research question directly (Rusch, Hall, & Griffin, 1986; Zirpoli, Snell & Loyd, 1987). These two studies compared groups of abused and nonabused clients living within institutional settings and found that some disabilities were significant in differentiating the abused from the nonabused clients.

In research conducted by Rusch, Hall, and Griffin (1986), 160 clients residing in a North Carolina institution for persons with disabilities were studied. Eighty of the clients represented all of the substantiated physical abuse cases occurring within the institution between 1977 and 1982. A control group of 80 nonabused clients was randomly selected from the remaining institutional population.

Records of all 160 clients were reviewed to determine the following characteristics of each client: age, sex, IQ (as measured by the Stanford-Binet Intelligence Scale), social maturity quotient (as measured by the Vineland Social Maturity Scale), physical disabilities, communications skills, and tendency to be aggressive (defined by exhibiting two or more serious aggressive episodes during a 6-month period). The two groups, abused and control, were compared on the above seven variables.

Rusch and his colleagues found no significant differences between the two groups on the basis of sex (although there were five more males in the abused group), and no significant differences between the two groups on mean IQ levels. However, 71% of the abused group scored in the profound level of retardation compared with 60% in the control group. Also, no significant differences

were found regarding the physical disabilities variable, although more clients in the abused group (49%) had physical disabilities compared to the control group (38%).

Significant differences were found on the age variable (more abused clients were found in the youngest age category), and on the social maturity quotient, with 76% of the abused group scoring in the profound range compared with 61% of the control group. Other significant differences were found between the number of clients demonstrating self-injurious behavior (16% for the abused and 5% for the control group), the number of clients who were verbal (38% for the abused compared to 59% for the control group), the number of clients who were ambulatory (86% for the abused and 73% for the control group), and the number of clients who were aggressive (51% of the abused and 11% of the control group). The difference between the two groups on the aggression variable was very strong. In the Zirpoli, Snell, and Lloyd (1987) study, 91 victims of physical abuse from five state training centers in Virginia for individuals with disabilities were compared to 91 randomly selected control clients from the same five facilities. The abused clients represented all confirmed cases of client abuse occurring from 1980 through 1985.

Records of each of the 182 clients were reviewed to determine the following characteristics: age, sex, level of functioning, auditory, visual, ambulation, speech ability, and the frequency of four challenging behaviors (aggression, disruption, rebelliousness, and hyperactivity).

Zirpoli and his colleagues (1987) found no significant differences between the two groups on the basis of age, sex, and on the clients' auditory, visual, ambulation, and speech skills. Significant differences were found between the two groups on the level-of-functioning variable. Over twice as many clients in the abused group were labeled severely disabled (59%) compared to the control group (25%), and half as many of the clients in the

abused group were labeled profoundly disabled (18%) compared with the control group (44%). No differences were found between the two groups on the number of clients labeled mild and moderately disabled.

In the area of challenging behaviors, the abused group had twice as many clients considered frequently aggressive, disruptive, rebellious, and hyperactive compared to the control group. As in the Rusch et al. study, the differences between the two groups on the basis of challenging behaviors was particularly strong.

Summary and Recommendations

Are children with disabilities at greater risk for physical abuse than other children? The answer to this question depends upon the condition of a host of other variables concerning the child's caregivers and environment. Having a disability alone does not place a child at greater risk for abusive treatment. As previously stated, *most* parents of children with disabilities cope very well with the additional demands of a child who requires additional supports. But unless we provide caregivers with the necessary support, we place children at risk for maltreatment. Not all caregivers who were abused as children develop into abusive parents. Given the appropriate and necessary support, some are able to break the cycle of abuse and establish healthy, functional families.

Given the variables that are associated with abuse, how can we help in breaking the cycle? Some solutions require significant changes in national priorities and attitudes. Parents and educators, however, are in the best position to advocate for these changes. Four fundamental changes are outlined here. First, we must put an end to the widespread tolerance of physical punishment against children. As parents and educators, we can start in our own homes and educational settings.

Second, we must advocate for

highest priority status for our nation's children and the issues related to their protection and enrichment (physical, mental, and emotional). This means full funding for Head Start (only 30% of our nation's children who qualify for Head Start are being served), the Women, Infants and Children (WIC) program, and other effective programs that serve our nation's impoverished children.

Third, we must ensure that all caregivers, regardless of background or income, are provided with the appropriate community support necessary to provide their children with a protecting, healthy, and enriching environment. This means appropriate prenatal care for *all* women, appropriate medical care for *all* children, and quality day care and educational services for *all* children, regardless of family income or ability to pay. These are sound investments for the future of our nation's children *and* our nation.

Lastly, in direct regard to children with disabilities, families of children with disabilities must be provided the necessary support to live as a family unit and participate in all community activities. This means full inclusion of persons with disabilities into our society and an end to the isolated, segregated settings forced upon many families with a disabled member. Family isolation is a significant contributor to child abuse that can be dramatically decreased by greater societal acceptance of all people with disabilities.

How well we advocate for and achieve the above objectives may well answer our primary question. Are children with disabilities at greater risk for abuse and other forms of maltreatment? It depends. And it depends upon what we do to change the contributing variables to this national tragedy.

References

Bell, R. Q. (1968). A reinterpretation of the direction of effects in studies of socialization. *Psychological Review, 75,* 81–95.

Bousha D. M., & Twentyman, C. T. (1984). Mother-child interactional style in abuse, neglect, and control groups: Naturalistic observations in the home. *Journal of Abnormal Psychology, 93,* 106–114.

Diamond, L. J., & Jaudes, P. K. (1983). Child abuse in a cerebral-palsied population. *Developmental Medicine and Child Neurology, 25,* 169–174.

Dunlap, W. R., & Hollingsworth, J. S. (1977). How does a handicapped child affect the family? Implications for practitioners. *Family Coordinator, 26,* 286–293.

Egeland, B., Jacobvitz, D., & Papatola, K. (1984, May). *Intergenerational continuity of parental abuse.* Proceedings from the Conference on Biosocial Perspectives on Child Abuse and Neglect, Social Science Research Council, York, ME.

Fontana, V. J. (1971). *The maltreated child.* Springfield, IL: Thomas.

Frisch, L. E., & Rhoads, F. A. (1982). Child abuse and neglect in children referred for learning evaluation. *Journal of Learning Disabilities, 15,* 583–586.

Garbarino, J. (1982). *Children and families in the social environment.* New York: Aldine.

Gelles, R. (1973). Child abuse as psychopathology: A sociological critique and reformation. *American Journal of Orthopsychiatry, 43,* 611–621.

Gill, D. (1970). *Violence against children: Physical child abuse in the United States.* Cambridge, MA: Harvard University Press.

Hoffman, E. (1981). Policy and politics: The Child Abuse Prevention and Treatment Act. In R. Bourne & E. H. Newberger (Eds.), *Critical perspectives on child abuse* (pp. 157–170). Lexington, MA: Lexington Books.

Ingraham v. Wright, 498 F. 2d 248 (5 Cir. 1977).

Johnson, C. F., & Showers, J. (1985). Injury variables in child abuse. *Child Abuse and Neglect, 9,* 207–215.

Lorber, R., Felton, D. K., & Reid, J. B. (1984). A social learning approach to the reduction of coercive processes in child abusive families: A molecular analysis. *Advances in Behavior Research* and *Therapy, 6,* 29–45.

MacMillian, D. L. (1982). *Mental retardation in school and society.* Boston: Little, Brown.

Martin, H. P. (1972). The child and his development. In H. C. Kempe & R. E. Helfer (Eds.), *Helping the battered child and his family* (p. 93). Philadelphia: J. B. Lippincott.

Martin, H. P., Beezley, P., Conway, E. F., & Kempe, C. H. (1974). The development of abused children: A review of the literature and physical, neurologic, and intellectual findings. *Advances in Pediatrics, 21,* 25–73.

Meier, J. H. (1985). *Assault against children: Why it happens and how to stop it.* Austin, TX: PRO-ED.

Patterson, G. (1983). Stress: A change agent for family process in M. Rutter & N. Gar-

mezy (Eds.), *Review of child development research* (pp. 235–264). Chicago: University of Chicago Press.

Pianta, R., Egeland, B., & Erickson, M. F. (1989). The antecedents of maltreatment: Results of the mother-child interaction research project. In D. Cicchetti & V. Carlson (Eds.), *Child maltreatment: Theory and research on the cause and consequences of child abuse and neglect* (pp. 203–253). New York: Cambridge University Press.

Rogers, D. E. (1978). *Hear the children crying.* Trenton, NJ: Fleming H. Revell.

Rose, T. L. (1983). A survey of corporal punishment of mildly handicapped students. *Exceptional Education Quarterly, 3*(4), 9–19.

Rosenbaum, A., & O'Leary, K. (1981). Children: The unintended victims of marital violence. *American Journal of Orthopsychiatry, 51,* 692–699.

Rusch, R. G., Hall, J. C., & Griffin, H. C. (1986). Abuse-provoking characteristics of institutionalized mentally retarded individuals. *American Journal of Mental Deficiency, 90,* 618–624.

Sakemiller, L. L. (1986). *Child abuse of handicapped children.* Unpublished master's thesis, Bowling Green State University, Bowling Green, OH.

Sandgrund, H., Gaines, R., & Green, A. (1974). Child abuse and mental retardation: A problem of cause and effect. *American Journal of Mental Deficiency, 79,* 327–330.

Starr, R. H., Jr. (1982). A research-based approach to the prediction of child abuse. In R. H. Starr, Jr. (Ed.), *Child abuse prediction: Policy implications* (pp.105–134). Cambridge, MA: Ballinger.

Straus, M. A. (1983). Ordinary violence, child abuse and wife beating: What do they have in common? In D. Finkelhor, R. J. Gelles, G. T. Hotaling, & M. A. Straus (Eds.), *The dark side of families: Current family violence research* (pp. 194–223). Beverly Hills, CA: Sage.

Straus, M. A., Gelles, R. J., & Steinmetz, S. K. (1980). *Behind closed doors: Violence in the American family.* New York: Anchor Press.

Zigler, E. (1979). Controlling child abuse in America: An effort doomed to failure. In R. Bourne & E. H. Newberger (Eds.), *Critical perspectives on child abuse* (pp. 171–207). Lexington, MA: Lexington Books.

Zirpoli, T. J. (1990). Problems in paradise. *TASH Newsletter, 16,* 4.

Zirpoli, T. J. (1986). Child abuse and children with handicaps. *Remedial and Special Education, 7*(2) 39–48.

Zirpoli, T. J., Snell, M. E., & Loyd, B. H. (1987). Characteristics of persons with mental retardation who have been abused by caregivers. *The Journal of Special Education, 21,* 31–41.

The Inclusion Revolution

Joy Rogers

JOY ROGERS is Professor of Counseling and Educational Psychology at Loyola University Chicago. She also serves as a member of the Board of Education of Matteson School District #162.

Six-year-old Joseph Ford seemed an unlikely revolutionary. This exceptionally bright, cute little boy sought only to enter the first grade of the public "magnet school" attended by his older sisters. But Joe lived in Chicago where school officials had very different plans for him.

They were adamant that Joe should attend a segregated school for children who, like him, had physical disabilities. Children with such severe physical disabilities as Joe simply did not go to the city's outstanding magnet schools.

School officials extolled the benefits of all the physical therapy Joe would receive in the segregated school and insisted that he could not be educated in a magnet school. Joe's mom reasoned through the problem somewhat differently. She knew no amount of physical therapy would "cure" his cerebral palsy and that he would eventually have to earn his living using his superior intellect.

After a year-long struggle involving federal regulatory agencies and the highest officials in the school system, Joe won entry into the magnet school.

Even after he was allowed to enroll, the work was not over for Joe and his family. They had to overcome such barriers as school employees with negative attitudes, staff who often lacked skill at modifying instruction for him, and odd traditions (such as segregated school buses) within the school district. Joe's experience has been paralleled by hundreds of children in hundreds of communities throughout the country as parents have increasingly demanded and won integrated schooling for their children with disabilities. Parents whose children have severe learning and behavior problems have fought to assure that their children will have classmates who behave appropriately as role models. Pioneering kids like Joe have opened the schoolhouse doors in each of their communities for others to follow.

What's happened to Joe? He continues to thrive and is now a successful third grader. He is a bright, loving young man with strikingly mature values and an excellent chance to seize the future his parents have always believed he can attain. Not every child in a school which claims to be using inclusion has been as fortunate.

So Many Words

Many different terms have been used to describe inclusion of students with disabilities in "regular" classes. None of these terms actually appears in federal law, but all have been used to express varying beliefs about what the law means — or should mean.

Mainstreaming: This term has generally been used to refer to the selective placement of special education students in one or more "regular" education classes. Mainstreaming proponents generally assume that a student must "earn" his or her opportunity to be mainstreamed through the ability to "keep up" with the work assigned by the teacher to the other students in the class. This concept is closely linked to traditional forms of special education service delivery.

Inclusion: This term is used to refer to the commitment to educate each child, to the maximum extent appropriate, in the school and classroom he or she would otherwise attend. It involves bringing the support services to the child (rather than moving the child to the services) and requires only that the child will benefit from being in the class (rather than having to keep up with the other students.) Proponents of inclusion generally favor newer forms of education service delivery such as the ones under the heading, "What Does Inclusion Look Like?"

8. CHILDREN WITH PHYSICAL AND HEALTH IMPAIRMENTS

Full Inclusion: This term is primarily used to refer to the belief that instructional practices and technological supports are presently available to accommodate all students in the schools and classrooms they would otherwise attend if not disabled. Proponents of full inclusion tend to encourage that special education services generally be delivered in the form of training and technical assistance to "regular" classroom teachers.

Regular Education Initiative: This phrase was coined by a former federal education official, Madeline Will, and has generally been used to discuss either the merger of the governance of special and "regular" education or the merger of the funding streams of each.

It is not generally used to discuss forms of service delivery.

Does Federal Law Require Inclusion?

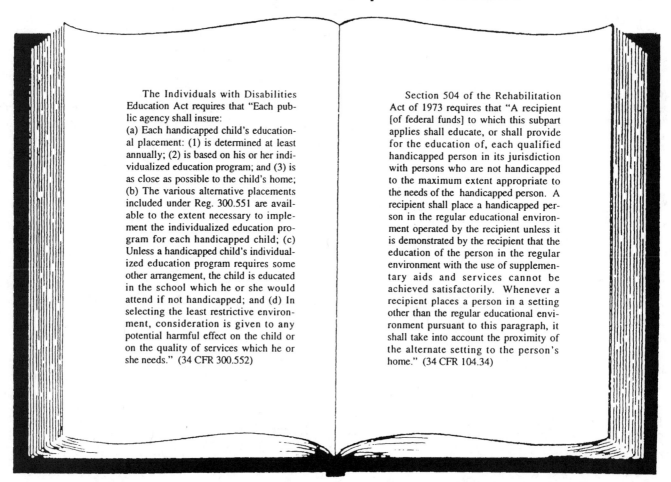

The Individuals with Disabilities Education Act requires that "Each public agency shall insure:
(a) Each handicapped child's educational placement: (1) is determined at least annually; (2) is based on his or her individualized education program; and (3) is as close as possible to the child's home; (b) The various alternative placements included under Reg. 300.551 are available to the extent necessary to implement the individualized education program for each handicapped child; (c) Unless a handicapped child's individualized education program requires some other arrangement, the child is educated in the school which he or she would attend if not handicapped; and (d) In selecting the least restrictive environment, consideration is given to any potential harmful effect on the child or on the quality of services which he or she needs." (34 CFR 300.552)

Section 504 of the Rehabilitation Act of 1973 requires that "A recipient [of federal funds] to which this subpart applies shall educate, or shall provide for the education of, each qualified handicapped person in its jurisdiction with persons who are not handicapped to the maximum extent appropriate to the needs of the handicapped person. A recipient shall place a handicapped person in the regular educational environment operated by the recipient unless it is demonstrated by the recipient that the education of the person in the regular environment with the use of supplementary aids and services cannot be achieved satisfactorily. Whenever a recipient places a person in a setting other than the regular educational environment pursuant to this paragraph, it shall take into account the proximity of the alternate setting to the person's home." (34 CFR 104.34)

In plain language, these regulations appear to require that schools make a significant effort to find an inclusive solution for a child. How far must schools go? In recent years, the federal courts have been interpreting these rules to require that children with very severe disabilities must be included in the classroom they would otherwise attend if not disabled even when they cannot do the academic work of the class if there is a potential social benefit, if the class would stimulate the child's linguistic development, or if the other students could provide appropriate role models for the student. In one recent case of interest, a court ordered a school district to place a child with an IQ of 44 in a regular second-grade classroom while rejecting the school district's complaints about expenses as exaggerated (Board of Education,

Sacramento City Unified School District v. Holland, 786 F.Supp. 874 (ED Cal. 1992)). In another case a federal court rejected a school district's argument that a child would be so disruptive as to significantly impair the education of the other children (Oberti v. Board of Education of the Borough of Clementon School District, 789 F.Supp. 1322 (D.N.J. 1992)). Educators need to be aware of such developments in the federal courts because court findings in one case tend to set precedent for future courts considering similar matters. These developments suggest that parents are increasingly able to go to the courts to force reluctant school districts to include their children in "regular" classes in situations where the child may not be able to "keep up" with the standard work of the class.

Why Try Inclusion?

Two different lines of reasoning have converged in the inclusion movement. The first line of reasoning is the civil rights argument that segregated education is inherently unequal and, therefore, a violation of the rights of the children who are segregated. The second line of reasoning is that empirical analysis of the outcomes from established special education programs indicate that they just haven't worked. In spite of the steady expansion of a costly special education bureaucracy, the children served in special education programs have not shown the expected benefits in development of academic, social, or vocational skills.

In some schools, special and "regular" education personnel co-exist side by side, but do not work together. Teachers have separate classrooms, are paid from separate budgets, and work with different curricular materials. Scarce resources are hoarded rather than shared. In an inclusive school, resources are more efficiently used and reach the maximum number of children.

The "Down Side" of Inclusion

In one school claiming to be using inclusion, an observer noted 44 second graders watching a filmstrip as a science lesson with only one teacher in the room. The 44 children included a group of special education students, a group of limited English proficient students, and a "regular" class. Two other teachers assigned to the group were out of the classroom. Few educators would attempt to defend this kind of instruction as inclusion — nor could it easily be defended as science instruction either! Inclusion cannot be viewed as a way of eliminating special education costs. It is simply a way of reconceptualizing special education service delivery: the traditional model requires bringing the child to the special education services and the inclusion model requires bringing the special education services to the child.

Similar problems have arisen where school administrators have tried to assign several children with severe disabilities to the same classroom. Although mild disabilities are relatively common (affecting about one child in ten), severe disabilities are far less common (affecting only about one child in a hundred). Thus, if four or five children with severe disabilities are placed with the same class of about 25 children, it is statistically extremely unlikely that the classroom is actually the room to which all of those children would possibly have been assigned if they had not been disabled. This is not inclusion. Such arrangements tend not to be beneficial to any of the children in the class — and create extremely frustrating work environments for the teachers who are assigned to such classes. It is easy to see why teachers in such situations might feel ineffective or exploited! Inclusion works when all staff members in the school accept their fair share of responsibility for all the children who live within the school's attendance area.

How Does Inclusion Affect Classmates?

Some misguided efforts at inclusion have simply moved children with disabilities into general education classrooms and left them for their classmates to teach. Although tutoring others can often be a good way to learn for both the included child and the tutor, if peer tutoring becomes the predominant mode of instruction, then neither child is receiving appropriate services.

The presence of an included classmate should provide opportunities for growth for the entire class.

- Classmates can develop a sense of responsibility and the enhanced self-esteem which results from such responsibility
- Classmates' understanding of the range of human experience can be enhanced.
- Classmates can benefit from their disabled classmates as role models in coping with disabilities. As a result of advancements in medical science, most of those presently nondisabled children will survive to become persons with disabilities themselves one day.
- Classmates are enriched by the opportunity to have had friends with disabilities who successfully managed their affairs and enjoyed full lives.

Effective teachers do not permit a classroom environment in which any child is the victim of ridicule. They arrange learning environments in which every child has opportunities to lead and to experience successes, and they value diversity because it helps them prepare their students to be capable citizens in a democracy.

What Are "Supplementary Aids and Services?"

Classroom teachers have sometimes been disappointed to discover that every included child does not come with his/her own full-time aide. The determination about what supplementary aids and services are needed is unique for each child and is specified in the child's Individualized Educational Program (IEP). Very few children have individual aides either in special education classes or when included in general classes. Indeed, managing paraprofessionals adds another time-consuming duty for which some teachers are poorly prepared. An incident in one school illustrates how aides can actually interfere with inclusion. In that school the child's individual aide befriended the classroom aide. The result was that instead of being with his classmates at lunch time, that child was seated alone with the two adult aides who enjoyed each others' company at lunch. Aides are very important in some situations, but the addition of adults in a classroom is not a panacea.

The most common supplementary aids and services are actually consultation and training for the teacher. For example, a teacher receiving a blind student for the first time may need initial guidance in how to arrange the classroom and may need continuing suggestions on how to adapt his or her lesson plans to help the blind student understand the concept to be taught.

Electronic aids and services are becoming increasingly common. Some students will use computers, speech synthesizers, FM amplification systems, etc. Other very important aids and services may be much less technologically sophisticated. Simple accommodations such as large print books, preferential seating, behavior management programs, or a modified desk are sufficient for many students with severe disabilities to be successfully included.

In schools where inclusion works well, it is important for the classroom teacher to have regular access to support staff who can help the teacher find equipment or procedures which permit all the children in the class to benefit from the instruction.

Some children need life-sustaining equipment previously unfamiliar in educational settings. Some children need suctioning, clean intermittent catheterization, or frequent positioning changes. Some children need daily medication, access to an epinephrine "pen," or blood sugar monitoring. Necessary supports may include both the equipment and the trained personnel needed to do these tasks. If children are carriers of communicable diseases for which immunization is available, necessary supports for their teachers can include immunization against those diseases.

People who have not seen children with disabilities successfully included in public school classes sometimes create barriers to inclusion because they may fear what they do not understand.

In some communities, teachers have feared that they will be asked to do new or difficult tasks without sufficient training and support. Administrators may fear loss of state or federal reimbursement unless special education students are placed in special education classrooms. Parents of nondisabled students may fear that their children will not get a fair share of the teacher's attention. Parents of the students with disabilities may fear that their children will lose special services which have been helpful.

However, a rapidly growing "track record" of inclusion indicates that, when done with care, inclusion does not create unreasonable demands on teachers or deprive classmates of learning opportunities. Indeed, inclusive classrooms offer some unique benefits for all who participate.

What Does Inclusion Look Like?

Effective inclusion is characterized by its virtual invisibility. One cannot go to look at the special education classrooms in an inclusive school because there are none. Children with disabilities are not clustered into groups of persons with similar disabilities, but are dispersed in whatever classrooms they would otherwise attend. There are not lots of little rooms labeled "LD Resource," "Emotionally Disturbed," "Speech," or "Trainable." In an inclusive school, special education teachers do not have their own classrooms, but are assigned to other roles such as team teaching in classrooms that serve both disabled and nondisabled students together.

The schools that most readily adopt the concept of inclusion are generally those that already embrace instructional practices which are designed to provide challenging learning environments to children with very diverse learning characteristics. Such practices include heterogenous grouping, peer tutoring, multi-age classes, middle school structures, "no-cut" athletic policies, cooperative learning, and development of school media centers which stimulate students' electronic access to extensive databases for their own research.

Each of these innovations has been demonstrated in numerous studies to enhance teachers' capacities to meet the individual needs of students.

What If The Included Student Can't Keep Up With The Class?

Each included student has an Individualized Education Program (IEP) which specifies what he or she needs to learn and, sometimes, that may not mean that the student will be learning the same things as the other students. The teacher's job is to arrange instruction that benefits all the students — even though the various students may derive different benefits. For example, most of the students in the class may be learning the total number of degrees in the angles of a triangle while the included student may be learning to recognize a triangle. Good teachers maximize the opportunities for all students to learn even though they may be learning at different levels. In general, good teachers help their included students to accomplish just as many as possible of the goals of the classroom and to function just as close as possible to the way that their peers function. Good administrators do not evaluate teachers with included students on the basis of the average academic achievement scores of their classes, but rather on the progress made by all the students.

An Inclusion Checklist For Your School

_____ 1. Do we genuinely start from the premise that each child belongs in the classroom he or she would otherwise attend if not disabled (or do we cluster children with disabilities into special groups, classrooms, or schools)?

_____ 2. Do we individualize the instructional program for all the children whether or not they are disabled and provide the resources that each child needs to explore individual interests in the school environment (or do we tend to provide the same sorts of services for most children who share the same diagnostic label)?

_____ 3. Are we fully committed to maintenance of a caring community that fosters mutual respect and support among staff, parents, and students in which we honestly believe that nondisabled children can benefit from friendships with disabled children and disabled children can benefit from friendships with nondisabled children (or do our practices tacitly tolerate children teasing or isolating some as outcasts)?

_____ 4. Have our general educators and special educators integrated their efforts and their resources so that they work together as integral parts of a unified team (or are they isolated in separate rooms or departments with separate supervisors and budgets)?

_____ 5. Does our administration create a work climate in which staff are supported as they provide assistance to each other (or are teachers afraid of being presumed to be incompetent if they seek peer collaboration in working with students)?

_____ 6. Do we actively encourage the full participation of children with disabilities in the life of our school including co-curricular and extracurricular activities (or do they participate only in the academic portion of the school day)?

_____ 7. Are we prepared to alter support systems for students as their needs change through the school year so that they can achieve, experience successes, and feel that they genuinely belong in their school and classes (or do we sometimes provide such limited services to them that the children are set up to fail)?

_____ 8. Do we make parents of children with disabilities fully a part of our school community so they also can experience a sense of belonging (or do we give them a separate PTA and different newsletters)?

_____ 9. Do we give children with disabilities just as much of the full school curriculum as they can master and modify it as necessary so that they can share elements of these experiences with their classmates (or do we have a separate curriculum for children with disabilities)?

_____ 10. Have we included children with disabilities supportively in as many as possible of the same testing and evaluation experiences as their nondisabled classmates (or do we exclude them from these opportunities while assuming that they cannot benefit from the experiences)?

This checklist may help school personnel in evaluating whether their practices are consistent with the best intentions of the inclusion movement. Rate your school with a + for each item where the main statement best describes your school and a 0 for each item where the parenthetical statement better describes your school. Each item marked 0 could serve as the basis for discussion among the staff. Is this an area in which the staff sees need for further development? Viewed in this context, an inclusive school would not be characterized by a particular set of practices as much as by the commitment of its staff to continually develop its capacity to accommodate the full range of individual differences among its learners.

What Skills Do Teachers Need In Inclusive Classrooms?

Most experienced teachers are quick to note that the students who come to them are increasingly needful of special attention. Whether or not the students are classified as special education students, the complexity of social problems which impact on children in the nineties means that far more children need extra help. In addition to schoolwork, children may need help finding adequate food, being safe from abuse, and developing motivation to learn.

The diversity of children in today's schools is often already very great. The inclusion of a child with a disability into this mix is most likely to add one child who has more needs than the others, but not needs that are more severe than needs already represented in the class. The best teachers in inclusive classrooms are simply the best teachers. The best teachers teach each individual student rather than try to gear instruction to the average of a group. The best teachers have a high degree of "with-itness," that is, they are highly aware of the dynamics of their classrooms. The best teachers are versatile. They are comfortable using many different teaching techniques and can readily shift among them as needed. The best teachers enjoy and value all their students—attitudes which are visible to others as they teach.

Inclusion has become such a value laden word that it is currently very difficult to state opposition to inclusion. However the pressure to appear to be inclusive may create many problematic practices that either do not have inclusive effects or, in some cases, do not fit within the existing knowledge base of educational practice. Thus, extensive debate on the question of whether "inclusion" is a good idea has produced much heat, but little light. More useful outcomes are likely to result when the staff of a school works together to determine how it can meet the needs of those specific children who live in its attendance area. The preceding checklist (see page 5) may help school personnel in evaluating whether their practices are consistent with the best intentions of the inclusion movement.

Helpful Resources

1. *Winners All: A Call for Inclusive Schools.* This 1992 report is available from the National Association of State Boards of Education, 1012 Cameron Street, Alexandria, Virginia 22314. It features descriptions of how various schools, school districts, and states have transformed their schools into effective learning environments for all children.

2. *Report Card to the Nation on Inclusion in Education of Students with Mental Retardation.* This 1992 report is available from The ARC, 500 E. Border Street, S-300, Arlington, Texas 76010. It provides comparative data analyzing the degree of success at fostering inclusion among the various states.

3. *Special Education at the Century's End: Evolution of Theory and Practice Since 1970.* This 1992 collection of readings is edited by Thomas Hehir and Thomas Latus and is available from *Harvard Educational Review*, Gutman Library, Suite 349, 6 Appian Way, Cambridge, Massachusetts 02138. The readings are particularly useful in developing an understanding of how the concept of inclusion arose within special education.

4. *Integrating General and Special Education.* This 1993 volume is edited by John Goodlad and Thomas Lovitt and is available from Macmillan Publishing Company, 866 Third Avenue, New York, New York 10022. The chapters represent a wide variety of viewpoints about how general and special education can work more effectively together.

5. *Techniques for Including Students with Disabilities: A Step-by-Step Practical Guide for School Principals.* This 1992 volume by E. John Shinsky is available from Shinsky Seminars Inc., 3101 North Cambridge Road, Lansing, Michigan 48911. It provides numerous reproducible checklists useful in developing readiness for inclusion among school personnel.

6. *Behind Special Education.* This 1991 volume by Thomas Skrtic is available from Love Publishing Company, Denver, Colorado 80222. It offers a conceptual analysis of issues in both general and special education underlying contemporary calls for change.

7. *Regular Lives.* This 1988 video was produced by Syracuse University and is available from the Council for Exceptional Children, 1920 Association Drive, Reston, Virginia 22091. It illustrates students of different ages in inclusive settings.

8. *Curriculum Considerations In Inclusive Schools.* This 1992 volume edited by William and Susan Stainback is available from Brookes Publishing Company, P.O. Box 10624, Baltimore, Maryland 21285-0624. Its chapters suggest inclusive strategies useful in various educational settings.

Physically Challenged Students

Diane Knight

Donna Wadsworth

Diane Knight is Assistant Professor and Donna Wadsworth is Instructor, Special Education, Department of Curriculum and Instruction, University of Southwestern Louisiana, Lafayette.

Recent U. S. Department of Education figures indicate that approximately 147,000 students are being treated for physical disabilities, of which 41,000 are orthopedically handicapped, 43,000 are other health impaired and 63,000 are multiple-handicapped. Approximately 17,000 students are technology-dependent and this number is expected to rise.

Until recently, students with severe health problems who needed continuous medical monitoring received their academic instruction in the isolated settings of residential facilities, hospitals and homes. Now, however, historic education laws have opened public school classroom doors to "medically fragile" or physically challenged students. These laws include Section 504 of the Vocational Rehabilitation Act of 1973 (PL 93-112), the Education for All Handicapped Children Act of 1975 (PL 94-142) and its 1986 Amendments (PL 99-457), and the Individuals with Disabilities Act of 1990 (PL 101-476).

The Council for Exceptional Children defines medically fragile students as requiring "specialized technological health care procedures for life support and/or health support during the school day. These students may or may not require special education" (Council for Exceptional Children, 1988, pp. 5-6). Students qualifying as "other health impaired" have "limited strength, vitality, or alertness, due to chronic or acute health problems, . . . which adversely affects their educational performance" (Sirvis, 1988, p. 42). Physical disabilities may include a variety of neurological or musculoskeletal impairments such as cerebral palsy, epilepsy, spina bifida, muscular dystrophy, arthritis or scoliosis. Severe, chronic illnesses include asthma, cystic fibrosis, diabetes, leukemia, sickle-cell anemia and hemophilia.

Physically challenged students are the fastest growing population of children receiving special education services. Advances in medical technology ensure declining mortality rates and improve the chances of preventing or curing many diseases and disorders. Recent U. S. Department of Education figures indicate that approximately 147,000 students are being treated for physical disabilities, of which 41,000 are orthopedically handicapped, 43,000 are other health impaired and 63,000 are multiple-handicapped (Hallahan & Kauffman, 1991). Approximately 17,000 students are technology-dependent and this number is expected to rise (Caldwell, Sirvis, Todaro & Accouloumre, 1991).

While school district central office personnel face the legal, financial and administrative issues associated with these students, regular classroom teachers and special education professionals must

From *Childhood Education*, Vol. 69, No. 4, Summer 1993, pp. 211-215. © 1993 by the Association for Childhood Education International. Reprinted by permission of the authors and the Association for Childhood Education International, 11501 Georgia Avenue, Suite 315, Wheaton, MD.

Physically challenged children may bring various types of unfamiliar equipment into the classroom.

form a team to effectively serve this growing population. The following specific suggestions provide pre-school, elementary and middle grade teachers with some immediate assistance necessary for the day-to-day, successful integration of students with physical and medical difficulties. The tips focus on parent involvement, peer interaction, environmental/training considerations and instructional adaptations.

Parent Involvement

Family members can provide key information about the student's abilities, interests, strengths and weaknesses. Parental insights complement information obtained from school sources and provide a general picture of the student's needs and capabilities (Bernheimer, Gallimore & Weisner, 1990). Teachers must acknowledge parents' anxiety, while channeling their concern into healthy, constructive contributions. Teachers can promote maximum parental involvement in the following ways:

■ *Medical History.* Obtain the student's complete medical history, including names, addresses and telephone numbers of attending physicians. When possible, secure parental permission to contact physicians in a medical emergency or with questions. Make careful notes about the student's need for medication (dosage, frequency) and regularity of ongoing medical treat-ments (chemotherapy, radiation, dialysis, suctioning). Question parents about the student's physical limitations, stamina and endurance levels, as well as side effects of medication/treatment (appetite loss, lethargy, hair loss, mood swings). Educators should become familiar with danger signs, such as a specific localized pain in a student with sickle-cell anemia, seizure activity in a student with epilepsy or a severe cut or bruise on a student with hemophilia.

Parents must understand that school attendance increases the risk of exposure to diseases. Teachers should inform parents immediately about any potential health threats. Such notification is particularly important for students who have undergone cancer treatments or organ transplants, as they are more susceptible to contagion.

■ *Emergency Care Plans.* Emergencies can result from medical equipment failure, natural disasters or physiological breakdown. Consult parents as to what person or agency should be notified in an emergency. As a general rule, inform local telephone and electric companies, fire and police departments, ambulance services, as well as the nearest hospital emergency room, about technology-dependent students. Avenues of emergency transportation in the community and alternate routes of transportation should be explored well in advance of any crisis. Trial runs might be conducted to ensure smooth operation during an emergency.

■ *Parent Participation.* Parents of technology-dependent or other health impaired students and parents of non-health impaired students may have differing concerns. A harmonious balance needs to be established in attending to their concerns, beginning with the initial contact. Continuous communication between school and parents cannot be overemphasized.

Anxiety levels and potential stressful situations can be alleviated by being sensitive to parents' needs. Concentrate on the positive aspects of issues or situations, not on "problems." Encourage parental observation in the classroom at the time of first placement. Discourage overprotectiveness and encourage parents to allow their child to attempt new activities independently. Serve as a resource for parents, helping them to realize their assets and strengths through support groups, community involvement or as school volunteers.

Peer Interaction

The self-esteem of a physically challenged student has a critical effect on learning. To enhance self-image, the education team must be constantly mindful of ways to involve these students in classroom activities. Maximum socialization must be promoted to ensure a positive mainstreaming experience. In order to accomplish this objective, however, teachers must first be comfortable with their own understanding of physical disabilities and have parental support (American Cancer Society, 1980; Chekryn, Deegan & Reid, 1987). The following strategies may help foster positive peer interaction:

■ *Orientation to Equipment.* When a physically disabled student initially joins the class, any unfamiliar equipment should be introduced to all students. Orthopedically handicapped students may use wheelchairs, walkers or braces. Technology-dependent students may require ventilators, suctioning machines and nebulizers. Such machines feature sounds, alarms, lights, cords, hoses and gauges that may prove frightening at first.

■ *Peer Socialization.* Special care to promote "normalization" must be exercised. Peer acceptance will be strengthened by involving the disabled student in all daily activities (academic classes, art, music, physical education, cafeteria, playground, extracurricular events). Adapt situations to facilitate active participation and increase chances of success. For example, a student with a physical disability could hit the ball, but not run, during a baseball game.

Educators must be careful to avoid the appearance of giving "special privileges" to physically challenged students. If not handled appropriately, non-health impaired students may come to resent the frequent snacks given to a student with diabetes or the extra attention (therapy) paid to the student with cystic fibrosis.

■ *Classroom Management.* Parents and the education team must jointly generate a consistent behavioral management program that will fit within preestablished classroom

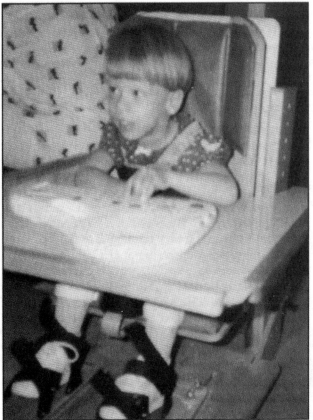

Activities like music can promote peer socialization.

Donna Wadsworth

rules, while not compromising special health care needs. To further promote peer acceptance, this plan should be as similar as possible to that for the other students. The teacher must be careful to feel "empathy" for the student, not "sympathy." Although it may be tempting to "give in" to the wishes of a student with a physical disability or life-threatening illness, such treatment will be detrimental. A mentor (another student or adult) can prevent possible behavioral problems by assisting the student with physical tasks or being available to talk, listen and understand.

Environmental/Training Considerations

Depending on health constraints, regular classroom placement of these students may be on a limited basis or for an extended period of time. Modifications in the structure and daily routine of the classroom may be necessary to accommodate students with physical disabilities. Some students can benefit from the use of specially constructed adaptive positioning equipment designed to foster social interaction, learning and independence. Other students will require continuous repositioning to relieve pressure points or to prevent the development of deformities (Sirvis, 1988). The following tips should be considered in regard to classroom environment and teacher training:

■ *Scheduling.* Specialized equipment should be integrated in a manner that does not detract from the existing learning centers, equipment, furniture and routine of the classroom. Some physically disabled students may receive health care services at regularly scheduled times throughout the day, while others will require services as the situation demands. For technology-dependent students, such services (ventilating, breathing treatments, tube feeding) may conflict with the time allotted and/or required for instructional tasks. As much as possible, how-

ever, interruptions for medical intervention should be nondisruptive to peers and planned at times of minimal social interaction (rest times, individual study times).

One-to-one assistance may be periodically needed for missed instruction. For students with other health impairments experiencing a remission in health, the school team may need to work closely with the homebound teacher to ensure learning continuity.

■ *Spatial Requirements and Mobility.* The school building must be accessible in its entirety to ensure maximum normalization. Students with orthopedic impairments need lowered shelves and hooks for easy storage and retrieval of instructional materials and personal belongings. Lowered water fountains and handrails in bathrooms facilitate the acquisition of personal hygiene and self-help skills. Lowered doorknobs and ramps allow the student to achieve independence in mobility.

Students who are technology-dependent have additional environmental restraints. Adequacy of electrical outlets and power sources, space for equipment and supplies, appropriate lighting and availability of water need to be considered. Whenever possible, students with physical disabilities should use the same types of desks as other students; this will foster uniformity and self-esteem.

It is prudent to maintain easy access to replacement equipment, should a breakdown/failure occur. Wheelchairs, braces and walkers may need repair on a moment's notice. In addition, manual backup for the power source (12 volt battery) and equipment for technology-dependent students (supplemental oxygen, resuscitator bag, suctioning catheter, extra trachea tubes) should be immediately available and may be stored in the regular classroom.

■ *Specialized Training.* Team members and parents should stress the development of academic, language, motor and social skills; methods for fostering these skills

can be the focus of inservices/workshops. In addition, general training sessions designed to disseminate information regarding types and usage of equipment, warning signs for pending crises, repositioning techniques, CPR and universal precautions/infection control will alleviate anxiety and promote collaboration.

Instructional Adaptations

The total development of physically disabled students depends upon professionals from a variety of disciplines sharing their expertise (Lowenthal, 1992; Taylor, Willits & Lieberman, 1990). The team must adapt instructional materials, methods and assessments, while providing direct instruction that is as close to grade level and/or age expectation as possible. Close adherence to approved curriculum guides and minimum standards should occur, while fostering problem-solving skills, creativity and individuality. The following strategies can help teachers adapt instructional materials:

■ *Support Service Assistance.* Because of health constraints, many physically disabled students receive supplemental services from other educators and health care professionals. In many instances, it is both possible and desirable for the teacher to reinforce these learned skills in the regular classroom.

Activities promoting motor skill development (stamina and endurance, mobility, motor planning, range of motion) should be planned in conjunction with the physical therapist, occupational therapist and/or adaptive physical education teacher. Augmentative communication techniques (signing, communication boards, switches) may be necessary for students with vocal cord paralysis, disease-affected musculature, spinal muscular atrophy or tracheotomy installation. The services of a speech/language therapist may be required.

■ *Lesson Plan and IEP (Individualized Education Plan) Development.*

Regular classroom teachers should actively participate in IEP development if a student in their classroom also receives special education instruction. Such participation will allow teachers to develop lesson plans that reflect the student's strengths and weaknesses and to write specific objectives in behavioral terms, reflecting the student's needs and achievement expectations.

The special education teacher can be a valuable resource in designing and implementing specific behavioral and instructional interventions. Daily contact is recommended to ensure lesson continuity, skill reinforcement, task completion and mastery learning. Appendix A reflects simple adaptations, which may be necessary when teaching physically challenged students.

Conclusion

In the past, poor integration of the education system and the medical field made it difficult for physically challenged students to participate in regular classroom activities. Today's societal demands call for the pooling of knowledge from a variety of professionals to provide timely, cost-effective and time-efficient schooling.

The tips in this article are designed to raise the awareness level of educators and, at the same time, assist them in making the inclusion of physically challenged students a more pleasant, nonthreatening experience. Independence, normalcy and acceptance can be the positive outcome.

References

American Cancer Society. (1980). *When you have a student with cancer.* (80-(100m)-No. 2613-LE). New York: Author.

Bernheimer, L. P., Gallimore, R., & Weisner, T. S. (1990). Ecocultural theory as a context for the individual family service plan. *Journal of Early Intervention, 14,* 219-233.

Caldwell, T. H., Sirvis, B., Todaro, A., & Accouloumre, D. S. (1991). *Special health care in the school.* Reston, VA: Council for Exceptional Children.

Chekryn, J., Deegan, M., & Reid, J. (1987). Input on teachers when a child with cancer returns to school. *Children's Health Care, 15,* 161-165.

Council for Exceptional Children. (1988). *Final report: CEC ad hoc committee on medically fragile.* Reston, VA: Author.

Hallahan, D. P., & Kauffman, J. M. (1991). *Exceptional children: Introduction to special education* (5th ed.). Englewood Cliffs, NJ: Prentice Hall.

Lowenthal, B. (1992). Collaborative training in the education of early childhood educators. *Teaching Exceptional Children, 24,* 25-29.

Sirvis, B. (1988). Students with special health care needs. *Teaching Exceptional Children, 20,* 40-44.

Taylor, R. L., Willits, P., & Lieberman, N. (1990). Identification of preschool children with mild handicaps: The importance of cooperative effort. *Childhood Education, 67,* 26-32.

Appendix A

Instructional Adaptations for Physically Challenged Children

1. Prevent paper and objects from slipping by using pads of paper, tape, clipboards, metal cookie sheets and magnets, photo album pages with sticky backings and plastic cover sheets, dycem (plastic) placed under paper and objects, or plastic photo cubes for displaying and storing materials.
2. Place a rubber strip on the back of a ruler or use a magnetic ruler to measure or draw lines.
3. Use calculators to perform computations.
4. Use felt tip pens and soft lead pencils that require less pressure. Improve grip on writing utensils by placing rubber bands, corrugated rubber or plastic tubing around the shaft. A golf practice ball or a sponge rubber ball may also be used.
5. Permit use of electronic typewriters, word processors or computers. Typing aids can include a pointer stick attached to a head- or mouthpiece to strike keys, a keyboard guard that prevents striking two keys at once, line spacers that hold written materials while typing and corrective typewriter ribbons that do not require the use of erasers.
6. Use lap desks or a table-top easel with cork that allows work to be attached with push pins.
7. Provide an "able table" that adapts to varying positions and angles and may be attached to a wheelchair or freely stood on a tray (elastic straps hold books/materials in place, while knobs adjust angles).
8. Write or type at tables/desks that adjust to wheelchair heights.
9. Provide two sets of books/workbooks—one for home and one for school use.
10. Tape assignments, lectures and activities that require extensive writing.
11. Allow a peer to carbon copy or photocopy class notes and provide written copies of board work.
12. Design worksheets/tests that allow students to answer in one of the following modes: one-word answers, lines placed through correct answers, magnetic letters moved on metal cookie sheets to indicate responses, wooden blocks placed on correct answers or containers with different categories in which answers can be dropped.
13. Use color-coded objects that are easy to handle and do not slip to indicate responses to polar questions: true/false, same/different, agree/disagree/don't know.
14. Select materials that are available on talking books or cassette tapes for students unable to hold books.
15. Use communication boards or charts with pictures, symbols, numbers or words to indicate responses.
16. Extend testing/assignment time and/or allow oral responses.

Children with Special Gifts and Talents

Who is a child with special gifts and talents? What "gift" are we discussing here? At first blush, most people will provide the simple answer, high IQ (intelligence quotient). In fact, the child with special gifts and talents may have a very average, or even below average, IQ.

Federal legislation has defined children who are gifted and talented in five areas of high performance capability: creativity, leadership, art, specific academic field, and overall intelligence. Thus, while a high IQ child would fall under the rubric of gifted, so would a child with an outstanding ability in one academic area only, or a child with a charismatic ability to take the lead, or a child skilled in music, painting, sculpture, photography, writing, acting, public speaking, or other artistic endeavors. Why is creativity listed separately from art? Creativity has been called the highest expression of giftedness, but no one definition of it is universally accepted. In general, creativity is believed to express a way of thinking which is divergent (different, moving away) from the typical way of thinking. It is original and involves more elaboration, fluency, and flexibility than the norm.

Federal legislation defines children with special gifts and talents not only in terms of creativity, general intelligence, specific academic skills, leadership, or art, but also in terms of their needs. They require services or activities not ordinarily provided by the school in order to fully develop their capabilities.

Should children with special gifts and talents be provided with special educational services? They are not included in the categories of children for which PL 94-142 mandates free and appropriate public education. The Omnibus Education Bill of 1987 provided modest support for development of special projects for the gifted and preparation of staff to educate the gifted. States, however, must pay for any gifted programming. Some states will accept the bills; most will not.

One of the controversies that looms largest in any state's or municipality's decisions about providing special educational services for children with special gifts and talents is assessment. Who will decide which children give evidence of high performance in creativity, general intelligence, specific academic skills, leadership, or art? What measures or evidence can be used as yardsticks by which to judge performance?

A child who scores 130 or above on a standardized IQ test is usually defined as intellectually gifted. Many professionals question both the validity and the reliability of IQ tests as measures of intelligence. IQ tests may fail to identify students from culturally or linguistically diverse groups, students raised in poverty, creative students, leaders, artists, and/or gifted underachievers. An IQ test also requires accomplishment across multiple areas of academic skills (e.g., math, verbal comprehension, performance in spatial tasks). IQ tests may fail to identify students with high performance capability in a very specific academic field.

The assessment of children with special gifts and talents should include multiple measurements. Recommended instruments of assessment are teacher nominations, peer nominations, parent nominations, self-nominations, achievement tests, recitals or other evidence of performance skills, creativity tests, and aptitude tests. While such a combination of procedures is desirable, few schools have the time or the financial resources to carry out such a complete evaluation of special gifts and talents.

What causes children to develop special gifts and talents? Most people seem to believe that pushy parents are, at least in part, responsible. Parents, so the mythology goes, begin teaching them their gifts or talents in infancy, or perhaps even prenatally. The parents expect the children to do great amounts of work practicing and perfecting their gifts or talents. The parents set high standards and expect the children to do their best at all costs. The parents shape the children to be aggressive, assertive, and competitive. While this may be the picture for a few children, it is far from the truth for most children with special gifts and talents. In fact, many parents have few, if any, special gifts or talents of their own. They are embarrassed by their child. They often apologize for, and downplay, their child's aptitudes.

Are children born with their special abilities, their divergent thought processes, their willingness to excel? If parents do not provide any environmental stimulation, it must originate from inside the child—right? Do gifted and talented children have congenital internal motivation, creativity, or special capabilities? No research has yet documented the causes of special gifts and talents. Research has suggested, however, that some very gifted individuals hide their own special abilities in order to be more socially acceptable. They display feelings of inferiority, guilt, fear, and low self-esteem, and their behavior is that of underachievement, low persistence, and an absence of goals.

Teachers have a responsibility to provide the most appropriate education in the least restrictive environment for every child (zero reject). Is the regular education classroom least restrictive or more restrictive for a child with special gifts and talents? Many creativity experts feel that the regular education classroom is very restrictive. The most appropriate educational setting for them would be one in which their special gifts and talents could be encouraged. Special services that enhance gifts and talents include resource room pull-out, community mentors, independent studies, special classes, special schools, and academic acceleration. Each student with a special gift or talent should have an individualized education program (IEP). It should be annually updated to accommodate the child's changing needs.

The first article in this unit discusses the absence of special educational services for a vast number of America's children with special gifts and talents. The author believes we are shortchanging the gifted in our public schools. The second selection points out the unevenness in the process of selecting children for gifted and talented programs. Poor and minority students are frequently overlooked. The author provides several suggestions for improving assessment procedures. The third article addresses the issue of math underachievement in gifted girls, and how this can be ameliorated. The fourth article suggests ways to better meet the needs of gifted and talented preschoolers.

Looking Ahead: Challenge Questions

Are public schools shortchanging the gifted? Defend your answer.

How can we improve the assessment of children with special gifts and talents?

Why do you think gifted girls can or cannot change their attitudes toward mathematics?

What activities are most beneficial for gifted and talented preschoolers?

HOW SCHOOLS ARE SHORTCHANGING THE GIFTED

Sally M. Reis

SALLY M. REIS, a professor of educational psychology at the University of Connecticut, is a researcher at UConn's National Research Center on the Gifted and Talented. Her studies on gifted education were the basis of the U.S. Department of Education's report, National Excellence: A Case for Developing America's Talent, *released in October.*

After only a few months, Andi decided that she didn't want to go to school anymore because she already knew most of what was being taught in her first-grade class. While her classmates struggled to add single-digit numbers, she had begun to teach herself multiplication and division and was fascinated with negative numbers, word problems, and logic problems. She begged her parents to help her to learn these skills, but they were unsure how much they should help her, fearing the impact her precocity might have on her subsequent school experience.

Her parents were justified in their concerns. Because schools have focused for decades on lifting up the lowest achievers, they are shortchanging the brightest students. High-ability children are not challenged in most classrooms and endure a steady diet of dumbed-down textbooks, and repetition of skills that they have mastered years ago. They suffer from the elimination of many forms of advanced or accelerated classes because it has become politically incorrect to separate students on the basis of ability. Furthermore, a widely used teaching technique called cooperative learning assigns the highest- achieving students to position of peer teacher—essentially pressing them into service as teacher aides.

Recent studies by the National Research Center on the Gifted and Talented portray a disturbing pattern of what happens in U.S. classrooms to high-ability students. For example, a survey of third- and fourth-grade teachers in several thousand public and private schools around the country revealed that fewer than half had ever received specific instruction in how to teach gifted students. Not surprisingly, given this lack of training, most teachers make at most minor modifications in the regular curriculum to meet the needs of gifted students.

Another study entailing daily observation of third- and fourth-grade classrooms around the country revealed that more than 80 percent of the time, high-ability students received the same kind of instruction, of the same material, as the rest of the class. In a typical summary, a classroom observer reported that "the gifted student was inattentive during all of her classes. She appeared to be sleepy, never volunteered, and was visibly unenthusiastic about all activities."

By underchallenging such students, U.S. schools delay and even halt these youngsters' mental development. If instructional materials are not above the students' level of knowledge or understanding, learning is less efficient and intellectual growth may stop. It is, for example, not surprising to find a bright first grader in an urban school who reads on a fifth-grade level—and who is reading only slightly above grade level when he or she enters fifth grade.

Because the work is too easy for them, many of our brightest students acquire poor work habits. A recent study conducted by the publisher of *Who's Who Among*

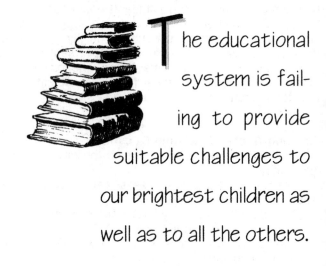

The educational system is failing to provide suitable challenges to our brightest children as well as to all the others.

From *Technology Review*, April 1994, pp. 38-45. Reprinted by permission of *Technology Review*. © 1994.

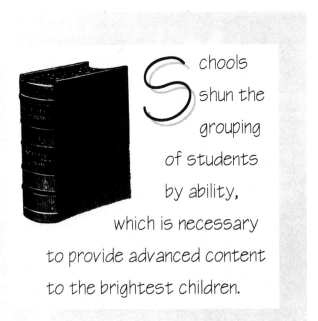

Schools shun the grouping of students by ability, which is necessary to provide advanced content to the brightest children.

American High School Students found that most high-achieving students study an hour or less a day. My own research on underachieving students in urban high schools has found a similar problem. In one representative response, a student commented: "Elementary school was fun. I always got A's on my report card. I never studied when we were in class and I never had to study at home."

Given this lack of rigor, it is not surprising that this country's most talented students are hard pressed to compete in a global community. One study compared U.S. high-school seniors taking Advanced Placement courses in math and science with top students in 13 other countries. Although these students represent the top 1 percent of students in the nation, on an international basis they ranked:

- *13 OUT OF 13 IN BIOLOGY*
- *11 OUT OF 13 IN CHEMISTRY*
- *9 OUT OF 13 IN PHYSICS*
- *13 OUT OF 13 IN ALGEBRA*
- *12 OUT OF 13 IN GEOMETRY AND CALCULUS*

The picture is actually even bleaker than these figures suggest, since a higher percentage of the total school population in other countries takes these advanced classes than in the United States. When the results are controlled to eliminate this source of difference, American students scored last in all subject areas. "Our top-performing students are undistinguished at best and poor at worst" in comparison to their counterparts in other countries, according to a Department of Education report on this country's inadequate treatment of the gifted. The report, entitled *National Excellence: A Case for Developing America's Talent*, was distributed in October to every school district in the nation and made front page headlines

These sobering statistics may provide one explanation for why graduate school enrollments of U.S. students in mathematics and science have substantially declined in the last two decades while the number of foreign-born graduate students has increased. In 1992, for example, 44 percent of the doctorates in mathematics and physical sciences, and 60 percent in engineering, granted in the United States went to non-citizens.

Our most advanced students need educational experiences different from those they are currently receiving. Without these services, talents may remain unnurtured: We can't develop the potential of a budding concert musician by providing him or her with ordinary music classes for one or two hours a week. We can't produce future Thomas Edisons or Marie Curies by forcing them to spend large amounts of their science and mathematics classes tutoring students who don't understand the material.

Didn't We Learn That Last Year?

In great part, the lack of challenge for gifted students stems from the unwillingness of schools to group students according to their abilities. The movement over the past decade to eliminate tracking—the relatively permanent (at least for the school year) placement of students into a class or group for students of a certain level—is creating special problems for high-ability students. The anti-tracking movement is based on the belief that such grouping is too often a self-fulfilling prophecy: kids labeled as "smart" flourish with stimulating instructional methods and interesting material, while those deemed "slow" stagnate in a backwater of low expectations, dulled by rote learning of basic skills.

Distaste for tracking has led to the erroneous presumption that all forms of grouping are bad. But some ability grouping is necessary for providing advanced content to high-ability students. Teachers have traditionally used some form of flexible instructional grouping to target appropriate levels of challenge and instruction for the wide range of abilities and interests in their classrooms, particularly in reading and math. Unfortunately, in their zeal for egalitarian equality, schools have turned away from ability-based grouping even within classrooms. Our survey of third- and fourth-grade classrooms found that students identified as gifted received instruction in homogeneous groups only about 20 percent of the time they were in school. This homogenization results in a "one size fits all" curriculum that is usually tailored to students in the middle of the class or, worse yet, to students who achieve at the lowest level.

Another trend that is potentially detrimental to gifted students is cooperative learning, in which small groups of students work together on assigned classwork. In one

*T*alented youngsters often find opportunities to do creative problem solving in extracurricular activities. Teams of kids participating in typical Odyssey of the Mind contests design weight-bearing structures made of lightweight material (top), build and race vehicles powered by a variety of energy sources (middle), and design a vehicle propelled by rowing for an "around the world" contest (bottom). Results can be impressive: one 18-gram structure held 1,200 pounds.

typical form of cooperative learning, a teacher assigns one bright child, two average children and one below-average student to a group. The smart student is supposed to help the others, and, in theory, all will benefit. Teachers have employed this method for decades, and it can indeed be a sound pedagogical technique.

Unfortunately, some bright students are not interested in teaching others, and some cannot explain how they've acquired advanced concepts. What's more, a student who is tutoring others in mathematics may refine some of his or her basic skills and knowledge but will not encounter the challenge necessary for the most advanced types of work.

Because most elementary-school classes are composed of kids with a wide range of abilities, textbooks must be written so that the less-able students at each grade level can understand them. Social studies books, for instance, now "teach" second- and third-grade students concepts that they grasped when they were two or three years old—that people live in families, for instance, and that they buy food at a store. When California educators tried to find textbooks that would challenge the top third of their students, no publisher had a book to present. The publishers suggested instead the reissuing of books from the late sixties—damning evidence of the "dumbing down" of textbooks over the past 25 years.

Although this phenomenon first received popular attention 10 years ago in the scathing Department of Education report, *A Nation at Risk*, the trend is not new. Textbooks began their slide in the 1920s as the children of immigrant and uneducated families began entering schools in large numbers. In response to this influx, books introduced fewer and fewer new words, and the words that were introduced were repeated more often. This trend continued through the 1950s in all subject areas: reading, social studies, mathematics, and science.

How far have books fallen? Take a look at the following two excerpts. The first passage comes from a fifth-grade history book published in 1950:

After a time Captain Jones had command of another ship, the "Bonhomme Richard." It was an old vessel and not very strong. But in it the brave

Top, middle: Local universities can provide intellectual stimulation that schools do not. An Iowa State summer program gives gifted 7th-12th graders a chance to work closely with researchers. Bottom: Third graders in a mixed-ability class in Alabama use enrichment exercises originally devised for gifted youngsters. Such practices partly compensate for the absence in most schools of ability-based grouping.

captain began a battle with one of England's fine ships. The cannons on the two ships kept up a steady roar. The masts were broken, and the sails hung in rags above the decks. Many of the men on the "Bonhomme Richard" lay about the deck dead or dying. The two vessels crashed together, and with his own hands the American captain lashed

them together. By this time the American ship had so many cannon-ball holes in its side that it was beginning to sink. The English captain shouted: "Do you surrender?" "Surrender? I've just begun to fight," John Paul Jones roared back at him. It was true. The Americans shot so straight and fast that the English sailors dared not stay on the deck of their ship. Their cannons were silent. At last the English captain surrendered.

Contrast that lively (albeit melodramatic) account with the dreary description of the same event from a fifth-grade textbook now in wide use:

The greatest American naval officer was John Paul Jones. He was daring. He attacked ships off the British coast. In a famous battle, Jones' ship, the "Bonhomme Richard," fought the British ship "Serapis." At one point in the battle Jones' ship was sinking. When asked to give up, Jones answered, "I have not yet begun to fight." He went on to win.

The poor quality of textbooks would not matter so much if schools treated the books as merely one of many teaching tools. Unfortunately, that is not the case. In too many elementary schools, textbooks dominate classroom instruction, constituting 75 to 90 percent of teaching time. In effect, textbooks determine what is taught in the classroom. The result is a curriculum bogged down with repetition. Imagine the frustration of a precocious reader who enters kindergarten reading at a relatively advanced level and spends the next two years being "taught" the letters of the alphabet and beginning letter blends. That's hardly the way to spark enthusiasm in an eager young mind.

Unfortunately, such glacial progress is the norm. Topics begun at the end of one grade are typically continued well past the beginning of the next. Overall, students in grades two to five encounter 40 to 65 percent new content, an equivalent of new material just two or three days per week. By eighth grade, this amount has dropped to 30 percent, just one and a half days per week. In mathematics, for example, popular textbooks present a steadily diminishing amount of new material each year through the elementary school years, according to studies by James Flanders, a noted mathematics researcher and elementary-school textbook editor at the University of Chicago. Instruction in addition and subtraction is repeated during every elementary school year. In Taiwan and Japan, by contrast, fifth graders study elementary algebra. In Holland, practice in multiplication and division is considered completed after third grade.

"There should be little wonder why good students, and even average or slower-than-average students, get complacent about their mathematics studies," says Flanders. "They know that if they don't learn it now, it will be retaught next year." Most of the new content in any textbook, naturally, is found in the second half of the book. The result, notes Flanders, is that "earlier in the year, when students are likely to be more eager to study, they repeat what they have seen before. Later on, when they are sufficiently bored, they see new material—if they get to the end of the book."

Gifted students could gain much simply from streamlining of the curriculum to reduce repetition. Such "compacting" excuses high-ability students from plowing through material that they have already mastered. A study of compacting by the National Center for the Gifted and Talented showed that teachers could eliminate as much as 40 to 50 percent of the usual material without affecting achievement scores in reading, math computation, social studies, and spelling. In fact, students whose science and math curriculum was compacted scored significantly *higher* than their counterparts in a control group given the full curriculum. Such is the benefit of relieving boredom.

Compacting the curriculum spares gifted students from repeating already mastered material and creates time for more stimulating activities.

THE GUTTING OF GIFTED EDUCATION

During the 1970s and 80s, a diverse array of services arose to meet the needs of high-ability students, such as math competitions, training in the invention process, and consultations by classroom teachers with specialists in gifted education. But budget pressures, exacerbated by the lingering recession, have forced gifted education into a full-scale retreat.

The reductions affect programs in several ways. Some school districts now offer gifted programs only at certain grade levels; typically, it is the elementary-school grades that get cut first. Some districts have dropped special components such as an arts program; and others have cut personnel. In many states, the position of state director of gifted education has been scaled back; other states, such as Massachusetts, have eliminated the positions entirely. Even states with laws mandating special attention for gifted students—including, Alaska, Florida, South Dakota, Utah, and Virginia—have eliminated or put in jeopardy some 15 percent of their programs.

In states without such a mandate, such as Connecticut, Delaware, North Dakota, and Wyoming, the impact is more dramatic: one in three programs in these states were reduced or threatened with reduction in the 1991–92 academic year (the last year for which such figures are available). In one school district in Connecticut, financial constraints have reduced the gifted program staff from seven teachers to two. Resource-room time for independent study, research, and critical and creative thinking are no longer provided to middle- and high- school students; gifted elementary-school students spend only one hour a week in a resource room catering to their special abilities. Several of the states that require services for the gifted, including Oklahoma

and Alaska, are considering repeal of their mandates. And two states that had passed legislation to require gifted education—Mississippi and Maine—have postponed implementation because of lack of funding.

One parent summarized her frustrations when her son's program was cut:

I remember my son coming home and telling me he was upset and angry because they were doing a chapter on telling time in his fourth-grade class. He learned to tell time before he entered kindergarten and he said, "I know all of this stuff. I've known all of the math work all year." And I tried to explain that other students needed to learn about time. And he was very angry and said to me, "But what about me?" And I didn't know what to say to him.

PROVIDING A CHALLENGE

Despite these cutbacks, promising programs have become available that allow gifted and talented students to leave their regular classroom to pursue individual interests and advanced content. For example, many local districts have created innovative mentorship programs that pair a bright elementary-school student with an adult or high school student who shares a common interest. And some schools, acknowledging that they do little different for gifted students within the school day, provide after-school enrichment programs, or send talented students to Saturday programs offered by museums, science centers, or local universities.

Some large school districts have established magnet

schools to serve the needs of talented students. In New York City, for example, the Bronx High School of Science has helped nurture mathematical and scientific talent for decades, producing Nobel laureates and other internationally known scientists. More recently, 11 states have created separate schools, such as the North Carolina School for Math and Science, for talented students. In many states, "governor's schools" provide intensive summer programs in a variety of advanced content areas. It is clear, however, that these opportunities touch a small percentage of students who could benefit from them.

Over the past several years, some of the most exciting offerings for gifted students have come from private organizations. For example, Future Problem Solving of Ann Arbor, Mich., runs a year-long program in which teams of four students apply information they have learned to some of the most complex issues facing society, such as the overcrowding of prisons or global warming. At regular intervals throughout the year, the teams mail their work to evaluators, who review it and offer suggestions for improvement. The program challenges students to think, to make decisions, and to come up with unique solutions to problems. (One team in Connecticut, for example, proposed converting surplus military submarines into additional prison space.)

Although not developed solely for gifted students, Future Problem Solving is widely used in gifted programs because they typically have the inclination to pursue such additional projects. Gifted students also are more often able to afford the time for such activities, after breezing through much of their regular schoolwork. In a similar effort, called Odyssey of the Mind, teams of students design structures and machines. In one typical project, students had to design and build a balsa wood structure to support the most weight possible. Costs to the schools for these programs are modest—$55 per student team for Future Problem Solving, $135 for Odyssey of the Mind. For these fees, the schools receive background materials on the topic and access to the network of evaluators (typically, teachers who are coaching teams at other schools).

Another national program, operated by the Center for Talented Youth and Academic Programs at Johns Hopkins University, recruits and provides testing and program opportunities for precocious youth. Each year, Talent Search offers both the mathematics and verbal portions of the Scholastic Aptitude Test—usually taken by high-school juniors and seniors—to thousands of interested 12- to 14-year-olds (typically seventh and eighth graders). Those who score above that year's mean for college-bound seniors become eligible for a number of programs operated by Talent Search, including summer seminars in advanced subjects and enrollment in college courses. By taking advantage of the courses offered by Talent Search, a talented youth could complete two or more years of math in one year. Unfortunately, school districts do not have to honor these credits and could require a student who took geometry during a junior-high-school summer to take it again as a high-school sophomore.

Enrichment opportunities for the brightest students are not limited to math and science. To enter the annual History Day contest, students can work individually or in small groups on research projects related to a historical event, person, or invention related to a given theme. Drawing on primary source materials such as diaries, as well as information gathered in libraries, museums, and interviews, students prepare research papers, projects, media presentations, and performances as entries. The entries are judged by local historians, educators, and other professionals; each June, state finalists compete for a nationwide prize.

While these programs are valuable supplements, the smartest kids would also benefit greatly if existing schools simply became more flexible in their assignment of children to grade levels. Why, for example, do we have or even need 12 grades that students must pass through in sequence? Why can't students progress through a series of competencies in an ungraded setting, thus earning time to pursue advanced curricula or an area of individual interest or talent?

Unfortunately, most educators these days discourage a broad range of useful, and once common, acceleration practices—starting kindergarten or first grade at a younger age, skipping grades, or entering college early. This reluctance stems from a misguided anti-

Gifted kids would benefit greatly if schools became more flexible. Why must students pass through twelve grades in sequence?

intellectualism that discourages policymakers from promoting excellence in our schools and allows them to pay less and less attention to nurturing intellectual growth. Anti-acceleration policies—often justified on the social harm that the gifted student might experience—also tacitly acknowledges the anti-intellectualism of children: kids labeled as gifted have traditionally been ostracized by their peers.

Indeed, bright students seeking to avoid harassment learn to hide their academic prowess, such as by ceasing to participate in class discussions. Consider the experiences of an exceptional student who pleaded with her school board to save the gifted program:

> In my 12 years in school, I have been placed in many "average" classes—especially up until the junior- high-school level—in which I have been spit on, ostracized, and verbally abused for doing my homework on a regular basis, for raising my hand in class, and particularly for receiving outstanding grades.

THE GIFTED'S GIFT TO SCHOOLS

Gifted programs have developed an impressive menu of curricular adaptations, independent study and thinking-skill strategies, grouping options, and enrichment strategies. Many of these innovations could be used to improve education for all students, not just those who score highly on intelligence or achievement tests. In particular, programs for teaching the gifted tend to focus not on memorizing facts but on practicing the skills of knowledge acquisition and problem solving.

In fact, most students would benefit from this approach to instruction. With knowledge accumulating at an unprecedented pace, it is at least as important to teach kids how to obtain and analyze information as it is to convey an existing set of facts. Educators should therefore reassess the need for content-based instruction for students of all ability levels. Bright students fortunate enough to be receiving special attention are already experiencing the joys of independent, self-directed learning. This kind of schooling is more challenging and more fun than conventional classroom work. Why not apply it more generally?

Joseph Renzulli and I at the University of Connecticut have developed an approach to do just that. Our "schoolwide enrichment model" has been field tested and implemented by hundreds of school districts across the country. This approach seeks to apply strategies used in gifted programs to the entire school population, emphasizing talent development in all students through acceleration and a variety of other strategies.

Of course, not all students can participate in all advanced opportunities. But many children can work far beyond what they are currently asked to do; they rise to the level of expectations. In addition, the infusion of some of these techniques may help us identify other young people with untapped potential for academic achievement, leadership, and creativity.

Ideas for improving education have been around for decades, if not centuries. More will undoubtedly surface as long as thoughtful people have the courage and vision to try new ways to solve the endless array of problems that a changing society places on the doorsteps of its schools. Amidst all of these restructuring efforts, we cannot afford to ignore our most talented children. It is they who set the pace. By pushing these children to stretch and develop their intellectual gifts, we can raise the standard of schooling for all.

Poor and Minority Students Can Be Gifted, Too!

Our daily practices must reflect the recognition that gifted students come from all walks of life.

MARY M. FRASIER

Mary M. Frasier is President, National Association for Gifted Children, and Associate Professor, Educational Psychology Coordinator, and Program for the Gifted Director, Torrance Center for Creative Studies, 422 Aderhold Hall, University of Georgia, Athens, GA, 30602.

Despite all efforts toward equity in schools, minority and poor students remain noticeably absent from gifted programs. The most frequent explanation for their low representation in such programs is performance on an IQ test below the cutoff score set by a state department, school district, or school system. Other explanations describe the limitations of a low socioeconomic environment to stimulate and support the development of higher intellectual capacities. Finally, there is the persistent attitude that giftedness simply cannot be found in some groups (Frasier 1987).

Improving Nomination Methods

Such negative attitudes are reinforced by narrow nomination and screening methods that limit the access of underinvolved populations to these programs. As Gallagher (1983) noted, "if you don't get a chance to come to bat, you don't get a chance to hit." To give these students their chance, we can expand the methods used to appraise children's potential.

We can create nomination forms that incorporate behavioral traits, such as the 15 indicators of giftedness delineated by Hagen (1980, pp. 23-26). The use of these dynamic (rather than static) traits requires nominators to observe, for example, a student's use of language rather than just to rely on appraisal of language in a test situation.

Second, parents and other representatives of the underinvolved groups can help educators reword items on rating scales (such as the Scale for Rating Behavioral Characteristics of Superior Students, Renzulli and Hartman 1971), so

Sternberg's Triarchic Theory of Intelligence and Gardner's Theory of Multiple Intelligences became major breakthroughs in expanding the definition of _intelligence_.

that the ratings more accurately reveal the manifestations of giftedness within a cultural group.

Third, teachers can develop vignettes of poor and minority students they have taught to serve as prototypes of successful students. Nominators can then use these vignettes as examples to help others recognize students who are demonstrating potential for achievement. The development of vignettes is enhanced by incorporating behavioral traits of successful students from disadvantaged backgrounds. (See Ross and Glaser 1973 for a particularly useful source of such traits.)

The intent of these approaches is to broaden concepts of what giftedness looks like in minority and low socioeconomic populations. Then, as teachers and parents become aware of the varied manifestations of giftedness, they are better prepared to recognize—and nominate for programs—many more poor and minority students.

Expanding The Definition of _Intelligence_

Another barrier to equity in gifted programs is the continuing but outmoded emphasis on the IQ as the _sine qua non_ of giftedness. When program acceptance is based solely on this limited criterion, minority and poor students do not fare well. Thus, a more nearly complete definition of _intelligence_ is part of the solution to eliminating barriers.

A few years ago, Torrance (1979) demonstrated that we can learn much about children's potential by examining indicators of intelligence that do not depend on prelearned solutions to problems. He developed the Torrance Tests of Creative Thinking, figural and verbal, to assess children's responses to open-ended problem-solving situations. Corroborating this concept, Sternberg (1982) advocated that ability be evaluated not only through the measurement of one's manipulation of *entrenched concepts* (familiar) but also one's ability to deal with *nonentrenched concepts* (unfamiliar).

Recently, Sternberg's (1981) Triarchic Theory of Intelligence and Gardner's (1983) Theory of Multiple Intelligences became major breakthroughs in expanding the definition of *intelligence*, foretelling the end of reliance on factor-analytic, psychometric measures such as IQ. Clark's (1988) research on brain/mind functioning has further supported a broad concept of giftedness, one that includes talent other than academic.

These developments, combined with the findings of other researchers (Baldwin 1984, Renzulli 1978, Treffinger and Renzulli 1986, and Tannenbaum 1983), have led to a more sophisticated array of best practices in identifying potential for gifted performance. These practices include:

● seeking nominations from a variety of persons, professional and non-professional, inside and outside school;

● applying knowledge of the behavioral indicators by which children from different cultures dynamically exhibit giftedness in the development of nomination forms;

● collecting data from multiple sources, objective and subjective, including performances and products;

New information is causing us to reconsider the misconception that poor homes are necessarily illiterate or incapable of supporting intellectual development.

● delaying decision making until *all* pertinent data can be collected in a case study (Frasier 1987).

Also noteworthy are the productive efforts of Tonemah (1987) and of the American Indian Research and Development Center in Norman, Oklahoma, in identifying gifted and talented American Indian students using creativity indicators. These and other developments are helping us to make headway, but there is more that we can do.

What Else Needs to Be Done?

As efforts continue to break down barriers to equity, we are encountering other challenges in serving poor and minority students well. We often fear that their deprived backgrounds will put them at a loss in a program that assumes familiarity with certain content and experiences. Thus, we typically *adapt* curriculum to try to fit or adjust the students to the curriculum. For example, minority and poor children are placed in pre-gifted programs designed to remediate language and performance deficiencies. Upon successful completion, they may then be certified for placement in a gifted program. What is more promising is to emphasize *accommodation* by changing the structure, function, or form that produces an enhanced learning environment. Examples of curriculum accommodations would be to emphasize high expectations for achievement, establish clear standards of excellence, and provide assistance in securing mentors.

Second, new information is causing us to reconsider the misconception that poor homes are necessarily illiterate or incapable of supporting intellectual development. Recent findings indicate that the qualities of home life that promote achievement are similar, regardless of income level (Bradley et al. 1987, Coleman 1969, Murphy 1986, Rosenbaum et al. 1987, Scott-Jones 1987, Slaughter and Epps 1987). For example, the entire August 1988 issue of *Ebony* magazine—in particular, the article "Model Youths: Excelling Despite the Odds" (Brown 1988)—compels us to reexamine notions and expand realities regarding the extent of support for intellectual development in the black community. As we reconceptualize the role of families in promoting intellectual achievement, we can better recognize their strengths and resources and work in partnership with them.

Third, we must strengthen counseling options to provide the social and emotional support these students

need to gain confidence in their abilities (Exxum 1979, 1983; Colangelo 1985; and Frasier 1979). With adequate support, they can manage the conflict inherent in being identified gifted, gain access to the information they need to make good academic and vocational decisions, and resolve the problems of social interaction within their culture and the culture of the larger society. See Comer (1987) for an excellent program that defines the total academic, social, and psychological support needed to enhance the achievement of minority and poor students.

The Reality of Diversity

An encompassing perspective of giftedness and improved assessment methods will help us to remove the barriers that so often keep poor and minority students out of programs for the gifted. The gifted in our schools are a diverse group, made up of children from all racial groups, at all ages, and at all socioeconomic levels.

References

Baldwin, A.Y. (1984). *The Baldwin Identification Matrix 2 for the Identification of the Gifted and Talented: A Handbook for Its Use.* New York: Trillium Press.

Bradley, R.H., S.L. Rock, B.M. Caldwell, P.T. Harris, and H.M. Hamrick. (1987). "Home Environment and School Performance among Black Elementary School Children." *Journal of Negro Education* 56, 4: 499-509.

Brown, R. (1988). "Model Youth: Excelling Despite the Odds." *Ebony* 43, 10: 40-48.

Clark, B. (1988). *Growing Up Gifted.* Columbus, Ohio: Merrill Publishing Company.

Colangelo, N. (September 1985). "Counseling Needs of Culturally Diverse Students." *Roeper Review* 8, 1: 33-35.

Coleman, A.B. (November 1969). "The Disadvantaged Child Who Is Successful in School." *The Educational Forum* 32, 1: 95-97.

Comer, J.P. (March 1987). "New Haven's School-Community Connection." *Educational Leadership* 42: 13-16.

Exxum, H.A. (1979). "Facilitating Psychological and Emotional Development of Gifted Black Students." In *New Voices in Counseling the Gifted*, edited by N. Colangelo and R.T. Zaffran. Dubuque, Iowa: Kendall/Hunt Publishing Co.

Exxum, H.A. (February 1983). "Key Issues in Family Counseling with Gifted and Talented Black Students." *Roeper Review* 5, 3: 28-31.

Frasier, M.M. (1979). "Counseling the Culturally Diverse Gifted." In *New Voices in Counseling the Gifted*, edited by N. Colangelo and R.T. Zaffran. Dubuque, Iowa: Kendall/Hunt Publishing Co.

Frasier, M.M. (Spring 1987). "The Identification of Gifted Black Students: Developing New Perspectives." *Journal for the Education of the Gifted* 10, 3: 155-180.

Gallagher, J.J. (May 22, 1983). "Keynote Speech." *International Conference on Gifted Students*. Ontario, Canada: Sheridan College.

Gardner, H. (1983). *Frames of Mind: The Theory of Multiple Intelligences*. New York: Basic Books.

Hagen, E. (1980). *Identification of the Gifted*. New York: Teachers College Press.

Murphy, D.M. (1986). "Educational Disadvantagement: Associated Factors, Current Interventions, and Implications." *Journal of Negro Education* 55, 4: 495-507.

Renzulli, J.S. (1978). "What Makes Giftedness? Reexamining a Definition." *Phi Delta Kappan* 60: 180-184, 261.

Renzulli, J., and R. Hartman. (1971). "Scale for Rating Behavioral Characteristics of Superior Students." *Exceptional Children* 38, 1: 243-248.

Rosenbaum, J.E., M.J. Kulieke, and L.S. Rubinowitz. (1987). "Low-Income Black Children in White Suburban Schools: A Study of School and Student Responses." *Journal of Negro Education* 56, 1: 35-52.

Ross, H.L., and E.M. Glaser. (1973). "Making It Out of the Ghetto." *Professional Psychology* 4, 3: 347-356.

Scott-Jones, D. (1987). "Mother-as-Teacher in the Families of High- and Low-Achieving Low-Income Black First-Graders." *Journal of Negro Education* 56, 1: 21-34.

Slaughter, D.T., and E.G. Epps. (1987). "The Home Environment and Academic Achievement of Black American Children and Youth: An Overview." *Journal of Negro Education* 56, 1: 3-20.

Sternberg, R. (1981). "A Componential Theory of Intellectual Giftedness." *Gifted Child Quarterly* 25, 2: 86-93.

Sternberg, R. (1982). "Nonentrenchment in the Assessment of Intellectual Giftedness." *Gifted Child Quarterly* 26, 2: 63-67.

Tannenbaum, A.J. (1983). *Gifted Children: Psychological and Educational Perspectives*. New York: Macmillan Publishing Co.

Tonemah, S. (1987). "Assessing American Indian Gifted and Talented Students' Abilities." *Journal for the Education of the Gifted* 10, 3: 181-194.

Torrance, E.P. (1979). *Torrance Tests of Creative Thinking: Norm-Technical Manual*. Bensenville, Ill.: Scholastic Testing Service.

Treffinger, D., and J.S. Renzulli. (February 1986). "Giftedness as Potential for Creative Productivity: Transcending IQ Scores." *Roeper Review* 8, 3: 150-154.

Gifted Girls in a Rural Community: Math Attitudes and Career Options

ABSTRACT: This study was designed to determine the feasibility of improving gifted girls' attitudes toward mathematics. This study was conducted in three school districts in an isolated rural setting. Subjects were 24 gifted girls in Grades 4-7. A control group also contained 24 gifted girls at the same grade levels. On pretest, using the Mathematics Attitude Inventory *(MAI), no significant differences were found between groups in their attitudes toward math. The intervention program included problem-solving activities, math-related career options, and self-esteem issues. MAI posttest scores after the 18-week program indicated that the program was effective in changing attitudes toward mathematics of gifted girls in a rural environment.*

JULIE LAMB

ROBERTA DANIELS

JULIE LAMB (CEC #185), educator for gifted children, Paragould, Northeast Arkansas School District. ROBERTA DANIELS (CEC #345), Director of Gifted Education, Special Education Department, Arkansas State University, Jonesboro, Arkansas.

☐ For many years, researchers (Armstrong, 1979; Boswell & Katz, 1980; Fennema & Sherman, 1977; Fox, 1980) have been interested in educational and career barriers between females and the field of mathematics. Early research (Fennema & Sherman) indicated that males outperformed females in math achievement at the junior high and high school level but also found significant differences in attitudes toward math between the two groups. More than 10 years ago, Armstrong concluded that the development of attitudes that affect females' math achievement begins around age 13. Armstrong's research included a survey of 1,452 13-year-old students and 1,788 high school seniors and offered strong evidence that stereotypical expectation of parents, peers, and teachers influenced females' decisions not to participate in math. Thus, females' lack of positive attitudes toward math has been attributed to stereotyping rather than a lack of ability.

More recently, Kerr (1988) contended that gifted girls are rewarded for intellectual achievement at early ages; but by adolescence, they are rewarded for social conformity, which may include seeing math as masculine. In a 1984 study, Flemming and Hollinger examined internal barriers for gifted girls, which may prohibit their success in mathematics. These barriers included the following:

1. An avoidance of math because it is not feminine.
2. An exhibition of a lack of ability in math due to the lack of social expectation.
3. A lack of seeing math as necessary for obtaining their educational and career goals.

Gifted girls in rural settings may be particularly influenced by social conformity which affects their attitudes toward math due to cultural beliefs of the community. The demise of the one-room schoolhouse has not eliminated traditional rural values, which include sex-role stereotyping that may discourage gifted girls' participation in math and science (Howley, Pendarvis, & Howley, 1988; Southern, Spicker, & Davis, 1987).

From *Exceptional Children*, Vol. 59, No. 6, May 1993, pp. 513-517. © 1993 by The Council for Exceptional Children. Reprinted by permission.

By limiting their academic choices in math at adolescence, gifted girls also limit their occupational choices. Boswell and Katz (1980) found that girls who had a deficiency in high school mathematics courses did not have an appropriate background to enter technical fields of study in college. Further, many gifted girls fail to realize the potential of their early years, settling for jobs well below their abilities (Shaffer, 1986). In a study of the lives of 22 women who had been identified as gifted girls, Shaffer found that only 3 women reported having challenging careers. Gifted women, who have not fulfilled their academic potential and do not have challenging careers, may be largely regretful (Kerr, 1988). Gifted females in rural societies are no exception to the need for fulfilling career potential that may likewise benefit the rural communities (Howley et al., 1988).

Fox and Tobin (1988) have offered suggestions for improving math attitudes of gifted females, based on research conducted with 24, mathematically talented, 7th-grade girls. The girls were involved in exploration of math-related careers through four minicourses pertaining to geometry, statistics, probability, and computer science. During the program, the girls met with women scientists and mathematicians to examine engineering, medical research, and space exploration. Results of pre- and postmeasures of attitude and career interest demonstrated the effectiveness of the model that had a positive impact on the gifted females' math attitudes and career awareness.

As gifted girls participate in programs to deter negative attitudes toward mathematics, there is an increased opportunity to maximize career options as young adults. Because research (Armstrong, 1979; Boswell & Katz, 1980; Kerr, 1988) has described a change in attitude beginning with adolescence, the present intervention program began at the elementary level. The purpose of this study was to determine if an intervention program implemented in an isolated rural setting and designed to improve gifted girls' attitudes toward mathematics would produce positive math attitudes.

METHODS

Subjects

Forty-eight girls identified as academically gifted ranging from 4th to 7th grade participated in this study. The numbers per grade for the experimental group were as follows: 6 fourth graders, 4 fifth graders, 6 sixth graders, and 8 seventh graders. The control group contained 5 fourth graders, 7 fifth graders, 4 sixth graders, and 8 seventh graders. The 48 girls were included in the gifted program (which is a cooperative program that exists in three isolated rural communities' schools), based on scores from standardized aptitude and achievement tests and teachers' recommendations. Twenty-four girls from one school comprised the experimental group that received the intervention program. The control group consisted of 24 girls from the remaining two schools.

Though gifted girls from only one rural school district comprised the experimental group, the schools are demographically close—within an 18-mile radius. Each school is located in a small community (i.e., 3,000 or less in population). Similarities in socioeconomic status of the three communities are consistent: Each contains small merchant businesses, small factories, and crop farming.

Procedures

A quasi-experimental design using a pretest, posttest, and control group was used for the study so that control for threats to internal validity of maturation and selection was established. To control for possible variations between the control and experimental groups, a pretest using the *Mathematics Attitude Inventory* (MAI) (Sandman, 1980) was administered to all 48 gifted girls.

The MAI is a 48-item, self-rating scale. According to Sandman (1980), the test reports attitude toward math teachers, anxiety toward math, value of math in society, self-concept in math, enjoyment of math, and motivation in math. Eight questions in each of the six categories comprise the self-rating scale. Each question was answered according to a 4-point Likert scale (strongly agree, agree, disagree, or strongly disagree). The possible maximum score was 192 points, with a possible minimum score of 48 points.

A statistical analysis using *t*-test scores revealed that there were no significant differences between the experimental and control groups' scores for all six categories on the pretests. The total mean scores for the pretests, as measured by the MAI, were 140.38 for the experimental group and 142.17 for the control group, resulting in a *t*-test score of .26.

The MAI reports a maximum score of 32 and a minimum score of 8 for each of the six subtests. Subtest scores for the experimental and control groups on the girls' attitudes toward their math teacher, anxiety toward math, value of math in society, self-concept in math, enjoyment of math, and motivation in math are shown in Table 1. It should be noted that a high score on the anxiety toward math subtest reports low anxiety. There were no significant differences between the scores of the experimental and control groups on any of the subtests of the MAI.

The experimental group received the intervention program, which consisted of an 18-week treatment. The gifted girls were told at the first class meeting that they would be involved in a

TABLE 1
Pretest Scores of Experimental and Control Groups of Gifted Girls

Math Attitude	Experimental		Control			
	Mean	(SD)	Mean	(SD)	t	p
Attitude toward						
math teacher	22.33	(8.13)	24.88	(5.34)	1.28	.207
Anxiety	24.67	(4.43)	25.08	(4.62)	.32	.751
Value of math in society	26.75	(3.12)	26.29	(3.29)	.49	.623
Self-concept in math	24.25	(4.07)	24.54	(4.13)	.25	.806
Enjoyment of math	21.83	(4.86)	20.75	(4.64)	.79	.434
Motivation	20.54	(5.75)	20.63	(4.54)	.06	.956
Total	140.38	(25.97)	142.17	(21.70)	.26	.796

Note: $N = 24$ in each group. Differences not significant.

special unit pertaining to math. They were informed that they would be doing some fun activities and were given an overview of the activities they would encounter. The experimental group discussed the importance of the career decisions that each would encounter and how math-related careers were one available option. However, the group was not told that the unit was being implemented to determine if their attitudes toward math would change.

The intervention program included attitude and career awareness activities based on *Just Around the Corner* (Roberts, 1982) and *Math for Girls and Other Problem Solvers* (Downie, Slesnick, & Stenmark, 1981). The gifted girls developed problem-solving strategies according to *Problem of the Week* (Fisher & Medigovich, 1981) and *Mental Math in the Middle Grades* (Hope, Reys, & Reys, 1987). These materials contain both individual and group activities dealing with attitudes about mathematical decisions, career information in the area of math, and problem-solving strategies. Activities for the experimental group, Grades 4-7, were grouped according to units, for approximately 2 weeks per unit. The gifted girls in Grades 4-6 met daily for 30 min for 18 weeks for the intervention program. The 7th-grade girls met 2 days per week for 1 hr each meeting during the semester to receive the intervention program.

According to Fox and Tobin (1988) and Kerr (1988), intervention programming should encourage gifted girls to obtain a positive self-concept pertaining to mathematical concepts. The present intervention included six units. Unit 1 included activities to enhance self-esteem, such as the following:

1. Making lists of "Things I Do and Don't Do Well" and ways to improve the areas of lesser confidence.

2. Participating in role play to demonstrate optimistic and pessimistic attitudes.
3. Debating the effects of self-perception as it relates to task commitment.

After exploring the importance of a positive attitude in all pursuits, students went on to Unit 2, which emphasized appreciating math as a useful tool in daily events. This unit, involving school peers and the community, began with a "Math Appreciation Day." Other activities examined the work of people who dealt with mathematical processes in their daily lives, explored the usefulness of mathematical knowledge for particular industries in the community, and developed budgets for the girls' families after investigating how money and math processes coincide.

Unit 3 was designed to improve girls' problem-solving abilities (Fisher & Medigovich, 1981). In Unit 4, the girls developed a math newspaper, *Math Rap*, for the school. The girls created math games, puzzles, comics, and news about activities in their math classes.

Though not all models developed to involve females in math to promote positive attitudes have incorporated the same strategies, all have reported the importance of career awareness in math-related fields (e.g., Boswell & Katz, 1980; Fox & Tobin, 1988; Shaffer, 1986). Therefore, Unit 5 dealt with occupations in math-related fields. Resources were made available by the school and community libraries, the school counselor, and community industries so that the girls could research different occupations. Female guest speakers with math-related occupations were invited from industries in the community.

While participating in Unit 6, the 24 girls in the experimental group provided a tutoring service for a variety of students, at which time they showed a high level of confidence. The final intervention strategies included problem-solving

TABLE 2
Posttest Scores of Experimental and Control Groups of Gifted Girls

Math Attitudes	Experimental		Control		t	p
	Mean	(SD)	Mean	(SD)		
Attitude toward						
math teacher	25.96	(6.45)	23.33	(5.17)	1.56	.126
Anxiety	29.49	(2.41)	24.71	(4.51)	4.55	.001*
Value of math in society	30.46	(1.77)	25.42	(3.94)	5.71	.0001*
Self-concept in math	28.83	(2.04)	23.96	(3.91)	5.42	.0001*
Enjoyment of math	28.13	(2.69)	21.13	(3.36)	7.96	.0001*
Motivation	26.17	(3.20)	21.00	(4.59)	4.53	.001*
Total	169.00	(14.77)	139.54	(21.85)	5.47	.0001*

Note: N = 24 in each group.
*p < .05.

RESULTS

Statistical differences at the .05 level of significance in math attitudes of gifted girls were found between the experimental and control groups for the posttest scores. The total mean score of the posttests for the experimental group was 169.00; the control group's mean score was 139.54. Differences between the total mean scores of the posttests for the experimental and control groups resulted in a *t*-test score of 5.47. There were statistical differences significant at the .05 level in five of the six subtests (i.e., anxiety, value of math in society, self-concept in math, enjoyment of math, and motivation in math) (see Table 2). The gifted girls' posttest scores did not significantly differ in their attitudes toward their math teacher. As regular classroom math lessons continued routinely throughout the duration of the intervention program, attitudes for the classroom teachers did not vary.

Although no statistical differences at the .05 level of significance were reported on the pretest scores for any of the six subtests, experimental group scores increased after participation in the intervention program. Based on the results of the statistical analysis of the posttest scores, it was concluded that the intervention program designed to improve the math attitudes of the gifted females from that isolated rural area made a significant difference in the 24 gifted girls' math attitudes as measured by the MAI (Sandman, 1980).

CONCLUSION

Armstrong (1979) and Boswell and Katz (1980)

have reported that sex differences in mathematics achievement were not due to ability but some attitudinal factors. Kerr (1988) asserted that stereotypical expectations placed on girls relative to math involvement were the most influential factor affecting girls' choices to participate in math. According to Howley et al. (1988), gifted girls from rural areas are even less likely to participate in math because of traditional values of a rural community that may view involvement in math and math-related careers as a "masculine" trait.

The concern of some researchers (Fox & Tobin, 1988; Kerr, 1988; Shaffer, 1986) has focused on the loss of career potential and future happiness of gifted females who limit themselves in math due to internal barriers (via attitude). If these contentions are true, this study provides evidence that systematic intervention programming can positively influence the attitudes of gifted females toward math.

Further research needs to be conducted on populations in other isolated rural areas. It might be noted that a cursory glance at the raw data of this study revealed that large gains were obtained in the 4th and 5th grade. Further analysis in future studies should consider comparing the attitudes of larger groups of gifted girls by grade level to determine at which level intervention programs should be implemented for the most benefit.

A limitation of this study exists in the selection process. Location and the number of available gifted girls prevented the subjects from being randomly selected. The gains made by the experimental group are very likely due to the variety and extent of activities provided in the intervention program. Another factor that cannot be statistically supported by this study but had a possible effect on the findings, may be linked to the researcher as a female role model. Thus, further research is likewise recommended concerning

activities to reinforce skills from Unit 3 and concluded with the administration of the MAI as a posttest.

female role models' effect on gifted girls' math attitudes, particularly in rural settings.

If young gifted girls are to reach their potential mathematically, they must possess positive attitudes. The evidence from this study indicates that math attitudes of gifted females can be influenced. Thus, gifted females (even those from rural areas) can develop potential that will broaden career choices.

REFERENCES

Armstrong, J. M. (1979). *Achievement and participation of women in mathematics*. (Report No. NIE-G-7-0061). Denver, CO: Education Commission of the States. (ERIC Document Reproduction Service No. ED 184878)

Boswell, S. L., & Katz, P. A. (1980). *Nice girls don't study mathematics*. (Report No. NIE-G-78-0023). Boulder, CO: Institute for Research on Social Problems. (ERIC Document Reproduction Service No. ED 188888)

Downie, D., Slesnick, T., & Stenmark, J. (1981). *Math for girls and other problem solvers*. Berkeley, CA: Dale Seymour.

Fennema, E., & Sherman, J. (1977). Sex-related differences in mathematics achievement, spatial visualization and socio-cultural factors. *American Educational Research Journal, 14*, 51-71.

Fisher, L., & Medigovich, W. (1981). *Problem of the week*. Palo Alto, CA: Dale Seymour.

Flemming, E. S., & Hollinger, C. L. (1984). Internal barriers to the realization of potential: Correlates and interrelationships among gifted and talented female adolescents. *Gifted Child Quarterly, 28*, 135-140.

Fox, L. H. (1980). *The problem of women and mathematics*. New York: Library of Congress, Department of Cataloging in Publication Data. (ERIC Document Reproduction Service No. ED 211353)

Fox, L. H., & Tobin, D. (1988). Broadening career horizons for gifted girls. *The Gifted Child Today, 11*(1), 9-12.

Hope, J., Reys, B., & Reys, R. (1987). *Mental math in the middle grades*. Palo Alto, CA: Dale Seymour.

Howley, A. A., Pendarvis, E. E., & Howley, C. B. (1988). Gifted students in rural environments: Implication for school programs. *Rural Special Education Quarterly, 8*(4), 43-50.

Kerr, B. A. (1988). Raising career aspirations of gifted girls. *Vocational Guidance Quarterly, 32*(1), 37-43.

Roberts, D. R. (1982). *Just around the corner*. Little Rock: Arkansas Department of Education.

Sandman, R. S. (1980). *Mathematics Attitude Inventory*. Minneapolis: Minnesota Evaluation Center, University of Minnesota.

Shaffer, S. M. (1986). *Gifted girls: The disappearing act*. Washington, DC: Mid-Atlantic Center for Sex Equity. (ERIC Document Reproduction Service No. ED 301 994)

Southern, W. T., Spicker, H. H., & Davis, B. I. (1987). The rural gifted child. *Gifted Child Quarterly, 31*(4), 155-157.

We would like to thank John Enger of Arkansas State University for assistance with the statistical analysis and Beverly Shaklee of Kent State University for assistance with revisions.

Manuscript received December 1991; revision accepted April 1992.

Meeting the Needs of Gifted and Talented Preschoolers

Suzanne M. Foster

Suzanne M. Foster is a Doctoral Fellow in the Department of Elementary Education, Ball State University, Muncie, Indiana. She assists in the supervision of undergraduates who teach reading to local elementary school students.

Gifted preschool children are rarely served by special preschools for the gifted. There is a shortage of these kinds of programs in the United States. In 1982 there were only 18 such programs identified (Karnes & Johnson, 1991). If they are in preschool programs, gifted children may or may not be receiving enrichment. The current emphasis on inclusion makes it doubtful that preschool programs for the gifted will be publicly funded in the near future. Preschool teachers need to take responsibility for meeting the needs of this group, as well as the needs of other special needs children in their classroom. How can teachers help these children develop their potential? What kinds of things can be done in the regular preschool classroom?

Gifted preschoolers enjoy many of the same activities that non-gifted children enjoy but to a greater degree and in more depth and detail (Wolfe, 1989). If the preschool class is studying a unit on the human body, the teacher could go into more detail for the gifted children. This can be done through a learning center with models of the heart, brain and lungs. Many of the gifted and non-gifted children would love to see and touch the models. The gifted children would be able to understand the concepts in greater depth as their curiosity and thinking were stimulated. While these models would interest many of the children, they would also meet the needs of the gifted children.

Information Lovers

Many gifted preschoolers love to learn information. They are like sponges in their ability to absorb concepts and new ideas. Samantha, for example, loved dogs and focused for weeks on learning all about the different breeds. She loved to go to the grocery store and read the dog food labels and collect pictures of dogs. The teacher can provide enrichment by focusing on the special interests of children like Samantha and integrating these interests into the curriculum. Through books, field trips, the arts and resource people, a teacher can expand gifted children's knowledge and introduce them to new ways of thinking about a subject they are interested in.

For example, gifted children who are interested in bees can be enriched by a unit on bees. The book corner could have books of various levels of difficulty on bees and related insects. The teacher could discuss wasps and help the children see the similarities and differences between bees and wasps. The teacher could stretch the children's knowledge through discussions, asking both higher and lower level questions. Materials such as empty wasp nests and honeycombs could be displayed on the science table. A beekeeper could be invited to the school to relate his/her experiences with the children. The gifted children would be fascinated by all the details as the other children benefited as well.

Many gifted preschoolers are very verbal; they easily absorb new vocabulary and are often interested in learning to read. Many show a fascination with books and some gifted

Reprinted from *Children Today,* Vol. 22, No. 3, 1993, pp. 28-30.

199

children teach themselves to read before they enter kindergarten. Activities that introduce advanced vocabulary would be an excellent source of enrichment for gifted preschoolers. A unit on the oceans could be expanded for the gifted children by showing all the children a video of coral reefs. The gifted children would enjoy learning the names of the animals that live in the reefs—names like banner fish, anemones and clown fish. The teacher could print word cards with the names of the animals that live in the reef so the gifted children could use them to make sentences and stories.

The Need For Play

Play is one of the best ways for children to learn. According to Johnson, Christie and Yawkey (1987) children need at least a 30- to 50-minute block of uninterrupted time during their free play period to enact an episode in dramatic or consecutive play. It takes time for them to organize themselves and their materials and work out their ideas. Gifted preschoolers especially need these longer time blocks because they often are able to create extensive sociodramatic play episodes and build complicated block structures. They may get so involved in their play that they are reluctant to stop and move on to something else. They need to play with their intellectual peers to experience the joys of playing with someone who can understand them and help create these dramatic play episodes.

For example, five-year-old Jane often played at home with Megan, a non-gifted friend. Megan was not as advanced in her dramatic play as Jane was and would play the same role again and again with little imagination or variation. Jane would try to involve Megan in more complicated roles but would give up and go off to read a book by herself when Jane didn't respond. When Jane played with Beth, her gifted peer, the dramatic play would last for hours, with both children playing joyfully. Dramatic play can be especially

enriching for gifted preschoolers who have the imaginations and concepts to carry out elaborate play episodes.

Thematic Units

Thematic units in science and social studies are an excellent way to meet gifted children's intellectual needs. The units, along with appropriate field trips, can provide much of the enrichment a gifted preschooler needs. The block and dramatic play areas, art, music and literacy centers can all be coordinated around the theme. Some possible themes are:
- Pioneers
- The Ocean
- Dinosaurs
- Space
- Animals and Habitats.

Depending on the children's interest levels, the thematic unit can be as much as a month long. The unit should allow for more detail for the gifted preschoolers. For example, if the class is studying space exploration, props such as pieces of dryer hose for breathing equipment, space helmets, walkie talkies, a refrigerator box for a space ship and food in plastic bags could be put in the dramatic play center. The gifted children in the center will probably be organizing the play and helping the others create more complicated story lines. If the children are absorbed in their dramatic play, extending the play time will benefit all the children while meeting the needs of the gifted children.

Reading the children such books as *The Magic School Bus Lost in the Solar System,* and then inviting all of them to dictate individual stories using this theme to make their own books is a way to extend this theme. Later, the teacher could read to the gifted children more of the details in this book, which has two levels. This activity suits the needs of the gifted child, who may dictate more elaborate stories and spend more time illustrating them.

A field trip to a planetarium would fascinate most children while it enriches the gifted preschoolers, who

would love learning the names of the stars and constellations. A visit from an aerospace engineer or an astronomer who could share how their occupations related to space would be another way to provide enrichment.

Activities For Gifted Preschoolers

There are many other activities teachers or parents can do with gifted preschoolers. Examples of these are:
- reading higher level books to the children. Gifted 4-year-olds might enjoy listening to such books as *The Trumpet of the Swan* by E.B. White. They often enjoy paging through books about science and nature. The book corner should have books reflecting different interests and reading levels.
- teaching the children to use computers. Some programs such as *Dinosaurs and Facemaker* are enjoyed by gifted young children (Alvino, 1988).
- introducing them to music appreciation by letting them listen to Vivaldi, Bach and Raffi.
- introducing them to art appreciation by teaching them about great artists and different art styles, taking them to the art gallery, and reading them picture books with high quality illustrations such as *Animalia* by Graeme Base.
- providing a variety of manipulative materials—such as parquetry blocks, peg boards and Jumbo Cuisenaire Rods—to encourage math development (Alvino, 1989).
- teaching critical thinking skills and problem solving by introducing them to simple logic puzzles and mazes.
- providing art activities rather than crafts. A craft activity can intimidate gifted children, who are perfectionists and become frustrated when their project doesn't look like the model.

Ideas From Parents

Parents of gifted preschoolers are an ideal source of ideas. Here is a list of activities collected from parents of gifted preschoolers:

- Teach them to play card games of all kinds, e.g. War, Slap Jack, checkers, *Monopoly, Chutes and Ladders* and chess. They learn to read words and numbers, count and reason from these activities.
- Immerse them in literature by having books in every room to encourage their desire to learn to read.
- Leave writing and drawing materials out at all times for them to use, and have a special drawer of "junk" materials that can be used to create projects.
- Let them be chemists: Give them your old spices, vinegar and baking soda and let them see what happens.
- Make a list with them of all the materials they would need if they were buying a pet; figure the costs with them and take them comparison shopping.

- Give them coupons and let them choose items they would like to buy.
- Let them plan a party of their choice, designing the invitations, making the guest list and arranging for the activities and refreshments. Then hold the party.

Conclusions

Gifted preschoolers provide a special challenge to teachers and parents alike. Child care specialists, childhood development workers and educators need to remember that although gifted preschoolers may think like 8-year-olds, they are still preschoolers. The key to enriching gifted preschoolers lies in knowing their interests and offering activities and materials to expand these interests. Gifted preschool children can test the patience of both parents and teachers. Interesting and challenging activities at home and in preschool will help channel their energy and intellectual curiosity in positive ways. It is the job of parents and teachers to see to it that these children receive appropriate educational experiences so that boredom and underachievement don't occur (Koopmans-Dayton and Feldhusen, 1987).

References

Alvino, J. (1989). *Parents' Guide to Raising a Gifted Toddler.* Boston: Little, Brown and Company.

Base, G. (1986). *Animalia.* New York: Harry N. Abrams, Inc.

Cole, J. (1991). *The Magic School Bus Lost in the Solar System.* New York: Scholastic.

Karnes, M.B. and Johnson, L.J. (1991). The Preschool/Primary Gifted Child. *Journal for the Education of the Gifted,* 14(3), 267-283.

Koopmans-Dayton, J.D. and Feldhusen, J.F. (1987). A Resource Guide for Parents of Gifted Preschoolers. *Gifted Child Today,* 10(6), 2-7.

White, E.B. (1970). *The Trumpet of the Swan.* New York: Harper & Row.

Wolfe, J. (1989). The Gifted Preschooler: Developmentally Different but Still 3 or 4 Years Old. *Young Children,* 44(3), 41-48.

Early Childhood Exceptionality

Public Law 94-142, The Individuals with Disabilities Education Act, was amended by PL 99-457 in 1986. PL 99-457 is a federal mandate calling for early childhood special education for infants and preschoolers with disabilities. The infants and preschoolers need only to be at-risk for developmental disabilities according to standardized measurements. They do not yet have to be diagnosed as having a specific condition of exceptionality (e.g., mental retardation, visual impairment). "At-risk" can be determined by birth difficulties such as low birth weight, prematurity, small-for-gestational age status, or apnea in the neonatal period. It can also be determined by delays in motor development, cognitive development, language development, self-help skills, play skills, and personal-social skills in infancy and early childhood. Child Find is the agency responsible for identifying infants and toddlers at-risk of disabilities and for determining their eligibility for special educational services.

The assessment of young children eligible for early intervention is difficult. It is usually multidisciplinary, comprehensive, and prolonged. As much as possible, the assessment is conducted at the home of the child in a nonthreatening manner. Appropriate diagnostic instruments and procedures are supplemented with direct observations of behavior. Each child is assessed more than once by each member of the multidisciplinary team to ensure that opinions are not based on a good day or a bad day. As much as possible, parents and other significant caregivers are interviewed and included in the assessment procedures. These careful measures do not always guarantee that every at-risk child will be correctly included in or excluded from early intervention programs.

The causes of early childhood exceptionality are often linked to prenatal or neonatal factors: maternal gestational infections, drug use, alcohol use, malnutrition, radiation exposure, or stress; premature birth, low birth weight, birth injuries, or neonatal respiratory distress and anoxia. Current guesstimates are that one-half of all early childhood disabilities are preventable with improved prenatal and neonatal care. While cause and effect cannot be proved, there are positive correlations between early childhood exceptional conditions and environmental fac-

tors such as inadequate nutrition, inadequate health care, child abuse, mental illness of primary caregiver(s), drug abuse by primary caregiver(s), very young or older (over 35) mothers, and economic poverty.

When an infant or toddler is accepted into an early childhood intervention program, an individualized family service plan (IFSP) is developed. According to PL 99-457, IFSPs must include planned services for both the exceptional child and his or her family. The family participates in its development, reviews it every six months, and helps to evaluate progress and update its goals every year. Services to the child may include educational remediation for problems with language, motor skills, cognitive skills, personal-social skills, play skills, and self-help skills, singly or in any combinations.

Services for the family may include teaching them to help their child use special equipment (e.g., hearing aids, braces), teaching behavioral management, teaching about nutritional needs, health needs and normal child development, helping them explain the exceptional child's disability to siblings, neighbors, friends, and other significant persons, and helping them deal with their fears, anger, guilt, and anxiety about their child's disability. The IFSP always names a case manager from the profession most closely related to the child's exceptional condition. The case manager supervises the special services to ensure compliance with PL 99-457's mandate for cooperation among child, parents, and professionals.

Early childhood special education programs may be home-based, center-based, or combined home-center programs. Home-based or combined home-center programs make it easier to involve parent(s) or primary caregivers in all of the recommended special educational services. Home care is usually more natural, less expensive, and more time intensive than center care. However, home care may not be possible if parents must work outside the home, if parents do not want to help provide special services, or if the child's remediation requires peers or support personnel or services that cannot be brought to the home.

Center-based early childhood intervention makes it easier to provide experts in several disciplines for all the recommended special educational services. Center care introduces children to peers and introduces parents to other parents sharing similar concerns. It is also easier to evaluate progress, ensure quality child care, and reassess IFSPs when the child can be observed on a daily basis. However, center care can be expensive, involve long-distance transportation, and leave parents feeling unwanted or unneeded.

The benefits from early intervention, whether home-based, center-based, or combined home-center programs, are legion. The central nervous system has more plasticity (ability to change) in infancy and early childhood. While early intervention may not cure the disability, it can often reduce its impact on later growth and development. Problems that are often secondary to the exceptional condition can be prevented or at least alleviated. Parents become more involved with their children with disabilities. They learn better ways of coping with the stresses produced by the child's problems and adapt more readily to the life changes that inevitably occur.

The first article selected for this unit is a position paper of the Association for Childhood Education International. It affirms the mandates of PL 99-457. It addresses the issues of access to early intervention, quality assurance, and preparation of personnel to provide special services to infants and toddlers. The second article discusses the practice of enrolling young children with disabilities in inclusive preschools with nondisabled peers. What attitude barriers exist? What strategies can address them? The third article defines what kinds of assistive technology (such as computer software) might be appropriate for early childhood special educational programming. The final selection discusses the advantages of toy libraries for infants and toddlers with exceptionalities. Toy libraries can help implement the special services of home-based, center-based, and home-center programs.

Looking Ahead: Challenge Questions

More people are becoming aware of the need to provide greater support for infants and toddlers with disabilities and their families. What constitutes quality care?

What staff-development activities can change teacher attitudes, classroom practices, and child outcomes when children with disabilities are enrolled in inclusive preschools?

Can assistive technology be beneficial to infants and toddlers with disabilities?

How important is play in early childhood intervention? Will a toy library help assure that infants and toddlers with disabilities engage in play?

Infants and Toddlers with Special Needs and Their Families

A Position Paper of the Association for Childhood Education International by David Sexton, Patricia Snyder, William R. Sharpton and Sarintha Stricklin

David Sexton is Professor and Chair and William R. Sharpton is Associate Professor, Department of Special Education and Habilitative Services, University of New Orleans, Louisiana. Patricia Snyder is Assistant Professor, Department of Occupational Therapy, Louisiana State University Medical Center, New Orleans. Sarintha Stricklin is Instructor, Human Development Center, LSU Medical Center.

Several recent trends reflect increased interest in developing and providing services for infants and toddlers with special needs and their families. First, evidence is mounting that indicates early intervention is valuable for diverse groups of very young children who exhibit a variety of special needs and for their families (Guralnick, 1991). Second, legal safeguards were established for the rights of individuals with disabilities, which have important implications for service-providing agencies and individuals. Third, there is much discussion about lowering the age for entering public schools (Gallagher, 1989). Fourth, more people are becoming aware of the need to provide greater

support for child and family care (Kelley & Surbeck, 1990; Shuster, Finn-Stevenson & Ward, 1992).

Finally, a consensus is emerging that the functions of early intervention, child care and early childhood education (birth through age 8) are inextricably bound together; that "quality" or "best practices" cannot be achieved without systematically addressing the interrelationships among all three fields (Kagan, 1988, 1989; Mitchell, 1989; Salisbury, 1991; Sexton, 1990). In fact, Burton, Hains, Hanline, McLean and McCormick (1992) suggest that if quality early intervention, child care and early childhood education services are ever to become a reality, then it will be necessary to formally unify the three historically distinct fields.

Recognizing the widespread concern for infants and toddlers, including those with special needs and their families, the Association for Childhood Education International (ACEI) addresses three related issues in this position paper: 1) access to services, 2) quality assurance and 3) preparation of personnel. The final section offers some major conclusions and recommendations related to infants and toddlers with special needs and their families.

From *Childhood Education*, Annual Theme Issue, 1993, pp. 278-286. © 1993 by the Association for Childhood Education International. Reprinted by permission of the authors and the Association for Childhood Education International, 11501 Georgia Avenue, Suite 315, Wheaton, MD.

ACCESS TO SERVICES

ACEI reaffirms its belief that all young children and their families have a fundamental right to quality care, education and special intervention.

ACEI leads the way in advocating for the right of all children and their families to quality care and education. For example, ACEI/Gotts issued a position paper on this fundamental right in 1988. Although children with special needs and their families are not explicitly addressed, the paper clearly argues for complete, open access to care and education as one of the most fundamental rights of all young children, including infants and toddlers.

Many other professional organizations support ACEI in its position on open access to services. In its guidelines for developmentally appropriate practices, the National Association for the Education of Young Children (NAEYC) unequivocally takes the position that all young children deserve access to a quality program (Bredekamp, 1987). The Division for Early Childhood (DEC) of the Council for Exceptional Children (CEC) issued a position paper supporting the right of young children with disabilities to education and care in settings with typically developing children (McLean & Odom, 1988). The Association for Persons with Severe Handicaps (TASH) adopted the position in 1988 that people with disabilities must have opportunities to achieve full integration into society (Meyer, Peck & Brown, 1991).

ACEI also recognizes the need for comprehensive and ongoing screening, monitoring and assessment services for all infants and toddlers and their families. The goal of such services must be to facilitate early identification of children's special needs and ensure provision of appropriate interventions. Early identification activities should be an integral part of a comprehensive early childhood system, birth through age 8, and needed interventions should be embedded within typical child care, education, home and health routines.

Further, ACEI recognizes and supports the legal right of children with special needs and their families to regular child care and education services. The 1991 amendments (P.L. 102-119) to Part H of the Individuals with Disabilities Education Act (IDEA) (P.L. 101-476) require early intervention services to be provided in regular settings with typically developing children, as appropriate for each child. The term "natural environments" is used to refer to regular settings for typically developing age peers.

In 1990, the Americans with Disabilities Act (ADA) was signed into law. The ADA rules went into effect January 26, 1992. All public accommodations are now prohibited from discriminating against individuals because of a disability. Under Title III of the Act, the law specifically includes nursery schools, child care centers and family child care homes in the definition of "public accommodation" (Rab, Wood & Stanga, 1992; Surr, 1992).

ACEI recognizes that increasingly diverse populations of infants and toddlers represent great challenges to child care and education systems and affirms the need for immediate action to support these systems.

The population of infants and toddlers entering or seeking entry into child care and education systems is changing to include special needs and at-risk children. Service providers and decision-makers must respond to these changes if children and families are to reach their full learning and developmental potential (Stevens & Price, 1992). "Special needs" and "at-risk" are popular terms used to describe an extremely heterogeneous population (Hrncir & Eisenhart, 1991). Care must be taken to consider the extreme diversity within a particular special needs or at-risk subgroup. For example, the popular media image of "crack babies," as Griffith (1992) notes, is that they are all severely affected and little can be done for them. In fact, the effects vary dramatically from infant to infant and are moderated or exacerbated considerably by other factors.

The special needs population requires particular attention not only because of its diversity, but also because of the large numbers needing services. As the following statistics illustrate, we clearly need to take immediate action.

- Each year, some 425,000 infants are born who will manifest a disability within the first four years of life (Garwood, Fewell & Neisworth, 1988). At the end of 1990, only approximately 600,000 children with special needs, birth through 5, were receiving intervention services (Hebbeler, Smith & Black, 1991).
- Some 350,000 to 375,000 newborns each year have been exposed prenatally to drugs, including alcohol (Pinkerton, 1991; Stevens & Price, 1992). Fetal alcohol syndrome (FAS) is now recognized as the leading known cause of mental retardation in the Western world. Conservative estimates indicate that approximately one in 500 to 600 children in the U. S. are born with FAS and one in 300 to 350 are born with fetal alcohol effects (FAE) (Burgess & Streissguth, 1992; see also, Cohen and Taharally, 1992).
- Each year, 412,000 infants are born prematurely (Bartel & Thurman, 1992).
- An estimated 16 percent of all American children (3 to 4 million children) have blood lead levels in the neurotoxic range (Neddleman, 1992).

■ Human immunodeficiency virus (HIV) has become the greatest infectious cause of pediatric mental retardation in the U. S. In October of 1992, the Centers for Disease Control (CDC) reported 3,426 cases of acquired immunodeficiency syndrome (AIDS) among children under the age of 13 and estimated that several times as many children are infected with HIV (Seidel, 1992).

■ An estimated 3,000,000 to 4,000,000 Americans are homeless (Eddowes & Hranitz, 1989; Heflin, 1991). The number of children in the U. S. who are homeless on any given night range from 68,000 to 500,000 (Linehan, 1992).

Much recent rhetoric by politicians and policymakers centers on ensuring that all children are ready to enter school (e.g., *America 2000*). In a recent survey of U.S. state expenditures, however, half of the states spend less than $25 per child on the care and education of young children and one-third of the states spend less than $17 per child (Adams & Sandfort, 1992). Feeg (1990) reminds us that the U. S. is ranked 18th among industrialized nations in infant mortality and compares poorly in protecting and immunizing well children.

These facts clearly indicate the need for immediate action at national, state and local levels to ensure that additional dollars are made available to support child care, education and health systems in providing high quality, comprehensive services for all children. Such support is critical as these systems begin to upgrade early care and education services for more traditional populations, while simultaneously providing quality services for less familiar, special needs populations.

ACEI affirms the position that child care and education reform movements must be inclusive, addressing the needs of infants and toddlers with special needs and their families within the broader context of society.

Recently, movements to "restructure" or "reform" the education and child care systems have gained much momentum. One such movement is *America 2000* (U. S. Department of Education, 1991), a set of six national education goals developed by President Bush and the nation's governors. The first goal is of particular relevance to infants and toddlers with special needs and their families: "By the year 2000, all children in America will start school ready to learn." While this goal, widely touted as the cornerstone of *America 2000*, clearly focuses attention on the importance of learning during the early years, significant inherent problems remain.

First, children with special needs or disabilities are not specifically mentioned in this or any of the other goals. It is imperative that national programs value and include the needs of *all* children. The second problem is defining "readiness" according to an expected level of skills and abilities children should possess prior to school entry. Such an approach serves a gatekeeping function of keeping some children out and ignores the central question of how "ready" the education system is for the child (Kelley & Surbeck, 1991; Willer & Bredekamp, 1990). Gatekeeping to exclude children with special needs and their families from the mainstream, whether implemented consciously or unconsciously, is nothing new and is certainly not even remotely related to "restructuring" or "reform." As Bowman (1992) notes:

What is a special-needs child? The usual answer is a child with a disability that prevents him or her from functioning effectively. But is the disability always in the child? I suggest that in most instances, the disability is not in the child, but in the misfit between the child and the environment. (p. 106)

ACEI receives support for this position from DEC which issued a position statement on the first goal of *America 2000*, and from NAEYC, which endorsed the DEC statement (Holder-Brown & Parette, 1992).

ACEI strongly supports refocusing the reform and restructuring movements to recognize that school success is dependent upon families receiving the comprehensive health, education and social services they need in order to support children's development and learning, beginning with prenatal care. Willer and Bredekamp (1990) and Kelley and Surbeck (1991) argue for a restructured early childhood care and education system that extends well before and beyond the school and classroom to encompass health and human services.

An important step in this direction is the new Family Leave Law, which combines parental leave with disability insurance so that all families at all economic levels can afford to take time off to care for their children (Bond, Galinsky, Lord, Staines & Brown, 1991). New resources must be invested and current ones redirected to ensure that restructuring and reform efforts focus on making the system "ready" to respond to the needs of all children and their families.

QUALITY ASSURANCE

Quality assurance must not be overlooked when attending to the crisis in child care, health care and early childhood education (Daniel, 1990; Kagan, 1988; Willer, 1987). Quality assurance issues for infants and toddlers with special needs and their families must be addressed within the context of ensuring that *all* young children benefit from developmentally appropriate practices. An integrated service system should be designed to support, and not supplant, the role of families.

All young children and their families have a right to expect that child care, health care, and education and intervention systems are designed to enhance and promote their well-being. To ensure that quality services are delivered, some definable, measurable quality indices must be established, validated and adopted by health, child care, education and intervention systems. Such an outcome requires the collaboration of individuals representing multiple agencies and programs, both private and public, as well as consumers. These stakeholders must undertake systematic efforts toward evaluating and developing the context for collaboration, including:

- setting clear and manageable goals
- developing an operational structure that matches the goals
- developing mandates that are facilitative
- arranging for joint leadership
- pooling existing resources and identifying new ones
- establishing processes and policies that are clearly understood. (Kagan, 1991)

ACEI affirms that standards for quality infant and toddler programs must be validated and adopted for all young children, benefiting children, their families and all of society.

Several professional groups support ACEI (ACEI/Gotts, 1988) in advocating for quality assurance standards for child care and early childhood education programs, including NAEYC (Bredekamp, 1987) and the Alliance for Better Child Care (National Association for the Education of Young Children [NAEYC], 1987). Also, the Division for Early Childhood of the Council for Exceptional Children (DEC/CEC) recently published quality indicators for early intervention programs (Division for Early Childhood/CEC, 1993).

The care and education standards promulgated by the early childhood and early intervention communities are similar in philosophy and content. The similarities most likely result from the growing recognition that all children benefit from care environments that are safe, responsive, developmentally appropriate and competency-enhancing. Care environments that meet these and other identified standards should promote children's well-being and, from a transactional/ecological perspective, that of families and society (Bronfenbrenner, 1986; Hamburg, 1991).

A large consensus group comprised of parents, practitioners, policymakers, researchers and advocacy groups from all early childhood communities must collaborate to ensure that appropriate standards for all children are validated and adopted. The accreditation process developed by NAEYC (1986) is certainly a welcome step in this direction.

ACEI recognizes that government regulation through child care licensing is one of the primary policy mechanisms for establishing and overseeing quality care (Kagan, 1988; Phillips, Lande & Goldberg, 1990). The battle continues on a state-by-state basis to establish licensing standards, with many states seeing an erosion in established standards due to nonenforcement or exemption (Lindner, 1986; Willer, 1987). There is no denying that quality early childhood programs require time and money, as well as commitment and broad-based support. Resources must be available to develop and maintain high quality programs that meet the needs of children, parents and staff.

ACEI affirms the position that quality child care and education systems must promote full inclusion.

The most important indicators that must be present in early childhood quality assurance standards include those that address program policies, structures and practices supporting full inclusion of special needs children in settings designed for their age peers without disabilities (Demchak & Drinkwater, 1992; Hanline & Hanson, 1989; Salisbury, 1991). As Campbell (1991) notes, "More than any area of special education, the benefits of noncategorical programming where young children with disabilities are educated with those with typical development have been empirically supported"(p. 473).

Inclusion benefits both children and families. For example, children with and without disabilities benefit developmentally and socially from interaction in a child care environment that individualizes care and promotes ongoing regular contact among children (Demchak & Drinkwater, 1992; Odom & McEvoy, 1988). Families whose children experience inclusion frequently cite the development of empathy, respect for differences and respect for individuals as important outcomes for both themselves and their children.

Campbell (1991) makes the compelling argument that, beyond the cited benefits of inclusion, the real issue is whether we can justify removing children from the normal life experiences to which they are entitled by virtue of being young children. ACEI shares this view, affirming that infants and toddlers with special needs and their families should not be excluded from such experiences or from systems designed to serve all children and families. Developing one quality inclusive system of care, education and intervention can result in improved services for all children and families.

ACEI affirms the position that quality child care, health care and education systems must be integrated and that individualized, or personalized, care and education must be provided all infants and toddlers and their families.

The unique characteristics of all infants and toddlers must be considered in developing quality care, education and intervention programs. As a group, infants and toddlers with special needs are extremely heterogeneous. Individualized care, education and intervention must be provided to capitalize on the unique characteristics of each child and family. In fact, provisions of Part H of IDEA require that intervention for infants and toddlers having known or suspected disabilities include an Individualized Family Service Plan (IFSP) that systematically focuses on the individual family's priorities, resources and concerns (Sexton, 1990).

Kelley and Surbeck (1990) note that individualization, or "personalization," of care is also essential for typically developing infants, toddlers and their families. No accepted, single standard exists regarding the nature of services provided young children prior to school entry. ACEI endorses the principle that services for infants and toddlers with special needs should be designed according to the same standards as those for all other infants and toddlers. Programs adhering to such standards will provide care and education that are individualized, family-directed and culturally normative.

ACEI affirms the position that quality child care and education systems must embed needed interventions for infants and toddlers with special needs within the natural routines, schedules and activities of child care and home settings.

Quality child care and education systems must develop and utilize environments that promote active engagement of children with peers, adults and materials (McWilliam & Bailey, 1992). The learning environment should not be structured by strict schedules or insistence that children remain seated and quiet. Space, equipment, people and materials should be arranged instead to free children to move, choose and busy themselves. As Olds (1979) notes, "For all its manifestations, the environment is the curriculum" (p. 91). The true curriculum for infants and toddlers is everything they experience during the day (Bredekamp, 1987; Hignett, 1988).

Programs serving infants and toddlers with special needs should embed needed interventions within the natural routine or schedule of the child's day (Sexton, 1990). Needed special therapies (e.g., occupational, physical, speech, etc.) should be integrated within caregiving routines. Busenbark and Ward (1992) argue for integrated therapy that:

- lends itself to the inclusion and active involvement of nondisabled peers

Table 1: Core Competencies for Personnel Preparation

- Organize learning environments that are safe, healthy and stimulating.
- Promote all children's physical, intellectual, social, adaptive and communicative competence.
- Select curriculum and teaching/intervention strategies that: a) are developmentally appropriate, b) address all areas of development, c) are responsive to a wide variety of individual needs and d) are based on normal routines.
- Facilitate the success of children in all learning situations.
- Collaborate with families in all aspects of care, education and intervention.
- Ensure that all practices are respectful of and sensitive to cultural diversity.
- Integrate academic and practical experience via field experiences such as practicum, student teaching/internship and technical assistance/support at the job site.
- Maintain a commitment to professionalism via interdisciplinary and interagency teaming, continuing education, and systems change through individual and group advocacy.

- is delivered in the child's natural environment
- affords opportunities for modeling intervention strategies for staff and families during caregiving routines
- promotes focusing on child and family goals that are realistic, appropriate, functional and meaningful
- improves the child's social interaction skills
- builds a strong collaborative partnership among therapist, program staff and parents.

PREPARATION OF PERSONNEL

All disciplines concerned with infants and toddlers and their families agree that overall program quality or developmental appropriateness is determined directly by the knowledge and skills of the individuals caring for and serving this population (Bredekamp, 1987, 1992; Granger, 1989; Klein & Campbell, 1990; Kontos, 1992; Sexton, 1990). Available data indicate, however, enormous personnel problems that demand immediate attention. Granger (1989) reports that the annual personnel turnover rate in child care and early childhood programs not located in public schools is as high as 40 percent. Kontos (1992) also estimates that the annual turnover rate among child care providers is approximately 40 percent. The results of several national surveys (Bailey, Simeonsson, Yoder & Huntington, 1990; Meisels, Harbin, Modigliani & Olson, 1988; U. S. Department of Education, 1990) and state surveys (Hanson & Lovett, 1992; McCollum & Bailey, 1991; Sexton & Snyder, 1991) clearly note that:

- there are critical shortages of early intervention personnel across disciplines
- these critical shortages are predicted to continue, or even worsen, in the future
- there is a dearth of training content at both undergraduate and graduate levels related to working with infants and toddlers who have special needs and their families.

How adequately these and related personnel preparation issues are addressed will determine the future of our youngest children and the education profession (Bredekamp, 1992). A personnel system must be developed that addresses both preservice and inservice education needs.

ACEI promotes collaboration among the fields of early childhood education, child care, early intervention and supporting disciplines in the design and delivery of personnel training.

One key issue in personnel preparation is whether preservice and inservice training programs for early interventionists should be developed and delivered in isolation or in collaboration with general early childhood and care programs. Miller (1992) argues convincingly against educating personnel to work with either "regular" or "special needs" young children. Concerns over segregated personnel preparation programs have resulted in collaborative efforts among numerous professional groups, such as NAEYC, Association for Teacher Educators (ATE) and DEC, to achieve consensus on personnel preparation issues (Bredekamp, 1992).

ACEI endorses such efforts as absolutely necessary and, in addition, advocates inclusion of related professional groups (e.g., American Occupational Therapy Association and American Speech and Hearing Association) in future efforts. Joint collaboration has the potential to help ensure that full inclusion of infants and toddlers with special needs and their families becomes a reality.

An integrated personnel preparation system is imperative for numerous reasons. First, Part H of IDEA mandates that infants and toddlers with special needs be cared for and served in natural environments available to their typically developing age peers. Therefore, personnel in education and care settings will increasingly educate and care for infants and toddlers with special needs within these more natural and normalized environments. Early interventionists will spend much more of their time providing technical assistance to education and care personnel, collaborating with them on transition and inclusion issues.

IDEA, Part H, also requires that specific early intervention services must be delivered by interdisciplinary teams. Collaboration and joint training must occur across related disciplines such as occupational and physical therapy, audiology, speech and language therapy, social work and psychology. An integrated and collaborative preservice and inservice training system is an efficient, effective mechanism to address shared and related competencies.

Second, a consensus is growing among historically distinct fields that, if quality child care, education and intervention are to be provided all infants, toddlers and their families, an interdisciplinary approach to personnel preparation must build on "core" competencies identified by different professional groups (Burton et al., 1992; Demchak & Drinkwater, 1992; Miller, 1992; NAEYC, 1988). These core competencies should serve as a basis for developing an integrated personnel system. For example, personnel competency domains (Table 1) have been identified by the Council for Early Childhood Professional Recognition in its Child Development Associate (CDA) requirements for infant and toddler caregivers (Council for Early Childhood Professional Recognition, 1992); NAEYC, in its developmentally appropriate practice guidelines (Bredekamp, 1987); and DEC, in its recommendations for certification of early childhood special educators (McCollum, McLean, McCartan & Kaiser, 1989).

There is also growing recognition across fields that inservice or outreach training must receive priority within any personnel preparation system (Bruder & Nikitas, 1992; Granger, 1989; Kontos, 1992; Miller, 1992). Bailey (1989) defines inservice education as the process by which practicing professionals participate in experiences designed to improve or change professional practice. Given the high turnover rates in all areas of child care, education and intervention and the paucity of preservice training programs, inservice or outreach training opportunities must be coordinated, interdisciplinary and immediate. Kontos (1992) presents convincing data that indicate inservice training and technical assistance result in improved child care, as well as a dramatically lower turnover rate for family care workers.

ACEI also recognizes the importance of including administrators in any personnel preparation system. Specific competencies related to integrated early care, education and intervention must be included in preservice and inservice leadership training programs. The extent to which education, care and intervention personnel employ integrated and collaborative practices is directly related to an administrator's ability to identify, nurture and reward such behaviors.

ACEI affirms the right of all infants, toddlers and family members to child care, education and intervention delivered by trained personnel who have appropriate certification and/or licenses and who are adequately and equitably compensated.

One important step in establishing any field as a profession is some means to assess each individual's work performance and to license or credential those deemed competent according to criteria developed by the profession (Radomski, 1986). National surveys across fields, however, clearly indicate the lack of a credentialing or certification system that recognizes and monitors an individual's competency in the education, intervention or care of very young children.

After completing a survey of child care regulations in the U.S., Phillips et al. (1990) concluded:

Among the most disturbing findings in the state-by-state analysis is the lack of attention given to specialized training for child care providers. It is the rare state that requires both pre- and in-service training of center- or home-based staff; many more states fail to require either form of training. (p. 175)

Data reported by NAEYC (1988) indicate that only 24 states and the District of Columbia certify early childhood teachers as distinct from elementary teachers. Only three states define early childhood to be birth through age 8, as does ACEI. Furthermore, in a national survey of personnel standards for Part H of IDEA, Bruder, Klosowski and Daguio (1991) found that few regulatory standards were specific to personnel providing services to infants and toddlers.

ACEI recognizes the importance of formal licensing or credentialing of early childhood educators, care providers and early interventionists for at least two reasons. First, and most important, studies have consistently found developmentally appropriate practices are best predicted by the combination of an individual's formal education and training in child development/early childhood education and his/her exposure to supervised practical experiences (Fischer & Eheart, 1991; Snider & Fu, 1990). Evidence indicates that these same factors also affect the quality of services provided by early interventionists (Kontos & File, 1992).

Second, a credentialing or certification system based on national standards of care, education and intervention for all infants and toddlers, but flexible enough to accommodate the unique needs of different states, could focus the efforts of historically distinct fields to join forces and empower personnel. As Bredekamp (1992) observes:

The most overwhelming barrier to all our work on behalf of children is always financial; we know that we must improve compensation to ensure that we attract and keep the best and brightest in our profession, but we have not figured out how to get the money. (p. 37)

Bellm, Breuning, Lombardi and Whitebook (1992) report that real earnings by child care teachers and family child care providers have actually decreased by nearly one-quarter since the mid-1970s. Historically, professionals have not organized around the issue of compensation, perhaps perpetuating the general perception that child care, education and intervention are basically unskilled labor and that anybody can "watch" children (Modigliani, 1988; Morin, 1989; Phillips et al., 1990). ACEI solicits the support and collaboration of other professional groups to help ensure an integrated system that recognizes and monitors the competencies of personnel via formal credentialing or certification and that equitably rewards individuals accordingly.

CONCLUSIONS

Recent efforts to develop a comprehensive system of intervention for infants and toddlers with special needs and their families have provided opportunities to examine service access and quality issues. The key question in formulating public policy, particularly under Part H of IDEA, is: Should we create or continue a segregated system for early intervention or should we focus on collaborative efforts to support and improve general child care and education systems? It is becoming clear that one inclusive child care and education system is needed. Moreover, a collaborative approach is required if needed special interventions are to be embedded within the system.

The building of such a system entails constructive attention to:

- ensuring access to services for all children
- developing and enforcing quality control assurance standards
- training personnel and administrators to meet the needs of an extremely diverse population in developmentally appropriate ways.

Such a system also requires public policies that provide resources to achieve the collaboration necessary to improve child care and education. Such policies benefit all infants and toddlers and their families, as well as society in general. Now is the time for individuals and groups representing historically distinct areas to join forces with families and decision-makers in creating the best possible system of services and care for our youngest children—our most vulnerable, yet most valuable, resources.

References

Adams, G., & Sandfort, J. R. (1992). State investments in child care and early childhood education. *Young Children, 47*(6), 33-35.

Association for Childhood Education International/E. E. Gotts. (1988). The right to quality child care. Position paper. *Childhood Education, 64*, 268-275.

Bailey, D. B. (1989). Issues and directions in preparing professionals to work with young handicapped children and their faimilies. In J. Gallagher, P. Trohanis, & R. Clifford (Eds.), *Policy implementation and P.L. 99-457: Planning for children with special needs* (pp. 97-132). Baltimore, MD: Paul H. Brookes.

Bailey, D. B., Simeonsson, R. J., Yoder, E. E., & Huntington, G. S. (1990). Preparing professionals to serve infants and toddlers with handicaps and their families: An integrative analysis across eight disciplines. *Exceptional Children, 57*(1), 26-35.

Bartel, N. R., & Thurman, S. K. (1992). Medical treatment and educational problems in children. *Phi Delta Kappan, 74*, 57-61.

Bellm, D., Breuning, G. S., Lombardi, J., & Whitebook, M. (1992). On the horizon: New policy initiatives to enhance child care staff compensation. *Young Children, 47*(5), 39-42.

Bond, J. T., Galinsky, E., Lord, M., Staines, G. L., & Brown, K. R. (1991). Beyond the parental leave debate: The impact of laws in four states. *Young Children, 47*(1), 39-42.

Bowman, B. T. (1992). Who is at risk and why. *Journal of Early Intervention, 16*, 101-108.

Bredekamp, S. (1987). *Developmentally appropriate practice in early childhood programs serving children from birth through age 8.* Washington, DC: National Association for the Education of Young Children.

Bredekamp, S. (1992). The early childhood profession coming together. *Young Children, 47*(6), 36-39.

Bronfenbrenner, U. (1986). Ecology of the family as a context for human development research perspectives. *Developmental Psychology, 22*, 723-742.

Bruder, M. B., Klosowski, S., & Daguio, C. (1991). A review of personnel standards for Part H of P.L. 99-457. *Journal of Early Intervention, 16*, 173-180.

Bruder, M. D., & Nikitas, T. (1992). Changing the professional practice of early interventionists: An inservice model to meet the service needs of Public Law 99-457. *Journal of Early Intervention, 16*, 173-180.

Burgess, D. M., & Streissguth, A. P. (1992). Fetal alcohol syndrome and fetal alcohol effects: Principles for educators. *Phi Delta Kappan, 74*, 24-30.

Burton, C. B., Hains, A. H., Hanline, M. F., McLean, M., & McCormick, K. (1992). Early childhood intervention and education: The urgency of professional unification. *Topics in Early Childhood Special Education, 11*(4), 53-69.

Busenbark, L., & Ward, G. (1992). Service delivery for preschool children with disabilities. *Early Childhood Report, 3*(9), 67.

Campbell, P. H. (1991). An essay on preschool integration. In L. H. Meyer, C. A. Peck, & L. Brown (Eds.), *Critical issues in the lives of people with severe disabilities* (pp. 473-477). Baltimore, MD: Paul H. Brookes.

Cohen, S., & Taharally, C. (1992). Getting Ready for Young Children with Prenatal Drug Exposure. *Childhood Education, 69*, 5-9.

Council for Early Childhood Professional Recognition. (1992). *The child development associate assessment system and competency standards: Infant/toddler caregivers in center-based programs.* Washington, DC: Author.

Daniel, J. (1990). Child care: An endangered industry. *Young Children, 43*(2), 27-32.

Demchak, M. A., & Drinkwater, S. (1992). Preschoolers with disabilities: The case against segregation. *Topics in Early Childhood Special Education, 11*(4), 70-83.

Division for Early Childhood/CEC. (1993). *DEC recommended practices: Indicators of quality in programs for infants and young children with special needs and their families.* Reston, VA: Author.

Eddowes, E. A., & Hranitz, J. R. (1989). Educating children of the homeless. *Childhood Education, 65*, 197-200.

Feeg, V. D. (1990). Health issues in a changing society. In E. Surbeck & M. F. Kelley (Eds.), *Personalizing care with infants, toddlers and families* (pp. 52-61). Wheaton, MD: Association for Childhood Education International.

Fischer, J. L., & Eheart, B. K. (1991). Family day care: A theoretical basis for improving quality. *Early Childhood Research Quarterly, 6*, 549-563.

Gallagher, J. J. (1989). The impact of policies for handicapped children on future early education policy. *Phi Delta Kappan, 71*, p. 121-124.

Garwood, S. G., Fewell, R. R., & Neisworth, J. T. (1988). Public Law 94-142: You can get there from here! *Topics in Early Childhood Special Education, 8*(1), 1-11.

Granger, R. C. (1989). The staffing crisis in early childhood education. *Phi Delta Kappan, 71*, 130-134.

Griffith, D. R. (1992). Prenatal exposure to cocaine and other drugs: Developmental and educational prognoses. *Phi Delta Kappan, 74*, 30-34.

Guralnick, M. J. (1991). The next decade of research on the effectiveness of early intervention. *Exceptional Children, 58*, 174-183.

Hamburg, S. K. (1991). The unfinished agenda must be met. *Young Children, 46*(4), 29-32.

Hanline, M. F., & Hanson, M. J. (1989). Integration considerations for infants and toddlers with multiple disabilities. *Journal of the Association for Persons with Severe Handicaps, 14*, 178-183.

Hanson, M. J., & Lovett, D. (1992). Personnel preparation for early interventionists: A cross-disciplinary survey. *Journal of Early Intervention, 16*, 123-135.

Hebbeler, K. M., Smith, B. J., & Black, T. L. (1991). Federal early childhood special education policy: A model for the improvement of services for children with disabilities. *Exceptional Children, 58*, 104-112.

Heflin, L. J. (1991). *Developing effective programs for special education students who are homeless*. Reston, VA: Clearinghouse on Handicapped and Gifted Children, Council for Exceptional Children.

Hignett, W. F. (1988). Infant/toddler care, yes: But we'd better make it good. *Young Children, 47*(6), 73-77.

Holder-Brown, L., & Parette, H. P., Jr. (1992). Children with disabilities who use assistive technology: Ethical considerations. *Young Children, 47*(6), 73-77.

Hrncir, E. J., & Eisenhart, C. (1991). Use with caution: The "at-risk" label. *Young Children, 46*(2), 23-27.

Kagan, S. L. (1988). Current reforms in early childhood education: Are we addressing the issues? *Young Children, 43*(2), 27-32.

Kagan, S. L. (1989). Early care and education: Beyond the schoolhouse doors. *Phi Delta Kappan, 71*, 107-112.

Kagan, S. L. (1991). *United we stand: Collaboration for child care and early education services*. New York: Teachers College Press.

Kelley, M. F., & Surbeck, E. (1990). Infant day care. In E. Surbeck & M. F. Kelley (Eds.), *Personalizing care with infants, toddlers and families* (pp. 62-70). Wheaton, MD: Association for Childhood Education International.

Kelley, M. F., & Surbeck, E. (1991). *Restructuring early childhood education*. Bloomington, IN: Phi Delta Kappa Educational Foundation.

Klein, H. K., & Campbell, P. (1990). Preparing personnel to serve at-risk and disabled infants, toddlers, and preschoolers. In S. J. Meisels & J. P. Shonkoff (Eds.), *Handbook of early childhood intervention* (pp. 679-699). New York: Cambridge.

Kontos, S. (1992). *Family day care: Out of the shadows and into the limelight*. Washington, DC: National Association for the Education of Young Children.

Kontos, S., & File, N. (1992). Conditions of employment, job satisfaction and job commitment among early intervention personnel. *Journal of Early Intervention, 16*, 155-165.

Lindner, E. W. (1986). Danger: Our national policy of child carelessness. *Young Children, 41*(3), 3-9.

Linehan, M. F. (1992). Children who are homeless: Educational strategies for school personnel. *Phi Delta Kappan, 74*, 61-66.

McCollum, J. A., & Bailey, D. B. (1991). Developing comprehensive personnel systems: Issues and alternatives. *Journal of Early Intervention, 15*, 57-65.

McCollum, J. A., McLean, M., McCartan, K., & Kaiser, C. (1989). Recommendations for certification of early childhood special educators. *Journal of Early Intervention, 13*, 195-211.

McLean, M., & Odom S. (1988). *Least restrictive environment and social interaction*. Reston, VA: Division for Early Childhood, Council for Exceptional Children.

McWilliam, R. A., & Bailey, D. B. (1992). Promoting engagement and mastery. In D. B. Bailey & M. Wolery (Eds.), *Teaching infants and preschoolers with disabilities* (2nd ed.) (pp. 229-255). New York: Macmillan.

Meisels, S. J., Harbin, G., Modigliani, K., & Olson, K. (1988). Formulating optimal state early childhood intervention policies. *Exceptional Children, 55*(2), 159-165.

Meyer, L. H., Peck, C. A., & Brown, L. (1991). *Critical issues in the lives of people with severe disabilities*. Baltimore, MD: Paul H. Brookes.

Miller, P. (1992). Segregated programs of teacher education in early childhood: Immoral and inefficient practice. *Topics in Early Childhood Special Education, 11*, 39-52.

Mitchell, A. (1989). Old baggage, new visions: Shaping policy for early childhood programs. *Phi Delta Kappan, 70*, 665-6723.

Modigliani, K. (1988). Twelve reasons for the low wages in child care. *Young Children, 43*(3), 14-15.

Morin, J. (1989). We can force a solution to the staffing crisis. *Young Children, 44*(6), 18-19.

National Association for the Education of Young Children. (1986). Accreditation: A new tool for early childhood programs. *Young Children, 41*(4), 31-32.

National Association for the Education of Young Children. (1987). Alliance for Better Child Care (ABC). *Young Children, 42*(4), 31-33.

National Association for the Education of Young Children. (1988). Early childhood teacher education. Traditions and trends: An executive summary of colloquium proceedings. *Young Children, 44*(1), 53-57.

Neddleman, H. L. (1992). Childhood exposure to lead: A common cause of school failure. *Phi Delta Kappan, 74*, 35-37.

Odom, S. L., & McEvoy, M. A. (1988). Integration of young children with handicaps and normally developing children. In S. L. Odom & M. B. Karnes (Eds.), *Early intervention for infants and children with handicaps: An empirical base* (pp. 241-268). Baltimore, MD: Paul H. Brookes.

Olds, A. R. (1979). Designing developmentally optimal classrooms for children with special needs. In S. J. Meisels (Ed.), *Special education and development: Perspectives on young children with special needs*. Baltimore, MD: University Park Press.

Phillips, D., Lande, J., & Goldberg, M. (1990). The state of child care regulation: A comparative analysis. *Early Childhood Research Quarterly, 5*, 151-179.

Pinkerton, D. (1991). Substance exposed infants and children. Reston, VA: Clearinghouse on Handicapped and Gifted Children, Council for Exceptional Children.

Rab, V. Y., Wood, K. I., & Stanga, J. (1992). Training child care providers on the impact of the ADA. *Early Childhood Report, 3*(8), 5-8.

Radomski, M. A. (1986). Professionalization of early childhood educators: How far have we progressed? *Young Children, 41*(5), 20-23.

Salisbury, C. L. (1991). Mainstreaming during the early childhood years. *Exceptional Children, 58*, 146-155.

Seidel, J. F. (1992). Children with HIV-related developmental difficulties. *Phi Delta Kappan, 74*, 38-40, 56.

Sexton, D. (1990). Quality integrated programs for infants and toddlers with special needs. In E. Surbeck & M. F. Kelley (Eds.), *Personalizing care with infants, toddlers and families* (pp. 41-50). Wheaton, MD: Association for Childhood Education International.

Sexton, D., & Snyder, P. (1991). *Louisiana personnel preparation consortium project for Part H*. New Orleans, LA: University of New Orleans.

Shuster, C. K., Finn-Stevenson, M., & Ward, P. (1992). Family day care support systems: An emerging infrastructure. *Young Children, 47*(5), 29-35.

Snider, M. H., & Fu, V. R. (1990). The effects of specialized education and job experience on early childhood teachers' knowledge of developmentally appropriate practice. *Early Childhood Research Quarterly, 5*, 68-78.

Stevens, L. J., & Price, M. (1992). Meeting the challenge of educating children at risk. *Phi Delta Kappan, 74*, 18-23.

Surr, J. (1992). Early childhood programs and the Americans with Disabilities Act (ADA). *Young Children, 47*(5), 18-21.

U. S. Department of Education. (1990). *Twelfth annual report to Congress on the implementation of the Education for Handicapped Act*. Washington, DC: Office of Special Education and Rehabilitative Services.

U. S. Department of Education. (1991). *America 2000: An education strategy*. Washington, DC: Author.

Willer, B. (1987). Current reforms in early childhood education: Are we addressing the issues? *Young Children, 42*(6), 41-43.

Willer, B., & Bredekamp, S. (1990). Redefining readiness: An essential requisite for educational reform. *Young Children, 45*(5), 22-24.

Preschool Mainstreaming: Attitude Barriers and Strategies for Addressing Them

"Imagine for a moment that you have a child who today is happy, healthy, attending his or her local school, and progressing normally. Reflect for a moment on where you would want the child to go to school should he or she be in a car accident and become unable to walk without assistance and unable to learn as quickly" (Forest, 1992).

Deborah F. Rose and Barbara J. Smith

Deborah F. Rose, M.S.W., is a research associate at Allegheny-Singer Research Institute, and Barbara J. Smith, Ph.D. is a research scientist at Allegheny-Singer and the executive director of the Division for Early Childhood of the Council for Exceptional Children.

This article is adapted from "Attitude Barriers and Strategies for Preschool Mainstreaming," a paper in the Policy and Practice in Early Childhood Special Education Series.

The regulations governing the Individuals with Disabilities Education Act (IDEA) require that children with disabilities be placed in the Least Restrictive Environment (LRE) in which the individual child will learn (1991, 34 CFR § 300.550). Placement decisions—made by public school placement teams consisting of school administrators, teachers, parents, related service personnel, or whoever is appropriate for an individual child—must determine (1) the "regular educational environment" where the child would be educated were she or he not identified and labeled as eligible for special education and related services, and (2) whether the special education and related services can be appropriately delivered in that setting. Additionally, decisions to educate children in settings other than the "regular educational environment" can occur only when "the nature and severity of the handicap is such that education in regular classes with the use of supplementary aides and services cannot be achieved satisfactorily" (1991, 34 CFR § 300.550).

School districts have exercised a variety of options in order to meet the LRE requirements of the IDEA. School districts that operate preschool programs for typically developing children have integrated children with disabilities into their public school classrooms. Districts that do not offer preschool services to typically developing children have collaborated with community-based preschool and child care programs to deliver special education and related services in natural preschool environments (Smith & Rose, 1991). Many districts, however, are encountering policy and attitudinal barriers to placing preschool children with disabilities in community programs. Each of the key players—members of the placement team, as well as teachers and administrators in community-based programs—holds a set of beliefs about where children with disabilities are best educated, the role of the family in the child's early education, and the quality of community-based programs.

Are attitudes a problem?

A recent national survey of special education program and policy officials; program directors of child care, Head Start, and special-education services; and parents collected information about the greatest barriers to preschool mainstreaming, including issues of education policy, attitudes, and curricula and methods.

Nearly 60% of the survey respondents cited attitudes as a barrier to preschool mainstreaming. Those identifying attitudinal barriers varied by position; for example, all responding parents, compared to fewer than one third of child care directors, believed that attitudes were a barrier to mainstreaming.

What are the attitude barriers and strategies?

The types of attitudes reported on the survey were categorized according to the following concerns: (a) turf, (b) teacher preparedness, (c) awareness, (d) "someone will lose," and (e) communication/collaboration/respect. Although numerous attitude barriers were cited, few solutions to those barriers were offered by the survey respondents. The strategies discussed here represent op-

From *Young Children,* Vol. 48, No. 4, May 1993, pp. 59-62. © 1993 by Deborah F. Rose and Barbara J. Smith, St. Peter's Child Development Center, Inc., 2500 Baldwick Road, Suite 15, Pittsburgh, PA 15205. Reprinted by permission.

tions suggested by survey respondents or case-study subjects and expert consultants to the project.

Turf issues

Barriers. History and tradition are the things of which turf issues are made. The pride that the special-education community feels in the provision of services to children with disabilities was evident in survey responses to the attitude question. Survey respondents reported that many special educators are "holding on to the segregated systems of educating children" because of these turf issues.

The location of the preschool program (school based versus community based) was another concern expressed by survey respondents. As more children with disabilities are placed in community-based preschools that are not under the direct purview of the public school system, special educators report concern about how "their" children are being educated. Special educators believe that they have been trained specifically to provide "the best" education experiences for children with disabilities. Survey respondents reported a loss of control over the very methods, techniques, and curricula that they were taught would be most effective when educating children with disabilities. Respondents also expressed concern about the receptivity of community-based programs to technical assistance from special educators. With the changing role of special education in some states, it is not surprising that turf issues are recognized as barriers to mainstreaming. Survey respondents also expressed concerns about job security.

Some respondents reported that they believe that more intensive services can be provided to children and families if the public and private education systems are kept separate.

Strategies. Placement teams should have representation from parents and community providers. Encouraging an airing of the values that are brought to the table by each team member affords the best opportunity to discuss turf barriers. Frequent, structured, ongoing discussions will allow a sharing of team members' expertise and the opportunity for all team members to become familiar with one another. The school and the team should establish a vision statement about preschool mainstreaming. If the public school administrator does not consider facilitating group discussions to be one of her personal strengths, someone who has expertise could be solicited to this end. Perhaps a nearby university or human-service provider could supply such expertise.

Some of the strategies listed here in other categories will also help to address turf issues.

Teacher preparedness issues

Barriers. Often public school personnel must meet different teacher certification requirements than Head Start or community-based preschool teachers. This difference in personnel requirements has contributed to public school personnel harboring some doubts about the expertise of community-based and Head Start teachers. Survey respondents reported concern about having children with disabilities placed in community-based preschool settings due to a lack of available resources and support personnel. Some respondents reported that parents may be reluctant to have their child placed outside the public school system due to a lack of teacher training related to the needs of children with disabilities.

Community-based providers expressed concerns about their own ability to educate children with disabilities, particularly those with severe disabilities or medically fragile children. Child care teachers reported that special educators lack basic child development knowledge that child care teachers believe they have.

Survey respondents reported that the curricula of some pre-K and kindergarten programs have an academic focus. This academic orientation can appear to preclude the placement of children with disabilities in those classrooms.

Strategies. Improved communication and training between and among the various service systems may effect change. Historically, regular-education teachers have been prepared for the inclusion of children with disabilities by being provided information about the disability characteristics of such children and legal requirements (Ayers & Meyer, 1992). This type of preservice training does nothing to provide the teacher with the tools needed to effectively teach children who do not learn typically. Most regular-education teachers have been informally adapting curricula and methods to fit the individual learning needs of typical children. Community service providers need to be supplied with the best information and technologies related to the learning needs of children who do not learn typically. They also should have available to them ongoing consultation from special-education personnel.

Special education has excelled at individualizing education for children with diverse learning needs. Additionally, special education has long recognized the role of the child as a social being—a precursor to productive adult social interactions (Ayers & Meyer, 1992). Early childhood special education has a "family focus" that can be shared as well, whereas the "regular" early childhood field has a strong background in child development to share.

Joint training can be used as a means of sharing each program's expertise. If the attitude barriers truly lie with different preservice training requirements, then providing the community-based program with the expertise of special-education personnel should decrease the teacher-preparedness barriers. Providing special-education personnel with training conducted by community-based personnel allows community-based providers to feel more valued, as well as offering special-education personnel the opportunity to gain some of the community-based providers' child-development expertise.

Including parents who wish to participate in the training will afford them the opportunity to see the public and private systems work cooperatively and to share their expertise. Providing an opportunity for parents not only to participate in the training but to provide training to the team on their areas of expertise can increase the parents' stake in the process.

Awareness issues

Barriers. Survey respondents reported that more information sharing is needed at all levels with respect to children with disabilities. A lack of understanding was reported related to specific disabilities, medical needs, early childhood programming and services, curricula and methods, and integration efforts. All of the survey groups except parents reported these concerns. The parents of typically developing children were not surveyed, but respondents reported that parents, in general, appear to be uninformed about research findings related to the benefits of integration for all children.

Strategies. A number of systems are already in place for the information-sharing activities that appear to be needed. Some states have their own technical-assistance systems, while the federal government funds Regional Resource Centers and the National Early Childhood Technical Assistance System (see Sources for further information). These technical-assistance networks have access to current research findings related to integration. Part of the mission of each of these technical-assistance networks is to provide awareness materials.

Visiting model programs that are already integrating children with disabilities provide teachers and parents with the opportunity to talk with their counterparts. Seeing a high-quality integrated preschool program in action may dispel a great number of fears. Arrange a roundtable discussion for all participants to discuss the successes and challenges of their program. Talk openly about the difficulties encountered when the program began and the ways that the host program handled the challenges; for example, recount your training needs and fiscal concerns. The host program has the unique perspective of having lived through the challenges and successes of integration and should prove a useful resource.

Communication/collaboration/respect issues

Barriers. Parents reported that the people making decisions about their children do not really know the issues because the decision makers do not have children with disabilities themselves. Public school personnel believe that community providers are not receptive to technical assistance from the special-education community.

Attitude barriers to communication, collaboration, and respect all seem to stem from the same source—misinformation about other people and programs. This lack of information sharing has been reported to occur at all levels (local, state, and federal). It is difficult to have respect for a program about which little is known and where no relationship with the provider exists.

"Public school officials at the [sic] state and local level do not make information available about preschool mainstreaming," stated one survey respondent. Similarly, respondents reported that information about specific programs such as Head Start or child care programs was not being effectively communicated.

Strategies. In the words of one survey respondent, "Special educators who begin collaborating with 'regular' early childhood teachers often talk about unexpected learning they experience—learning about typical behavior and developmentally appropriate approaches. The unanticipated 'lesson' is that children with special needs are *children* first

and values begin to shift." Administrators must make a commitment to providing teachers and related service personnel with the necessary time away from their classrooms to collaborate effectively with their counterparts. Providing common planning time during the school day will allow personnel to talk with one another (Ayers & Meyer, 1992).

As the literature on transdisciplinary teaming suggests, to collaborate effectively requires an amount of "role release" or skill trading among participants (McCollom & Hughes, 1988). When collaboration is truly encouraged, the participants can freely share their knowledge with others, knowing that, in return, they will gain knowledge from the other participants.

Some state departments of education have demonstrated a commitment to collaboration by defining their statewide integration philosophy and encouraging each local school district to adopt the state's philosophy. The New Mexico State Department of Education has issued a "full inclusion" statement that outlines their rationale and expressed commitment to the advancement of inclusionary schools.

"Someone will lose" issues

Barriers. Respondents expressed concern for the early educational experiences of children with disabilities as well as typically developing children in integrated placements. Some respondents reported that parents of both typically developing children and children with disabilities were concerned that integration could have a negative effect on the services their children receive.

—*Attitudes related to typically developing children.* Respondents expressed the concern that typically developing children in integrated preschool placements would not receive a quality preschool experience because the children with disabilities would require an inordinate amount of time and attention from the classroom teacher. Respondents also expressed the fear that the child with a disability would be too disruptive to the classroom and would pull

Early childhood special education has a "family focus" that can be shared, whereas the "regular" early childhood field has a strong background in child development to share.

resources from the typically developing children.

—*Attitudes related to children with disabilities.* Many survey respondents reported that public school personnel are reluctant to take advantage of community-based preschool placements because they fear a loss of control over the child's education— a revisiting of the turf issues discussed earlier. Specifically, the public school special-education personnel are concerned that they will not be able to adequately supervise the child's individual education program (IEP). Survey respondents reported that parents and public school personnel are reluctant to have children placed in regular-education classrooms because they fear that their child will not receive the specialized instruction or intensity of services that may be provided in specialized settings. One respondent expressed resistance to community-based preschool programs as follows: "public school programs are 'better' with certified teachers and greater resources." One survey respondent reported that "it is still a common belief among parents and educators that students with disabilities will be 'happier' and get better 'special' services in traditional special-education settings."

Strategies. Integration can only be considered successful if it is done in a thoughtful way with careful consideration of all of the supports that will ensure success. Indeed, the law requires that the necessary services and supports be provided (34 CFR § 300.550). Community-based teachers who believe that they lack the expertise and training to effectively teach children with disabilities must be provided with the necessary training and afforded the opportunity for frequent meetings with team members, including special-education personnel. Both community-based teachers and special-education personnel could benefit from visiting model preschool mainstream sites where they could see that all children benefit from being together.

Parents of children with disabilities, as well as parents of typically developing children, who are reluctant to have their children participate in integrated programs must be respected. Perhaps they would feel differently if they were aware of the benefits associated with mainstreaming. They should be provided the wealth of current research findings that report positive outcomes related to mainstreaming preschoolers.

Conclusion

Public school placement team members hold opinions related to the children with whom they work, the parents of those children, and community-based service providers. Each of them also has her or his own definition of, and attitude about, the philosophy of inclusion or mainstreaming. Exploring these attitudes as a group that includes the community service provider and parents will likely result in more appropriate individualized placement decisions for the children and families being served.

Both regular- and special-education personnel need to be prepared through preservice and in-service training to become a part of a new school community, a community that recognizes that all children learn, all children contribute, and all children belong. Children with disabilities in mainstream settings must receive at least what they were receiving in specialized settings. Mainstreaming is meant to enhance the child's education through provision of a normalized social context for learning.

Staff-development activities can be employed in the hopes that changes will occur in teacher attitudes, classroom practices, and child outcomes (Guskey, 1986). Guskey believes that there is a temporal sequence to these events. Staff-development activities lead to changes in teachers' classroom practices through providing specific tools for the teachers' use. The teachers' new learning can lead to changes in child outcomes, and improved child outcomes should lead to changes in teachers' beliefs and attitudes.

Sources for further information

Council for Administrators in Special Education (CASE) of the Council for Exceptional Children, 615 16th Street, N.W., Albuquerque, NM 87104, 505–243–7622

The Division for Early Childhood (DEC) of the Council for Exceptional Children, 1920 Association Drive, Reston, VA 22091, 703–620–3660

National Association of State Directors of Special Education (NASDSE), 1800 Diagonal Road, Suite 320, King Street Station 1, Alexandria, VA 22314, 703–519–3800

National Early Childhood Technical Assistance System (NEC–TAS), Suite 500, NCNB Plaza, Chapel Hill, NC 27514, 919–962–2001

National Head Start Resource Access Program, Administration for Children, Youth and Families, Office of Human Development Services, U.S. Department of Health and Human Services, P.O. Box 1182, Washington, DC 20013, 202–245–0562

U.S. Office of Special Education Programs Early Childhood Branch, 400 Maryland Avenue, S.W., Washington, DC 20202, 202–732–1084

References

Ayers, B., & Meyer, L.H. (1992, February). Helping teachers manage the inclusive classroom: Staff development and teaming star among management strategies. *The School Administrator*, 30–37.

Forest, M. (1992). Full inclusion is possible. *The inclusion papers: Strategies to make inclusion work* (pp. 14–15). Toronto, Canada: Inclusion Press.

Guskey, T.R. (1986). Staff development and the process of teacher change. *Educational Researcher, 15*(5), 5–12.

Individuals with Disabilities Education Act. (1991, October). 34 CFR § 300.550, 20 U.S.C. (secs. 1411–1420).

McCullom, J.A., & Hughes, M. (1988). Staffing patterns and team models in infancy programs. In J.B. Jordan, J.J. Gallagher, P.L. Huntinger, & M.B. Karnes (Eds.), *Early childhood special education: Birth to three* (pp. 129–146). Reston, VA: Council for Exceptional Children/Division for Early Childhood.

Smith, B.J., & Rose, D.F. (1991). *Identifying policy options for preschool mainstreaming.* Monograph. Pittsburgh, PA: Research Institute on Preschool Mainstreaming, Allegheny-Singer Research Institute. (ERIC Document Reproduction Service No. ED 338 403)

Children With Disabilities Who Use Assistive Technology: Ethical Considerations

Loreta Holder-Brown and Howard P. Parette, Jr.

Loreta Holder-Brown, Ph.D., has been a leader in personnel preparation, training teachers and related service professionals. Loreta is a professor of special education at the University of Alabama, where she chairs the Program for Orthopedically Handicapped and Other Health Impaired in the Area of Special Education.

Howard P. Parette, Jr., Ph.D., has given national and international presentations and has published extensively in the area of technology service delivery for young children with disabilities.

Technology is increasingly being used by all children in our society to enhance educational opportunities and quality of life. Interactive computer programs and self-correcting/programmed learning games are commonplace in many classrooms for young children. Velcro fasteners on shoes and jackets enable children to successfully dress themselves. Tape recorders and listening stations allow teachers to individualize instruction for one child while working with other children in group activities. Such inexpensive technologies that do not require sophisticated skills to use are readily available.

Although technology is important for all children, it is especially critical for children with disabilities who depend on assistive technology for mobility, communication, and learning. The impetus for the use of technology with these children evolves from the passage

Loreta Holder-Brown

of Public Law (P.L.) 101–476, the *Individuals with Disabilities Education Amendments of 1990.* This legislation amends P.L. 99–457, the *Education of the Handicapped Amendments of 1986,* through which states could provide early intervention services to children who have developmental disabilities, children who are at risk, and their families. This legislation expands the scope of services that may be provided to young children with disabilities and identifies assistive technology as a specific service that is provided to young children. The law also mandates that these children be served in the least restrictive environment. These mandates have implications

not only specific to the implementation of programs serving young children who have disabilities but also for regular child care and education programs, such as Head Start (which for many years required that children with disabilities compose 10% of the service population).

Definition of assistive technology

"Assistive technology" may be defined as any item, device, or piece of equipment that is used to increase, maintain, or improve the functional abilities of persons with disabilities [P.L. 100–407, *Technology Related Assistance for Individu-*

als with Disabilities Act of 1988, 29 U.S.C. 2202, Section 3(1)]. Assistive technologies for children with disabilities range from such simple devices as adapted spoons and switch-adapted, battery-operated toys to complex devices such as computerized environmental control systems. These items, devices, or equipment may be commercially made, acquired off the shelf, or customized. The definition of assistive technology in P.L. 101–476 is consistent with that in P.L.

ethical considerations emerge that should be of concern.

Ethics and technology

As personnel in child care, Head Start, kindergarten, and other preschool settings provide services to young children with disabilities, these personnel will be involved with occupational therapists, physical therapists, speech/language pathologists, nurses, and

ment of other professionals (e.g., the occupational therapist, physical therapist, or speech/language pathologist) (Parette, Hourcade, & VanBiervliet, in press). These professionals may see the child and her needs from a different and more limited perspective than do early childhood educators who are trained to view the "whole child."

Like all areas of human endeavor, the use of technology in preschool and other early childhood settings must be guided by values and philosophies (Cavalier, 1986; Weinrich & Gerstein, 1987). Many important ethical considerations should guide early childhood professionals as they identify or adapt technologies for young children with disabilities such as cerebral palsy, spina bifida, visual impairment, or hearing impairment. These considerations are described below.

Increasingly, young children with disabilities will be afforded opportunities to participate in early childhood education settings. Dissemination of information relating to the use of assistive technologies is expected to increase, too.

100–407. The concepts found in these mandates not only open new vistas for children with disabilities but present new challenges for all professionals who provide services to preschool children.

Emerging challenge to early childhood professionals

Day care providers and other professionals will frequently be required to participate in the development and implementation of programs for preschoolers who are disabled (see "DEC Position Statement on Goal One of America 2000" on next page). Familiarity with assistive technologies will be of considerable importance to these providers as they participate in team decision-making processes (Parette, Hourcade, & VanBiervliet, in press). As caregivers and other teachers begin to acquire an expanded information base regarding assistive technologies, they must, in turn, use this information to aid in selecting and using equipment in their settings. In this process, certain

parents. Part of the team's assignment is to ensure that all dimensions of the child's present levels of performance are considered. This team approach is most effective when persons having expertise in instructional programming, including technology and its applications, work cooperatively with parents and early childhood professionals who provide the children's day-to-day care and education.

Serving as part of a team

Personnel in early childhood programs for the nondisabled will be required by law to participate in multidisciplinary team processes and may be expected to assume important responsibilities as team members. Unfortunately, many professionals have had inadequate training and/or experience with technology and its applications. When professionals are not prepared for the responsibility of selecting devices for children and using them in service settings, they may rely too heavily on the judg-

Selection of appropriate technology

"Appropriateness" has several dimensions. P.L. 99–457 was defined to encompass any need the child has relating to learning and/or development, including the need to learn basic self-help skills and to develop appropriate social interaction, cognitive, and language skills. Assistive technologies can play critical roles in assuring not only the provision of appropriate learning experiences in these areas but also the child's mobility or ability to communicate.

From a more traditional perspective, a technology is appropriate for all children when its application meets one of three criteria.

First, a technology should respond to (or anticipate) specific, clearly defined goals that result in enhanced skills for the child.

Second, a technology should be compatible with practical constraints, such as available resources or the amount of training required to enable the child, his family, and the early childhood educator to use the technology.

Third, a technology should result in desirable and sufficient outcomes (Office of Technology Assessment, 1982).

Some basic considerations for children with disabilities are related to (1) ease of training the child and his family to use and care for the technology; (2) reasonable maintenance and repair, with regard to time and expense; and (3) monitoring of the technology's effectiveness.

Maintenance of a child focus. During the process of identifying the child's needs, developing a plan, and securing funding for assistive technology, professionals sometimes have a tendency to let the interesting technology, rather than the child and her educational needs, become the focus of attention. For example, a talking computer with a colorful display could capture the attention of team members and be recommended for use even if a less sophisticated approach might be more effective. Technology is not an end in itself; it is a means to provide increased experiences, opportunities, and independence for children who have disabilities. When used in early childhood settings, technology should generally facilitate gradual behavior changes in the child that are observable and have social validity (Evans & Meyer, 1985; Snell & Bowden, 1986).

Limited knowledge of the technology. Given the many types of technology that are available, it is difficult, if not impossible, for any one person to remain informed of all new technological developments that might potentially be appropriate for a child. This may result in the professional's recommendation of a familiar technology that may not be the most appropriate to meet the child's needs. It is

---

DEC Position Statement on Goal One of America 2000

The Division for Early Childhood (DEC) of the Council for Exceptional Children (CEC) developed a position statement on America 2000 and the first goal: "All children will start school ready to learn." They requested NAEYC support for this position statement, and it was given after staff review that confirmed that the statement is congruent with existing NAEYC position statements. The position statement is reproduced below.

"Schools should be ready to accept and effectively educate all children. Schooling will succeed or fail, not children.

When we say *all* children, we do mean all—including children with disabilities, children placed at-risk for school failure, children of poverty, children who are non-English speaking, children with gifts and talents.

Reaching Goal One requires healthy and competent parents, wanted and healthy babies, decent housing, and adequate nutrition.

Quality early education and child care should be a birth right for all children. These services must be comprehensive, coordinated, focused on individual family and child needs, and available to all families that need and choose to use them.

It is not appropriate to screen children into or out of early education programs. All children must be given a legitimate opportunity to learn.

Education in the 21st century must attend to children's social and emotional growth and development, not merely focus on academic outcomes.

Early educators must be schooled in and encouraged to use a wide variety of developmentally appropriate curricula, materials, and procedures to maximize each child's growth and development.

Achieving long-term academic goals does not imply that young children be drilled in English, science, and math. These academic goals are best achieved when young children are provided with environments that encourage their eager participation, exploration, and curiosity about the world.

No important social aims are ever achieved by rhetoric. Reaching this goal will require strong and continuing leadership, a wise investment in human and related capital, and collaboration between families, service providers, government, and business."

---

crucial to explore all reasonable technology options before recommending an approach. Because a large number of human and environmental factors exist that can affect technology selection and usage, and given the wide range of assistive technologies available, it is important to use a multidisciplinary approach. The strengths of each discipline's knowledge base can then be used to increase the probability that the most effective educational or early intervention solution will be developed for each child. It is important for personnel and parents to use technical assistance centers that provide information and training with regard to the use of technology for children with disabilities, as well as vendors and professionals (e.g., orthotists, prosthetists, and computer consultants) to gain more information about appropriate and available technology.

Developmental relevance. Although attitudes toward technology are changing, personnel working in early childhood programs may view a particular kind of technology as a means of entertaining a child (Childers & Podemski, 1984; Griffin, Gillis, & Brown, 1986). The use of computers is an excellent example. Many times computers are not incorporated into the curriculum for the child but instead are used merely to keep the child occupied. Educators of the nondisabled often face the same problems with technology. Computers, televisions, and other technology can be and often are used inappropriately with nondisabled children as well as with disabled children. Early childhood educators are continually faced with making optimal use of technology to provide appropriate programming on the developmental level of young children. The same rigorous standards of developmental appropriateness applied to other strategies and materials must be applied to the use of assistive technologies not only for children who have disabilities but for all children.

Often education for children with disabilities may be as simple as enabling a child who has cerebral palsy to write by modifying a pencil. One trap to avoid with children with disabilities involves the recommendation of an assistive device that does little to promote long-term increased independence. For example, encouraging the use of a wheelchair because transporting a child using a wheelchair is easier than teaching the child to use a walker or other support devices may be detrimental. Extended inappropriate use of a wheelchair may result in atrophy of leg muscles and perhaps prevent the child from learning less restrictive means of mobility in the future.

Self-perception and the perception of others. In our society people have had a tendency to focus on children's disabilities rather than on their abilities, thus contributing to the belief that these children are abnormal or deviant and have less worth than able-bodied persons. It is important that assistive technologies do not unnecessarily draw attention to disabilities but rather assist the child to more fully participate in friendships and activities. In some instances this will mean selecting an assistive technology that will be most accepted in the child's environment, rather than the technology that best performs the task. For example, a head pointer (i.e., a rod attached to a headband or helmet) might be technically the best approach for a child to access a computer keyboard; however, it may make the child look different and subject him to ridicule. The child could use a keyguard, touch screen, light pen, or scanner to serve the same purpose and be accepted more readily by peers, family, and the public.

Dignity of choice. Efforts must be made to select and apply technology in a manner that acknowledges and promotes individual dignity and the opportunity for personal choice (Pfrommer, 1984; Guess, Benson, & Siegel-Causey, 1985; Cavalier, 1988). Children and their families have a right and a responsibility to actively participate in the educational planning process. Some people think that only specialists—for example, occupational and physical therapists—have the necessary knowledge and experience to make decisions about which technology to use, but the desires of the child and his family are also relevant. The child and his family have unique expertise concerning their activities, their goals, and the environment in which they live. Failure to use this expertise may result in the failure of the assistive technology to meet the needs of the child and his family. For example, failure to provide the child and his family the opportunity to choose the "voice" characteristics of a communication system may result in the child's reluctance or refusal to independently use the device (Parette & VanBiervliet, 1990). In addition, ignoring child and parental desires or failing to even ask them questions conveys the message that they are unimportant in the educational process. Encouraging participation in the decision-making process does not mean presenting the child and her parents with a plan and asking for their consent; encouraging participation implies sharing assessment information, information relating to strengths and weaknesses of all of the alternatives, and encouraging and facilitating the family's active participation in the creation of a plan.

Charity. Since the nineteenth century, when schools for the deaf and the blind were founded, many people have considered children with disabilities as burdens of public charity (Wolfensberger, 1969); hence, some people believe that these children should be grateful for the charity they receive. Any technology that is then prescribed is viewed as being better than nothing. This may result in the use, or attempted use, of a technology because it is available (e.g., donated by a local vendor) rather than appropriate. Basing decisions regarding assistive technologies primarily on the child's need for that technology to improve or maintain her functional abilities across environments is critical.

Limitations imposed on the technology. Unfortunately, many technologies that are acquired for children with disabilities are viewed as school property instead of technology that increases the independence and functioning of the child *across environments*. Augmentative communication systems are an excellent example and are often purchased for use only in the early childhood program setting. The use of the technology may be further limited to specific times (e.g., the child may be able to use the technology only when she is working on language skills with the speech pathologist). The child is then unable to communicate except in those settings at specified times. When the child enters another environment or returns home, she has no means of expressing her needs, wants, or ideas. Limiting the child's access to assistive technologies that are crucial to functioning across environments will disrupt learning and severely limit learning opportunities. Personnel working in early childhood settings must consider the child's total needs when developing and implementing program plans involving assistive technology and ensure easy access to the assistive technology in all environments.

Individual rights and social equity. Problems in obtaining full funding of P.L. 99–457 and other service initiatives may result in administrators' reluctance to embrace the idea of providing expensive technologies to young children with disabilities (Mendelsohn, 1989). Because most preschool and early childhood programs have limited funds, resources must be used in an efficient manner. This implies the need to examine a range of technologies that might be appropriate for a particular child, and to give the cost factor careful consideration. The most expensive technologies are not always the best ones to meet the needs of young children with disabilities. Frequently, the most appropriate

choice is a low-tech solution requiring minimal training and low maintenance. It is crucial to remember, however, that the first priority in the selection of assistive technologies for all children must be the technology's appropriateness for meeting the child's educational and life goals.

Conclusions

Increasingly, young children with disabilities will be afforded opportunities to participate in early childhood education settings. Dissemination of information relating to the use of assistive technologies is expected to increase, too. This suggests that early childhood professionals will be called upon to assume new competencies enabling them to effectively participate in team processes and ethical decision making regarding the selection and use of assistive technology for preschool children. If we work together on this, we will be able to increase children's abilities to interact with others and to exercise control over their environment.

Plans that are developed and appropriate assistive technology that is provided will shape the early experiences of these children and provide the foundation upon which much future learning will occur. It is critical that careful consideration be given to the ethical implications of technologies. Unquestionably, these decisions will have a far-reaching impact on the lives of children with disabilities.

References

Cavalier, A. (1986). The application of technology in the classroom and workplace: Unvoiced premises and ethical issues. In A. Gartner & T. Joe (Eds.), *Images of the disabled-disabling images* (pp. 129–142). New York: Praeger.

Cavalier, A. (1988). *Technology assistance: Devices, techniques, and services for people with cognitive impairments. Testimony to the Select Subcommittee on Education of the Committee on Education and Labor of the U.S. House of Representatives.* Arlington, TX: Association for Retarded Citizens.

Childers, J.H., Jr., & Podemski, R.S. (1984). Removing barriers to the adoption of microcomputer technology by school counselors. *The School Counselor, 31,* 229–233.

Evans, I., & Meyer, L. (1985). *An educative approach to behavior problems: A practical decision model for interventions with severely handicapped learners.* Baltimore: Paul H. Brookes.

Griffin, B.L., Gillis, M.K., & Brown, M. (1986). The counselor as a computer consultant: Understanding children's attitudes toward computers. *Elementary School Guidance and Counseling, 20,* 146–149.

Guess, D., Benson, H., & Siegel-Causey, E. (1985). Behavior control and education of severely handicapped students: Who's doing what to whom? And why? In D. Bricker & J. Filler (Eds.), *Severe mental retardation: From theory to practice* (pp. 230–244). Reston, VA: Council for Exceptional Children.

Mendelsohn, S. (1989, March). *Payment issues and options in the utilization of assistive technology.* Paper presented to the National Workshop on Implementing Technology Utilization, Washington, DC.

Office of Technology Assessment. (1982). *Technology and handicapped people.* Washington, DC: U.S. Government Printing Office.

Parette, H.P., & VanBiervliet, A. (1990). *Assistive technology guide for young children with disabilities.* Little Rock, AR: UALR Press.

Parette, H.P., Hourcade, J.J., & VanBiervliet, A. (in press). Technology teams and the exceptional child: Teacher guidelines for the evaluation of assistive devices. *Teaching Exceptional Children.*

Pfrommer, M.C. (1984). Utilization of technology: Consumer perspective. In M. Gergen & D. Hagen (Eds.), *Discover '84: Technology for disabled persons. Conference papers* (pp. 237–343). Menomonie, WI: Stout Vocational Rehabilitation Center.

Snell, M., & Bowden, D. (1986). Community-referenced instruction: Research and issues. *Journal of the Association for Persons with Severe Handicaps, 11*(1), 1–11.

Weinrich, S.G., & Gerstein, M. (1987). Guidelines for counselors in the selection and use of computer software. *Elementary School Guidance and Counseling, 22*(1), 53–61.

Wolfensberger, W. (1969). The origin and nature of our institutional models. In R. Kugel & W. Wolfensberger (Eds.), *Changing patterns in residential services for the mentally retarded* (pp. 59–171). Washington, DC: President's Committee on Mental Retardation.

Play for ALL Children
The Toy Library Solution

Sara C. Jackson
Linda Robey
Martha Watjus
Elizabeth Chadwick

Sara C. Jackson is Assistant Professor, Department of Special Education, University of Southern Mississippi—Gulf Coast, and Director of Toy Library—Coast, funded by the Hasbro Children's Foundation of New York. Linda Robey, Martha Watjus and Elizabeth Chadwick have been Research Assistants, Education Department, University of Southern Mississippi—Gulf Coast.

Affirming its importance in infant and child development, play is a central theme of most early childhood programs. Play "provides children with opportunities for developing mastery and competence in cognitive, social and physical skills" (ACEI/Isenberg & Quisenberry, 1988, p. 142). Yet, its value seems to have eluded many educators of young children with disabilities, as well as their parents.

There are several reasons for this phenomenon. Educational programs for young disabled children have traditionally emphasized direct instruction of specific skills, in many cases leaving little time for play. Also, parents sometimes find it difficult to engage in playful interaction with their disabled children. More paramount, yet related to the first two reasons, is the serious shortage of appropriate toys available to the child with special needs.

PLAY FOR CHILDREN WITH DISABILITIES—A PROBLEM

Lack of Play Opportunities

Although play has always been an integral part of the regular preschool curriculum, this has not been true for the child with disabilities (Widerstrom, 1983). Many preschool programs for the disabled still emphasize teaching specific skills, especially self-help skills, resulting in limited opportunities for the disabled youngster to simply "play" (Sinker, 1990). According to Thurman and Widerstrom (1990), "the traditional nursery school emphasis on play has been rejected as too nondirective and too haphazard" (p. 120). The benefits of play for optimal child development are well discussed in the research literature, yet neither spontaneous nor structured play as a method of enhancing cognitive, physical and social growth is generally stressed in programs for children with disabilities.

Playtime at home also may be less available for the child who has special needs. Parents of disabled children often have difficulty playing with their infants and toddlers. Their anxiety about the fragile condition of a disabled youngster can inhibit a spontaneous playful attitude. Also, many disabled children are less responsive than nondisabled children to their parents' attempts at play. In fact, some infants with disabilities are extremely irritable, cry incessantly and do not appear to enjoy being held (Ainsworth, 1973).

Another barrier to playful interaction between parent and disabled child is the added stress experienced in caring for the child (Bailey & Wolery, 1984). Unfortunately, with extra demands on their time and emotions, little energy is left over for quality playtime with their child. Sometimes parents feel so much pressure to teach their special child certain skills that they forget to relax and have ordinary playful interaction with the youngster (Gerlock, 1982).

Parents may be unaware that, while play is the spontaneous activity of most children, their disabled child may need to be "taught" how to play with toys or other children. Moreover, parents generally have not been encouraged to emphasize play in their relationship with their child. Even the editors of *Exceptional Parent* (October 1990) acknowledge that play has been low on their editorial priority list over the last 20 years (Schleifer & Klein, 1990).

Lack of Appropriate Toys

In addition to lack of adequate school and home playtime, ordinary toys themselves present profound difficulties. Many commercial toys are unsuitable for a significant percentage of children

From *Childhood Education*, Vol. 68, Fall 1991, pp. 27-31. © 1991 by the Association for Childhood Education International. Reprinted by permission of the authors and the Association for Childhood Education International, 11501 Georgia Avenue, Suite 315, Wheaton, MD.

with special needs; their disabilities make it physically difficult or impossible to play with ordinary toys. To overcome this obstacle to play, appropriate new toys and specially adapted toys have been developed (Domroese, 1985). Unfortunately, these toys are not widely marketed, making them expensive and often difficult to obtain. Furthermore, parents may have to purchase several expensive adaptive switches before finding one their child is able to activate.

THE TOY LIBRARY SOLUTION—AN EXCITING CONCEPT

Attempting to solve these problems, some communities have established toy lending or play libraries. People are beginning to recognize play's value in nurturing the cognitive, physical and social development of all children—especially those with disabilities (Juul, 1987). Additionally, growing emphasis on the importance of the family experience for the disabled child has led to the development of specialized toys and adaptive switches.

Both educators and lawmakers now affirm that the best interventions must involve the entire family unit (Swick, 1989). As primary caretaker, a parent is the child's first teacher and greatest motivator. This essential role of the family has been emphasized in recent legislation, the Education of the Disabled Act Amendments of 1986 or Public Law 99-457. The law focuses on training and support for the child within the context of the family. Unlike P.L. 94-142, which requires an Individual Education Plan (IEP), P.L. 99-457 mandates an Individual Family Service Plan (IFSP) for infants and toddlers. This realization of the vital role of parents and family in early intervention is consistent with the philosophy and procedures of toy libraries.

Toy libraries for disabled youngsters and their families support both the spirit and the intent of P.L. 99-457. Through the loan of specially adapted toys and parent training in appropriate play techniques, these libraries promote family involvement in early intervention efforts for youngsters with special needs. The toy library is an ideal way to expand children's play opportunities as well as accommodate the family in its early intervention efforts.

Development of Adapted Toys
Recent technological advancements have greatly increased the availability of useful toys for children with special needs. Steven Kanor, pioneer in the field of toy adaptation, has used his expertise as a biomedical engineer to design capability switches that activate toys with minimal pressure or movement (Cole, 1982). For those with severe disabilities, he has even designed voice-responsive and light-activated switches. By enabling them to enjoy ordinary toys, he has both enriched their lives and increased their opportunities for individual growth and development.

These "special" toys are adapted by taking an ordinary battery-operated toy and bypassing the usual means of turning it on by using a new switch to activate the toy, one that can be operated by disabled children. Many types of switches have been engineered to match the needs of an individual child. The plate switches are operated by minimal pressure, using any part of the body. Other switches are voice-activated or require merely a puff of breath or a tilt of the head. All switches and toys are interchangeable. This enables the child to play with the entire inventory of toys, using the one switch that best suits his/her needs.

While computer technology provides the means to modify ordinary commercial toys for use by children with special needs, the toys may never be widely marketed. The toy library is currently the best way to make these adapted toys available to large numbers of children.

Toy Library History
Two basic types of toy libraries now operate in the United States. Lekotek, a toy library first developed in Scandinavia and specifically designed for youngsters with disabilities (Juul, 1988), stresses integration of the special needs youngster into family and community. With a primary focus on family support, Lekoteks emphasize play techniques, schedule monthly family visits and lend specially adapted toys. They are generally staffed by professionals and funded by the local community.

Another type of toy library is based on the British model. Unlike the Lekotek, it is usually staffed by nonprofessional volunteers and is often privately funded. In both Britain and America, this type of library has expanded its mission to serve not only disabled children, but other groups of needy or at-risk youngsters (Domroese, 1985)—children whose access to toys is limited due to poverty and/or chaotic home environments.

The toy library movement in the United States has followed both the Scandinavian and the British models. First formed in the early 1980s in Illinois, Lekoteks have since spread to other states (Domroese, 1985). Besides lending toys to children with disabilities, the Lekotek now offers a leader training course, publishes materials on play and toys and encourages computer use.

Toy libraries similar to the more informal British models have also increased in the U.S. Many were initially linked to public libraries, such as the Learning Games Libraries in Illinois and the ToyBrary Project in Nebraska. Some have expanded their mission to include the economically disadvantaged, children in shelters and those in hospitals. Many operate mobile units, providing door-to-door service and lending educational toys to families with special needs children (Stone, 1983). Funding has often been provided by state education agencies.

Toy Libraries in the U.S.
—A Growing Movement

The state of Illinois has established a network of Learning Games Libraries in various communities, the first opening in Oak Park in 1976. This library, a project of the Illinois Council for Exceptional Children and the Illinois Library Association, provides developmental learning materials (games and toys) to children with learning problems or physical disabilities. The additional 12 libraries that have grown out of this pilot project now operate under the auspices of the Learning Games Libraries Association in Oak Park.

In Nebraska, the State Department of Education (Special Education Branch) and the Nebraska Regional Library System have collaborated to form the ToyBrary, a toy lending library for parents and children. Begun in 1977, ToyBraries now number 15 throughout the state, enabling children in rural areas to benefit from the materials offered. Primarily geared to the child with special needs, the toys and games available for loan emphasize parental involvement.

Three Florida agencies provide assistance to disabled children through the use of specially designed toys and adaptive switches. The Communications Systems Evaluation Center is administered by the Orange County School System. Valencia Community College in Orlando operates the CITE Program (Center for Independence Training and Evaluation), while the Florida Diagnostic and Learning Resources System directs 18 centers throughout the state. The Miami center houses a toy lending library; several others are directly involved in play training programs for disabled children and their families.

These agencies utilize recent advances in science and technology to evaluate and help exceptional children realize their full potential. Children who play with special toys and switches can eventually succeed in using more sophisticated tools such as computers.

Several other states have opened toy libraries, often through their public library systems. In Los Angeles County alone, more than 30 toy libraries reach 15,000 children annually. A $25,000 grant has been given to the Wisconsin Public Libraries to establish circulating toy collections. In Maryland, the Howard County Library Children's Department circulates 1,300 toys each month. Staff members are trained to advise parents on how to use the toys effectively with their children.

Between 1985 and 1988, the number of toy libraries in the United States doubled, from 125 to 250. The National Lekotek Center reports that currently 52 certified Lekoteks operate throughout the United States. More than a million children and families are served annually by toy libraries nationwide (Myers, 1988).

How To Begin

To determine the feasibility of establishing a toy lending or play library in your community, it is advisable to explore existing facilities in your state. A personal on-site visit is preferable; calling or writing for information is certainly recommended. Contacting other state agencies or national organizations may also prove helpful (see Resources). In brief, before starting a toy library consider the following: funding (state sponsored, private or part of state library system), library space, cataloging system, staff (volunteer or paid) and effective publicity (see Suggested Readings and Toy Sources).

Conclusion

Much has been written about learning and socializing through play and its vital role in both child development and early childhood education. Fortunately, its importance in the development of the exceptional child is also becoming more broadly acknowledged. The growing number of toy libraries in the U.S. has enabled more teachers and parents to use play and toys as invaluable learning tools for youngsters with special needs.

As Isenberg and Quisenberry (1988) state in a position paper of the Association for Childhood Education International (ACEI), "The time has come to advocate strongly in support of play for all children" (p. 138). Thanks to the toy library, *all* children can now engage in play, including those with disabilities.

References

Ainsworth, M. D. S. (1973). The development of infant-mother attachment. In B. M. Caldwell & H. Riciutti (Eds.), *Review of Child Development Research* (1-94).

Association for Childhood Education International. J. Isenberg & N. Quisenberry. (1988). Position paper. Play: A necessity for all children. *Childhood Education, 64,* 138-145.

Bailey, D. B., & Worley, M. (1984). *Teaching infants and preschoolers with handicaps.* Columbus: Charles E. Merrill.

Cole, L. (1982, December 19). Toys: Not only playthings. *Daily News,* p. w-3.

Domroese, C. (1985, October). *Learning games libraries: Help for the at-risk child—A growing movement in Illinois.* Paper presented at the Council for Exceptional Children/Division on Early Childhood, National Early Childhood Conference on the Child with Special Needs, Denver, CO.

Gerlock, E. (1982). *Parent group guide: Topics for families of young children with handicaps.* Nashville, TN: John F. Kennedy Center for Research on Education and Human Development, Families, Infant, and Toddler Project.

Juul, K. D. (1987, Winter). Toy libraries for children with special needs. *Learning Games Libraries Association Newsletter.* (Available from Learning Games Libraries Association, P.O. Box 4002, Oak Park, IL 60303)

Juul, K. D. (1988, Spring). Lekoteks in

Norway. *Learning Games Libraries Association Newsletter.*

Myers, S. M. (1988, January). *U. S. A. Toy Library Association Newsletter.* (Available from U. S. A. Toy Library Association, 2719 Broadway, Evanston, IL 60201)

Schleifer, M. J., & Klein, S. D. (1990, October). Recreation and play. The time is now. *Exceptional Parent,* p. 20.

Sinker, M. (1990). Play is play—Whether or not you can walk or talk. *Child's Play,* 7(1), 3.

Stone, M. (1983, Winter). Toy libraries. *Day Care and Early Education,* pp. 19-21.

Swick, K. J. (1989, November). Working with parents of children with special needs. *An Exceptional Student Education Newsletter,* 11(3), 11-13. (Available from Florida Diagnostic and Learning Resources System/South, Dade County Public Schools, Miami, FL)

Thurman, S. K., & Widerstrom, A. (1990). *Infants and young children with special needs* (2nd ed.). Baltimore, MD: Paul H. Brooks.

Widerstrom, A. (1983). How important is play for disabled children? *Childhood Education,* 60, 39-49.

Suggested Readings

Adaptive Play for Special Needs Children by C. R. Musslewhite. College Hill Press, San Diego, CA, 1986.

An Invitation to Play: Teacher's Guide by C. Zieher. Wisconsin Department of Public Instruction, Madison, WI, 1986.

Early Childhood Special Education: Birth to Three by J. B. Jordan, J. J. Gallagher, P. L. Huntinger & M. B. Karnes (Eds.). Council for Exceptional Children, Reston, VA, 1988.

Helping the Mentally Retarded Acquire Play Skills by P. Wehman. Charles C. Thomas, Springfield, IL, 1977.

Learning Materials Catalog. Learning Games Libraries Association, Oak Park, IL, 1986.

Learning Through Play by P. Chance. Gardner Press, New York, 1979.

Looking at Children's Play: A Bridge Between Theory and Practice by P. Monigham-Nourot, B. Scales, J. Van Hoorn & M. Almy. Columbia University, New York, 1987.

Play and Education: The Basic Tool for Early Childhood Learning by O. Weininger. Charles C. Thomas, Springfield, IL, 1979.

Play as a Medium for Learning and Development: A Handbook of Theory and Practice by D. Bergen (Ed.). Heinemann, Portsmouth, NH, 1988.

Toys for Growing: A Guide to Toys That Develop Skills by M. Sinker. Yearbook Medical Publishers, Chicago, 1986.

"Developmental Toys" by J. T. Neisworth (Ed.) *Topics in Early Childhood Special Education,* 5(3), 1985.

"They Too Should Play" by C. C. Hirst & E. Y. Shelley. *Teaching Exceptional Children,* 21(4), 26-28, 1989.

Resources

Florida Diagnostic & Learning Resources System/South, 9220 S.W. 52nd Terrace, Miami, FL 33165 (305-274-3501).

Learning Games Libraries Association, P.O. Box 4002, Oak Park, IL 60303 (312-386-1687).

Lekotek of Georgia, Inc., 3035 N. Druid Hills Rd., Atlanta, GA 30329 (404-633-3430).

Los Angeles County Toy Loan Program, 2200 N. Humbolt St., Los Angeles, CA 90031 (213-586-6615).

National Lekotek Center, 2100 Ridge Ave., Evanston, IL 60204 (708-328-0001).

Nebraska ToyBrary Project, 301 Centennial Mall S., Lincoln, NE 68509 (402-471-2471).

Toy Library-Coast, USM—Gulf Park, Long Beach, MS 39560 (601-867-2636).

United Cerebral Palsy of Westchester, Mobile Toy Library for Disabled Individuals, King St. & Lincoln Ave., Rye Brook, NY 10706 (914-937-3800).

USA Toy Library Association, 2719 Broadway Ave., Evanston, IL 60201 (708-864-8240).

Toy Sources

Able Net, Inc., 1081 10th Ave. S.E., Minneapolis, MN 55414 (800-322-0956).

Crestwood Co., P.O. Box 04606, Milwaukee, WI 53204 (414-461-9876).

Jesana, Ltd., P.O. Box 17, Irvington, NY 10533 (800-443-4728).

Kapable Kids, P.O. Box 250, Bohemia, NY 11716 (800-356-1564).

Kaye's Kids, Division of KAYE Products, Inc., 1010 E. Pettigrew St., Durham, NC 27701-4299 (919-683-1051).

Rifton—For People with Disabilities, Rt. 213, Rifton, NY 12471 (914-658-3141).

Steven J. Kanor, Inc., 385 Warburton Ave., Hastings, NY 10706 (914-478-0960).

Switch Works, P.O. Box 64764, Baton Rouge, LA 70896 (504-925-8926).

The Capable Child, 8 Herkimer Ave., Hewlett, NY 11557 (516-872-1603).

Therapeutic Toys, Inc., P.O. Box 418, Moodus, CT 06469 (800-638-0676).

Transition to Adulthood

Public Law 94-142, *The Individuals with Disabilities Education Act,* was amended by PL 101-476 in 1990. Public Law 101-476 extended the age through which children with disabilities are entitled to a free and appropriate education to age 21. It also suggested guidelines to be implemented by public schools to assist high school students with disabilities make the transition from school to adulthood activities such as work, independent living, and community participation. While many special education programs had been making efforts to help youth with disabilities prepare for paid employment prior to PL 101-476, few special services were provided to help adolescents move from the world of family and school, to the world of independent living and full community participation. Thus, PL 101-476 called for a transition movement with multiple goals and much more extensive special preparatory services.

Transitions from school to adulthood are described as vertical transitions. In addition to vertical transitions, PL 94-142 and its amendments also require horizontal transitional services. These are services to ensure smoother transitions from preschool to elementary school, elementary to middle school, middle to high school, high school to post-secondary education (e.g., technical school, college); or transitions from special classes to regular classes, or vice-versa, or transitions from special schools to regular schools, or vice-versa. Horizontal transitions generally require less in the way of special preparatory services than vertical transitions.

All transitions involve life changes. Transitions are not easily accomplished even by adults in excellent physical and mental health! We should not expect them to be easy for children and youth with disabilities. Transitions require planning, extra effort, and a commitment to completing the process.

Vertical transitions from the world of school to the world of work, independent living, and community should be anticipated very early in the life of children with disabilities. Their individualized education programs (IEP) should reflect a concern with post-school life as early as elementary school. By middle school and high school, children with disabilities should have an individualized transition plan (ITP) as well as, or as a part of, their IEP.

The world of work is constantly changing. It is very difficult to begin an ITP for future employment for a child in elementary school, especially not knowing what work opportunities will exist in a future decade, or how the child's interests will evolve. Employment preparation begins with an assessment of the interests and capabilities of each child with a disability. A child with a handicap should be allowed to explore many possible avenues of future employment and make some informed choices. Options and preparation should be commensurate with the reality of the capabilities of the student. Most students have more abilities than people think. There is a wide range of employment available to adults with disabilities, from work in a sheltered workshop, to supportive employment with mentors, coaches, and counseling, to independent employment in real jobs. Preparation for employment may range from the functional curriculum of the school, to vocational education, vocational rehabilitation or adult education; to technical or trade school; to college or university.

Employment preparation for children and youth with disabilities involves student input, parent input, special education input, and multidisciplinary cooperation. By high school, many adolescents with disabilities may become involved in learning functional employment skills in some community-based setting. Should vocational apprenticeship programs be included in the ITP of every adolescent with an exceptional condition? It is dangerous to group all disabled adolescents together as a group who need a vocational-technical track for their education. If a school has tracking, the assignment of students with disabilities to academic tracks, vocational tracks, general education tracks, or special education tracks must be nondiscriminatory. It should be based on testing and evaluation procedures across disciplines, including aptitude tests as well as IQ and achievement tests. No student should be placed in a specific track on the basis of a disability or on the basis of a single test score.

Once an adolescent makes the transition from school to work, whether in competitive employment, supported employment, or sheltered employment, follow-up procedures should be instituted and continued for one to two years. Students who enter competitive employment work side by side with nondisabled coworkers and are evaluated by their employers. They may need assertion training, or empowerment skills to ensure nondiscriminatory wages and promotion, or assistance to change jobs if they desire. Students who enter supported employment are initially provided with supported employment specialists or job coaches. They receive on-the-job training, support, and supervision. This support is gradually reduced as they become competent in their jobs. Students who work in sheltered workshops continue to receive training, support, and supervision on their jobs.

Adolescents with disabilities are entitled to appropriate special educational services to help them make the transitions to independent living and community-civic responsi-

bilities as well as employment. Independent living may range from complete autonomy in a home or apartment, to partial autonomy with a spouse or roommate in a home or apartment, to residence with a live-in aide, to life in a group home. Parents or custodial caregivers once kept individuals with disabilities in their childhood homes for most of their adult lives. This is no longer considered the most appropriate placement. School curriculum should include lessons on independent living such as meal preparation and clean up; home deliveries (e.g., mail) and delivery pick-ups (e.g., trash); using money and paying bills; and making modifications to ensure that doors, toilets, sinks, and appliances are accessible and in working order.

Special educational curriculum should also be provided to adolescents with disabilities to help them make the transition from the shelter of family-school life to responsible community life. Students should be taught to drive or to use public transportation. They need to know how to read maps and schedules. They have the right to vote or even to run for public office. They have the right to due process and may sue, or be sued. They should learn

social conventions (greetings, conversation skills, manners), grooming and clothing styles, access to medical care, and other interpersonal behaviors that will enhance their self-efficacy and self-esteem. When transitions from school to community go awry, it is more frequently from a lack of social living skills than from a lack of work skills. While much has recently been done to improve life transitions of persons with disabilities, much is left to be done.

The first article in this unit discusses the current needs of the transition movement with a view of both past and future concerns. The second article addresses the problems of fitting functional transitional curricula into an inclusive education model.

Looking Ahead: Challenge Questions

What are the current problems and issues regarding transition from the world of school to the worlds of work, independent living, and community responsibilities?

Is a functional curriculum compatible with an inclusive education model? When do you start a functional curriculum for children with disabilities?

Transition: Old Wine in New Bottles

ABSTRACT: *The transition movement of the 1980s was preceded by two similar movements: (a) the career education movement in the 1970s and (b) the work/study movement in the 1960s. These three movements are described and compared to provide an historical context for understanding current problems and issues regarding transition. Some broad social issues, such as educational reform, are then examined to illustrate the potential influence of such issues on the future development of policy that will affect the transition movement.*

ANDREW S. HALPERN

ANDREW S. HALPERN (CEC Chapter #216) is a Professor in the Division of Teacher Education at the University of Oregon, Eugene.

One of my favorite books within the special education literature was written several years ago by Sandra Kaufman. Sandra is the mother of three children, one of whom, Nicole, is a daughter with mental retardation. During Nicole's childhood, Sandra and her husband Matt struggled, often unsuccessfully, to find ways of dealing with Nicole's problems. When Nicole was in her early 20s, however, and living in her own apartment, Sandra went back to school and became associated with the anthropological studies of mental retardation being conducted by Robert Edgerton. As part of her work in this area, Sandra decided that she would conduct a "field study" of her own daughter. A book eventually emerged out of this effort, which Sandra entitled *Retarded Isn't Stupid, Mom!* (Kaufman, 1988).

Although Nicole's story covers the full span of her life, the essence of Kaufman's book deals with Nicole's transition from adolescence into adulthood. This transition, as you might expect, was a struggle, not only for Nicole but for her parents and siblings as well. Although the hopes and aspirations of all concerned often remained high, there were times when the pathway had so many obstacles that the temptation to give up became almost insurmountable. In one particularly poignant example, Nicole burst into tears after attempting to buy a card for a friend's wedding shower. After purchasing the card, she discovered that it was worded in such a way for a man

to give to a woman. Nicole's despair was apparently very great as she contemplated one more piece of evidence of her self-perceived incompetence, which caused her to question her value as a human being.

Sandra recounted her own reaction to this incident through a conversation with Matt:

"How does she take it?" I cried. "Everywhere she turns, the world screams at her that she's inadequate. She's barred from all the fun that [her brother and sister] enjoy. She's denied privileges they are given as a matter of course. She's excluded from the better paying, more interesting jobs. She's told she's too incompetent to have a baby. . . . She can't even buy a card in a store without being mortified. No wonder she's despondent."

Matt stared out the front window.

"And then," I continued, "we add to her problems. 'Go to work every day. Plan your time carefully. Eat right. Go to bed early. Clean your apartment. Budget your money. Use birth control.' That's what she hears from dawn to dusk. It's all so . . . rational, so middle class. Why does she have to live this way? Where is it written? Good God. She climbs mountains each day just to survive."

Matt looked at me. "So what are you saying?"

I shivered, "I guess I'm no longer sure I know what's best for her. There are many kinds of success. Maybe the best thing for her would be all-night sessions with friends, a baby or two, SSI for income. . . ."

He was incredulous. "Could you really accept that? An aimless life in which each day is lived for itself?" (Kaufman, 1988, pp. 132-133)

From *Exceptional Children*, Vol. 58, No. 3, December/January 1992, pp. 202-211. © 1992 by The Council for Exceptional Children. Reprinted by permission.

Sandra Kaufman's anguished question about what's best for Nicole cuts to the heart of the transition movement for people with disabilities. Six years ago, Madeleine Will (1984a) defined a "new" federal initiative called "transition": "The transition from school to working life is an outcome-oriented process encompassing a broad array of services and experiences that lead to employment." A year later, I argued (Halpern, 1985) that the goals of transition should never be confined to employment, but should encompass all appropriate dimensions of adult adjustment and involvement in the community. Now, in the 1990s we no longer debate the appropriateness of a broader set of goals for transition. Instead, we have more appropriately turned our attention to the question of how to make transition work in our local communities. We have acknowledged that transition, from the perspective of families, is not only about services and social goals. From a phenomenological perspective, transition is better defined as "a period of *floundering* that occurs for at least the first several years after leaving school as adolescents attempt to assume a *variety* of adult roles in their communities."

A REVIEW OF HISTORICAL MOVEMENTS

The question of how to make transition work is complex and must be addressed at several levels, including policy development, program capacity development, and program implementation in local communities. The issues being addressed were obviously not invented in 1984, and we have experienced several broad social movements during the past three decades that have attempted to deal with these issues. Like old wine in new bottles, these issues have been addressed with varying levels of success by each new approach that has emerged to attack the old issues.

Cooperative Work/Study Programs

During the 1960s, a popular approach that emerged to address these issues was the work/study program, conducted cooperatively between the public schools and local offices of state rehabilitation agencies (Halpern, 1973; 1974; Kolstoe & Frey, 1965). The general goal of these programs was to create an integrated academic, social, and vocational curriculum, accompanied by appropriate work experience, that was designed to prepare students with mild disabilities for eventual community adjustment. The administration of these programs was generally structured by *formal* cooperative agreements between the schools and the rehabilitation agency.

The centerpiece of each cooperative agreement involved the assignment of a portion of each teacher's day (usually one half) to the role and duties of a work coordinator. This, in turn, led to a significant increase in the number of students who participated in work placements as part of their high-school program. The formal relationship between a local school and the vocational rehabilitation agency also facilitated the efficient referral of students to become clients of the rehabilitation agency, which in turn eased the transition of students from school to the adult community.

Despite the tremendous growth and prosperity of this program during the 1960s, it basically died during the 1970s, primarily as a consequence of two intrinsic flaws. The first of these flaws derived from the funding mechanism that was generally used to support the program. This funding mechanism involved certifying the teacher's time (and accompanying salary) spent being a work coordinator as "in-kind" state contribution of dollars to the rehabilitation agency's budget. Because the majority of the rehabilitation agency's budget comes from federal allocations, at a ratio of several federal dollars for each matching state dollar, this certification of an already existing expenditure (the teacher's salary) as "in-kind" matching dollars became a clever way of generating additional federal rehabilitation dollars at no real additional expense to the state.

There was a hitch, however, in the federal regulations governing the certification of in-kind dollars for matching purposes. According to these regulations, if a person's salary from another agency was certified as rehabilitation matching money, then the proportion of that person's time represented by the "certified" salary had to be *supervised* by a representative of the rehabilitation agency. As you can imagine, school principals were not thrilled by the prospect of somebody other than themselves supervising their teachers. Although "creative" ways were often improvised for fulfilling this supervision requirement, it frequently emerged as a point of contention in the day-to-day implementation of the work/study agreement.

A second problem emerged from the "similar benefits" requirement of the 1973 amendments to the vocational rehabilitation act. This requirement, in a nutshell, stipulates that the rehabilitation agency cannot pay for services that are the legitimate responsibility of some other agency. Since the schools were *not required* to provide work experiences to their special education students during the 1960s, the provision of this service could be construed as a *rehabilitation* service under the terms of the cooperative agreement, thereby providing a justification for the generation of federal matching rehabilitation dollars (so long as the supervision requirement was met). A dramatic change occurred, however, with the passage of Public Law 94-142 in 1975, which required that every child with a disability is entitled to "a free and *appropriate* public education." Interpreters of this new law determined that "work experience" could be construed as a component of an "appropriate" education during high school for many students with disabilities. Such an interpretation made it risky for the rehabilitation agency to purchase this service, because it might be regarded as the responsibility of the schools and would then be governed by the rules concerning similar benefits.

In combination with several other constraints, the supervision and similar benefits requirements of the rehabilitation legislation led to the near demise of the cooperative work/study program during the 1970s. The needs being addressed through the program, however, were still very much alive. A new movement came into being during this period of time called "career education," which held some promise for addressing the persistent needs. The old wine was about to receive a new bottle.

Career Education

Unlike the work/study movement, which focused on the delivery of services within a specific type of interagency agreement, the career education movement was much more general in its articulation and diffuse in its implementation. In fact, the initial impetus for career education did not even mention the needs of people with disabilities. The beginning of the career education movement is often identified as occurring in 1970, when Sidney Marland, then the Commissioner of Education, declared career education to be the top priority of the U.S. Office of Education. Almost immediately following this pronouncement, a federal initiative began to emerge, with the awarding of approximately $90 million in demonstration grants through funding structures that were already available under Parts C and D of the 1968 Vocational Education Act (Hoyt, 1982). Most of these grants were concerned with career education for the *general* population of students.

During the decade of the 1970s, the movement progressed in several directions, including increased federal visibility (although not accompanied by increased federal support), extension of the concept to include a clear focus on the needs of people with disabilities, and formal endorsement of the concept by The Council for Exceptional Children (CEC) (Brolin, 1983; Cegelka, 1979; Hoyt, 1982). Each of these trends is worthy of comment.

Federal visibility for the career education movement was clearly enhanced in 1974 when the Office of Career Education was established within the U.S. Office of Education. The legislative mandate for the movement was crystallized in 1977 with passage of P.L. 95-207, the Career Education Implementation Incentive Act. In addition to providing a general impetus to career ed-

ucation, this act also specifically mentioned people with disabilities as an appropriate target population for services that would be facilitated through the act.

In 1976, the Division of Career Development was approved as a 12th division of The Council for Exceptional Children. In 1978, CEC formally endorsed the concept of career education through the publication of a position paper on the topic. The significant involvement of this organization in the career education movement laid the foundation for preserving the movement in special education irrespective of federal involvement. Such a foundation was indeed needed in 1982, when P.L. 95-207 was repealed by Congress, consistent with a preplanned federal intent to use this legislation only as a source of "seed money" to nourish the development of the movement (Hoyt, 1982).

When one reflects on the accomplishments of the career education movement—and these accomplishments were many—it is interesting to observe that a commonly accepted definition of "career education" never did emerge. Definitions that emerged from the field ranged from a narrow focusing of goals on the preparation of students for paid employment to a much broader concern with all aspects of adult life. Attempting, perhaps, to mediate between these two positions, the policy adopted by CEC contains elements of both extremes:

> Career education is the totality of experiences through which one learns to live a meaningful, satisfying work life. Within the career education framework, work is conceptualized as conscious effort aimed at producing benefits for oneself and for others. Career education provides the opportunity for children to learn, in the least restrictive environment possible, the academic, daily living, personal-social and occupational knowledge and specific vocational work skills necessary for attaining their highest levels of economic, personal and social fulfillment. The individual can obtain this fulfillment through work (both paid and unpaid) and in a variety of other societal roles and personal life styles including his/her pursuits as a student, citizen, volunteer, family member, and participant in meaningful leisure time activities. (*Position Paper,* 1978).

In many ways, the career education movement can be viewed as an expansion of the work/study movement that preceded it. The work/study movement was fairly narrow in its goals, generally restricted to secondary education, largely focused on serving students with mild mental retardation, typically implemented in programs reserved for students with disabilities, and formally structured as an interagency collaboration. The career education movement was diffuse in its goals, oriented to both elementary and secondary education, available to students with and without disabilities, implemented in both regular and special education environments, and broadly structured as a general education movement. Both movements were spawned through opportunities presented by federal legislation and were nurtured largely through federal financial participation. The work/study movement died as an inadvertent consequence of federal legislation and regulation, and the career education movement was intentionally disowned as a federal initiative. Both predecessors left a legacy for the emergence of the transition movement in the 1980s.

Transition

Only 2 years after the repeal of the Career Education Implementation Incentive Act in 1982, a new federal transition initiative emerged on the scene (Will, 1984a) in the form of a "position paper" from the Office of Special Education and Rehabilitative Services (OSERS). The essence of this paper involved the articulation of a "transition model," which has come to be known as a "bridges" model. This model describes three types of services (bridges) that are needed to facilitate the transition from school to work.

The first bridge, labeled "transition without special services," refers to the use of *generic* services available to anyone in the community, even if special accommodations are necessary within these services for people with disabilities. Postsecondary education, such as that provided in a community college, is mentioned as a prime example of a generic service.

The second bridge, "transition with time-limited services," refers to *specialized,* short-term services where the presence of a disability is usually required to qualify a person for access to the service. Vocational rehabilitation is offered here as an example.

The third bridge has been labeled "transition with ongoing services." As the model developers point out, this bridge did *not* in 1984 represent a widely existing service delivery system. Exemplified by "supported employment," it was relatively new (Will, 1984a, 1984b) and had made its presence known primarily in demonstration projects that were themselves supported by federal grants and contracts. The rehabilitation amendments of 1986, however, identified supported employment as a *regular* program, paving the way for an increased funding level over time.

The target of the OSERS transition model, as I mentioned before, has been restricted to "employment." Perhaps anticipating some concern about the narrowness of this goal, the choice of employment is justified in words such as the following (Will, 1984a):

> This concern with employment does not indicate a lack of interest in other aspects of adult living. Success in social, personal, leisure, and other adult roles enhances opportunities both to obtain employment and enjoy its benefits.(p. 1)

> The focus on employment as a central outcome of effective transition provides an objective measure of transition success. (p. 2)

What the author of this policy seemed to be suggesting was that the nonvocational dimensions of adult adjustment are significant and important only in so far as they contribute to the ultimate goal of employment. Whether or not one agrees with the restricting of transition goals to employment, the impact of this policy was swift and deep. Almost immediately following publication of the OSERS policy on transition (Will, 1984a), requests for "transition" proposals began to appear in a wide array of federal programs dealing with disability. This trend was enhanced through the introduction of transition and supported employment components into new legislation that pertained to people with disabilities. The newest amendments to P.L. 94-142, now called the "Individuals with Disabilities Education Act (P.L. 101-476), contain several important new initiatives in the area of transition, including the requirement that all IEPs address transition goals no later than the student's 16th birthday.

Comparison of the Three Movements

Because the transition movement is still in full force today, it is impossible to evaluate the impact of the movement from an historical perspective. Certain comparisons with the work/study and career education movements, however, allow us to examine the transition movement within the broader context of its antecedents.

The transition movement's early focus on employment was narrower than the stipulated goals of either the work/study or career education movements. All three movements acknowledged that the dimensions of adult adjustment extend beyond employment, but only the transition movement adopted a clearly restrictive position on this issue. The reason for this restrictive position was not a lack of appreciation for the complexity of adult adjustment. Rather, it was the sense of the policymakers that a more limited objective would be more feasible, fundable, and easier to evaluate than a program with multiple objectives.

In a similar "restrictive" vein, both the transition and work/study movements focused their efforts on the limited time span of high-school years through early adulthood, whereas the career education movement covered a much broader span of human development. On the other hand, the transition movement provides the broadest focus on the types of *adult* service agencies that need to be directly involved in the partnerships with the public schools in order to facilitate the movement from school to work.

CURRENT NEEDS AND CONCERNS

Where, then, do we stand after 30 years of programs that have been designed to prepare young people with disabilities for adult roles in their communities? A candid answer to this question is that we still have a long way to go. In the area of curriculum and instruction, we are still frequently deficient in *what* we teach, *how* we teach, and *where* we teach. Curriculum content still tends to focus too much on remedial academics and not enough on functional skills. Instructional design often ignores the issues of maintenance and generalization without which we have no reason to believe that the skills being taught in the classroom will be used in the community settings where they are relevant. The location of instruction is frequently in the school-based classroom, even though a community-based setting would often be more appropriate.

Other concerns, in addition to curriculum and instruction, leave us less than satisfied with the current state of affairs. Integration of high-school students with disabilities into the mainstream remains a cloudy issue, both with respect to its desirability and its implementation. Too many students drop out, and those who remain often receive a meaningless certificate of attendance rather than some form of useful diploma. Transition planning is often ineffective or even nonexistent. The array of adult services is insufficient to meet the needs of those who leave school, and parents or other relatives must often assume the lifelong role of case manager for their child or children with disabilities.

These unresolved issues and concerns can be addressed in several ways.

1. New policies can be developed to structure the ways that we think about needs and priorities.
2. The capacity to address unresolved issues and concerns can be enhanced through legislation, resource allocation, and careful planning for the development of new programs and services.
3. New programs and services can be implemented, evaluated, and refined in local communities, drawing on the policy-development and capacity-building efforts that provide a foundation for local activities.

All three levels of effort—policy development, capacity building, and the effective implementation of new programs—can be enhanced through the collection and dissemination of appropriate follow-along information that documents the experiences of students while in school, and the outcomes that they achieve after leaving school. All of these efforts to address the unresolved problems of transition must work in tandem if widespread impact is eventually to occur.

LOOKING TOWARD THE FUTURE

Each of these approaches to facilitating change is worthy of extended discussion and analysis. Much has also been written about these various approaches, particularly those that involve capacity building and new program implementation. Perhaps the area that is least often considered is the set of conditions that influence the development of policy. Nearly 20 years ago, when I was a relative newcomer to our profession, I had the good fortune to be invited by Michael Begab to a conference on the sociology of mental retardation. At this conference, the gifted sociologist Amitai Etzioni made an interesting observation about the relationship between "special interest" concerns, such as the field of disability, and the broader concerns of society as a whole. He admonished us to avoid myopia, lest we become so caught up in our narrow concerns that we neglect to understand and respond to the broad social problems and issues that exert great influence on our society as a whole. He used the metaphor of attempting to cross the ocean in a 16-foot wooden boat with a 10-horsepower motor. For such a voyage to have even a chance of being successful, one must move with the waves and not against them.

Relevant Social Issues

If Etzioni was correct in his thinking, to make significant headway with the problems of transition for young adults with disabilities, we must first understand the broad social issues that have an impact, or a potential impact, on our narrower set of concerns. As one way of addressing this purpose, I spent a 3-month period (March-May, 1990) doing a very informal study of "relevant social issues." My method involved carefully reading newspapers and news magazines and cutting out and collecting anything that seemed in any way relevant to me at the time. I eventually gathered several hundred clippings and did an informal content analysis of my collection, which yielded the following categories: educational reform, our current health care crisis, increasing levels of poverty in our children, the movement of our society toward increased ethnic diversity, and the growing social implications of financing and managing our federal budget deficit. I have chosen to discuss educational reform to illustrate the influence of the broad social context on policy development that pertains to transition for students with disabilities.

Educational Reform

Much has certainly been written and discussed on the topic of educational reform over many years. In collaboration with the National Governors Association, a recent framework for crystallizing at least some of the major concerns was provided by President Bush in his 1990 State of the Union message. As part of this message, he outlined his preference for six national goals to be met by the year 2000. These goals were then embellished 15 months later with a set of proposed strategies in a document entitled *America 2000: An Education Strategy* (Bush, 1991). The goals include the following:

1. Every American child must start school prepared to learn, sound in body and sound in mind.
2. The high-school graduate rate in the United States must increase to no less than 90%.
3. All students in Grades 4, 8, and 12 will be tested for progress in critical subjects.
4. American students must rank first in the world in achievement in mathematics and science.
5. Every adult must be a skilled, literate worker and citizen, able to compete in a global economy.
6. Every school must be drug free and offer a disciplined environment conducive to learning.

Many of these goals have either clear or potential relevance for the transition programs that are of concern to us. *We* are concerned about functional illiteracy, and approximately 20% of the *entire* adult American population is unable to perform basic math calculations or read at a rudimentary level of effectiveness. *We* are concerned about high-school dropouts, and approximately 30% of *all* American students drop out of school. The commonality of concerns is easy enough to identify, and the examples that emerged in the news clippings were quite numerous. Some seemed to have particularly important ramifications for our narrower set of interest. For example:

- Should vocational apprenticeship programs, such as those found in Germany, be developed as a strong and viable alternative to the college preparation programs that are the cornerstone of high schools in our country?
- Should the federal government get into the business of determining and measuring minimum education competencies?
- Can all students be educated together, or is some sort of tracking system desirable?
- Should schools be the instruments of social reform, or should they stick to the business of education?
- What should be the role of parents in dealing with the education of their children?

Vocational Apprentice Programs. Although vocational education programs in the United States have a long history of their own, some interesting aspects of the vocational apprentice program in Germany have received recent public attention from the national syndicated columnist, William Raspberry, who visited these programs, along with a contingent of educators from Indiana. He introduced this topic with his perceptions of the haphazard manner in which many American youngsters begin their work careers:

Typically, they leave high school to look for work wherever they can find it—sometimes with help from family friends, sometimes going full time into jobs in which they worked part time during high school. Only after a succession of random jobs, it seems, do they stumble upon something with real career potential—a permanent job with clear prospects for advancement that pays enough to support a family. . . . The delayed transition to adulthood signals to the youngsters that, no matter what we say, there is little real relationship between what they learn in school and their ability to make their way in the world.

Raspberry then presented his viewpoint, which praised the potential of Germany's apprentice program to address these issues that he had raised. The essence of this program, as he reported it, involves a refocusing of the last 2 or 3 years of public education to include 3 or 4 days a week pursuing an on-the-job apprenticeship, with only 1 or 2 days a week in the classroom. There are 380 apprenticeable skills in Germany, and the minimum competencies are standardized across the country. Government regulates the standards, and employers have no obligation to participate in the program.

But the employers do, in fact, participate. They pay for the cost of training even though there is no obligation, or even expectation, that the apprentice will continue to work for the employer who provides the training. "Employers consider the training expenses an unremarkable investment in the competency of Germany's work force and, therefore, an investment in their own long-term survival." Many companies train far more people than they have any possibility of ever hiring. Raspberry speculated that the employers are motivated to participate because they have real control over *what* is taught and *how* skills are taught. As for the value of this approach, he asked rhetorically, "Who would you rather have teach your child a job: A master craftsman or a school teacher?"

The extended involvement of the business sector in the educational enterprise is a topic of intensifying discussion in our country, with many businesses expressing a strong interest in participating. As we continue to explore innovative ways for businesses to become integrally involved in the education of all students, new models and opportunities likely will emerge that provide good opportunities for students with disabilities. To continue with the imagery of Etzioni's metaphor, this may be a wave worth catching.

Federal Involvement in Minimum Competencies. The federal government has entered the business of education in many ways. P.L. 94-142 and the OSERS transition initiatives are obvious examples in our field. The minimum competency strand of educational reform, however, has begun to explore the limits of federal intervention in education.

In response to President Bush's goal of testing student achievement in Grades 4, 8, and 12, the National Assessment Governing Board (NAGB) voted in December 1989 to ask Congress for a substantial expansion of the National Assessment of Educational Progress (NAEP) test that it has been operating for the past 20 years. The purpose of this expansion would be to develop new and better tests to address the President's goal. Opposition to this proposal has been strong and from many sources including the National Congress of Parents and Teachers Association (PTA), the Council of Chief School Officers, the National Education Association, and the National Association of Secondary School Principals.

The voices of opposition present several arguments. The multiple-choice formats that tend to dominate standardized tests measure only certain kinds of learning that emphasize fact recall. Because there are no commonly accepted definitions of minimum competency, developing a single standardized form of assessment is impossible. If the outcomes of such assessment are used to distribute sanctions and rewards, schools will slavishly pursue good scores regardless of their educational relevance.

The NAGB, of course, has some arguments of its own. Without accountability, they assert, society has no way of evaluating educational outcomes. Furthermore if schools are allowed to develop their own assessments, they will tend to set easy standards that make their programs look good.

It is too early to predict the outcome of this controversy. The potential impact on transition programs for students with disabilities is also uncertain. If a national competency assessment program is strengthened, will this result in a raising of minimum competency standards and increased difficulty in earning a high-school diploma, thereby decreasing the number of special education students who can earn a diploma? On the other hand, would a good set of standardized measures help to provide a valid paradigm for evaluating the impact of instruction and distributing financial resources to education programs? The eventual outcome of this debate will most certainly affect transition programs for students with disabilities.

Tracking and Mainstreaming. The issue of student tracking is not new to the field of special education. The concept of educating students with disabilities in the least restrictive environment was a cornerstone of P.L. 94-142, and the mainstreaming movement and regular education initiative (REI) have emerged as attempts to embody this concept. As we all know, these attempts have not been uniformly supported within special education, with both the success and appropriateness of such efforts being challenged, especially at the secondary level.

Concerns about mainstreaming have also emerged from the perspective of regular education. Within this context, the issue is often expressed as a concern about the appropriateness of tracking systems for organizing classroom instruction. A recent opinion presented by the syndicated columnist, Paul Greenberg, (1990, April 22) provides a perspective on this issue. He stated:

> The latest fad in Educanto is to eliminate "tracking," the grouping of students by ability. Such an approach might make sense to simple laymen like you and me, but the educationists have just about decided that it's ineffective—not to say elitist, racist, fascist and possibly even old-fashioned. Can any more serious indictment be imagined? . . . The newest approach is to throw kids together regardless of ability or knowledge; it is assumed that the superior knowledge and skills of the sharpest will rub off on the the rest. Uh-huh. This is the kind of assumption that would make Pollyanna look like a hard-bitten cynic. . . . In the days of the one-room school house, older or brighter students often took charge of the younger ones, rather than being challenged by new material. It had its advantages, but not that many. Mainly it was a matter of necessity. . . . Are we, in the name of progress, headed back to that system? If so, you can be sure it'll be given some multisyllabic name (how does "cooperative learning" sound?) and hailed in educational journals as a great advance. Educanto marches on.

Greenberg's stinging sarcasm is hardly a careful or fair evaluation of tracking or mainstreaming, but it does represent an important public perception that needs to be addressed. The issue gets even cloudier when we consider the legal requirement that tracking, if it is done, must be nondiscriminatory. The basic concern that seems to be involved in this debate is how to achieve excellence in education for *all* students, while acknowledging that their needs, abilities, and educational goals are diverse. In any case, it seems almost certain that decisions concerning tracking and cooperative learning in regular education will spill over into decisions concerning mainstreaming and REI for students with disabilities.

Schools and Social Reform. One of the three columns written by Raspberry about the apprentice program in Germany raised an interesting companion issue about the role of schools as instruments of social reform. His beginning sense of this issue emerged from an awareness that amateur sports in Germany have no connection with educational institutions, which relieves the schools of any responsibility for such budget-draining items as sports stadiums, uniforms and equipment for athletes, bands and cheerleaders, buses to transport these people to events, and coaches' salaries. He also noticed that German schools did not tend to support any form of school transportation, lunchrooms, or most extracurricular activities. His conclusion?

> One of the reasons German youngsters seem more serious than ours is that German schools are more businesslike and career-oriented than ours. While there are exceptions, schools are for those who want to learn something and are not used as day care centers or personality enrichment programs.

Schools in the United States, of course, tend to move in a completely different direction. Good schools are often viewed as those that "do it all." School personnel are expected not only to teach, but also to transport, feed, coach, counsel, advise, and support student development in a myriad of extracurricular activities. Furthermore, schools are expected to play a major role in solving serious social problems, such as drug abuse, child abuse, poverty, health problems, and teen-age pregnancy.

For example, beginning in October 1990, a new federal law requires all teenage parents on welfare to enroll in a high-school completion program if they don't already have a diploma or a GED. Failure to comply will result in a dramatic reduction of welfare benefits. These high expectations for our schools to serve as a major agent of social change are likely to remain intact for a long time. As the debate concerning school responsibilities unfolds, each decision to maintain or expand these multifaceted responsibilities will have obvious fiscal and programmatic implications. At some point, both money and energy will run out. Programs for students with disabilities will have to compete for both resources.

Role of Parents. The role of schools as agents of social change cannot be separated from the role of parents. The relationship is almost symbiotic; a partnership is most desirable, but whatever the schools don't do will be foisted upon parents, and vice versa. What, then, is a proper delineation of responsibilities?

Public sentiment seems to place a majority of this responsibility upon the schools. Columnist Mike Royko (1990, April 16) takes issue with this sentiment through a dialogue with his fictitious blue collar philosopher, Slats Grobnik.

> "Where did President Bush find this dummy?" asked Slats Grobnik, looking up from his newspaper.

Oh, let's leave poor Dan Quayle alone.

"I don't mean Quayle. It's this secretary of education."

Ah, you mean Lauro Cavazos.

"Yea, whatever his name is. What a klutz."

That's a rather harsh appraisal. After all, the man is our nation's highest education official. Show some respect.

"Yeah? Haven't you read what he said about high school dropouts?"

I know that it is considered a grave crisis, particularly among minority groups, so Bush has set up task forces to look into the problem.

"Nah, I mean the latest. This guy Cavazos went to one of these task force meetings and talked about whose fault it is that so many Hispanic kids drop out of school."

I assume he blamed the school systems, as everyone does.

"Yeah, he mentioned that. But he didn't stop there. He started talking like a looney.... He said that it's not just the schools that aren't doing their job, it's the parents of the dropouts."

I don't understand. Why are you calling him a dummy? You've been saying the same thing for years.

"I know, but I'm not the secretary of education, or the president, or a mayor or any other politician or mucky-muck. So it's OK for me to say it. But this stiff don't seem to know that what he said is a big no-no."

But if he believes it to be true, and if you agree, why shouldn't he come out and say it?

"You're as dumb as he is. I'll tell you why. Because this ain't the old days. We got a new set of rules now. When there is a problem—or a grave crisis, like they call it—you gotta blame society, or the government or the one I like the best—the failure of institutions. You never blame people. But what this guy went and did is blame people. And that's against the rules. So that's why he's a dummy. He don't know how to play the game."

Slats goes on to point out that politicians who don't play by the rules eventually lose their jobs.

Royko's blue collar philosopher may be on to something important here. If our needed educational reforms can only be accomplished with the assistance of parents, and if some parents want to abdicate this responsibility, and if policymakers are afraid or unable to confront the issue, many of the problems that currently bedevil the schools will remain unresolved. Students with disabilities, of course, will be caught up in the vortex of these unresolved problems, which must inevitably have an impact on the opportunities that are available within special education and transition programs, whether or not parents of students with disabilities are actively involved in these programs.

CONCLUSION

This short excursion in the area of educational reform, of course, is only one example of many general social concerns that set the parameters and conditions for the development of policy concerning transition programs in our field. A similar analysis of other concerns, such as the health care crisis in the United States, would undoubtedly yield other insights into policy issues that are likely to affect transition programs. The outcomes of policy development in these broader social issues will provide definite opportunities and limitations for structuring the changes that we are attempting to implement in our narrower field of concern.

Within this narrower field, we have already learned a great deal about how to improve program capacity and how to implement specific programs that take advantage of this capacity. Our literature is full of many fine examples of such efforts. From the perspective and influence of broad policy, however, the transition movement of the 1980s may or may not be the program of the 1990s that will emerge to address the needs of adolescents with disabilities as they prepare to move into adulthood. The transition movement, if it remains viable, should be responsive to the broad issues and concerns of our general society. If "transition" eventually disappears as a rallying call for programs, however, this should not be cause for alarm. Something new will undoubtedly take its place, because many of the underlying problems being experienced by adolescents and young adults with disabilities are likely to remain in need of further attention. If necessary, the old wine will find yet another new bottle.

REFERENCES

Brolin, D. (1983). Career education: Where do we go from here? *Career Development for Exceptional Individuals, 6,* 3-14.

Bush, G. (1991). *America 2000: An education strategy.* Washington, DC: U.S. Department of Education.

Cegelka, P. (1979). Career education. In M. Epstein & D. Cullinan (Eds.), *Special education for adolescents: Issues and perspectives* (pp. 155-184). Columbus, OH: Charles E. Merrill.

Greenberg, P. (1990, April 22). Latest "educationist" fad on the wrong track. *The Register-Guard* (Eugene, OR), p. 3C.

Halpern, A. (1973). General unemployment and vocational opportunities for EMR individuals. *American Journal of Mental Deficiency, 80,* 81-89.

Halpern, A. (1974). Work-study programs for the mentally retarded: An overview. In P. Browning (Ed.), *Mental retardation: Rehabilitation and counseling* (pp. 120-137). Springfield, IL: Charles C Thomas.

Halpern, A. (1985). Transition: A look at the foundations. *Exceptional Children, 51,* 479-486.

Hoyt, K. (1982). Career education: Beginning of the end, or a new beginning. *Career Development of Exceptional Individuals, 5,* 3-12.

Kaufman, S. (1988). *Retarded isn't stupid, Mom!* Baltimore: Paul H. Brookes.

Kolstoe, O., & Frey, R. (1965). *A high school work-study program for mentally sub-normal students.* Carbondale, IL: Southern Illinois University Press.

Position paper on career education. (1978). Reston, VA: The Council for Exceptional Children.

Royko, M. (1990, April 16). Education secretary takes a risk. *The Register-Guard* (Eugene, OR), p. 9A.

Will, M. (1984a). *OSERS programming for the transition of youth with disabilities: Bridges from school to working life.* Washington, DC: Office of Special Education and Rehabilitative Services, U.S. Department of Education.

Will, M. (1984b). *Supported employment for adults with severe disabilities: An OSERS program initiative.* Washington, DC: Office of Special Education and Rehabilitative Services, U.S. Department of Education.

This article is an edited version of a keynote address delivered on three different occasions: at a regional conference on transition in Seattle, Washington, June 4, 1990; at a state conference on transition in Auburn, Alabama, April 18, 1991; and at a national conference on transition in Sydney, Australia, June 27, 1991.

Manuscript received June 1990; revision accepted February 1991.

Is a Functional Curriculum Approach Compatible with an Inclusive Education Model?

Gary M. Clark

Gary M. Clark (*CEC Chapter #665*), *Professor, Department of Special Education, University of Kansas, Lawrence.*

A nagging question for many special education teachers at elementary, middle school, and high school levels is the question of what to teach. What is most important for students to know or be able to do both now and in the future?

Instruction has always involved deciding on what to teach (curriculum) and how to teach it (methods, materials, and activities). Special education in its earliest years was left to develop its own discipline around both of these areas. As a separate educational system, it went about this in a variety of ways, but most often it started with the general education curriculum as a base and modified it to fit the expected performance levels of the students. Most of the modifications were accomplished by adapting instruction; for example, devising new ways of teaching reading (Fernald method or the Gillingham approach) and mathematics (Cuisenaire rods, abacas, etc.) or new materials, and not by modifying the content itself.

Looking back, this approach to academics was a logical first step. Many of the children placed in special education classes during those early years had mild levels of learning and behavior disorders. Hopes were high that specialized methods and materials could

remediate their difficulties and help them achieve in the general education curriculum with other children, although at a slower pace. As special education identification and placement began to include children with moderate to severe disabilities, the next logical step was to consider some changes not only in *how* children with special needs are taught, but also in *what* they are taught. The term *functional academics* was used early on to reflect the shift away from traditional academics.

In the 1970s, the field of special education moved from being the sole provider of special education content and instructional strategies and techniques to being a system that would provide and support a continuum of educational options. Most of the options developed, however, placed the responsibility for curriculum back in the hands of general education. Before long those early questions regarding the generalizability and relevance of traditional academics for students with moderate and severe disabilities evolved into the current questions regarding functional outcomes for all students with disabilities.

Functional outcomes of education— that is, the ability to live and work as a part of the community satisfactorily— may or may not result from traditional academic curricula. What makes it so difficult for parents and educators to deal with this fact is that the idea of providing a more functional curricu-

lum for more functional outcomes seems to preclude full inclusion, especially given today's increased emphasis on academics in public education. This special focus section of *TEACHING Exceptional Children* looks at a functional curriculum approach and how it might work within an inclusive education context.

What Is a Functional Curriculum Approach?

A variety of writers have defined functional curricula, or what is sometimes referred to as *life skills instruction* (cf. Brolin, 1991; Brown et al., 1979; Clark, 1991; Cronin & Patton, 1993; Falvey, 1989; Mithaug, Martin, & Agran, 1987). While there is a common theme imbedded in these and other perspectives described in the literature, there is still a possibility of miscommunication when the term *functional* is used.

The basic notion of functionality implies the usefulness of something or usefulness for somebody. Given that, it is clear that what is functional for one person is not necessarily functional for another person or what is a functional use for an object in one situation may not be functional in another situation. A cane may be functional for a person who needs support for mobility, but it has no usefulness for someone who does not need it. Likewise, the cane can be func-

From *Teaching Exceptional Children*, Vol. 26, No. 2, Winter 1994, pp. 36-39. © 1994 by The Council for Exceptional Children. Reprinted by permission.

tional as a support tool for walking but without function in swimming. For our purposes, functional curriculum must have a specific context and focus for children and youth with disabilities. The context and focus arise from the need of all persons with disabilities to have the life skills to make a successful transition from school to adult living (Brolin, 1991; Clark & Kolstoe, 1990; Halpern, 1985; Polloway, Patton, Epstein, & Smith, 1989). From this perspective, the concept can be defined as follows:

A functional curriculum approach is a way of delivering instructional content that focuses on the concepts and skills needed by all students with disabilities in the areas of personal-social, daily living, and occupational adjustment. What is considered a functional curriculum for any one student would be the content (concepts and skills) included in that student's curriculum or course of study that targets his or her current and future needs. These needs are based on a nondiscriminatory, functional assessment approach.

How Do You Determine What Is Functional Knowledge or a Functional Skill?

The answer to this question depends upon the answers to a variety of related questions:

- Is the instructional content of the student's current educational placement appropriate for meeting the student's personal-social, daily living, and occupational adjustment needs? That is,
- Does the content focus on necessary knowledge and skills to function as independently as possible in the home, school, or community?
- Does the content provide a scope and sequence for meeting future needs?
- Do the student's parents think the content is important for both current and future needs?
- Does the student think the content is important for both current and future needs?

- Is the content appropriate for the student's chronological age and current intellectual, academic, or behavioral performance level(s)?
- What are the consequences to the student of not learning the concepts and skills inherent in the current educational placement?

As these questions imply, the determination of functionality with a specific focus on transition to adult living does not depend on a particular point of view about where a student is educated. A student in a segregated, self-contained special school or class may not be receiving a functional curriculum any more than a student in an inclusive education model. This is not to say that there may not be positive benefits associated with various current placement alternatives. If those benefits do not include life skills instruction at all or in sufficient amount, however, the educational placement is not providing an appropriate functional curriculum. If parents and students choose general education as the desirable primary or even exclusive placement, a functional curriculum must be planned within that context. The Special Focus article by Field, LeRoy, and Rivera gives an example of a student-centered functional curriculum determination.

Current functional curriculum models focus directly on knowledge and skills that need to be taught and leave the delivery procedures and instructional environment decisions to users. Some of the better known models include the Community-Referenced Curriculum (Smith & Schloss, 1988), Community Living Skills Taxonomy (Dever, 1988), Hawaii Transition Project (1987), and Life Centered Career Education model (Brolin, 1991). Of these, the Life Centered Career Education (LCCE) model by Brolin is probably the best example of a comprehensive functional curriculum model across age levels and the most completely developed curriculum package for secondary school teachers (Brolin, 1992).

The LCCE model is organized around 22 competencies needed for adult living. The competencies are clustered across three basic domains: Daily Living, Personal-Social, and Occupa-

tional Guidance and Preparation. Each of the 22 competencies can be broken down into subcompetencies that may be appropriate for individualized education program (IEP) goals or short-term objectives. The curriculum content domains of the LCCE model, as well as the other models that are available, are directly on target for the planning of transition services mandated for students 16 years of age and older under Public Law 101-476 (IDEA), the Individuals with Disabilities Education Act of 1990.

When Do You Start a Functional Curriculum?

Special educators who value life skills education have long held the view that a functional curriculum for children with disabilities should begin formally when these children enter the public schools (Kokaska & Brolin, 1985; Clark, 1979). The Division on Career Development and Transition of The Council for Exceptional Children established its position on early beginnings with a formal policy statement reflecting the view that many concepts and skills must be introduced at the awareness and exploration stages for elementary school children in order to make the most of instructional efforts during the secondary school years (Clark, Carlson, Fisher, Cook, & D'Alonzo, 1991). The Special Focus article by Beck, Broers, Hogue, Shipstead, and Knowlton demonstrates the possibilities of this practice for elementary school children in grades two through four.

Who Needs a Functional Curriculum?

All children and youth in public schools today should be provided an education that is specific enough to provide them with the knowledge and skills they need to perform age-appropriate roles while in school and to meet the demands of being family members, citizens, and workers as adults. As early as 1979, the Carnegie Council of Policy Studies in Higher Education stated in an educational reform paper that the public education approach to teaching basic skills and academic content was successful with only about two-thirds of the school population. Few would argue that a large proportion of the population of students who are at risk and many students with disabilities have difficulties using what schools provide for successful adult adjustment. Follow-up studies of former special education students, including the majority of students referred to as having mild disabilities, support the Carnegie study contention that another approach should be considered.

Many teachers who are assigned to resource rooms or collaborative programs either do not consider their students as needing functional curricula or perform their roles within whatever curricular offerings exist without concerning themselves with curriculum alternatives. Some states using noncategorical teacher endorsements complicate the issue by differentiating mild/moderate teaching endorsements from severe/profound teaching endorsements according to the different curricula used with the students in the two groups. That is, a functional curriculum is typically identified with students with severe disabilities, and all other students (i.e., those with mild to moderate disabilities) are assumed to be able to benefit sufficiently from the general education curriculum.

Logic, research data, and now the IDEA mandate to at least address functional curriculum needs through transition planning for students age 16 and above all lead to only one answer to the question of who needs a functional curriculum: All students with disabilities need such a curriculum, but each must be determined individually.

How Do a Functional Curriculum and a Traditional Curriculum Relate to One Another?

For some people, the relationship between a functional life skills curriculum and academics is a practical question. For others, it is a philosophical question that might be phrased more directly as "What is the place of a functional curriculum approach in the context of the inclusive education movement?" It is easier to deal with these questions if a distinction is made between a functional curriculum and a functional curriculum approach.

The term *functional curriculum* suggests a document or written guide that is in place and used for all students in a particular setting. While this could be the case, the definition given earlier implies that it could also be a specified program of instruction or course of study for an individual student. It may be tied to a group instructional setting if, in fact, it is used for most or all of the students in that setting, but this is not necessarily the case. If it is tied to a self-contained or separate delivery alternative, a high degree of responsibility is placed on special education teachers to demonstrate that the outcomes are not only satisfying to the students and their families, but also acceptable and desirable outcomes of the school's commitment to providing quality, integrated educational programs.

A *functional curriculum approach,* on the other hand, suggests that functional content is prescribed on the IEP, but that it has no restrictions regarding the type or location of instructional delivery. This perspective permits educators and families to look first to what a child's instructional content should be before determining where and how it should be provided. The functional curriculum approach places a high degree of responsibility on both general and special educators to make sure that the instruction is delivered effectively and with integrity, regardless of the delivery environment(s).

At present, the relationship between a functional curriculum approach and the traditional academic curriculum is a tenuous one. A lot is going on in public education that sends both discouraging and encouraging messages. The discouraging message is that general education is moving toward a more rigorous academic model and that effective schools and outcomes-based/performance-based education will focus on fostering higher achievement scores in the traditional subject matter areas and increased skills in higher-order thinking and problem-solving. The encouraging message is that some educators are viewing outcomes-based education more broadly than as simply increasing academic achievement scores and higher-order thinking. They are advocating functional, generalizable skills for responsible citizenship as the ends and academic skills as the means to those ends. This broader view of outcomes for education provides special educators and families who want a functional approach a window of opportunity to choose to be a part of a single educational system that takes responsibility for *all* students.

How Can Schools Develop a Functional Curriculum Approach and Promote Inclusive Education?

Even a functional curriculum delivery system that is based on a special class model can incorporate many aspects of inclusion. The very nature of life skills instruction depends upon age-appropriate skills and experiences with age peers who do not have disabilities. A transition perspective of preparing students to leave school and assume adult roles depends upon real-life, community-based skills and experiences for learning and generalization. This means that a highly inclusive model can organize and present instruction together with students without disabilities, but it must meet the functional, community-based needs of all students. Functional skills instruction must be planned deliberately and implemented with families and general education teachers. Implementation of this type of planning and collaboration becomes increasingly more difficult and complex as students move from elementary to high school settings. This may affect both the nature and the quality of both functional skills acquisition and inclusion.

Three ways of developing and implementing a functional curriculum within an inclusive education philosophy are presented in the three Special Focus articles that follow. The three approaches reflect a "bottom-up" model, a student-centered model, and a "top-down" model. Each article illustrates not only what can be done but also what has been done in certain situations and settings. Each reflects a high degree of commitment to the notion of the importance of functional life skills and integration outcomes. Your task as a reader is to determine which one, if any, fits your situation and decide what you can replicate or adapt to suit your needs.

References

Brolin, D. E. (1991). *Life centered career education: A competency based approach* (3rd ed.). Reston, VA: The Council for Exceptional Children.

Brolin, D. E. (1992). *Life centered career education (LCCE) curriculum program.* Reston, VA: The Council for Exceptional Children.

Brown, L., Branston, M., Hamre-Nietupski, S., Punpian, I., Certo, N., & Gruenwald, L. (1979). A strategy for developing chronological age-appropriate and functional curricular content for severely handicapped adolescents and young adults. *Journal of Special Education, 13*(1), 81-90.

Carnegie Council of Policy Studies in Higher Education. (1979). *Giving youth a better chance: Options for education, work, and service.* San Francisco: Jossey-Bass.

Clark, G. M. (1979). *Career education for the handicapped child in the regular classroom.* Denver, CO: Love Publishing.

Clark, G. M. (1991). Functional curriculum and its place in the regular education initiative. Paper presented at the Seventh International Conference of the Division on Career Development, The Council for Exceptional Children, Kansas City, MO.

Clark, G. M., Carlson, B. C., Fisher, S. L., Cook, I. D., & D'Alonzo, B. J. (1991). Career development for students with disabilities in elementary schools: A position statement of the Division on Career Development. *Career Development for Exceptional Individuals, 14,* 109-120.

Clark, G. M., & Kolstoe, O. P. (1990). *Career development and transition education for adolescents with disabilities.* Needham Heights, MA: Allyn and Bacon.

Cronin, M. E., & Patton, J. R. (1993). *Life skills instruction for all students with special needs: A practical guide for integrating real-life content into the curriculum.* Austin, TX: Pro-Ed.

Dever, R. B. (1988). *Community living skills: A taxonomy.* Washington, DC: American Association on Mental Retardation.

Falvey, M. (1989). *Community-based curriculum* (2nd ed.). Baltimore: Paul H. Brookes.

Halpern, A. S. (1985). Transition: A look at the foundations. *Exceptional Children, 51,* 479-486.

Hawaii Transition Project. (1987). Honolulu: Department of Special Education, University of Hawaii.

Kokaska, C. J., & Brolin, D. E. (1985). *Career education for handicapped individuals* (2nd. ed.). Columbus, OH: Merrill.

Mithaug, D., Martin, J. E., & Agran, M. (1987). Adaptability instruction: The goal of transitional programming. *Exceptional Children, 53,* 500-505.

Polloway, E. A., Patton, J. R., Epstein, M. H., & Smith, T. E. C. (1989). Comprehensive curriculum for students with mild handicaps. *Focus on Exceptional Children, 21*(8), 1-12.

Smith, M. A., & Schloss, P. J. (1988). Teaching to transition. In P. J. Schloss, C. A. Hughes, & M. A. Smith (Eds.), *Community integration for persons with mental retardation* (pp. 1-16). Austin, TX: Pro-Ed.

Credits/ Acknowledgments

Cover design by Charles Vitelli

1. Inclusive Education
Facing overview—United Nations photo by John Isaac. 6-8—Photos by Eric Hanson. 25-26—Photos by Robert LeRoy.

2. Children with Learning Disabilities
Facing overview—United Nations photo by L. Solmssen.

3. Children with Mental Retardation
Facing overview—United Nations photo by S. Dimartini.

4. Children with Behavioral Disorders and Autism
Facing overview—United Nations photo by Shelley Rotner. 80—Graphics by Jared Schneidman Design.

5. Children with Communication Disorders
Facing overview—United Nations photo by Marta Pinter.

6. Children with Hearing Impairments
Facing overview—United Nations photo by L. Solmssen.

7. Children with Visual Impairments
Facing overview—United Nations photo by L. Solmssen.

8. Children with Physical and Health Impairments
Facing overview—United Nations photo by John Isaac.

9. Children with Special Gifts and Talents
Facing overview—Photo by Elaine M. Ward. 186—Photos by OM Associates. 187—Photos (top, middle) by Iowa State University. 187—Photo (bottom) by Talents Unlimited.

10. Early Childhood Exceptionality
Facing overview—United Nations photo by John Isaac.

11. Transition to Adulthood
Facing Overview—United Nations photo by Milton Grant.

ANNUAL EDITIONS ARTICLE REVIEW FORM

■ NAME: _____ DATE: _____

■ TITLE AND NUMBER OF ARTICLE: _____

■ BRIEFLY STATE THE MAIN IDEA OF THIS ARTICLE: _____

_____

_____

_____

_____

■ LIST THREE IMPORTANT FACTS THAT THE AUTHOR USES TO SUPPORT THE MAIN IDEA:

_____

_____

_____

_____

_____

_____

■ WHAT INFORMATION OR IDEAS DISCUSSED IN THIS ARTICLE ARE ALSO DISCUSSED IN YOUR TEXTBOOK OR OTHER READING YOU HAVE DONE? LIST THE TEXTBOOK CHAPTERS AND PAGE NUMBERS:

_____

_____

_____

_____

_____

_____

_____

■ LIST ANY EXAMPLES OF BIAS OR FAULTY REASONING THAT YOU FOUND IN THE ARTICLE:

_____

_____

_____

_____

_____

■ LIST ANY NEW TERMS/CONCEPTS THAT WERE DISCUSSED IN THE ARTICLE AND WRITE A SHORT DEFINITION:

_____

_____

_____

_____

_____

ANNUAL EDITIONS:
EDUCATING EXCEPTIONAL CHILDREN,
Eighth Edition
Article Rating Form

Here is an opportunity for you to have direct input into the next revision of this volume. We would like you to rate each of the 42 articles listed below, using the following scale:

1. Excellent: should definitely be retained
2. Above average: should probably be retained
3. Below average: should probably be deleted
4. Poor: should definitely be deleted

Your ratings will play a vital part in the next revision. So please mail this prepaid form to us just as soon as you complete it.
Thanks for your help!

Rating	Article	Rating	Article
	1. Inclusion		22. Hearing for Success in the Classroom
	2. A Commentary on Inclusion and the Development of a Positive Self-Identity by People with Disabilities		23. The Roles of the Educational Interpreter in Mainstreaming
	3. Privacy of School Records: What Every Special Education Teacher Should Know		24. The Establishment Clause as Antiremedy
	4. Separate and Unequal		25. Developing Independent and Responsible Behaviors in Students Who Are Deaf or Hard of Hearing
	5. Peer Education Partners		26. Efficacy of Low Vision Services for Visually Impaired Children
	6. Selection of Appropriate Technology for Children with Disabilities		27. A Direct Service Program for Mainstreamed Students by a Residential School
	7. Enabling the Learning Disabled		28. Teaching Choice-making Skills to Students Who Are Deaf-Blind
	8. Young Children with Attention Deficits		29. Medical Treatment and Educational Problems in Children
	9. Identifying Students' Instructional Needs in the Context of Classroom and Home Environments		30. Physical Abuse: Are Children with Disabilities at Greater Risk?
	10. Adapting Textbooks for Children with Learning Disabilities in Mainstreamed Classrooms		31. The Inclusion Revolution
	11. Prenatal Drug Exposure: An Overview of Associated Problems and Intervention Strategies		32. Physically Challenged Students
			33. How Schools Are Shortchanging the Gifted
	12. Integrating Elementary Students with Multiple Disabilities into Supported Regular Classes: Challenges and Solutions		34. Poor and Minority Students Can Be Gifted, Too!
	13. The Effects of Social Interaction Training on High School Peer Tutors of Schoolmates with Severe Disabilities		35. Gifted Girls in a Rural Community: Math Attitudes and Career Options
	14. Autism		36. Meeting the Needs of Gifted and Talented Preschoolers
	15. They Can But They Don't—Helping Students Overcome Work Inhibition		37. Infants and Toddlers with Special Needs and Their Families
	16. Do Public Schools Have an Obligation to Serve Troubled Children and Youth?		38. Preschool Mainstreaming: Attitude Barriers and Strategies for Addressing Them
	17. The Culturally Sensitive Disciplinarian		39. Children with Disabilities Who Use Assistive Technology: Ethical Considerations
	18. Preschool Classroom Environments That Promote Communication		40. Play for All Children: The Toy Library Solution
	19. Toward Defining Programs and Services for Culturally and Linguistically Diverse Learners in Special Education		41. Transition: Old Wine in New Bottles
			42. Is a Functional Curriculum Approach Compatible with an Inclusive Education Model?
	20. Do You See What I Mean? Body Language in Classroom Interactions		
	21. Using a Picture Task Analysis to Teach Students with Multiple Disabilities		

(Continued on next page)

ABOUT YOU

Name_____ Date_____

Are you a teacher? ☐   Or student? ☐

Your School Name _____

Department _____

Address _____

City _____ State _____ Zip _____

School Telephone # _____

YOUR COMMENTS ARE IMPORTANT TO US!

Please fill in the following information:

For which course did you use this book? _____

Did you use a text with this Annual Edition?   ☐ yes   ☐ no

The title of the text? _____

What are your general reactions to the Annual Editions concept?

Have you read any particular articles recently that you think should be included in the next edition?

Are there any articles you feel should be replaced in the next edition? Why?

Are there other areas that you feel would utilize an Annual Edition?

May we contact you for editorial input?

May we quote you from above?
